POST-COMMUNIST TRANSITIONAL JUSTICE

Taking stock of the twenty-fifth anniversary of the collapse of the communist regimes of Central and Eastern Europe, this volume explores the ways these societies have grappled with the serious human rights violations of past regimes. It focuses on the most important factors that have shaped the nature, speed, and sequence of transitional justice programs in the period spanning the tumultuous revolutions that brought about the collapse of the communist dictatorships and the consolidation of new democratic regimes. Contributors explain why leaders made certain choices, discuss the challenges they faced, and explore the role of under studied actors and grassroots strategies. Written by recognized experts with an unparalleled grasp of the region's communist and post-communist reality, this volume addresses far-reaching reckoning, redress, and retribution policy choices. It is an engaging and carefully crafted volume, and it covers a wide variety of cases and discusses key transitional justice theories using both qualitative and quantitative research methods.

Lavinia Stan is Associate Professor in the department of political science at St. Francis Xavier University, Canada. She is an associate editor of the peer-reviewed *Women's Studies International Forum* and, most recently, the coauthor or coeditor of *Transitional Justice in Post-Communist Romania* (2013); *Church, State and Democracy in the Expanding Europe* (with Lucian Turcescu, 2011); and the three-volume *Encyclopedia of Transitional Justice* (with Nadya Nedelsky, 2013). Stan is also the author of more than fifty peer-reviewed articles published in such venues as the *European Political Science Journal*, *Problems of Post-Communism*, *Communist and Post-Communist Politics*, and *Europe-Asia Studies*.

Nadya Nedelsky is Associate Professor of International Studies at Macalester College. She is the author of *Defining the Sovereign Community: National Identity, Individual Rights, and Minority Membership in the Czech and Slovak Republics* (2009) and the coeditor of the three-volume *Encyclopedia of Transitional Justice* (with Lavinia Stan, 2013). She is author of the national report on the Czech and Slovak republics titled *How the Memory of Crimes Committed by Totalitarian Regimes in Europe Is Dealt with in the Member States* commissioned by the European Commission Directorate-General for Justice, Freedom and Security in 2009 as well as articles and book chapters on transitional justice.

Post-Communist Transitional Justice

LESSONS FROM TWENTY-FIVE YEARS OF EXPERIENCE

EDITED BY

LAVINIA STAN

St. Francis Xavier University, Canada

NADYA NEDELSKY

Macalester College

CAMBRIDGE
UNIVERSITY PRESS

CAMBRIDGE
UNIVERSITY PRESS

32 Avenue of the Americas, New York, NY 10013-2473, USA

Cambridge University Press is part of the University of Cambridge.

It furthers the University's mission by disseminating knowledge in the pursuit of education, learning, and research at the highest international levels of excellence.

www.cambridge.org
Information on this title: www.cambridge.org/9781107065567

First published 2015

A catalog record for this publication is available from the British Library.

ISBN 978-1-107-06556-7 Hardback

Contents

Figures, Tables, and Photos

FIGURES

TABLES

PHOTOS

Contributors

Robert Clegg Austin – Professor at the Munk School of Global Affairs, University of Toronto, Canada. His research interests are situated at the intersection of history and politics of Eastern Europe, state building, and transitional justice, with a focus on Albania. His book on Albania's interwar experience, *Founding a Balkan State*, was published in October 2012. He has also published extensively on transitional justice in post-communist Albania.

Andrew H. Beattie – Senior Lecturer in German and European Studies at the University of New South Wales in Australia. His research explores the ways in which Germans have dealt with the legacies of East German communism and Nazism, whether in memorials, museums, historiography, or transitional justice. His PhD thesis, awarded the Jean Monnet Thesis Prize by the Contemporary Europe Research Centre, Melbourne (2005), was published as *Playing Politics with History: The Bundestag Inquiries into East Germany* (2008).

Monica Ciobanu – Associate Professor of Sociology, State University of New York at Plattsburgh. Her research focuses on democratization, memory, truth, and justice in post-communism, with a focus on Romania. Her work on post-communist transitional justice includes numerous book chapters and articles in peer-reviewed journals.

Roman David – Lecturer in Political Science, Newcastle University, England. He has published extensively on lustration, rehabilitation, and transitional justice in Eastern Europe and Iraq. His *Lustration and Transitional Justice: Personnel Systems in the Czech Republic, Hungary, and Poland* (2012) won the Award for Concept Analysis from the International Political Science Association.

Constantin Goschler – Professor of Modern History at Ruhr-University Bochum, Germany. His research interests focus on the politics of memory in Germany and the history of intelligence agencies. He is the author or co-editor of *Robbery and Restitution: The Conflict over Jewish Property in Europe* (2007), *Schuld und Schulden: Die Politik der Wiedergutmachung für NS-Verfolgte seit 1945* (2005), and *Die Praxis der Wiedergutmachung: Geschichte, Erfahrung und Wirkung in Deutschland und Israel* (2009).

Brian Grodsky – Associate Professor of Comparative Politics at University of Maryland, Baltimore County. His research interests focus on human rights, transitional justice, democratization, global civil society, social movements, and U.S. foreign policy. His books include *The Costs of Justice* (2010) and *Social Movements and the New State: The Fate of Pro-Democracy Organizations When Democracy Is Won* (2012).

Cynthia M. Horne – Associate Professor of Political Science at Western Washington University. Her research interests include lustration laws, transitional justice, rule of law, and trust building. She is the author of *Post-Communist Economies and Western Trade Discrimination: Are NMEs Our Enemies?* (2006).

Duncan Light – Visiting Research Fellow at Manchester Metropolitan University, United Kingdom. He is a cultural geographer with research interests in the relationships between urban space, power, identity, and public memory, and he has also explored the relationships between tourism and national identity in Romania. He is the coeditor of *Post-Communist Romania: Coming to Terms with Transition* (2001) and the author of *The Dracula Dilemma: Tourism, Identity and the State in Romania* (2012).

Moira Lynch – Assistant Professor of Political Science at Loyola University Maryland. Lynch earned a PhD in Political Science from the University of Minnesota in 2012. Her research interests include transitional justice, human rights, norms and institutions, democratization, civil war, international law, and feminist international relations theory.

Bridget Marchesi – Doctoral student in the Department of Political Science at the University of Minnesota. Her research interests include transitional justice, human rights, democracy and democratization, and civil war.

Nadya Nedelsky – Associate Professor, International Studies Department, Macalester College. Her research interests include human and minority rights, nationalism, ethnicity, democratization, citizenship, and transitional justice, with an area focus on Central and Eastern Europe. She is the author of *Defining the Sovereign Community: National Identity, Individual Rights, and Minority Membership in the Czech and Slovak*

Republics (2009) and the coeditor, with Lavinia Stan, of the three-volume *Encyclopedia of Transitional Justice* (2013). She has also published chapters in edited volumes on transitional justice and articles in the journals *Ethnic and Racial Studies, Ethnicities, Nations and Nationalism*, and *Theory and Society*.

Olivera Simić – Lecturer in the Griffith Law School, Griffith University, Australia. Her research engages with transitional justice, international law, gender, and crime from an interdisciplinary perspective. She is the author of *Regulation of Sexual Conduct in UN Peacekeeping Operations* (2012) and the editor of *Civil Society and Transitional Justice in the Balkans* (2013).

Lavinia Stan – Associate Professor of Political Science, St. Francis Xavier University, Canada. Her research focuses on post-communist democratization, especially transitional justice, and religion and politics. She is the author or coauthor of *Transitional Justice in Post-Communist Romania* (2013); *Church, State and Democracy in Expanding Europe* (2011); and *Religion and Politics in Post-Communist Romania* (2007) and the coeditor of *Encyclopedia of Transitional Justice* (2013) and *Transitional Justice in Eastern Europe and the Former Soviet Union* (2009).

Jelena Subotic – Associate Professor of Political Science at Georgia State University in Atlanta. She is the author of *Hijacked Justice: Dealing with the Past in the Balkans* (2009) and numerous articles about human rights, transitional justice, identity politics, and the Western Balkans.

Aleks Szczerbiak – Professor of Politics and Contemporary European Studies at University of Sussex, United Kingdom. His research interests revolve around political parties and electoral politics, impact of European integration on national politics, and the politics of transitional justice in post-communist states. He is the author of "Poles Together? The Emergence and Development of Political Parties in Post-communist Poland" (2001) and "Poland Within the European Union: New Awkward Partner or New Heart of Europe?" (2012).

Helga A. Welsh – Professor of Politics and International Affairs at Wake Forest University, North Carolina. Her publications have focused on the history and politics of the former East Germany, German unification, transitional justice, and democratization processes in Central and Eastern Europe. She is the coeditor of *German Unification: Process and Outcomes* (1994) and the author of *Revolutionärer Wandel auf Befehl* (1989).

Craig Young – Reader in Human Geography at Manchester Metropolitan University, United Kingdom. His research centers on the cultural geographies and politics of identity in post-communist Eastern Europe. He is the coeditor of *Cosmopolitan Urbanism* (2006) and coauthor of papers in *Nationalities Papers*, *Europe-Asia Studies*, and *Transactions of the Institute of British Geographers*.

Foreword

Constantin Goschler

Twenty-five years of experience with post-communist transitional justice: congratulations! But what is this silver jubilee about? First, of course, it is related to the fall of communism in Eastern Europe. At the same time, the jubilee reflects the continued rise of transitional justice both as a concept in political science and as political practice. Looking back to the starting point of these two closely intertwined processes in Central and Eastern Europe, we are forced to consider the importance of the circumstances that marked that departure, which might be described as the "spirit of 1989." At the time, all over the world, from Latin America to Eastern Europe, dictatorship seemed to be on the retreat, and the combination of liberal democracy and market economy appeared to be the unrivaled winner of the Cold War and a model for the future. This mood was most prominently manifested in Francis Fukuyama's *The End of History and the Last Man*, published in 1992. There, the political scientist – walking in the footsteps of German philosopher Georg Wilhelm Friedrich Hegel (1770–1831) and Russian-born French philosopher Alexandre Kojève (1902–1968) – argued that "liberal democracy may constitute the 'end point of mankind's ideological evolution' and the 'final form of human government,' and as such constituted the 'end of history.'"[1] From such a perspective, transitional justice readily appeared as an instrument of the *Weltgeist* and consequently was taken as the ultimate toolbox for replacing totalitarian dictatorship with liberal democracy.

We need to recall this optimism because in the meantime the celebratory mood that characterized the early post–Cold War period has given way to a veritable hangover. True, historians are happy that history has not ended, but the combination of liberal democracy and liberal market has lost much of its charisma. During the same period, transitional justice has become both a globally accepted model and a highly contested issue. The volume at hand offers an outstanding contribution to this ongoing academic and political debate by delivering numerous answers and raising even more questions, making it exciting reading. Instead of simply making normative claims for desirable political outcomes, the volume offers empirically saturated and theoretically rich case studies that provide many counterintuitive findings and thereby shatter trusted beliefs. Hence, the academic reader and the political practitioner alike will get the best of both worlds from this volume: a clear perspective on the ambivalences and contingencies of transitional justice in post-communist Central and Eastern Europe and an insight on its best and worst practices.

Commendably, the volume at hand is not a compendium of national case studies. The editors have chosen a systematic approach, structuring the volume in four consecutive steps: causes, effects, challenges, and neglected factors and actors of transitional justice in post-communist Eastern Europe. By following this structure, the contributors to the book offer not only astounding discoveries on a wide range of Central and Eastern European cases but also invaluable starting points for widening our perspective on transitional justice challenges in other parts of the world. I highlight only a handful of their most significant contributions.

In 1945, the four Allied powers started a comprehensive denazification and reeducation program in defeated Germany, which since then often has been considered a model for successful transitional justice. When the program was launched, the infamous German international lawyer Carl Schmitt, who had lost his prominent academic position as a result of denazification, criticized the realization of "victor's justice," voicing a popular viewpoint. In December 1949, Schmitt caustically commented in his *Glossarium*, alluding to the double standard used for judging crimes: "There exist crimes against and crimes for humanity. Crimes against humanity are committed by Germans. Crimes for humanity are committed against Germans."[2] While Carl Schmitt is certainly a problematic witness, he nevertheless addressed a crucial problem of modern political ethics. Although the concept of transitional justice implicitly presupposes a pre-stabilized harmony of power and morality, in reality it always becomes an element of the struggle for power and even a highly useful tool for its execution. The contributors to the present volume are very sensitive to this problem, and several case studies show how transitional justice can be used to delegitimize political opponents and strengthen certain political positions. This dynamic has deeply affected outcomes and perceptions of transitional justice in post-communist Central and Eastern Europe.

Another common problem in the region is that several layers of violent histories come into play, but countries apply transitional justice very selectively. This volume explores the tension between the communist past and the Nazi Holocaust, two periods that severely affected Central and Eastern Europe. While "Eastern" attempts to redress the communist past have been confronted with "Western" expectations that the Holocaust should also be addressed in the range of transitional justice programs adopted after 1989, especially in the context of admission into the European Union, the present volume avoids such narrowness.[3] The chapters not only carefully take into account the problem of multiple violent and criminal pasts but also offer an expansive view of transitional justice's timeframe, which they see as ongoing. Hence, for these contributors transitional justice extends long after the dictatorship's ousting.

Tina Rosenberg's famous differentiation between "criminal regimes" in Central and Eastern Europe and "regimes of criminals" in Latin America[4] also points to an important problem affecting post-communist transitional justice. Because in Central and Eastern Europe the lines between victims and perpetrators are so blurred as to lead to "diffused guilt," transitional justice there has not always been popular with larger segments of the society. Discussing a variety of individual cases, the contributors to the present volume deal with the resulting dilemma: while transitional justice aims at establishing democracy, democracy is not always favorable to and supportive of transitional justice. The new post-communist elites have repeatedly pointed to transitional justice's unpopularity. Sadly, the Central and Eastern European experience confirms the experience of other regions where victims of bygone dictatorships may not hope for much solidarity within their societies – at least as long as they constitute a minority therein.

This leads to another fundamental dilemma that is astutely analyzed in the present volume. Two of the paramount aims of transitional justice – justice and reconciliation – do not easily go hand in hand. A major catchword of transitional justice is transparency, and its concrete manifestation is lustration, a reckoning program widely implemented in post-communist Central and Eastern Europe. Several case studies included in this volume deal with the relationship between justice and reconciliation. They argue that, despite widespread demands for ousting the once powerful secret police, the opening of the secret files they compiled had many unwanted and unpopular side effects. Chief among these problematic effects has been the unraveling of post-communist societies' still-fragile social fabric, whose members often remain prone to nostalgia for the lost security of the communist era.

Ultimately, the present volume convincingly makes clear that transitional justice is not a blueprint for democracy, market economy, and happiness. Rather, the contributors explore transitional justice as a complicated process that involves intimate interactions within post-dictatorial societies and among diverse international actors, thereby reflecting the tensions between global norms and local practices that often come into play in the field of human rights politics. Instead of proposing and upholding a teleological perspective, the volume shows both successes and failures of transitional justice in post-communist Central and Eastern Europe and offers keen-witted explanations for them. The superb volume at hand will push forward our understanding of transitional justice in many ways. Moreover, it will profoundly affect our general perspective on Central and Eastern European societies after 1989. The volume's analyses are deeply realistic and offer multiple explanations for why transitional justice is not just a highly ambivalent endeavor but also one that is worth pursuing.

NOTES

1. Francis Fukuyama, *The End of History and the Last Man* (New York: Free Press/ Macmillan, 1992).
2. Carl Schmitt, entry from December 6, 1949, cited in *Glossarium: Aufzeichnungen der Jahre 1947–1951*, ed. Eberhard von Medem (Berlin: Duncker & Humblot, 1991), 282.
3. John Torpey, *Making Whole What Has Been Smashed: On Reparations Politics* (Cambridge, MA: Harvard University Press, 2006), 52 f.
4. Tina Rosenberg, *The Haunted Land: Facing Europe's Ghosts after Communism* (New York: Random House, 1995).

Introduction: Post-Communist Transitional Justice at 25

Nadya Nedelsky and Lavinia Stan

The year 2014 marks the twenty-fifth anniversary of the collapse of the Eastern European communist regimes, after which Eastern Europe attempted to reckon with the many state-sponsored wrongs committed between 1945 and 1989. The region experimented with court trials of former communist decision-makers and other state officials, lustration (the banning or public identification of communist leaders, secret agents, and other compromised persons occupying certain post-communist public positions), access for ordinary citizens to the extensive secret documents compiled on them by the secret political police forces, temporary and permanent history commissions, official apologies and condemnations, restitution of property abusively confiscated from individuals and communities, rewriting history textbooks, rehabilitation of former political prisoners, compensation packages, as well as extensive memorialization projects involving relevant commemorations, monuments, and exhibitions. Most of these programs have been formulated, funded, and completed by domestic state and non-state actors, while a handful were supported by international actors.

We now have a generation's worth of experience with these wrenching processes. This period spans the tumult of the revolutions that brought about the collapse of the communist dictatorship to the consolidation of new democratic regimes with now-adult citizens who don't remember communism and have no direct experience with its repression and oppression. Our volume's thirteen chapters gather, from this remarkable period, key lessons for both theory and practice formulated by experts in the field of transitional justice with intimate knowledge of the region's communist misfortunes and post-communist travails. The purpose of this volume is *not* to present comprehensive summaries of each country's accomplishments and failures in redressing the human rights violations perpetrated by communist state officials – these are already available as peer-reviewed articles and book chapters. Instead, the present volume focuses on the most important factors that have shaped the nature, speed, and sequence of transitional justice programs in the region's first twenty-five years after communism.

The volume is divided into four parts, each dedicated to a different overarching but interrelated theme. Part 1 explores the *causes* of transitional justice, Part 2, its *effects*, Part 3, key *challenges*, and Part 4, *neglected actors and factors* in coming to terms with the communist past. This division of focus allows for targeted engagement with key theoretical debates in the broader context of now long-term regional transition. Let us take each in turn.

The three chapters in Part 1 ask why post-communist countries chose their strategies, examining transitional justice's relationship to the host of political goods that the key leaders of these new democracies have had to deliver, the negotiations and calculations factored in electoral politics by formations representing the government and the opposition, as well as the ideological and programmatic concerns that sometimes have convinced politicians to pursue or block reckoning with the past. These relationships are investigated across a number of countries as diverse as Albania, Poland, Croatia, and Serbia, which are sometimes examined in detail on their own or strategically positioned in theoretically fruitful comparative frameworks. Part 1 focuses on selected transitional justice programs, some of which were quintessentially Eastern European like lustration and access to secret archives, while others were imported into the region from other parts of the world after they proved their ability to rectify past wrongs, such as court trials and investigative commissions. The chapters explain why these programs were adopted rather early or rather late after the collapse of the communist regime, why their scope differed considerably from neighbor to neighbor, and why particular processes were sometimes completely abandoned in particular political circumstances.

Part 2 deals with the impact of post-communist transitional justice programs. Its two chapters use different data sets and methods. The first chapter is exclusively quantitative, resting on the Eastern European section of a large database of cases drawn from all continents and a variety of countries in transition. The second chapter combines an opinion poll with qualitative methods and instead of investigating all post-communist countries, as the first chapter does, focuses on developments in one state, the Czech Republic. Both studies seek to examine how lustration (including the public identification of former secret agents), court trials of former communist decision-makers, and retribution programs (including rehabilitation of former political prisoners) have affected post-communist rule of law and respect for human rights. The most important theoretical question this section addresses concerns the expected positive relationship between transitional justice and democratization, which underlies most reparation and retribution programs enacted in Eastern Europe.

Part 3 discusses the main challenges that have faced post-communist transitional justice. These chapters deal with four different themes that have emerged in the region as crucially important for any attempt to meaningfully reckon with past human rights violations, but have remained understudied to date: the problem of timing transitional justice programs and the importance of launching early versus late initiatives; the political choices made when new democracies have to address multiple and competing criminal pasts simultaneously; the way countries get inspiration from programs implemented elsewhere in the region through diffusion processes promoted by domestic, regional, and international actors; and the way honest inquiries into recent human rights abuses are impeded by the mythologization of the past for some political purposes. Again, conceptual and methodological plurality allows these chapters, when brought together, to contribute significant theoretical mileage. Two of the chapters included in this part focus on Balkan countries where the communist past has competed for attention from the political elite and the general population with a bloody post-communist revolution (Romania) or a devastating civil war (Serbia and Croatia). The other two chapters adopt a broader view, taking into consideration a number of post-communist countries' experience with transitional justice.

Lastly, Part 4 presents methods of coming to terms with the past that have been underexplored to date by scholars and practitioners working on post-communist Eastern Europe, and in doing so seeks to test the current limits of the definitions of "transitional justice." These understudied methods include history commissions, official commemorations, the changing of names of streets and localities, theatre productions, and unofficial disclosures of names of individuals connected to the communist political police forces. Here too chapters privileging processes unfolding in a particular country (Romania or the former Yugoslavia) are juxtaposed with chapters that survey all, or almost all, known cases registered in the region during the past twenty-five years. Given its case selection, Part 4 breaks new ground by underscoring the importance and numerous benefits, as well as the many shortcomings and possible dangers, of symbolic processes of coming to terms with the past that can be pursued by civil society actors.

This volume makes important contributions to the existing transitional justice literature. By discussing the efforts to reckon with the communist past across a number of Eastern European countries during the first twenty-five years of post-communist democratic transformation, the chapters offer welcome broad-based information on the practices, processes, and methods that have been pursued to date. In doing so, they often underscore ways of rectifying past wrongs that have gained little, if any, attention from scholars and practitioners. Beyond this, the volume contributes to the theory of transitional justice by investigating a number of outstanding questions still unanswered satisfactorily (the importance of diffusion or multiple "competing pasts"; the link between transitional justice and rule of law, trust, and respect for human rights; the possible contribution of non-state actors; the challenge of timing reckoning and the perils of ignoring its reconciliatory dimension; the various determinants of reckoning with the past), and by presenting several methods that have remained unstudied to date (vigilante justice, commemorations, as well as theatre productions). Indeed, the volume helps us to understand transitional justice in general and the post-communist politics of memory in particular, by proposing explanations for how some methods of redressing communist wrongs (such as property restitution, court trials, and memorialization) are more popular than others (most notably, radical lustration) in the post-communist context; why transitional justice stagnated or accelerated at different moments of time; whether delayed justice is worth pursuing at all or all reckoning must be conducted relatively early after the regime change; why post-authoritarian governments decide to reckon with some pasts, but not with others, and how they prioritize transitional justice relative to the business of running the country; and how the politics of memory has (or has not) facilitated the broader democratization process.

While many scholarly articles and book chapters have taken up some of these questions, our volume offers a unique contribution because of the breadth of its perspective. First, it brings temporal range, looking at developments in the region over the entirety of the post-communist period, spanning early to very recent developments. This offers a perspective simply unavailable to works written closer to the tumultuous period of revolution and regime transition and studies concerned with particular events taken in isolation. Second, it provides regional range, offering comparisons between country developments over this long period – something beyond the space limitations of the journal articles and individual chapters published to date. Third, the volume offers program range, offering studies focused on neglected ways of reckoning that push us to reconsider the definitional boundaries accepted to date. Last, it does all this with a view to highlighting both the most important and the most neglected factors shaping transitional justice in post-communist Eastern Europe.

PART I

Determinants of Transitional Justice

1

Transitional Justice and Political Goods

Brian Grodsky

Twenty-five years after the collapse of communism, the ghosts of yesterday remain very much alive. From Poland to the Balkans, various aspects of transitional justice have become part and parcel of a much broader political discourse touching on everything from political identity to regional integration. As in other parts of the world, in Eastern Europe the process of dealing with the human rights abuses of previous regimes promises to carry on for even longer than those regimes existed in practice. Transitional justice has already proven in the region to be anything but transitional.

This long-term nature of transitional justice and the extent to which it pervades other apparently unrelated policy spheres raise challenges to earlier theoretical work on the determinants of transitional justice policies. Central arguments in the literature focus on factors such as the relative power of new vis-à-vis old elites, the dominance and complicity of old elites' associates in new state structures, the nature of past human rights abuses, and societal fragmentation (for example, along ethnic or class lines). This chapter argues that all of these might help to establish the boundaries within which new elites shape transitional justice policies, but they do not fully account for the policies chosen. Here, I add one more piece to the complicated puzzle, arguing that political elites pursue transitional justice strategically, implementing popular programs only to the extent they do not interfere with the provision of other expected goods and services and pursuing even unpopular programs when they are perceived to facilitate the delivery of these expected goods.

I assess this argument based on media analyses and interviews with elites involved in transitional justice policies in Poland, Serbia, and Croatia.[1] The diversity of experiences during and after communism makes this group of cases a fruitful area to assess broad arguments derived from countries around the world. These cases vary in important ways, in particular with regard to the nature and scope of repression, the regime change, and the transitional justice programs on the table. Poland is the quintessential Central European case, where the worst years of repression ended in the 1950s and the communists ultimately negotiated power away to an opposition group (Solidarity). Serbia and Croatia, by contrast, registered multiple periods of repression, the last and most violent one taking place after communism and involving victims regarded by the public as enemies. While calls for, and mechanisms of, transitional justice were almost exclusively domestic in the Polish case, they emanated largely from outside actors in the latter two.

DETERMINING JUSTICE

Since World War II, political elites have struggled with the question of how to redress past human rights violations. For many transitional justice scholars, the decision of how to deal with the past (or not) is a function of the relative power of new political leaders vis-à-vis former leaders of the old regime. From an elite perspective, the path of political transition (negotiation or revolution) can influence the post-transition distribution of political power and, hence, the feasibility of various transitional justice policies. Following Huntington, proponents of this argument believe that where old elites have the power to direct change, they will in the process ensure for themselves amnesty and/or a strong enough hand in the new regime to ensure that transitional justice is weak or non-existent. Where members of the old regime are replaced by revolution, their weakness should result in much more aggressive forms of transitional justice.[2]

Proponents of the relative power theory, who define power more broadly by taking into account state structures, emphasize the continued presence in key power ministries of actors involved in earlier abuses. This, in turn, depends on the nature of the previous regime. In the South American context, the military is particularly relevant; in Eastern Europe, the police and secret services have received more attention. Their power, as an ostensibly cohesive, armed group, gives these actors the potential means to disrupt the transition; their complicity gives them a motive. Those applying an even broader definition of power, extending it to the level of societal support, argue that new elites avoid justice measures when they might inflame public opinion and increase instability, particularly where significant sectors of society were previously aligned with the old regime. Social structure (ethnic, religious, class) may preclude transitional justice if such policies could antagonize intra-societal relations. The role of memory and temporal as well as qualitative aspects of past abuses might set the parameters of activity. Accordingly, transitional justice is a function of relative power, but society – not members of the former regime – determines what is feasible.[3]

These arguments are heavily focused on what Welsh calls the "weight of the past," which in Central Europe includes such historical factors as level of communist-era repression (lower after 1956) and mode of transition (typically involving a significant role for the outgoing regime).[4] Some authors have noted that the most far-reaching lustration policies unfolded precisely in two states where the communist regime rapidly collapsed (Czechoslovakia and East Germany).[5] Others have contrasted otherwise similar states based on the level of communist-era repression, explaining that those facing more repression or fewer ways to oppose the old regime were inclined to more aggressively deal with the communist regime.[6] Like most analyses of post-communist transitional justice, some of these studies were focused largely on the single policy of lustration.

Not surprisingly, given the politicization of lustration, most scholars of post-communism also incorporate into their analysis the "politics of the present" – that is, the political setting, such as the political strength of post-communists, and contextual factors, such as fading memories and re-evaluations of the communist period. From this perspective, lustration laws depend on the ability to assemble pro-lustration coalitions in the legislature, sometimes by moderating policies to make them more politically feasible. In this vein, Calhoun claims that the adoption of liberal democratic values by post-communist states results in more lenient (thus more politically acceptable to former communists) lustration.[7] Others have found that lustration initiatives are more likely to come from those politicians who failed to fight the previous system and set out in the new one to prove their true anticommunist bona fides.[8] Still others play up the very politicization of transitional justice, portraying it as a contemporary game used by one set of politicians to weaken others.[9]

As the distinction between past and present is a false dichotomy in some contexts, some scholars have adopted a hybrid approach, showing how the two come together in ways that heavily influence transitional justice approaches. In a valuable study, Nalepa argues that new elites sometimes back away from lustration to avoid unearthing skeletons in their own closets (infiltration of communist-era dissident networks).[10] This may explain why in Poland and Hungary, where relatively more from communist-era opposition networks were recruited by the secret police, lustration came later than in the Czech Republic, which had fewer collaborators, meaning that former anticommunists taking power had fewer worries about embarrassing themselves.

AN INSTITUTIONAL APPROACH

Each of these studies identifies individual pieces of the transitional justice puzzle that, on their own, are important but when taken together become much more powerful. Using these various arguments as building blocks, I apply an institutional lens in which transitional justice policies are a function of both the constraints and opportunities of empowered actors. Many of the preceding arguments represent the former. For instance, powerful old elites can be a threat to aggressive transitional justice, particularly when they have voting power in primary institutions, control the means of violence, or manipulate public opinion in the new system. Similarly, social schisms based on roles in the previous regime can limit available transitional justice policies. This is particularly true when empowered politicians believe they need the support of a constituency with strong views on justice in order to maintain power past the next elections. However, politics are dynamic, and while these variables may set the stage for transitional justice decisions, they do not, I argue, dictate their direction.

I follow the underlying assumption in the literature that most new political elites, those excluded from power under the former system and empowered under the new, democratic one, tend to want to purse the most aggressive forms of transitional justice possible. I categorize these elites here as "post-oppositionists" – they are the one-time leaders of the opposition movement that preceded democratic breakthrough, who take power in the new democracy. Whether motivated by morality, pragmatism, or vengeance, those who argue for turning the other cheek tend to be outliers. Nevertheless, empowered proponents of transitional justice face various sources of (potentially conflicting) pressure for and against accountability policies, a function of past and present conditions. Moreover, they are much less likely to pursue forms of transitional justice that would ultimately endanger their political survival. At the end of the day, democratic leaders are accountable to constituents who expect government to provide essential goods and services. These political goods include everything from order, security, and civil liberties to anti-inflationary or pro-employment economic policies and international memberships (with their respective security or economic dividends). The provision of these goods, which is a central feature of political viability in a democratic state and features prominently in the good government literature, is critical to understanding how transitional justice plays out.

From a strategic perspective, political leaders concerned primarily with political survival must ensure that transitional justice policies are perceived by their constituents to further, or at a minimum not interfere with, the provision of those goods they can influence. This is most important for those actors with the greatest constitutional powers, since these actors suffer most when constituent expectations and policy outcome are out of sync. Those "primary actors" tasked with running the state (such as a prime minister) will face considerably higher expectations than those more ceremonial, "secondary" leaders (such as the monarch or weak president in a typical parliamentary system). As I will show, in primary institutions transitional justice is largely dictated by the following bottom line: where justice is seen as an impediment to the delivery of goods it should be eschewed, where it is viewed as beneficial it should be pursued. Impediments are measured in perceived opportunity costs; even if transitional justice has very little monetary cost, it may be seen as politically costly if it is viewed as a policyholder preoccupation or if the public is antagonistic toward a chosen policy.

These public attitudes govern the relationship between political goods and transitional justice policies. While such policies can be seen as political goods in and of themselves (for example, if criminal enterprises are disrupted by charging members involved in former rights violations), they can also be seen as competing for critical resources otherwise available for other programs that may be seen by voters as more pressing. Where the public is neutral or in favor of retribution (whether a function of the "politics of the past" or "politics of the present"), elites must demonstrate that such accountability measures do not interfere with their provision of expected goods. Where the public is staunchly opposed to aggressive forms of transitional justice, such as criminal accountability, primary actors will only pursue such policies if they can explicitly link them to their ability to better provide these goods – in essence, buying their constituents off.

While transitional justice preferences of secondary actors, facing far fewer demands and expectations, are more difficult to predict and apparently less consequential for policy output, they can affect the transitional justice debate indirectly, by using agenda setting, issue linkages, and public political pressure to increase or decrease primary actors' perceived costs of pursuing transitional justice. Introduction of transitional justice legislation or public statements, appeals, and campaigns by secondary actors might put primary actors on the defensive and force them to alter their policies. These pressures can ultimately result in the adoption of somewhat more or less aggressive policies than might be predicted by looking at primary actors alone.

By focusing on new elites' calculations of what publics want and expect from them, this institutional argument allows us to consider a range of variables featured prominently in the literature, which help set new elites' parameters of movement. In one country, transitional justice may face public opposition due to high levels of complicity, in another it may be intimately linked to identity, and in a third the public may have little interest at all. In each case, the perceived public support will indirectly affect new elites' calculus of how much people are willing to pay for transitional justice. Structural constraints, including the explicit costs and the opportunity costs of a particular policy (which may in part result from the power old elites continue to wield), affect this calculus and help inform elites about what forms of transitional justice are politically feasible.

EVIDENCE FROM THE POST-COMMUNIST WORLD

The three cases explored here, Poland, Croatia, and Serbia, allow us to look for replication in a variety of contexts.[11] In some ways, these cases are broadly comparable. As noted earlier, all have faced issues of accountability in the context of radical political and economic reform, they share a legacy of relatively similar communist-era human rights abuses and the persistence of formerly abusive institutions in post-communist times, and citizens in these states share many political cultural traits. However, these cases also diverge in ways that provide for a very broad test of the arguments posited here. They differ by transition type as well as temporal and qualitative aspects of human rights violations, making them representative of post-communist diversity and instrumental in understanding similar problems outside of the communist world. While Jelena Subotic's chapter in this volume focuses on the politicized reinterpretation of certain elements of communist and pre-communist history in the post-communist period, I concentrate here on violations perpetrated during the wars in the 1990s.

My analysis is based primarily on media analyses and elite interviews. The first stage of research for each case involved an international media review, based on broad keyword searches on *LexisNexis* (for example, "criminal prosecution" and "Yugoslavia"). In the countries where international reporting or translations of local publications were insufficient to establish a timeline of the events and political context from the time of political change to the period of research (2005), I then conducted a local media analysis (in Serbia, I searched *Danas* and *Politika*; in Poland, I searched *Gazeta Wyborcza* and *Rzeczpospolita*). Next, I conducted semi-structured, open-question elite interviews to gauge elite perceptions for why specific policies were pursued or eschewed. Although I focus on criminal accountability in this chapter, the project included measures from condemnations and victim compensation to truth commissions and administrative cleansings. I interviewed (in each of the local languages) four types of actors directly concerned with human rights developments in each state: members of the (former) opposition movements and current ruling elites, leaders of locally active non-governmental human rights organizations, representatives of foreign missions and intergovernmental organizations, and members of the (former) regime accused of rights violations. Interviewees were determined based on their position (in strong or weak institutions) and stance toward transitional justice. I also relied on the snowball method, requesting at the end of each interview names of actors prominent on both sides of the transitional justice debate, whom I also contacted. I conducted more than 150 interviews in the three countries, asking actors who were close to policy decisions what influenced the way these decisions were ultimately made.

Serbia

Slobodan Milošević, responsible for egregious human rights violations following the dismemberment of Yugoslavia, left office in the fall of 2000, when a democratic alliance dominated by two Serbian opposition parties, Vojislav Koštunica's Democratic Party of Serbia (DSS) and Zoran Djindjić's Democratic Party (DS), helped mobilize the population and oust Milošević. Despite Milošević's ouster, Serbia had a negotiated transition. Koštunica took control of the presidency and federal structures through an October 2000 "electoral revolution," but he became captain of a sinking ship (the federation), his position largely representative, secondary in authority to the prime minister's. The opposition consolidated power through the December 2000 republic elections, the product of negotiations with Milošević's associates. Djindjić subsequently became the Serbian prime minister, a primary institution responsible for running the day-to-day affairs of that government, representing 90 percent of Yugoslavia's population (with the remainder being accounted for by Montenegro). Yugoslavia's new leaders at both the federal and republic levels immediately faced external pressures to extradite alleged war criminals to the domestically unpopular International Criminal Tribunal for the Former Yugoslavia at The Hague (referred to here as the ICTY or The Hague).

The case of Serbia demonstrates the complicated nature of relative power explanations. According to a transition-based political elite argument, those who long opposed the Milošević regime (referred to here as post-oppositionists) should faithfully follow through on any (assumed) promises of amnesty that made the transition possible.[12] Electoral results, which left these post-oppositionists with control of 70 percent of parliamentary seats in the powerful Serb Republic, might cast doubt on this interpretation since post-oppositionists emerged as a powerful force despite the negotiated transition. Nevertheless, state-structure proponents would also warn that the continued dominance of old regime associates over the police and military leaderships should be enough to stymie proponents of criminal justice. With citizens also largely opposed to justice for war crimes, most relative power considerations suggest criminal justice was off the table.

However, Serbian republic leaders under the first two post-Milošević governments transferred more than twenty mostly high-ranking indictees to the ICTY. The greatest threat to this process, according to interviewees involved, came not from members of the Milošević regime, but from President Koštunica, himself a post-oppositionist. Milošević's arrest and extradition led to the first open split in the post-oppositionist camp and brought federal (military) and republic (police) security structures into armed conflict. Still, Djindjić maintained his policy of sluggish cooperation with the ICTY until he was murdered in 2003, purportedly for this policy. When Koštunica became prime minister in 2004, Yugoslavia's cooperation with the ICTY was initially frozen, but it then suddenly found new life in the twelve "voluntary surrenders," largely regarded as handovers, in the last quarter of 2004 and first quarter of 2005.

Outside of their institutional settings, both Koštunica and Djindjić should have avoided cooperation with the ICTY between 2000 and 2003. Neither seemed personally in favor of the ICTY, Koštunica labeling it a "monstrous institution"[13] and Djindjić questioning the veracity of its indictments. Cooperation with the ICTY was unpopular and opposed by a majority of Serbs, who viewed charges against fellow Serbs as disproportionate to the evidence and overwhelmingly believed their brethren would not receive a fair trial in The Hague. Cooperation was risky, as was dramatically demonstrated by Djindjić's assassination. While post-opposition forces wanted to see Milošević and his cronies in prison, they envisioned more benign domestic trials for corruption (a crime against the Serb people) over international trials for war crimes (committed against non-Serbs).

Officials from the United States (U.S.) and the European Union (EU), by consistently advocating for ICTY cooperation throughout the first years of the post-Milošević transition, provided the great push for international justice.[14] Western leaders dangled the carrots of ICTY-conditional foreign aid and membership in Western institutions (especially the EU) as an enticement. Why did Western pressures convince Prime Minister Djindjić to cooperate (if cautiously) with The Hague, while they were ineffective with regard to federal President Koštunica? How did Koštunica influence events despite occupying such a weak office? And why did Koštunica alter his policies several months after becoming prime minister?

The answer to the first and last questions, according to Serbian political leaders, is that cooperation is largely determined by institutional incentives. Those who worked closest to Djindjić are adamant that the prime minister and others in his party wanted to see Milošević stand trial at home and only subsequently, when this became increasingly impossible, at The Hague.[15] They also recognized that without cooperation with the EU their political careers were in jeopardy. Without Western carrots, including favorable EU negotiations and billions of dollars of much-needed aid, Serbian governing elites would have been unable to move closer to fulfilling popular aspirations for conditioned policies such as EU entry and provide for basic services such as electricity.

In public, Djindjić and other government officials simultaneously expressed discomfort with the ICTY and framed arrests and extraditions as a step toward modernization and re-integration into the international community. "We do not have the luxury of losing needed economic aid for not collaborating with the court in The Hague," he made clear.[16] Indeed, Milošević's provocative extradition took place just days before an important donors conference valued at more than $1 billion. Djindjić "didn't do this only for the money, but that was a very concrete issue for a prime minister," recalled one of his former advisors.[17] "Of course, financial support was important for us and the deadline for us really was a deadline," added one of Djindjić's deputies.[18]

The slow pace of cooperation with the ICTY was partly the effect of opposition from Djindjić's greatest political rival, President Koštunica, who used anti-cooperation calls to differentiate his party from Djindjić's. Based in a weak institution, Koštunica had much more to gain from populist anti-ICTY rhetoric than from Western aid. "It was Djindjić who was running the finances. Koštunica had absolutely no responsibility for running the country," pointed out a former Djindjić advisor.[19] Without counter-pressure from the secondary institution, elites admit that costs of cooperation would have been significantly lower and cooperation may have been more forthcoming.[20]

Therefore, Serbia's pro-transitional justice elites calculated that unpopular pro-ICTY policies could be trumped by other, especially economic, measures.[21] Parties favorable to transitional justice were not alone in this calculation. When the nature of goods appeared sufficient to win public acquiescence, even Serbia's most adamant opponents to cooperation submitted. Subsequently, Prime Minister Koštunica, who as president had opposed cooperation with the "despicable"[22] ICTY, orchestrated twelve "voluntary surrenders," largely regarded as handovers, in late 2004 and early 2005.[23]

Koštunica's dramatic policy change, a case of strategic conversion, responded to an EU deadline for the start of negotiations that would bring

Serbia one step closer to EU entry. Like his predecessors, Koštunica went out of his way to explain cooperation with the ICTY as "necessary" for entry into the EU.[24] According to his deputy, handovers to the ICTY were "in the interest of our county."[25] Cooperation with the Tribunal remained unpopular and there is no indication that Koštunica had become a Hague convert, but he, like Djindjić, altered his own strategic preferences, gambling that delivery of key goods would outweigh the unpopular decisions used to purchase them. Also similar to Djindjić, Koštunica strived to use international pressures to secure goods that among his potential electorate made up for the sins used to purchase them. The idea was not to simply weather public opposition but to use the increased availability of popularly demanded goods to minimize or even reverse it.

Croatia

One year before Milošević was deposed, a loose coalition of six opposition parties defeated the late Croatian strongman Franjo Tudjman's nationalist party in the 1999 "electoral revolution." In the run-up to those elections those opposing Tudjman's regime vowed to increase cooperation with the ICTY in order to secure Croatia's accession to the EU, so cooperation seemed likely when they began the year 2000 in solid control of the government and parliament. In an interview with the foreign press soon after he assumed the premiership, Ivica Račan affirmed that "we will certainly accelerate the process of cooperation with The Hague."[26]

The change in Račan's attitude only makes sense from an institutional viewpoint. In 2000–2003, Croatian post-oppositionists (those who had opposed the Tudjman regime and the 1990s wars) controlled the presidency (a secondary institution), the cabinet, and 65 percent of seats in parliament (both primary institutions), but were unwilling or unable to systematically carry out transfers of Croatian criminals to the ICTY or other criminal forms of justice – in stark contrast to relative power predictions. Instead, they pursued a spotty policy of criminal accountability (whether cooperation with The Hague or domestic criminal trials), avoiding activities that could be interpreted as unpatriotic by voters or Račan's ruling coalition, representing the 1999 opposition parties which were unified only in their pro-Western, anti-war, and anti-Tudjman policies. In contrast to public support relative power arguments, Croatian leaders were afraid not of confronting a divided and potentially violent Croatia but of humiliating Croats with a reassessment of their recent war years. As in Serbia, political strategy and personality politics, filtered through formal institutions, explain many of the transitional justice decisions taken in Croatia. And as in Serbia, society created the political landscape on which all of this played out.

Račan and other leaders of the former democratic opposition, like their counterparts across the border in Serbia, claim to personally have wanted to see war crimes violators punished – claims that nearly all interviewees from civil society backed up. They also realized that society was unprepared to allow this to happen on a large scale or at high levels at home, leaving The Hague as the only place where justice could succeed. If Račan sounded like a true internationalist in the foreign press just after coming to power, his enthusiasm for cooperating with the ICTY was far more bridled on the domestic stage, where political leaders understood that most Croats felt they were victims, not perpetrators, of war crimes, and those who defended Croatia were heroes. "The general approach here is that Croatia was attacked by Serbia and we had a right to defend ourselves," summarized the parliamentarian who drafted Croatia's ICTY cooperation law.[27]

As in Serbia, Croatian authorities faced diplomatic pressure for cooperation from the United States and the EU, a club most Croats hoped to join. Unlike in Serbia, however, foreign pressures on Croatia lacked focus and salience. Diplomatic pressure was diffusely dealt with the various war-related rights violations that continued to exist, so apart from pressing for cooperation with the ICTY, Westerners demanded Serb refugees' right of return and greater transparency for domestic war crimes trials of primarily ethnic Serbs. More importantly, the nature of the goods Račan was offered in return for cooperation (a distant EU membership) made the benefits of cooperation a difficult sell to constituents looking for concrete, immediate gains. In contrast to Serbia, there was no mention of Hague conditionality in the run-up to talks on $250 million in assistance from the International Monetary Fund. U.S. aid to Croatia was raised from $12 million under Tudjman to a still-meager $20 million under Račan, conditional on the Croatian government's cooperation with the ICTY and the return of Serb refugees. The EU officials admitted that while funding was theoretically contingent on political conditions, they lacked the unity to engage in the complicated task of pulling funding. Intra-Union cleavages hurt the EU's credibility, convincing many politicians and constituents in Croatia that the ICTY issue "will just blow over," as several interviewees put it. This left Račan without the tools necessary to use foreign carrots and sticks to convince Croatian constituents that criminal justice was in their best interest.

As a result, and despite his own preference for criminal trials, Račan primarily played anti-Hague cards in public. Upon taking office, he promised to balance Croatia's "international obligations" with his duty to respect "the right to freedom and actions which secured (the state)."[28] He attacked the ICTY sentences and resisted the Tribunal's demands to the point that his government just narrowly escaped Security Council condemnation. Račan warned the ICTY to avoid equalizing Serbian and Croat guilt, thus supporting the widely held view that the majority of war crimes were carried out by Serbs and not Croats. As Croatia's former United Nations representative explained, "Definitely no one was a saint, but Milošević was the devil."[29] Račan assured Croats repeatedly that he had a strong record of non-compliance with ICTY demands for extraditions and would never accept indictments dealing with Croatian offenses.

Therefore, although Croatia received a much smaller list of Hague indictments than Serbia, Račan fought the international community in almost every case. On a rare occasion when the ICTY demanded handovers of two Croatian generals (Rahim Ademi and Ante Gotovina), Račan at first refused, then conceded only after a personal visit by the ICTY Chief Prosecutor Carla del Ponte and a one-month wait, by which time Gotovina allegedly had been allowed to escape. In 2002, Račan refused to hand over General Janko Bobetko on health grounds. Račan was ultimately credited with encouraging the surrender of just two indictees, Pasko Ljubicic and Rahmi Ademi.

The distance and intangibility of their country's entry into the EU made it extraordinarily difficult for Croatian elites to convert cooperation with the ICTY into readily consumable political goods at home. Račan, whose government was destabilized after he encouraged the generals to surrender, was weary of facing an anti-ICTY Croatian electorate if his government ever collapsed while extraditing national heroes. Račan was primarily concerned that his inability to demonstrate that cooperation with the ICTY was necessary would hurt him in the "battle for neutrals," that is, the moderate Croatians who may have supported his policies but were wary of attacks on the war period.[30]

When Račan did cooperate, he attempted to use international carrots and sticks much as the Serbs (more successfully) did. Without the same clear ties between cooperation and political goods, Račan had to stretch. He warned of international isolation as a result of non-cooperation and sometimes struggled to create the appearance of threats (economic sanctions) that were in fact absent.[31] For the most part, outside of occasional crises related to a particular suspect, Račan worked to keep ICTY cooperation at the more mundane level and out of the public eye. With little to gain and much to lose from an open policy of cooperation, he agreed, for example, to some document handovers but publicly held his ground on "unacceptable" ICTY requests.[32]

According to interviewees, including Račan himself, Račan desperately wanted to cooperate and privately expressed frustration that even domestic non-governmental organizations supportive of transitional justice were insufficiently active for him to convince constituents that cooperation was right.[33] More importantly, Račan lacked the tools to show these constituents that Croatia and Croatians would ultimately gain from cooperation. As a result, Račan acted counter to his own preferences for aggressive justice and openly balked at Western demands for compliance. Particular episodes of compliance partly ensued because President Stjepan Mesić, protected by his weaker powers and constitutionally dictated term in office, adopted a more forceful pro-ICTY stance that helped win over a few supporters and lessened the bite of Račan's pro-justice moves, including transferring documents and people, to The Hague.

As in Serbia, when the nature of the goods appeared sufficient to win over public acceptance, even Croatia's most adamant opponents to transitional justice were converted. This occurred in 2005, one year after Ivo Sanader, an ardent nationalist who had orchestrated a 2001 protest in defense of General Gotovina, became prime minister. His cabinet faced a crisis when EU officials finally delivered a concrete sanction, indefinitely postponing accession negotiations until Croatia demonstrated resolve to capture Gotovina. Faced with the responsibility of crushing Croatia's EU aspirations, Sanader saw he had more to gain in the long term from cooperation than obstruction. As such, he ceased hoping aloud for Gotovina's voluntary surrender and became an active proponent of Gotovina's handover, freezing the general's assets and even promising he would personally arrest and extradite him if given the chance.

To supporters, Sanader was a selfless politician, promising on Croatian Radio that his actions were about "the future of Croatia" and risking the nationalist backlash that led to his party's major defeat in the 2005 local elections.[34] As Sanader said: "My government is entirely oriented towards solving the last outstanding issue" – meaning unblocking EU negotiations.[35] By December, Gotovina was in The Hague, thanks in part to Croatian intelligence, and EU negotiations had resumed. The gamble proved to be a wise one; in the 2007 elections, Sanader's party came out stronger than it had four years earlier (winning 36.6 percent as opposed to 33.9 percent of the electoral vote), and he held onto the premiership.

Poland

While the cases of Serbia and Croatia highlight how foreign actors can influence the availability of political goods and thereby affect opportunities and even policy preferences of domestic elites, most post-repressive states are neither subject to international judicial mechanisms nor faced with aid conditionality based on transitional justice policy. Poland, where one-time anticommunists from the Solidarity movement (referred to here as post-oppositionists) faced practically no international pressure in the transitional justice sphere, is a more typical case. Solidarity activists and Communist Party leaders negotiated Poland's transition to democracy in 1989, making Poland the first European country to abandon communism. In the process, former communists guaranteed themselves a place in the new government and 65 percent of seats in the primary, lower house of parliament (Sejm). Post-oppositionists were left with 35 percent of the Sejm and total control in the freely contested secondary, upper house of parliament (Senate).

Given the exclusively domestic nature of accountability influences, the relatively weak institutional strength of post-oppositionists and the unreformed nature of Poland's communist repressive apparatus, relative power proponents should expect Poland's new elites to avoid harsh transitional justice. Nevertheless, just two months after assuming power on promises of economic and political reform, post-oppositionists launched a truth process designed to prosecute former communist leaders. Immediately after the regime change, the anticommunist opposition forces were unified in their quest for aggressive transitional justice. Within several months, however, an institutional schism arose. Senators struggled to keep transitional justice on the agenda, while Sejm members strived to moderate Senate policies in order to ensure support from former communists and their allies for economic reforms demanded by voters. The result was, after 1989, a more watered down transitional justice policy.

Although a minority in the constitutionally powerful Sejm, the Solidarity leaders forced former communist legislators to accept a truth process that led directly to criminal investigations of communist decision-makers. The Special Commission to Investigate the Ministry of Internal Affairs was tasked with analyzing more than 100 unsolved deaths attributed to the security services and other Ministry departments during the 1980s. Power constraints forced the Sejm's Solidarity minority to limit the legal powers of the Commission and allow former communist representatives to serve on working groups that conducted the Commission's inquiries. Nevertheless, as Solidarity leader Bronislaw Geremek noted, the Commission was a major step toward ensuring that communist "crimes should be punished."[36] The Commission's findings were used directly for disciplinary action or, in 88 cases, sent to public prosecutors for further investigation and possible trial. While the problem of building cases for crimes committed years earlier contributed to a dearth of convictions, the political will of the anticommunist Solidarity to pursue transitional justice initially proved stronger than rigidly defined power constraints indicate. Not only did outnumbered Solidarity representatives in the Sejm not draw back from the former communists, but they also investigated the communist general who continued to head the Ministry of Internal Affairs.

In contrast to the solid support Solidarity leaders in both houses of parliament gave to the Commission, within one year the question of criminal accountability provoked an institutional split. In the fall of 1990, senators began pressing for an extension of the mandate of the Chief Commission for the Investigation of Hitlerite Atrocities (Glowna Komisija or the GK) to include all communist-era crimes through 1989. By the time the GK had been expanded into the Commission for the Prosecution of Crimes against the Polish Nation, the Sejm had severely limited its authority to only those communist-era rights violations committed up to 1956. Senators fought restrictions until the end, when one acknowledged the political reality: "It is literally a miracle that this bill passed at all."[37]

Evidence suggests that the divergence in preferences was influenced by attention to economic conditions. The investigative commission was launched in the summer of 1989, before Solidarity members in the Sejm needed the support of communist legislators to produce expected goods (economic reform legislation). By the time the GK legislation was introduced, Sejm anticommunist members needed political good will from their communist colleagues to guarantee the continuity of economic reforms already underway. By limiting justice to pre-1957 rights violators (mostly dead or retired), they hoped to minimize the risk of legislative deadlock in this and other critical spheres. With little impact on the provision of these goods, senators had no political stake in this process.

A broader survey of the transitional justice debate from this period provides additional evidence that Sejm members were more focused on the political goods side of transitional justice. In 1991, for example, the Sejm rejected a Senate rehabilitation and compensation bill that nullified politically motivated criminal sentences issued between May 1943 (when Stalin created a Polish army under General Zygmunt Berling) and 1989. Senators, who did not have to pay for policies that would spring from the law because they had no responsibility for the budget, considered their version of the bill an indirect attack on the entire communist period. They argued: "If we accept the date of December 31, 1956, then we *ex cathedra* state that after this date there was no repression, there were no illegitimate sentences and there was no communist system."[38] As with the GK legislation, Sejm members slashed the scope of the bill to 1944–1956, ostensibly fearing that streamlining payments for all communist-era victims could threaten the stability of Poland's extraordinarily fragile economy. Many worried about voter reactions to an expanded bill since, one Sejm member noted, "Compensation would have come at the expense of taxpayers. If this were to come from [former Internal Minister Czeslaw] Kiszczak's personal income, that would be another story."[39]

According to relative power logic, we might have seen an expansion of criminal accountability after former anti-communist oppositionists consolidated their grip on power (1991–1993). This did not occur for several reasons. Apparently most important was the crumbling of the Solidarity umbrella, which led to political instability, as evidenced by the hasty rise and fall of governments, and encouraged post-opposition elites (who could be subject to elections at any moment) to focus on economic reforms perceived to be most valuable for voters. The Jan Olszewski cabinet (1991–1992) fell due to its transitional justice initiatives, including the publication of a list of public officials who had allegedly served as communist-era secret police informants. It was not until center-right forces reasserted control of parliament in 1997 (following four years when the house was controlled by former communists), that they launched a bill to authorize the new Institute of National Remembrance (which absorbed the GK) to investigate and prosecute crimes committed up to 1989. Of course, taking back power from former communists opened up the possibility of more aggressive justice. Not coincidentally, though, this was also a time of relative prosperity, when Poland was hailed as Central Europe's "tiger" economy. Less burdened with demands for creating beneficial economic conditions than they had been in 1991, post-oppositionists had more room to maneuver.

Solidarity did not come to power in 1989 on a campaign to right past wrongs. However, at a time when most communist regimes in the region continued to rule, it took the Polish anticommunist opposition forces just two months to launch aggressive criminal investigations against still-powerful former communist officials. Few anticommunists today recall fearing that the old communist regime members would halt democratization as a result of transitional justice. However, many, particularly those in the Sejm, recount keeping one eye on their constituents throughout. Soon anticommunist legislators in the Sejm focused on economic reforms and reversed course in the transitional justice debate. Unconstrained by the need to provide core political goods, the senators ensured that transitional justice remained on the table between 1989 and 1991, thus leaving Sejm leaders the task of toning down the legislation most offensive to the former communists. This period of diminished transitional justice continued between 1991 and 1993, when the anticommunist opposition forces consolidated their power. Only in 1997, once post-oppositionists and other members of the center-right took control of the state during an economic upturn, did they resume pursuing transitional justice in earnest.

DISCUSSION

Analytical approaches to transitional justice focused on relative power arguments provide a useful set of potential constraints for decisions and outcomes but would benefit from a broader framework. Politics is in part about avoiding risk but also about gaining advantage. Transitional justice policies are rarely conducted in isolation and should be analyzed in the context of other policy issues. The saliency of particular policies and their impact on the transitional justice debate depends on the institutional forum. Primary actors, who depend on the provision of goods to maintain office, should see transitional justice against this backdrop and act accordingly. The power of the institutional argument in the three divergent cases described here demonstrates a need to reconsider the determinants of transitional justice in post-repressive states.

The case of the former Yugoslavia demonstrates how institutions impact relationships and shape political strategy. In Serbia, the opposition took the helm of a country emerging from a decade of war, where unreformed military and police forces complicit in previous atrocities made transitional justice risky from a relative power perspective. Nevertheless, republic leaders in the primary institution (first Djindjić and later Koštunica) gambled that western goods exchanged for cooperation with the ICTY would convince an overwhelmingly anti-ICTY electorate that they had performed optimally. As the leader of a secondary federal institution, Koštunica could not profit early in the transition from this cooperation since he would get no credit for the goods – whose distribution was out of his hands – that it brought to Yugoslavia. He therefore objected to it, thereby increasing Djindjić's political costs. Djindjić's utility of cooperation was measured in the number of voters who could be wooed to his DS as a result of largely material improvements. President Koštunica, whose institutional authority made it impossible to take credit for such material gains, pursued a populist strategy of anti-cooperation to win support for his DSS.

Ultimately, Koštunica's political gamble paid off, a fact that DS members explain as Western betrayal. "We did not have clear support from the West," commented one DS leader. "[Voters said] 'You are traitors, but you are bad traitors. Where is the money, where is the western way of life?'"[40] Still, as Prime Minister Koštunica subsequently adopted policies similar to Djindjić's when he was faced with similar utility calculations. The sluggish pace of the cooperation with the ICTY initiated by Djindjić continued even after Koštunica became prime minister, when he was forced to balance institutional incentives to ensure expected goods and a political reputation built on rejecting pressures from external actors who held those goods.

The same dynamics played out in Croatia. However, there a basic deficit in political goods that could be used to sell compliance with the ICTY caused the first post-Tudjman prime minister to balk at cooperation. By taking aim at anti-Hague sentiment, President Mesić may have lessened the burden on Prime Minister Račan, but only marginally. Račan's compliance was painstakingly slow, although he and others close to him claim he preferred to do more. Just as Račan was unwilling to take the political risk of cooperation with nothing clear to gain from such a policy, his successor, Sanader, found that changing conditions and positions left him with relatively more to gain from the cooperation he so long and so vigorously opposed. Sanader's gamble on EU accession over the protection of a local military hero proved to be politically judicious.

The Yugoslav cases may be a prototype for a new era of transitional justice where international actors play a greater role in what have traditionally been domestic policies. However, the institutional argument provides new insights even where international pressures are absent. In her chapter, Subotic finds that in Serbia and Croatia justice for communist-era crimes, a time that attracted significantly less foreign attention, was also highly politicized. The Polish domestic justice process shows the influence of institutions. From a relative power perspective, the Polish anticommunist opposition forces – who came to power through negotiation, held only a minority stake in the primary institution, and had few links with the post-communist bureaucracy – should have turned away from criminal prosecutions. However, they rapidly (and almost unanimously) pursued criminal accountability until the fate of popularly demanded economic reforms eroded cross-institutional solidarity. As predicted by the institutional argument, Sejm members who initially demonstrated pro-accountability preferences pursued transitional justice only insofar as it was compatible with the provision of goods, while senators sought to keep harsh transitional justice on the agenda. The result was an abortive course of criminal accountability.

The public played a different role in each case. In Poland, where voters were relatively neutral with respect to transitional justice, primary actors adjusted their own preferences to ensure delivery of goods came first; secondary actors, whose hands were not on the economic wheel, pressed a pro-justice position without risking voter impatience. Where voters were antagonistic to transitional justice (as in Serbia and Croatia), primary actors pursued accountability only when they knew it could be readily traded for those goods useful in convincing their publics it was worthwhile. This position was, in turn, partly influenced by the activities of secondary actors. In no case did the level of public support directly dictate policy.

Determined relative power proponents might read each of these cases as affirmations, not rejections, of their argument. In Poland, for example, one could reinterpret the power of the anticommunist opposition forces as stemming from their success in the first semi-free elections – where they won every seat they could contest. The former communists then projected power outward, ruling it prudent to approve limited criminal accountability today rather than face more extensive investigations if Solidarity won the next elections. However, this focus on *potential* rather than *actual* power is precisely one ingredient missing from the current literature, one that involves the extended time horizon/strategic thinking I bring to the debate. In hindsight, we see that economics more than transitional justice (as might be predicted by relative power theories) dominated the attention of the former anticommunist forces after they consolidated power in 1991. Only after center-right forces returned to govern during a period of relative economic prosperity (1997–2001) did they strengthen criminal accountability legislation that had been deliberately weakened in 1991. The economic dimensions of transitional justice that facilitated delayed criminal justice in Poland may partly account for long-term pressure for prosecutions of the sort seen in Chile, where early amnesties gave way to a desire to reopen the books.

The case of Serbia offers space for a more poignant attack on the institutional argument. There, post-oppositionists took power in the Serbian Republic only after negotiations that gave way to elections in December 2000, when they were ultimately the victors, with 70 percent of parliamentary seats. Elite-level relative power hypotheses would indicate just this sort of process would take place. However, this argument undermines the mechanism involved (there was no outright revolution, but rather a negotiated transition to elections), running counter to expectations generated by state structure or public support relative power explanations – both of which would predict lenient forms of transitional justice. This line of thinking also does not account for why President Koštunica abandoned his stance upon becoming the prime minister accountable to a parliament that had proportionally more members of the old elite than when Djindjić was in power.

This chapter has focused on elite perceptions of constituent demands and what political actors must do to stay in power. While weak parties and a lack of strong voter allegiances undermine electoral accountability, the fundamental lesson here is that political elites play the accountability game *as if* they were operating in a fully functioning democracy. In their attempts to pursue or counter transitional justice policy, they act within institutionally defined borders with the expectation that their behavior may expedite voter support for their party or slow down support for other parties. In Serbia and many other states in transition, leaders defined the transitional justice debate more than parties. Djindjić and Koštunica appear to represent, speak for and act for their party colleagues in the transitional justice sphere. In Poland, decisions were also made by political elites, perhaps with more internal debate, though party discipline was quite high in the 1989–1991 Sejm as a result of what Geremek called "this feeling of solidarity, that we were on the same side."[41] In Croatia, Račan constantly struggled to maintain the backing of a diverse coalition, making his preferred policies even more difficult to implement. In each case, decisions were made at the top echelons and were heavily affected by the policy's perceived costs and benefits.

In each of these cases, transitional justice was a function of multiple phenomena. Transitions, like justice processes, are messy and there is no one overriding determinant. The point of this chapter is to highlight the significance of one important theoretical explanation that has long been ignored. As I have demonstrated in each of these cases, the positions of old elites, former state actors and societal attitudes all mattered, because they established the parameters within which political elites saw room to maneuver. The logic of the institutional argument presented here helps to incorporate the three and redefine them less as sole, even competing, causal mechanisms than as critical intermediaries that play a role in a more complicated process. Neither is transitional justice simply about economics, as these cases might suggest. Instead, it is best seen as a function of political opportunities, where economics and various strands of relative power are important, but not the sole, influences on the path of justice.

This chapter has focused on events that transpired over the first fifteen years after the fall of communism. Twenty-five years on, these processes continue to play out in fits and starts. Looking at transitional justice from a more global perspective, this is no surprise. Transitional justice is rarely a one-time occurrence. It is a process that is born and matures in various phases and shapes as opportunities emerge over time. While this chapter has focused on criminal accountability, the same determinants can be traced to other forms of transitional justice, including victim rehabilitation, truth commissions, and lustration. In various countries of Central and Eastern Europe, new opportunities that emerge in the future will inevitably lead to new and renewed transitional justice processes.

NOTES

1. This chapter is based on my book, which also included Uzbekistan and analyzed determinants of seven major types of justice (cessation of abuses, apologies/condemnations, rehabilitation/compensation, truth commissions, administrative cleansings, criminal prosecutions of lower-level functionaries, and criminal prosecutions for those with command authority). Brian Grodsky, *The Costs of Justice: How New Leaders Respond to Previous Rights Abuses* (Notre Dame, IN: University of Notre Dame Press, 2010).
2. For example, Alexandra Barahona De Brito, Carmen Gonzales-Enriquez, and Paloma Aguilar, eds., *The Politics of Memory: Transitional Justice in Democratizing Societies* (Oxford: Oxford University Press, 2001), 11 and 162; Jamal Benomar, "Justice after Transitions," in *Transitional Justice: How Emerging Democracies Reckon with Former Regimes*, ed. Neil J. Kritz (Washington, D.C.: United States Institute of Peace Press, 1995), 31–41; Samuel Huntington, *The Third Wave: Democratization in the Late Twentieth Century* (Norman: University of Oklahoma Press, 1991), 230–231; Luc Huyse, "Justice after Transition: On the Choices Successor Elites Make in Dealing with the Past," *Law & Social Inquiry* 20, no. 1 (1995): 63; Guillermo O'Donnell and Philippe C. Schmitter, "Tentative Conclusions about Uncertain Democracies," in *Transitions from Authoritarian Rule: Prospects for Democracy*, eds. Guillermo O'Donnell, Philippe C. Schmitter, and Laurence Whitehead (Baltimore, MD: Johns Hopkins University Press, 1986), 28; Terence Roehrig, *The Prosecution of Former Military Leaders in Newly Democratic Nations* (Jefferson, NC: McFarland, 2002), 199; Daniel Sutter, "Settling Old Scores: Potholes Along the Transition from Authoritarian Rule," *Journal of Conflict Resolution* 39, no. 1 (1995): 121; Jose Zalaquett, "Balancing Ethical Imperatives and Political Constraints: The Dilemma of New Democracies Confronting Past Human Rights Violations," *Hastings Law Journal* 43, no. 1425 (1992): 1432.
3. Peter Baehr, "Controversies in the Current International Human Rights Debate," *Human Rights Review* 2, no. 1 (2000): 21; Allison Corey and Sandra F. Joireman, "Retributive Justice: The Gacaca Courts in Rwanda," *African Affairs* 103, no. 410 (2004), 73–89; Ruti Teitel, "Transitional Justice Genealogy," *Harvard Human Rights Journal* 16 (2003): 70; Jose Zalaquett, "Confronting Human Rights Violations Committed by Former Governments: Principles Applicable and Political Constraints," in *Transitional Justice: How Emerging Democracies Reckon with Former Regimes*, ed. Neil J. Kritz (Washington, D.C.: United States Institute of Peace Press, 1995), 1–19.
4. Helga A. Welsh, "Dealing with the Communist Past: Central and East European Experiences after 1990," *Europe-Asia Studies* 48, no. 3 (1996): 419–420.
5. Natalia Letki, "Lustration and Democratization in East-Central Europe," *Europe-Asia Studies* 54, no. 4 (2002): 537; Grazyna Skapska, "Moral Definitions in Constitutionalism in East Central Europe: Facing Past Human Rights Violations," *International Sociology* 18, no. 1 (2003): 199–218; Welsh, "Dealing with the Communist Past," 415.
6. John P. Moran, "The Communist Torturers of Eastern Europe – Prosecute and Punish or Forgive and Forget," *Communist and Post-Communist Studies* 27, no. 1

(1994): 95–109; Nadya Nedelsky, "Divergent Responses to a Common Past: Transitional Justice in the Czech Republic and Slovakia," *Theory and Society* 33, no. 1 (2004): 81.

7. Noel Calhoun, "The Ideological Dilemma of Lustration in Poland," *East European Politics and Societies* 16, no. 2 (2002): 494–520.
8. Andrzej S. Walicki, "Transitional Justice and the Political Struggles in Post-Communist Poland," in *Transitional Justice and the Rule of Law in New Democracies*, ed. A. James McAdams (Notre Dame, IN: University of Notre Dame Press, 1997), 190–193; Kieran Williams, Brigid Fowler, and Aleks Szczerbiak, "Explaining Lustration in Central Europe: A 'Post-Communist Politics' Approach," *Democratization* 12, no. 1 (2005): 30.
9. Despina Angelovska, "The Failure of Macedonian Post-Communist Transitional Justice: Lustration, between Cleansing and Parody," in *Transitional Justice and Civil Society in the Balkans*, eds. Olivera Simić and Zala Volcic (Springer, 2013), 56; Robert C. Austin and Jonathan Ellison, "Post-Communist Transitional Justice in Albania," *East European Politics & Societies* 22 (2008): 383; Csilla Kiss, "The Misuses of Manipulation: The Failure of Transitional Justice in Post-Communist Hungary," *Europe-Asia Studies* 58, no. 6 (2006): 927.
10. Monika Nalepa, "Captured Commitments: An Analytic Narrative of Transitions with Transitional Justice," *World Politics* 62, no. 2 (2010): 348.
11. For more on the role of foreign pressure in the Serbia and Croatia cases, see Brian Grodsky, "Exploring the Schelling Conjecture in Reverse: 'International Constraints' and Cooperation with the International Criminal Tribunal for the Former Yugoslavia," *European Journal of International Relations* 17, no. 1 (2011): 121–143.
12. While an outright promise of amnesty was apparently never offered, one actor involved in Milošević's arrest told me that he coyly promised Milošević he would be transferred to a local prison and not to the Hague, at least "at this moment." See author interview with Cedomir Jovanovic, February 3, 2005, Belgrade.
13. "Vojislav Koštunica, Moderate Nationalist and Old Milošević Foe," *Agence France Presse*, September 24, 2000.
14. Author interview with European Union Official 1, December 6, 2004, Belgrade; author interview with European Union Official 2, December 2004, Belgrade; author interview with European Union Official 3, November 16, 2004, Belgrade; author interview with United States Government Official, April 2005, Zagreb. Days excluded for some respondents who did not want them included.
15. Author interview with Advisor to Prime Minister Zoran Djindjić, February 11, 2005, Belgrade; author interview with Dragor Hiber, December 16, 2004, Belgrade; author interview with Cedomir Jovanovic, February 3, 2005, Belgrade; author interview with Zarko Korac, February 4, 2005, Belgrade.
16. "Talks Stall on Extraditing Milošević to Hague: Serb Minister," *Agence France Presse*, June 4, 2001.
17. Author interview with Advisor to Prime Minister Zoran Djindjić, February 11, 2005, Belgrade.
18. Author interview with Cedomir Jovanovic, February 3, 2005, Belgrade.
19. Author interview with Advisor to Prime Minister Zoran Djindjić, February 11, 2005, Belgrade.

20. Author interview with Milan St. Protic, December 20, 2004, Belgrade.
21. Author interview with Rebeka Bozovic, January 28, 2005, Belgrade; author interview with Miroslav Filipovic, February 2, 2005, Belgrade; author interview with Gordana Matkovic, December 9, 2004, Belgrade; author interview with Vuk Obradovic, December 20, 2004, Belgrade; author interview with Dusan Petrovic, December 9, 2004, Belgrade.
22. "Vojislav Koštunica, Moderate Nationalist and Old Milošević Foe."
23. "Serb General Pavkovic to Surrender to Hague," *Reuters*, April 22, 2005; Ellie Tzortzi, "Serb Ex-General to Surrender to Un," *Reuters*, March 3, 2005; Nicholas Wood, "Serbia Moves a Step Closer to the European Union," *New York Times*, April 13, 2005.
24. "Serbian Premier Confident Feasibility Study to Be Positive," *BBC Monitoring International Reports*, March 4, 2005; "Serbian Premier Says Cooperation with ICTY 'Necessary,'" *BBC Monitoring Europe – Political*, November 22, 2004.
25. "Serbia Ready to Arrest Two Indicted Generals – Official," SeeNews, March 14, 2005.
26. "Premier-Elect Says Political System Needs Changing," *BBC Summary of World Broadcasts*, January 13, 2000.
27. Author interview with Ivo Josipovic, March 18, 2005, Zagreb.
28. "New Premier on Croatia's Economy, Media, Relations with Hague Tribunal, Bosnia," *BBC Monitoring Europe – Political*, January 29, 2000.
29. Author interview with Ivan Simonovic, March 18, 2005, Zagreb.
30. Author interview with Ivica Račan, March 4, 2005, Zagred.
31. "Croatia: Premier Says Decision to Cooperate with Hague Tribunal Was Inevitable," *BBC Monitoring Europe – Political*, July 8, 2001; "Half of the Croats Support Extradition of War Crimes Suspects," *Deutsche Presse-Agentur*, July 9, 2001.
32. "Croatian PM Urges Support in War Crimes Confidence Vote," *Agence France Presse*, July 15, 2001.
33. Author interview with Ivica Račan, March 4, 2005, Zagreb.
34. "Croatian Prime Minister Asks Vatican for Help in Pushing for EU Membership Talks," *Associated Press Worldstream*, February 22, 2005.
35. "Croatian PM Tells BBC He Would Personally Arrest Indicted Gen Gotovina," *BBC Monitoring International Reports*, April 26, 2005.
36. Author interview with Bronislaw Geremek, January 20, 2004, Warsaw.
37. Senate, *Dziennik Ustaw* (I Kadencja, 45 posiedzenia, April 19, 1991), 185.
38. Senate, *Dziennik Ustaw* (I Kadencja, 45 posiedzenia, March 15, 1991), 195.
39. Sejm, "Sprawozdanie Stenograficzne," Sejm (Kadencja X, 49 posiedzenia, 1991), 185; author interview with Grazyna Staniszewska, December 17, 2003, Warsaw.
40. Author interview with Dusan Petrovic, December 9, 2004, Belgrade.
41. Author interview with Bronislaw Geremek, January 20, 2004, Warsaw.

2

Transitional Justice as Electoral Politics

Robert Clegg Austin

Albania's experience with communism (1944–1990), along with subsequent attempts at transitional justice, including lustration, separate it from the rest of what used to be called Eastern Europe. Its near-total failure to address the past in any sustained or even helpful way is also unique, even given the low levels of success elsewhere in the region. As is always the case, local conditions played a decisive role, and in Albania timing was everything. In Albania, unlike elsewhere, neither formerly persecuted people nor dissidents led the charge for justice. Instead a political class emerged, often with strong communist credentials, that sought to use transitional justice for different purposes, and was responsible for Albania's uneven and politicized approach to the past. Former political prisoners, who were the most vocal in the calls for justice, were used sometimes as props. Certain other facts make the Albanian case unique. The harshness of the communist era and even the interwar legacy made everything more difficult. The past ensured that the political and economic transition would be long. Transitional justice, in the Albanian context, was only a part of electoral politics for a single party, nothing more.

More than two decades after the collapse of the communist regime we can take stock of the role transitional justice played or did not play in Albania in establishing a new state based on the rule of law. Despite the rhetoric employed by anti-communist parties, the legislation it adopted and the trials it conducted, Albania did little to deal with its communist past in a meaningful way. On only two occasions, in 1995 and 2008/2009, could one identify a shallow attempt to provide citizens with something concrete. However, both attempts were overtly political, something most citizens understood from the beginning, and therefore lost meaning for a population that sought and deserved answers. By 2014, too much time had passed for Albania to seriously consider additional attempts. This means that Albanians never got the accounting they deserved and requested in 1992, and collaborators and perpetrators were largely left untouched.

With the defeat of the Democratic Party (DP) in 2013, transitional justice again left the agenda, this time for good. Not only did the elections of 2013 bring an end to lustration, but as the first post-communist elections that were not contested by the loser, they may indicate that Albania has finally turned a corner on other levels as well. This chapter analyzes the entire post-communist period, compares the two major legislative initiatives, and explains the changing context of Albanian domestic political life that served to create a unique set of conditions.

UNDERSTANDING THE LEGACY OF POLITICS AND BLACKMAIL

To understand how the process of transitional justice became captured by petty politics I will first examine political life under the ruling DP from 1992 to 1997 with a focus on initial economic charges against the old regime and the two forms of de-communization that the DP introduced: lustration and file access. The enactments of the Genocide Law and the Verification Law in 1995 were the first serious legislative attempts by the DP to lustrate former communists from a variety of post-communist public offices. I will follow these partisan laws and observe how the DP abused and misapplied them. I will then examine how these laws were quickly dismantled and rendered meaningless upon the accession of the Socialist Party in 1997 and the implications of its government, which lasted until 2005. File access, which was also first permitted with the introduction of the Verification Law in 1995, met the same fate as lustration. In essence, Albania was largely unsuccessful in implementing a serious program of transitional justice. The Democrats had only political purposes in mind, while the Socialists had no interest at all in reckoning with the crimes of the communist regime.

A FATAL MISTAKE

Albania's first multi-party elections in March 1991 were won easily by Albania's communists (known as the Party of Labor since 1948). The nascent DP, which emerged in late 1990 as the only opposition to the communists and was led by Sali Berisha and Gramoz Pashko, lacked adequate time to prepare. The DP also lacked strong connections to the villages, where more than 65 percent of Albanians lived and whose inhabitants feared that any change in government would result in large-scale property return and deprive them of their land, which would have been catastrophic given that prior to World War II Albania was essentially feudal. That said, de-communization was essentially delayed in 1991.[1] During this time we see elite reproduction, not elite replacement, with very few Albanians willing to dig too deeply into the recent past.

However, the vote was challenged, and the communists faced mounting opposition from the cities in the vote's aftermath. As a result, they were forced to form a new government that included the opposition forces. This move radically transformed the political landscape and opened up the possibility of a reckoning with the past. At their tenth and last congress in June 1991, the communists did some overdue house cleaning, renamed themselves the Socialist Party of Albania (SP), and brought in some younger, less tainted faces. The party quickly dropped all references to Stalinism and communism and hoped to quietly join the mainstream of the European Socialist left.

Some modest steps were taken toward de-communization in summer 1991. Act 7514 provided an apology to those who had suffered under the communist regime, setting up the basis for compensation. However, the first serious move against the old regime was the release of a crucial report by Genc Ruli, the DP Minister of Finance in the coalition "national salvation" government, in July 1991. The report, essentially an audit of the often luxurious spending of the communist elite, subsequently became the basis of the charges against members of the old regime. It made clear that the communists were to be held to account not for their political actions but instead for their economic crimes.

As former President Sali Berisha noted, there were practical reasons for choosing mundane economic issues over more serious ones. He suggested that the coalition government, which was dominated by communists, forced certain compromises. More importantly, the judiciary was so stacked with communists that political changes stood no chance in the courts. Time was needed to develop a completely new court system amenable to serious change. Since most of what the communists did lay within the laws they promulgated, the best route for the new leaders was to catch them on preaching austerity while practicing gluttony. In terms of its impact on the lustration process, however, the decision to start the investigation of the past with petty economic crimes was "a fatal mistake."[2]

The notion of living well while the population suffered was expected to strike a chord amongst the very poorest sections of society. However, as Kathleen Imholz noted, "No one doubted that the [Enver] Hoxha family lived well and enjoyed goods unavailable to other Albanians, but making these changes the sole subject of a criminal proceeding seemed to trivialize the more serious abuses of the Hoxha regime."[3] With the benefit of hindsight, one can say with certainty that the decision to move against the old elite based on economic crimes was a catastrophic blunder for three reasons. First, it alienated ordinary people who expected that communists would face real justice for real crimes not because of the alcohol they consumed, the food they ate, or the refrigerators they had. Second, it became nearly impossible afterwards to engage people when serious charges were finally laid later. Lastly, it ensured that whatever happened later would appear decidedly political in spirit.

Of the entire aged Politburo charged in 1993, the vast majority were handed prison sentences based on the facts set out in the Ruli report after being tried in March 1994. Some political charges were added based on events that took place after the bombing of the Soviet Embassy in 1951, the abolition of religion in 1967, and killings along Albania's borders. All were found guilty of financial abuses and violating fundamental human rights. However, the trials against the old leadership failed to generate public enthusiasm or wider discussion from the nascent civil society, which at that time was too weak to play a major role and the government made no attempt to open up a wider discussion of the past.

Separate from these processes was the trial of former Socialist Prime Minister and Party leader Fatos Nano. Possibly meant as a means to show the population that the DP was doing something, Nano was charged with corruption and abuse of office in a dubious and highly politicized trial. Nano was convicted in 1994 and sentenced to twelve years in prison. He was freed in the civil chaos of 1997 and subsequently pardoned. The trial against Nano failed to capture the public's attention and seemed to fit in with the general pattern of politicized trials designed to destroy the opposition.

LEGISLATING IN HASTE

In addition to the economic charges, the Democrats conducted a massive purge of the state sectors. When other analysts suggest that Albania went further than most other countries in the former communist bloc, they are generally referring to the virtual emptying of this sector. On December 3, 1991, the coalition government introduced Law 7526 On Labor Relations, amending the country's labor code. The change, which was set out, in official parlance, to strengthen reform, allowed the government to dismiss employees of state-owned firms or agencies without explanation or the right to appeal. This process was often done haphazardly and the vague terminology "allowed for political and personal favoritism to enter the process."[4] The Socialists suggested that about 250,000 people lost their jobs following the landslide DP victory in the March 1992 elections, many of whom were merely Socialist sympathizers or their relatives with no connection to the old regime. This tendency, which has been part of Albanian political life since then, has had catastrophic implications for the long term development of a professional civil service.

In 1995, three years after being elected, the DP government introduced legislation decidedly different from what started with the Ruli report – they now could remove communist wrong-doers from the government. However, most analysts conclude that the hasty introduction of legislation was directly linked to the impending election in 1996. There was a real fear that the DP could lose the elections following the defeat of their newly proposed constitution in a public referendum in 1994.[5]

In late 1995, the Parliament passed Albania's first two lustration laws (together, the "Lustration Laws"): Law 8001 of September 22, 1995, On Genocide and Crimes against Humanity Committed in Albania during Communist Rule for Political, Ideological or Religious Motives (the "Genocide Law"), and Law 8043 of November 30, 1995, On the Verification of the Moral Character of Officials and Other Persons Connected with the Defense of the Democratic State, subsequently amended pursuant to a Constitutional Court decision of January 31, 1996 (the "Verification Law").[6] In their context, scope, and implementation, the Lustration Laws were exploited by the DP to selectively purge Albanian politics not of anti-democratic individuals, but rather of anti-DP individuals, usually belonging to the Socialist or Social Democratic Parties.

THE GENOCIDE LAW

According to its preamble, the purpose of the inappropriately named "Genocide Law" was to assist and accelerate the prosecution of perpetrators of "crimes against humanity" committed under the auspices of the communist regime. Interestingly enough, the government could have laid these same charges even before introducing the Genocide Law. Rather than providing a statutory basis for prosecution, the Genocide Law was the government's way of flexing its political muscles and showing that rather than concentrating on the economic crimes, as it had done in 1993–1994, it was ready to tackle de-communization immediately.

The government was quick to implement the Genocide Law, and by January 1996, the general prosecutor had ordered the arrests of twenty-four former senior communist officials. Many had been accused, arrested, and tried for lesser economic offenses but were now faced with much more serious punishment under the Genocide Law.[7] The Genocide Law also provided for some political lustration. Article 3 stipulated that those persons who were convicted of being authors, conspirators, or executors of crimes against humanity and who had held certain positions (including former party members, members of the People's Assembly, presidents of the Supreme Court of Justice, general prosecutors, and full time agents and part-time collaborators of the Sigurimi, Albania's much feared secret police) prior to March 31, 1991, would be banned from being elected or nominated to positions in the upper levels of government, the judicial system, and the media until 2002.[8]

Lustration under the Genocide Law was very limited; former communist officials would only be banned from public office provided they were first convicted by the general prosecutor. Political lustration could not have been a primary purpose of the Genocide Law; a five-year ban from entering public office on someone serving a twelve-year jail sentence was entirely illusionary. Nor could one say that the Genocide Law was aimed to bring the more infamous survivors of the old regime to justice, as genocide and crimes against humanity had been indictable offences under the old Albanian penal code, and, if anything, the evidence would have been fresher in 1992 than it was four years later when the prosecutions finally began.[9]

The Genocide Law did not therefore really serve a legal purpose; it did not effectively lustrate and was superfluous to "genocide" prosecutions. Rather, the law was intended to make the public believe that the DP was taking lustration seriously and associated the most well-known former communists with the DP's de-communization campaign. However, what the law did prove at the time was the "political immaturity" of the DP.[10] A second law introduced only two months later, the Verification Law, would build on this campaign and further the DP's political interests even more.

THE VERIFICATION LAW

The Verification Law provided for a committee (the "Verification Committee") responsible for screening potential and actual members of the government, police, judiciary, educational system, and media to determine their affiliation with the communist-era organs and state police. To this end, the Verification Committee was granted exclusive rights to use the files of the former secret service and the Albanian Party of Labor (the Albanian communist party).

Article 1 of the Verification Law established an extensive list of positions that could be reviewed by the Verification Committee, including members of Parliament, president, member of central government, leaders of local governmental bodies, manager of banking, financial and insurance institutions, army officers, member of the secret services, chief of police, judge or state prosecutor, member of the diplomatic corps, director or rector of a school or higher education institution, or a director or editor in Albanian state radio or television.[11]

According to Article 2, the Verification Committee was permitted to screen actual or potential holders of the above-enumerated positions to determine if they had fallen into one of roughly twenty categories of employment between November 28, 1944, and March 31, 1991. Under Article 4 of the same law, the Verification Committee included seven members. Of the seven members, only the member appointed by the National Information Service would not be directly or indirectly appointed by Parliament. Although, once appointed, the Verification Committee was theoretically independent, the composition thereof could be changed at will by Parliament, and the Verification Committee's actual freedom is debatable.

Under Articles 7 and 9, any individual who wished to run in an election for a position listed in Article 1 had to first be reviewed by the Verification Committee. If the Verification Committee found that the candidate had held a position listed under Article 2, the candidate would be restricted from running until 2002. As for candidates for appointment to an Article 1 position, no mandatory review regime was established; no appointment candidates had the option of requesting a review by the Verification Committee. Even Rustem Gjata, who had upheld the law in his capacity as Constitutional Court president, acknowledged that the process was selective and only carried out on requests from certain institutions, resulting in only partial and thus flawed implementation.[12] Many people with questionable pasts escaped scrutiny due to their political allegiance to post-communist ruling parties that controlled the verification process.

Shortly after the Verification Law was introduced, it became apparent that it would be applied to the advantage of the ruling DP and to the extreme detriment of the political opposition. While a complete list of the 139 individuals barred from participating in the May 1996 elections is not available, it is likely that it included a disproportionate number of prominent opposition leaders. It is worth noting that because public disclosure required the assent of the investigated individuals, the names of the barred candidates were generally not released to the public.

The Verification Committee's decisions were essentially final, but the Committee was hardly independent with six of seven members appointed by the DP. Nearly a decade later, DP members such as Sali Berisha and Spartak Ngjela acknowledged that the partisan nature of the Verification Committee had a significant negative impact on its effectiveness and reception by the public.[13] The low ratio of DP candidates barred from the elections is also suspect.

The opposition parties quickly manifested their dissatisfaction with the Lustration Laws. The Social Democrat Party brought a complaint to the Constitutional Court challenging Article 3 of the Genocide Law, while, at the same time, the SP brought a complaint challenging both laws. The Constitutional Court rejected these complaints on January 31, 1996, and proposed only some relatively minor amendments to the Verification Law.[14] Interestingly enough, the Socialists did not protest publicly or openly, a fact suggesting that the law caused problems for their electoral campaign, likely because if the SP were to challenge the law beyond raising the issue of its constitutionality, they might open themselves to attacks from the DP and the international community for wanting to reintroduce communism.

Instead, the SP and other opposition parties framed their criticism of the DP in the context of the new electoral law introduced by Berisha, Law 8055 of February 1, 1996, on Amendments to Law 7556 On Elections to the People's Assembly of the Republic of Albania (the "1996 Electoral Law"), which amended the 1992 electoral law by including not only specific wording implementing the Lustration Laws in the local and parliamentary elections, but also re-zoning changes and a reduction in the number of proportional seats. These changes were disadvantageous to the opposition parties.[15]

On May 26, 1996, the Socialists, the Social Democrats, the Democratic Alliance, and others boycotted the elections, citing flagrant election procedure violations and expressing continued dissatisfaction with the 1996 Electoral Law. However, as Elez Biberaj points out, this boycott may have been to a large degree in response to the Lustration Laws.[16] The opposition parties were able to limit the scope of the Lustration Laws as early as September 9, 1996 due to significant international pressure faced by the DP and the roundtable discussions held by Berisha on September 4, 1996, as a result of which the DP amended the Verification Law to exempt candidates for local council or commune chairs, as mentioned above.[17] Regardless, that year the DP easily won what were Albania's most flawed elections with 122 seats in the 140 seat parliament.[18]

QUIET EXPIRATION

With the collapse of several highly integrated pyramid schemes in mid-January 1997 and the violent chaos that followed, the DP government was faced with an economic fallout with which they were unable to cope. By March 1997 anti-government protests had escalated to an armed revolt that pressured Berisha to form a "government of national reconciliation" with ten other political parties, including the rebel-backed SP, and to hold elections by

June 1997.[19] However, the new coalition government could not agree on the terms of the new election.

It was within this context that, on May 9, 1997, an Organization for Security and Cooperation (OSCE) mission led by Franz Vranitsky managed to broker a deal between the parties, drafting the six point "political contract." The contract called for a new electoral law increasing proportional representation, the appointment of an international election coordinator and, more importantly, significant amendments to the Lustration Laws.[20] The scope of the Verification Law was drastically reduced under the new amendments, which saw only former members of the ex-communist Politburo, former agents of the secret police or foreign intelligence agency, and individuals convicted of crimes against humanity included in the lustration process. Many opposition candidates were cleared by the Constitutional Court and the Court of Cassation of earlier charges, and were thus allowed to participate in the June elections. With such a limited application, the intended effect of the Verification Law was seriously undermined.[21]

The Socialists handily won the June 1997 elections, obtaining 101 of 155 parliamentary seats. The DP won only twenty-seven seats, and the former darling of Albania's fight against communism, Sali Berisha, seemed headed for political oblivion. Moreover, the Socialist coalition controlled a two-thirds majority in Parliament and was given significant power to further alter the implementation of the Lustration Laws.[22] Shortly after its victory, the SP began a replacement campaign of DP supporters that virtually mirrored, though less systemically, the DP bureaucratic purges that took place after 1992.[23] However, the SP did not resort to the pretext of lustration.

Berisha's catastrophic defeat in the internationally sponsored elections sent him and the DP into the political wilderness for the next eight years. In a normal environment, he probably should have stepped down, but in keeping with post-communists politics in the Balkans, retirement was not an option. Borrowing from the Socialists, he alternated between parliamentary boycotts, noisy street demonstrations, and a near-coup in 1998. The Socialists, as noted, never cared about transitional justice. As a result, these projects gradually expired, and talk about the past was merely part of the political infighting between the two major parties. Popular demands for renewing the discussion were noticeably absent, and it was not on the agenda for civil society groups either.

The new Socialist government moved quickly to strike down the effects of the Genocide Law, requesting that the Albanian courts re-examine the accusations of crimes against humanity that had been leveled under the Genocide Law against former communist officials. On October 20, 1997, the Supreme

Court acquitted all the accused, ruling that they could not be held liable for actions that were not illegal at the time they were committed.[24] No further convictions were made under the Genocide Law for the remainder of its active life, and it essentially became a dead letter.

Under the new government, the Verification Law also underwent further changes. Shortly after the election, a new Verification Committee was appointed by the predominantly DP parliament, with Nafiz Bezhani as its chairman. At Bezhani's suggestion, on January 15, 1998, Parliament changed the Verification Law again to further narrow the scope of lustration. Most notably, the amendments altered the wording of the previous law, which banned "officers" of the National Information Service (successor to the Sigurimi, abolished in July 1991) and of the Interior Ministry, to include only senior officers and department heads. It no longer called for the lustration of former communist judges and state prosecutors from civil service and changed collaboration with the Sigurimi in general to include only collaboration with the Sigurimi in political trials and investigations.

In 1998, Albania also finished its constitutional project, which contained only a faint allusion to lustration. Its Article 17 allowed for temporary removal by establishing two key points. First, "the limitation of the rights and freedoms provided for in this Constitution may be established only by law for a public interest or for the protection of the rights of others. A limitation shall be in proportion with the situation that has dictated it." Second, "these limitations may not infringe the essence of the rights and freedoms and in no case may exceed the limitations provided for in the European Convention on Human Rights."[25] However, the Socialist government never applied the article in any context. Article 17 would again re-surface in a new debate in 2008 and 2009 as reason to block new lustration legislation.

By May 1998, Bezhani announced that the Verification Committee had reviewed 3,000 members of civil service and had submitted the names of eighty-one for lustration, including only four members of Parliament (two Socialists and two Democrats). After conducting the review, Bezhani happily announced that the entire Albanian government was "pure" and free of communist influence. There is no record of any further Verification Committee activity until December 31, 2001, when Parliament quietly let the Verification Law expire.

The Socialists governed for eight years (from 1997 to 2005). They won a contested election in 2001 with a strong showing. The 2001 election, with all the accusations of fraud, was by far the longest election in Albanian history with multiple re-counts and re-voting. Despite the fact that Berisha was widely blamed for the collapse of the pyramid schemes, Albania's descent into chaos, as well as the loss of two elections, he nevertheless stayed on as party leader. Even by Balkan standards, this is quite remarkable. Since Albanian elections produce no losers, only contested results, there is no really compelling reason for leaders to step down. In the 2001 election, the OSCE again noted that Albanians were still a long way off from a truly free and fair election citing ballot box stuffing, biased coverage in favor of the government on state television, and a climate of hostility between the major parties.[26] The elections of 2001 solidified Socialist Party rule and pushed transitional justice off the table. Afterwards, the issue disappeared almost entirely from political discourse, and came back only eight years later in a highly politicized context. By 2014, one could only conclude that transitional justice, more off than on again, was dead.

CLOSING A CHAPTER

Separate from lustration and yet an integral component of transitional justice is the issue of file access. In Albania, the first legislative attempt to regulate the use of Sigurimi files was made with the introduction of the Verification Law in 1995. Prior to that law, the files had been illegally used by individuals with connection in government to coerce or intimidate their political opponents. The Verification Law did not significantly improve the situation; the partisan nature of the Verification Committee resulted in only a selective review of the files. Even then, the files were generally only used for political purposes rather than disclosure to the public. This put Albania at odds with some key suggestions from the Council of Europe.

When the Verification Law expired in 2001, so did the only piece of legislation providing for even limited access to the secret files. The most recent public attempt to put the issue of file access back on the table was a bill tabled by three legislators in 2004, and another attempt in 2008. The proposed draft law in 2004 called for a complete, radical, and unconditional opening of files. The proposed scope of the draft law was similar to the Verification Law, but it varied most notably in that it called for a more nonpartisan Verification Committee, and required that *all* state employees or officials might be investigated and that anyone with a communist past be dismissed from public office immediately.

Without the support of the two dominant parties, the Democrats and the Socialists, however, this draft law died almost as soon as it was brought forward. Some might hold up the failure of this law as evidence of the shadowy hand of former communists, for it seems strange to suggest that in a country with a history of pervasive oppression, unjust imprisonment, exile, and state murder, the public would not demand to know the identities and roles of their persecutors. Yet although the secret files have always remained closed to ordinary Albanians, there is no public clamor to see them opened, and access does not appear to be on the forefront of public debate.

Is it possible that the cause is nothing more than public apathy. Berisha noted that so long after the fall of communism, file access no longer has relevance for most Albanians, who would prefer to close that chapter of their lives. The string of illegal file misuses from 1992–1995 also seriously undermined public perceptions of the files' integrity. The partisan composition of the Verification Committee, its selective review process, and the conflicting findings of its various incarnations did not improve matters either.[27] By 2014 it would be very difficult for any Albanian to take the literal content of the files seriously, let alone what a government organ chooses to filter and publish. Not only were the files kept closed, but Albania never experienced what happened elsewhere in the region where individuals simply received access to a secret list of agents and informers and published the names in local media unofficially.[28]

Many believed that it is not too late for Albanians to be granted complete and unhindered access to the secret files, particularly if the new government led by the Democrats in 2005 brought a "new wave of lustration" fundamentally different than the flawed experience that came before.[29] Only an impartial, equal, and non-judgmental approach to Albania's history could effectively dispel its ghosts. Given all the potential pitfalls of opening the files and the grave concerns regarding the integrity and completeness of the files, Arben Imami exclaimed "enough is enough, let us move on" and thus Albania's failed attempt at file access will also be its last.[30] This expectation proved to be incorrect.

THE RETURN OF THE DEMOCRATS AND POLITICIZED TRANSITIONAL JUSTICE

Berisha entered the 2005 election campaign as the underdog. The Socialists played up on the legacy of 1997 with lurid footage of Albania's descent into chaos, while Berisha's "Clean Hands" coalition focused on offering a government that would finally deal with pervasive corruption and its lagging bid to make good on its pledge to join the European Union. In what was another highly contested election, Berisha made a comeback and, despite widespread accusations of fraud, he became prime minister in a coalition with one time enemy and former Socialist Prime Minister Ilir Meta, who emerged as a very costly kingmaker.[31] Berisha's return to power was remarkable. The Socialists, who more or less traded places with the Democrats, headed for the usual boycott, and Albania's political polarization continued. Once again, the OSCE was disappointed with the election, citing numerous irregularities most notably in the counting of ballots.[32]

It is not in the scope of this chapter to examine every detail of the struggle between the two major parties. In short, electoral politics in Albania have been, and remain to a large extent, completely poisoned since the first election in 1991. Democrats and Socialists have used an extraordinary number of illegal and dubious methods to ensure electoral victory. What distinguished the Democrats from their political enemies is that they applied transitional justice and pseudo-lustration along with manipulation during and after elections. The Socialists, still carrying too much baggage from the communist past, were not in a position to do the same.

THE 2009 ELECTION

The year 2008 was 1995 all over again. Fearing for its future, Berisha's DP again brought new legislation designed to undermine the Socialist opposition under the guise of reckoning with the past long after the 1995 legislation had expired. This time around, much had changed. Voters were more savvy, civil society more developed, judges less pliant, and Albania more integrated internationally to simply get away with things. Berisha seemed unwilling to recognize that so much had changed. Moreover, the proposed adoption of new legislation proved the point that if lustration is implemented too late after the regime change, it becomes manipulation and it erodes voter trust in the government and the new democracy. That is at least how opponents inside and out of Albania saw things.

Prime Minister Berisha used much of the same rhetoric that had been deployed in 1995 with one big difference. In 1995, Albania was a mere three years into a flawed democracy and by 2008 and 2009 the salience of the issue had long faded. Nevertheless, Berisha pushed for new legislation. Never lacking in hyperbole, Berisha said, "Albanian society must strive by all manner of means to part for good with its bitter past and do away with the consequences of the most savage dictatorship Europe had known after Hitler's. In 1991, Europe's thirty-seven democratic parties issued a declaration terming Enver Hoxha as the post-war Hitler. This draft was meant to solve some of the bitterest problems inherited from the Communist dictatorship."[33] Berisha went on to praise the 1995 law which he said was implemented with "fairness" and that it was only the Democrats' electoral defeat in 1997 that prevented Albania from becoming "another country."[34]

The essence of the new law was not radically different from 1995. Act 10034/2008 On the Integrity of High Administration Figures called for new verification of senior officials, elected or appointed, for potential involvement in the communist regime. Based again on the Czech model, the act evaluated only very senior officials and permitted their removal from posts, but no other penalties. If implemented, the new law would also have finally allowed every Albanian access to their personal secret files. That access, the government argued, was in keeping with Council of Europe Parliamentary Assembly Resolution 1096, which stated that the Council "welcomes the opening of secret service files for public examination in some former communist totalitarian countries. It advises all countries concerned to enable the persons affected to examine, upon their request, the files kept on them by the former secret services."[35] However, the Council of Europe did note that their hope was that lustration processes would conclude by the end of December 1999.

The law, which was subject to a very acrimonious debate in the Albanian parliament in December 2008, was passed on January 14, 2009. It was to come into force on January 30, 2009 and stay in force for five years. It was adopted as an ordinary law with the opposition parties boycotting the vote. Its only defense in parliament came from an hour long speech by Prime Minister Berisha. The U.S. Embassy immediately issued a strong statement that said they were "deeply concerned. This law raised serious legal, governmental and constitutional questions among Albania's international partners, including the United States." They called on the government of Albania to "take immediate steps in consultation with national and international experts to ensure that this law would meet international standards."[36] The U.S. Ambassador also noted that despite individual interventions from EU states, "EU Heads of Mission in Tirana were unable to come to consensus on a public statement and ended up issuing nothing."[37] The Socialist opposition immediately called the new law a pre-election strategy. More sinister and harder to prove was the accusation that Berisha had more than an election in summer 2009 in mind. For some, it was more an attempt to encourage prosecutors and judges involved in some high level corruption charges brought against members of Berisha's government to back off or risk their jobs.

Accusations of corruption were leveled against Berisha's inner circle relating to a road project linking the port city of Durres with Kukes on the northern border with Kosovo which suffered massive cost overruns. These changes targeted Transport Minister Lulzim Basha, who remained in the cabinet in 2009 as foreign minister and was a protégé of the prime minister.

As well, there was the Gerdec fiasco when a military depot blew up in March 2008 killing twenty-seven people.[38] While Albanians may have given up on transitional justice, they did hope that someone should be held accountable for the horribly botched government operation to destroy old munitions at Gerdec. The most likely person was Berisha's ally and Defense Minister, Fatmir Mediu. Then U.S. Ambassador John Withers II noted that many see "this as the truest sign of Berisha's growing desperation to shut down [a] number of investigations that threaten to implicate members of the Berisha family as well as members of his inner circle." According to Withers, Berisha was "running out of time and options for shutting down these investigations."[39]

International observers also picked up the suggestion that Berisha was trying to frighten the courts. By late December 2008, there had already been intense international pressure to abandon the law from the United States, the Council of Europe, and the OSCE. Even the Albanian President Baimir Topi recognized its problems. According to Wikileaks, Topi was afraid to take a strong stand and veto the law due to his fear that Berisha and his allies would "launch unrelenting and even physically violent attacks against" him.[40] This was an astonishing admission from the country's head of state.

The main criticisms of the law were lengthy. International and domestic experts noted that the law circumvented the Albanian Constitution, especially regarding the dismissal of judges and members of parliament. The law was a party process driven without needed consultation, it was vague and unclear especially on the vetting process, the committee reviewing cases would end up in the DP's control, and it appeared to deny due process to those under investigation. Since the opposition completely rejected the law they were unlikely to take on their two seats on the five member commission, leaving the government naming two representatives and possibly the third member intended to be decided by consensus. With the Socialists boycotting parliament altogether, consensus was therefore impossible.

Already in January 2009 the Council of Europe had offered its assistance to Albania in drafting a law that would meet the Council's standards of democracy – something it explicitly said the new law did not accomplish. The OSCE also suggested the law should be postponed until some compromise was found between Albania's two major parties. Given the overwhelming international opposition, the law went to Albania's Constitutional Court which Berisha wrongly concluded he had in his pocket. Its first step in February 2009 was to suspend the law pending a review. At the same time, the Court also sought an opinion from the Council of Europe's Venice Commission. For Prime Minister Berisha, this was a huge setback and he did not hide his disappointment with the Court claiming that its judges violated judicial ethics and were in open conflict of interest.[41]

The fact that the Court took a stand shocked observers who suggested the judges would eschew challenging Berisha. Nevertheless, it was a victory for judicial independence and Albania's shallow democracy which hitherto had seen only scant victories for the rule of law. The subsequent decision from the Constitutional Court and the opinion from the Venice Commission doomed Albania's last attempt at politicized lustration. Both parties agreed that the law did not comply with Albania's Constitution and with the rule of law. The opinion of the Venice Commission, released in October 2009, cited an extraordinary number of issues relating to the law. Notably, it argued that the law was enacted too long after the communist regime's collapse, that its mandate was too broad and imprecise, and that it was not consistent with the Albanian Constitution. Of particular concern were the processes envisioned for dismissal of key public officials such as the President, Prosecutor General, members of the Supreme Court, and members of the Constitutional Court. In the end, the Venice Commission concluded that the new law "was less protective than the constitutional one."[42]

The government argued that the law was needed due to certain details specific only to Albania. The key issue, as in the past, was the timing. It seemed obvious to everyone that it was a law that was part of the electoral struggle and the court challenges to some of Berisha's key allies. However, the Albanian government argued that certain facts specific to Albania justified the new law eighteen years after the collapse of the communist regime. Since the Genocide and Verification Laws of 1995 had fallen into disuse and subsequently expired, the process was therefore incomplete when the DP returned to power in 2005. Moreover, the DP argued, there was also renewed interest from the population in gaining access to the files. Despite Berisha's numerous rants, the law was killed by the combined forces of Albania's civil society and Constitutional Court, the international community, and the Council of Europe's Venice Commission. The comparison between 2009 and 1995 is telling. In 1995, Albanians got a very bad law that accomplished nothing, but the law did make it to the books. In 2009, Albania was a different place. Rule of law was securing a foundation, civil society was developed, and the DP was no longer able to simply get away with things like it was in 1995. The most important change was that in 1995, as a strong anti-communist government, Berisha was allowed tremendous leeway; in 2009, his list of international allies had grown much shorter.

CONCLUSION AND LESSONS LEARNED

As noted, Berisha did narrowly win the June 2009 elections without his lustration law or file access. His opponents in the SP cried foul, but he prevailed, putting Albania into another four year long cycle of political polarization. The Council of Europe's October 2009 opinion on the Lustration Law was followed by the Constitutional Court's ruling in March 2010 which annulled the law completely. The Court argued that the law was simply incompatible with Albania's constitution, among other already noted issues. That decision ended Albania's on and off again experiment with transitional justice. Despite his victory in 2009, the often stubborn and combative Berisha did not take up the issue again in his four-year term, which ended in 2013. It is worth noting that none of his loyalists ended up in jail either.

The failure of these laws the second time around was telling. In the first place, the public was once again ignored and the former political prisoners were brought out as cover for an open political agenda. Even file access, which appeared again in 2008, failed to catch the public's attention so much that even the OSCE Office in Albania called for not only more public consultation, but first and foremost some agreement between the two major parties on just what was trying to be accomplished. The experience between 1992 and 2013 tells us that the process in Albania was ultimately about political blackmail since nothing serious ever happened and Albanians never received the reckoning with their past that they deserved. First, they had to endure the show trials of aging former Politburo members, then they got a rigged trial against then SP leader Fatos Nano, to be followed by the 1995 Genocide and Verification Law. By then, it was too late to regain the population's trust in the process. That new laws and new ideas appeared only in 2008 and 2009, at a time when new elections were imminent and Berisha loyalists were facing charges, was simply too much for the Albanians and a whole series of other interested actors.

In the 2013 elections, Berisha's DP suffered a truly decisive defeat – so decisive that for the first time since 1996 the results were not contested. Berisha stepped down as party leader and handed his party to his protégé, Lulzim Basha. Serious transitional justice attempts are finished now. Nevertheless, the pseudo-lustration continues, designed not to root out old regime members, but rather, as had been the case so many times in the past, simply as a tool to create party loyalists in the state administration by tying jobs to party membership. The emptying of the public service when power changes hands remains in place. For the Socialists, the danger posed by those in power between 1944 and 1990 is irrelevant. Should the Democrats ever return to power, it remains to be seen whether or not the horrors of the communist past can still be hauled out of the closet to fight contemporary political battles against the Socialists. The fact that they failed in 2009 was one of the few positive signals that Albania's institutions were durable in what was an otherwise pathetic transition period.

As noted, Albania's experience with communism ensured that its transition would face all kinds of challenges. The absence of a domestic dissident movement, the relatively strong communist credentials of the early anti-communist opposition, and the political weakness of the formerly politically persecuted meant that transitional justice could not be applied in a serious or sustained way. By the time it was introduced, it was both too late and clearly too tied to domestic politics to be taken seriously, especially after previous trials served to trivialize the past. The second attempt was too late and everyone inside and out of Albania knew that. Timing did prove to be everything, leaving Albanians with at most rumor or conjecture as the only means to understand what happened during their long communist period.

While the Albanian case was unique in many aspects, it does offer some lessons. Obviously, the politicization of transitional justice had a huge price as it meant that ordinary citizens lost faith in it. However, the urge for political actors to politicize the process of coming to terms with the communist past has been hard to resist, and Albania is not alone in falling into that trap. Timing has proven to be key, as post-communist Albania allowed too many years to pass before enacting relevant legislation and designing transitional justice programs, thus making it impossible after 1990 to impartially reckon with communist crimes. Finally, even today Albania lacks a judiciary independent from the executive and legislative branches of the government, and corrupt and self-interested businessmen. There have been some gains in the direction of creating an independent judiciary, which is the key to further integration with the European Union, but Albanian courts were never up to the job of offering impartial transitional justice, including lustration. Given what Albanians experienced in 1944–1990, the absence of a serious and sustained reckoning with the past has represented a major setback and further poisoned an already fraught democratization process.

NOTES

1. For election results, see Robert C. Austin, "What Albania Adds to the Balkan Stew," *ORBIS* 37, no. 2 (Spring 1993): 263.
2. Interview with Rustem Gjata, Tirana, June 24, 2005.
3. Kathleen Imholz, "Decommunization in Albania," *East European Constitutional Review* 4, no. 3 (Summer 1995): 55.

4. Fred Abrahams, *Human Rights in Post-communist Albania* (New York: Human Rights Watch, 1996), 26.
5. President Berisha's government proposed a new constitution that created a powerful presidency. Some 56 percent of voters rejected it.
6. These were the first two laws on lustration, with the exception of a 1993 law (No. 7666) affecting only the certification of lawyers, which was struck down by the Constitutional Court. Unofficial English translations are reproduced in Abrahams, *Human Rights*, 140–149.
7. Abrahams, *Human Rights*, 41.
8. The (unofficial) translation in Abraham's *Human Rights* reads "perpetrators, promoters and implementers." However, the wording "authors, conspirators and executors" was used in an original English submission by the Albanian foreign minister to the Council of Europe and is clearer and more accurate. See *Explanatory Note Contained in a Note Verbale Handed to the Secretary General at the Time of Deposit of the Instrument of Ratification of Treaty No. 009: Protocol to the Convention for the Protection of Human Rights and Fundamental Freedoms*, October 2, 1996, available at: http://conventions.coe.int/Treaty/Commun/ListeDeclarations (accessed October 9, 2013).
9. Interview with Rustem Gjata, Tirana, June 24, 2005.
10. Interview with Genc Ruli. Tirana, May 5, 2006.
11. In a subsequent amendment, candidates for election to local councils or to the position of chairman of a commune were exempted from the scope of the Verification Law, while mayoral candidates and municipal prefects were still subject to the law. As a result, the number of prospective verifications on the municipal level dropped from 60,000 for 5,764 posts to just 800 for 64 posts. See discussion of Law 8151 of September 9, 1996, *On Amendments to Law No. 7573 On Elections of the Organs of Local Authorities* in *Explanatory Note contained in a Note Verbale handed to the Secretary General at the time of deposit of the instrument of ratification of Treaty No. 009: Protocol to the Convention for the Protection of Human Rights and Fundamental Freedoms*, October 2, 1996, available at: http://conventions.coe.int/Treaty/Commun/ListeDeclarations (accessed October 9, 2013).
12. Interview with Rustem Gjata, Tirana, June 24, 2005.
13. Interviews with Spartak Ngjela, Tirana, June 21, 2005, and Sali Berisha, Tirana, June 23, 2005.
14. Kathleen Imholz, "States of Emergency as Pretexts for Gagging the Press: Word Play at Albania's Constitutional Court," *East European Constitutional Review* 6, no. 4 (Fall 1997): 57–63.
15. Elez Biberaj, *Albania in Transition: The Rocky Road to Democracy* (Boulder, CO: Westview Press, 1998), 289.
16. Ibid., 298.
17. Ibid., 312. See also discussion of Law 8151 of September 9, 1996, On Amendments to Law No. 7573 *On Elections of the Organs of Local Authorities in Explanatory Note Contained in a Note Verbale Handed to the Secretary General at the Time of Deposit of the Instrument of Ratification of Treaty No. 009: Protocol to the Convention for the Protection of Human Rights and Fundamental Freedoms*, October 2, 1996, available at: http://conventions.coe.int/Treaty/Commun/Liste Declarations (accessed October 9, 2013).

18. For details on scandalous elections, see Office for Democratic Institutions and Human Rights, *Observation of the Parliamentary Elections Held in the Republic of Albania, May 26 and June 2, 1996*, July 2, 1996, available at: http://www.osce.org/odihr/elections/albania/13567 (accessed October 9, 2013).
19. Biberaj, *Albania in Transition*, 319–325.
20. Ibid., 331. The amendments were introduced on 13 May 1997 as Law 8215, amending the Genocide Law, and Law 8220, amending the Verification Law.
21. Kahtleen Imholz, "Albania," *East European Constitutional Review*, 6, no. 2 (Spring/Summer 1997): 2–5.
22. Biberaj, *Albania in Transition*, 335–337.
23. Ibid., 352–353.
24. Ibid., 353.
25. *Albanian Constitution*, 2008, available at: http://www.ipls.org/services/kusht/cp2.html (accessed October 9, 2013).
26. Office for Democratic Institutions and Human Rights, *Republic of Albania Parliamentary Elections 24 June-19 August 2001*, October 11, 2001, available at: http://www.osce.org/odihr/elections/albania/13560 (accessed September 25, 2013).
27. Interview with Gent Ibrahimi, Tirana, June 2005.
28. Lavinia Stan, "Vigilante Justice in Post-Communist Europe," *Communist and Post-Communist Studies*, 44, no. 4 (December 2011): 319–327.
29. Interview with Spartak Ngjela, Tirana, June 21, 2005.
30. Interview with Arben Imami, Tirana, June 24, 2005.
31. Ilir Meta broke with the SP and established a new party, the Socialist Movement for Integration. Meta's 5 seats ensured he received huge "incentives" to join Berisha's coalition.
32. Office for Democratic Institutions and Human Rights, *Republic of Albania Parliamentary Elections 3 July 2005*, November 7, 2005, available at: http://www.osce.org/odihr/elections/albania/16856 (accessed September 25, 2013).
33. "Berisha: All Files Will Be Opened," *Republika*, Tirana, November 27, 2007.
34. Ibid.
35. Council of Europe Parliamentary Assembly, *Resolution 1096 (1996) on measures to dismantle the heritage of former communist totalitarian systems*, available at: http://assembly.coe.int/main.asp?Link=/documents/adoptedtext/ta96/eres1096.htm (accessed October 9, 2013).
36. Cabledrum for this cable from Ambassador Withers, "Lustration Law Passes, but What Next?," Tirana, December 23, 2008, available at: https://www.cabledrum.net/cables/08TIRANA899 (accessed October 14, 2013).
37. Ibid.
38. Sentences were handed down in March 2012. As a member of Parliament, Mediu escaped punishment and blame. "Albania Blast Trial Sentences Disappoint Victims," *Balkan Insight*, March 13, 2012, available at: http://www.balkaninsight.com/en/article/light-sentences-in-albania-deadly-blast-trial (accessed October 10, 2013).
39. Cabledrum for this cable from the U.S. Ambassador in Tirana. "Lustration Law Passes, but What Next."
40. Cabledrum for this cable from the U.S. Embassy in Tirana, "President Topi Leaning Against Veto of Lustration Law," Tirana, January 13, 2009, available at: https://www.cabledrum.net/cables/09TIRANA18 (accessed October 10, 2013).

41. Albanian Telegraph Agency (ATA), February 16, 2009, as provided by BBC Monitoring.
42. Venice Commission, *Amicus Curiae Opinion on the Law on the Cleanliness of the Figure of High Functionaries of the Public Administration and Elected Persons of Albania*, Strasbourg, October 13, 2009, Opinion no. 524/2009, available at: http://www.venice.coe.int/webforms/documents/?pdf=CDL-AD(2009)044-e (accessed October 14, 2013).

3

Explaining Late Lustration Programs: Lessons from the Polish Case

Aleks Szczerbiak

The former Soviet Union and Eastern bloc is a growing area of research and academic discussion in transitional justice. An expanding political science literature looks at the measures taken by the former communist states to deal with past atrocities and overcome the legacy of communist dictatorship. Despite the existence of a large comparative literature on this topic, the late implementation of lustration and access to communist-era security service files – together with the intense, on-going, and recurring politicization of the issue – remains a puzzle. It is this puzzle, "late" lustration and communist security service file access programs, that this chapter addresses by surveying the explanations available in the existing literature and, based on the Polish case, developing a tentative explanatory framework that identifies more precisely why lustration recurs at particular times in particular forms.

The chapter first reflects on why Poland is a case of late (and recurring) lustration by examining the various attempts to introduce lustration and file access laws in that country in the twenty-five years since the country embarked on democratization. This began with a communist-forgiving approach exemplified by the so-called "thick line" policy that avoided radical transitional justice. The following years were punctuated by renewed efforts at securing transitional justice, before belated lustration and file access laws were finally adopted at the end of the 1990s. Attempts to extend these truth revelation processes in the mid-2000s culminated in the laws being amended in 2006 and 2007 to radically expand their scope. The chapter then examines whether and how the recent literature on lustration and transitional justice in post-communist Central and Eastern Europe helps us to understand late lustration in Poland. Finally, it considers how these transitional justice issues became entwined with other debates on improving the quality of post-communist democratization and using recent history to question the legitimacy of political opponents. This, I argue, occurred because the emergence of late lustration and file access was often linked to efforts to improve the quality of post-communist democracy and ultimately become entangled with the "politics of history."

WHAT IS LUSTRATION?

Lustration has been the most important (and controversial) transitional justice method used in post-communist Europe. The region was the first to embrace it comprehensively. There lustration has remained an important transitional justice tool so much so that, as Stan notes, many "observers have employed it as a yardstick for measuring the progress of transitional justice in Eastern European and the former Soviet Union."[1] Definitional debates over the term have focused on: (1) whether it should exclude from and limit access to certain offices or simply vet individuals to identify those who worked for and collaborated with the communist secret services and (2) whether vetting and exclusion should also encompass communist party officials above a certain level.[2]

In the Polish case, lustration aimed at revealing whether an individual (generally an occupant of or candidate for a particular post) had links with the communist regime that were kept secret from the public, such as working for or collaborating with the communist security services (Służba Bezpieczeństwa, SB). Leadership (or membership) in the Communist Party or employment in the communist bureaucracy were more openly known, and therefore not subject to lustration. Lustration includes all forms of vetting that may or may not lead to automatic exclusion from office. Consequently, lustration could include "simply vetting or screening individuals for past associations with the communist security services without any sanction necessarily following [other than the damage to their reputation that the disclosure of this information could cause] . . . [rather than necessarily also] then attempting to automatically exclude them from public life on the basis of such links."[3]

Although scholars such as David view lustration primarily as a "personnel policy,"[4] it can also be seen as a "truth revelation procedure"[5] because it involves revealing information (extracted from the communist secret archives) that was held secret before 1989. Lustration, in this sense, depends a great deal on access to the secret archives compiled by the communist political police. In Poland after the passage of the 1998 law – when journalists, historians, researchers, and some other individuals were granted access to security service files – there was a great deal of "informal" screening of individuals and groups not covered by procedures set down in lustration laws. This public identification of former communist secret collaborators from among post-communist elites before the first lustration law was adopted preceded the official lustration carried out by the government through its courts and the National Remembrance Institute (IPM). Consequently, it is only by examining *both* official lustration as a personnel and employment policy *and* unofficial public identifications based on access to communist secret files that one can properly understand why lustration made a late comeback in some post-communist states.

POLAND: A CASE OF LATE AND RECURRING LUSTRATION

In Stan's general typology of post-communist states' approaches to transitional justice – based on whether they instituted trials against former communist regime functionaries and enacted lustration laws and access to communist secret archives – Poland was classified as a "mild" case. In such countries, transitional justice was both delayed in time and less radical in scope than those countries that, to a greater or lesser extent, pursued all three processes strongly and vigorously through citizenship, electoral and/or screening laws (the former East Germany, the Czech Republic, and the Baltic states) but more advanced than those countries that adopted weak transitional justice approaches with only one or two of the methods outlined (Bulgaria and Romania) or those that resisted attempts to re-evaluate the past and seemingly followed a "forgive and forget" approach (Slovakia, Slovenia, Albania, and all of the Soviet successor republics except for the Baltic states).[6]

In Poland, the revelation of the links between post-communist public office holders and the communist secret police through official lustration and unofficial public identification of former agents was by far the most extensively used transitional justice mechanism, much more so than trials or compensation of victims of communist rule. While it was the first country in the region to overthrow communism, as a result of peaceful negotiations between the outgoing regime and the former opposition, Poland approved a lustration law more than eight years after the transition to democracy began. Most striking about the Polish case was the ongoing politicization of lustration, with communist secret archives generating public scandals that, as we shall see, contributed to the collapse of two governments. According to David, Polish discourses on lustration developed such a "poisonous" character due to the length of the pre-lustration period.[7] Its significant delay and recurrence are the most striking features of the development of lustration in Poland, features that need explanation and analysis.

In August 1989, Tadeusz Mazowiecki, a Catholic intellectual advisor to the Solidarity opposition movement and Poland's first non-communist prime minister since the country was incorporated into the Soviet bloc after World War II, announced that a "thick line" would be drawn between the past and the present. Although he was actually seeking to distance his government from the damage done to the national economy by the previous communist regime, the "thick line" was often cited as a metaphor epitomizing the lenient approach to the communist regime adopted by his administration. Despite attempts to "forgive and forget" by both the Mazowiecki government and the subsequent government of Jan Krzysztof Bielecki, who in late 1990 formed a cabinet with the help of parties that were heirs to the Solidarity anti-communist opposition movement, the issue of dealing with the communist past did not go away. Poland refrained from systematically verifying whether persons holding or running for public office had collaborated with the SB. The secret files therefore gained notoriety in the years prior to the initiation of a formal lustration program because various politicians often used "informal lustration" to discredit their political opponents.

Following the first fully free parliamentary election of October 1991, the Solidarity-linked lawyer Jan Olszewski formed a center-right government of "breakthrough." A weak and unstable minority coalition, Olszewski's cabinet had huge political ambitions and promised a clean break with both the communist past and the "forgive and forget" policy of the two previous cabinets. Consequently, in May 1992 the Sejm, the more powerful lower house of the Polish parliament, voted by 186 votes to 15 (with 32 abstentions) in favor of a resolution proposed by Janusz Korwin-Mikke from the small liberal-conservative Union of Real Politics (Unia Polityki Realnej, UPR) requiring the Interior Minister Antoni Macierewicz to publicly disclose within twenty-one days the names of all senior public officials occupying at the time the rank of provincial governor upwards and including members of parliament who had collaborated with the SB. Because the motion had been neither channeled thorough the relevant parliamentary committees nor debated in a plenary session, Macierewicz was provided with no guidelines on how this objective should be achieved.[8] Consequently, a special investigation bureau was established within the interior ministry to compile a list of collaborators based on the secret archives. On June 4, Macierewicz presented parliament and President Lech Wałęsa with secret lists of 66 leading public officials who had allegedly figured in the SB archives as collaborators. These lists included Wałęsa, who led the Solidarity trade union from its creation in the early 1980s until the democratic transition of 1989, and other former anti-communist opposition activists, including pro-lustration advocates such as Wiesław Chrzanowski, the Sejm speaker and leader of the clerical-nationalist Christian-National Union (Zjednoczenie Chrześcijańsko-Narodowe, ZChN), one of the parties formed by heirs to the Solidarity, and Leszek Moczulski, the leader of the radical anti-communist Confederation for an Independent Poland (Konfedracja Polski Niepodległej, the KPN).[9] These "secret lists" were immediately leaked to the press, and on June 5 the Olszewski government was dismissed by 273 votes to 119 (with 33 abstentions). The prime minister hinted that his cabinet had fallen victim to a conspiracy by dark political forces linked to the communist regime.[10]

The controversy that ensued from this failed attempt to introduce lustration was widely felt to have discredited the entire process, but the issue did not go away. Still, none of the various draft lustration laws presented to parliament from 1991 to 1997 made any progress. The 1993 parliamentary election, which brought the communist successor Democratic Left Alliance (Sojusz Lewicy Demokratycznej, the SLD) and the Polish Peasant Party (Polskie Stonnictwo Ludowe, the PSL) to government, and the 1995 presidential election where SLD leader Aleksander Kwaśniewski defeated Wałęsa suggested that the issue of how to deal with the communist past was being suppressed and moved off the political agenda. Nevertheless, at the end of 1995 outgoing President Wałęsa and Interior Minister Andrzej Milczanowski warned that the SLD Prime Minister Józef Oleksy was endangering Poland's security. According to them, Oleksy allegedly had been (and still was) a Russian spy who had passed on secret documents to a KGB agent. Oleksy declared his innocence and military prosecutors later dismissed the charges, but he was forced to step down as prime minister in April 1996.

The so-called "Oleksy affair" meant that the call to tackle the legacy of the SB began to gradually dominate political debate and echo in parliament, setting off a chain of events that culminated in the passage of a lustration law in April 1997.[11] The Sejm adopted a proposal sponsored by a three-party coalition comprising the governing PSL and two opposition parties successors to the Solidarity: the liberal centrist Freedom Union (Unia Wolności, UW) and the social democratic Labour Union (Unia Pracy, UP). The new law contained a number of provisions. First, all elected state officials from the rank of deputy provincial governor up to ministers, prime minister and the president, candidates for parliamentary candidates, barristers, judges, prosecutors, and public mass-media leaders (up to 30,000 in total) were required to submit written declarations stating whether or not they consciously worked for or collaborated with the SB from 1944 to 1990.[12] Second, all statements denying collaboration were transferred to a state prosecutor, the Public Interest Spokesman, who used the SB archives to assess their accuracy. Third, if the prosecutor found evidence that the declaration was false, the public official was to be tried before the lustration court. Fourth, office holders or candidates for office who made false statements were banned from public office for ten years. Fifth, verdicts could be appealed, but the appeal court's rulings were binding and anyone found guilty of being a "lustration liar" had to resign immediately once the court made its judgment. The lustration process could be reopened if the Supreme Court overturned the decision of the appeal court. No job loss ensued if the individual admitted to having been an SB collaborator. President Kwaśniewski was dissatisfied with the lustration bill because it did not define collaboration narrowly enough for him[13] and it did not offer all citizens access to their SB files.[14] Nonetheless, he did not veto the lustration bill, but signed it into law days before the 1997 parliamentary election.

The lustration process did not actually take effect until 1999 due to difficulty in finding twenty-one judges willing to conduct lustration trials and pass such sensitive moral and political judgments. That problem was solved, and the lustration law was thus made workable, after the election in September 1997 of the right-wing Solidarity Electoral Action (Akcja Wyborcza Solidarność, AWS), which formed a coalition government with the UW. In June 1998, the Sejm solved the problem of finding willing judges by amending the lustration law so that the Warsaw District Appeal Court was recognized as the lustration court. It also strengthened the law, transforming the lustration prosecutor (appointed by the head of the Supreme Court) from being simply the government's representative to a key figure whose role was expanded to conducting the process. Finally, it allowed individual members of parliament to initiate lustration trials directly themselves through the so-called "parliamentary denunciation" whereby they could demand the investigation of particular individuals.

At the end of 1998, the AWS-dominated parliament also established the Institute for National Remembrance (Instytut Pamięci Narodowej, the IPN), which, apart from investigating Nazi and communist crimes and informing and educating the Polish public about the country's recent past, became the custodian of the SB files. Researchers, journalists and historians were granted access to any secret files they wanted. Citizens who had been victims of SB surveillance had access to their own files. Those who were not victims of communist persecution or worked as SB collaborators (even if they had themselves been spied upon) could not access their own files or any other files. Like the 1997 lustration law the implementation of this file access legislation was delayed due to difficulties in agreeing on a procedure to elect, and then identifying a suitable candidate to act as the IPN's chairman. The IPN therefore did not function properly until 2000.

Following the 2001 parliamentary election that brought the SLD back to office in coalition with the PSL, attempts were made by the new government to weaken and narrow the scope of the lustration law. All such efforts were unsuccessful, except for an attempt to scrap the "parliamentary denunciation" provisions. At the same time, other developments during 2001–2005 once again brought the issues of lustration and file access to the fore and led to calls for strengthening existing truth revelation procedures or introducing more radical ones. First, calls for more radical lustration were linked to the fight against political corruption, which became more salient in Poland following the Rywin affair. In late 2002, film producer Lew Rywin offered veteran anti-communist opposition strategist Adam Michnik a bribe to arrange a change in a draft law aimed at limiting the print media's influence on radio and television. After 1989, Michnik had become proprietor of the Agora media conglomerate that published the influential liberal daily *Gazeta Wyborcza*, of which he was founder and editor-in-chief. Rywin claimed to act on behalf of what he called the "group in power," which wanted to remain anonymous but possibly included the SLD Prime Minister Leszek Miller. The Rywin affair was followed by a raft of further scandalous revelations involving SLD politicians and officials, as a result of which corruption moved to the top of the political agenda. These scandals were felt to exemplify the corrupt and croneyistic network that had allegedly colonized Polish capitalism and led to calls for more radical lustration and revelation of former SB networks as means of breaking this corrupt nexus.

Second, the very act of opening up the SB files by the IPN led to pressure for further truth revelation procedures. In February 2005, the allegedly slow pace at which the IPN made available the SB files, and its apparent failure to fulfill its mandate to publicly name secret agents, prompted journalist Bronisław Wildstein to disclose a "working" list of 240,000 persons on whom secret files existed (including former agents, military intelligence, secret collaborators, prospective candidates for collaboration, and victims) and post it on the Internet. The list contained no information on whether those named were victims or collaborators and no details regarding their date of birth or place of residence that would identify them from others with the same name. As well as leading to heavy criticisms of the IPN for allowing such a security breach, the list's publication increased pressure on the Polish authorities to open up the SB archives more widely.[15]

Third, calls for further lustration and file access were also spurred by the emergence of links between prominent Catholic clergymen and the SB. These began with the revelation by the IPN in April 2005 that Father Konrad Hejmo, an acquaintance of Pope John Paul II who for twenty years was the main link between the Polish-born pontiff and Polish pilgrims visiting Rome, had been a communist spy. At a press conference, the IPN's director

Leon Kieres said that it had proof that Father Hejmo, a Dominican monk, had collaborated with the SB in the 1980s under the codenames "Hejnal" and "Dominik." News of the allegations broke at a time when Poles were still mourning Pope John Paul II who had died three weeks earlier and Father Hejmo had played a central role organizing the pilgrimage of up to one million Poles who flocked to Rome for the former pontiff's funeral.[16] A series of further revelations about links between Catholic clergymen and the SB followed, peaking in January 2007 when the Archbishop of Warsaw Stanisław Wielgus resigned a few days after his consecration (but immediately prior to his public investiture) following revelations about his collaboration with the SB, which he had initially denied.[17]

Following the election of a government led by the center-right Law and Justice (Prawo i Sprawiedliwość, PiS) party in 2005, the Polish parliament passed a series of amendments – first at the end of 2006 and then, in a revised version after the President Lech Kaczyński refused to approve the original, at the beginning of 2007 – which led to a radical expansion of the scope of the lustration law. This legislation was also supported by the main opposition party, the centre-right Civic Platform (Platforma Obywatelska, PO). It was felt that the provisions of the previous law, whereby during lustration proceedings the Public Interest Spokesman conducted the initial screening and then directed questions to the IPN, slowed the lustration process down too much. Under the new law, to streamline the verification process, the Spokesman's office was abolished and replaced by a special lustration department within the IPN that determined which declarations raised suspicion and warranted investigation; those that did not were not subject to further investigation. The new lustration law, which came into force in March 2007, also broadened existing rules on disclosing collaboration to include all "people filling a public function," thus requiring (according to some estimates) up to 700,000 individuals (including, for the first time, teachers, academics, and journalists) to declare if they had been SB informants.[18]

In May 2007, the Polish Constitutional Tribunal gutted the new provisions when it ruled that large sections of the amended law violated Poland's constitution. First, it ruled that the definition of who held public offices was too broad and should not include academics, journalists, bank and stock exchange managers, tax advisers, school heads, managers of sports organizations, and those who worked for private enterprises. Second, it struck down provisions that, it argued, defined the state security organs too broadly. Third, it annulled penalties for failure to submit a lustration declaration. Fourth, it banned the publication of a list of so-called "secret collaborators" (Tajni Współpracownicy) and "operational links" (Kontakti Operacyjni).[19] Fifth, it limited the IPN chairman's discretion as to whether or not he could withhold access to files from journalists or academics. The Tribunal questioned neither the provisions for lustrating candidates for senior office nor those that required the loss of office for those submitting a false declaration. As Nalepa put it, "even with the provisions struck down by the Tribunal, the IPN still expanded its powers compared to what they were under the 1997 law."[20]

After 2007, the issue of lustration and file access became less salient in Polish politics. One might argue that this development was inevitable, given the passage of time since the collapse of communism. However, it was also because the Constitutional Tribunal's gutting of the new legislation created confusion as to what the new law's precise provisions were together with the fact that, in the snap parliamentary election held in the autumn of that year, the PO ousted the PiS from government. The PO had supported the 2006–2007 lustration law amendments and, if anything, adopted a more radical policy toward file access in the run-up to the 2005 parliamentary election when more right-wing conservative elements within the party were ascendant. At the same time, the party increasingly downplayed the issue in order to accommodate the liberal-left Polish cultural and media establishment, which had always been extremely wary of, and in some cases openly hostile to, radical lustration and file access.

Nonetheless, lustration and secret file access retained their capacity to flare up as major political issues. In 2008 the IPN was criticized for publishing a book by historians Slawomir Cenckiewicz and Piotr Gontarczyk, who suggested that Lech Wałęsa had been an SB informer in the early 1970s (discussed in more detail below).[21] The political debates surrounding the publication of this book led to a 2010 amendment to the law regulating the work of the IPN. The PO-led government hoped the law would make it easier to replace the IPN's chairman, Janusz Kurtyka, who was heavily criticized by the anti-lustration liberal-left media for allegedly being too closely aligned with the PiS.[22] Kurtyka died tragically in the April 2010 Smolensk air crash.

EXISTING APPROACHES TO EXPLAINING (LATE) LUSTRATION PROGRAMS

A growing number of scholars have attempted to develop comparative explanatory frameworks to analyze why and how the newly emerging democracies of Central and Eastern Europe have chosen to come to terms with their communist past and whether or not they attempted to secure some kind of historical justice. Authors such as Moran argue that the intensity of transitional justice programs in post-communist states depended on structural factors such as the nature of the previous communist regime and the injustices that it inflicted.[23] Huntington argues that "justice was a function of political power" and attempts to find a predictive link between the new regime's policy toward dealing with previous non-democratic leaders and the type of transition that a society underwent in its efforts to democratize, particularly the role that elite bargains played in the "mode of exit" from authoritarianism to democracy.[24] Such analyses account successfully for the lack of an *early* interest in lustration and pursuit of transitional justice in countries like Poland. However, the key problem with them, as with all those frameworks that try to explain such phenomena through historical and structural factors, is that they are too static and have problems in explaining what might have made the issue arise *subsequently* and in accounting for the often quite radical changes of trajectory in the way that they dealt with it.

Several attempts have tried to explain the recurrence of lustration and file access as issues of political contestation in countries like Poland. The "politics of the present" approach stressed the role of post-communist party competition as a key explanatory variable.[25] Other efforts refine historical-structural and transition-type approaches, sometimes by supplementing them with "politics of the present" type explanations.[26] Explanatory models that try to blend and synthesize communist and post-communist (and, in Stan's case, pre-communist) factors to explain variations in transitional justice – specifically why progressively more radical lustration and file access legislation was introduced in cases such as Poland – are ambitious and often produce complex explanatory frameworks. However, they are vague in explaining the precise mechanisms involved in how exactly and why particular historical legacies in a country like Poland produced *particular lustration outcomes* at *particular times*, why the issue recurred *in the way that it did* and *at the point in time that it did*. Here, much more contingent "agency" factors still come into play and not all of these can be traced back to historical-structural causes. In particular, these models do not take into account that the ebb and flow of lustration in cases like Poland may have been due to the fact that political elites changed their stance on the issue. Interestingly, although Stan argues that history "matters a lot," at the end of her account she also acknowledges that it "is not destiny" and that the "individual personalities of politicians assuming leading roles in speeding up or slowing down the transitional justice process, and awareness of developments and problems in neighbors make an imprint on how national elites approach the politics of memory."[27] This is an acknowledgment that "agency matters" too.

One of the key issues that arises when trying to explain with more precision why transitional justice recurs at particular times and in particular forms is the extent to which political strategy and calculation or ideological and programmatic motives are the key drivers of (late) lustration and truth revelation. A variant of the "politics of the present" approach, what might be termed the "political elite strategy explanation," is based on the notion that political actors responded rationally to impulses such as (actual or anticipated) popular and societal demand to further their own partisan interests. This angle was not developed explicitly in my own collaborative work with Williams and Fowler.[28] Our analysis did not close off the possibility that lustration may have been motivated by ideological conviction rather than political strategy alone. The clear implication of our argument (and Welsh's)[29] was that the issue was, to a large extent, instrumentalized as an element of inter-party competition.

A more recent attempt to develop such a political elite strategy explanation for late lustration by Nalepa is rooted in a much more explicitly rational-choice framework and based on the idea that, when determining their strategic choices, supporters of lustration used the issue in a calculating way for party advantage.[30] Notwithstanding problems with Nalepa's account at an empirical and factual level, one of the biggest problems with her "skeletons in the closet" model – and other variations of the "politics of the present" explanatory framework that focus on strategic political and electoral factors (including my own previous work on this topic) – is that it argues that transitional justice was almost completely instrumentalized by strategic, office-seeking political elites. This approach underestimates the importance of normative factors and the extent to which the motives of those pushing for transitional justice may have been genuinely programmatically and ideologically driven more than being rooted in strategic considerations. Even those pro-lustration political actors and parties that saw the sponsorship of truth revelation procedures as a useful tool to gain advantage over their competitors were not solely (or even mainly) strategically motivated and may also have been committed to these policies for ideological and programmatic reasons. Stan is surely correct to say that "it (is) difficult to argue that normative considerations of justice are entirely absent,"[31] and that "to reduce the complexity of the politics of memory to the level of recognizing it only as a manipulating tool used in the cut-throat battles waged by power-thirsty political parties or to relegate it to the grey zone of illusory and unattainable myths ignores the Eastern Europeans' need to know the truth about the communist regime, to confront their own personal history, and to obtain justice and absolution."[32]

LUSTRATION AND POST-COMMUNIST DEMOCRATIZATION

Another approach to accounting for different patterns of post-communist lustration and transitional justice – including the recurrence of debates and changes of trajectory, as in the Polish case – places greater emphasis on precisely such ideological-programmatic factors.[33] These accounts are based on the idea that political elites believed, or came to believe, that a more radical approach to such issues was both necessary and desirable from a normative perspective. They also envisage scenarios where some elites who always believed that lustration was necessary came to subsequently find themselves in a position where they were able to implement it.

A good example of how an academic explanatory debate about the timing of lustration becomes linked with more normative approaches is Horne's argument that the emergence of late lustration was linked to efforts to improve the quality of post-communist democracy.[34] This directs our attention to the important point that in many countries, such as Poland, examining political discussions about lustration separately from other political developments under-estimates the extent to which discussions of these issues have often become entwined with other, broader post-communist democratization discourses on issues such as the public's right to information about the background of its public representatives, officials, and authority figures, and the need to tackle corruption. These relate to the relationship between transitional justice and the perceived failures of post-communist democratization as much as to questions of historical justice and dealing with the communist past, with lustration posited as a project designed to implement democratic renewal and to enhance the quality of democracy in these states. This is interesting, because the normative literature on post-communist transitional justice has often posited liberal democratic legal-ethical arguments both for and against adopting radical lustration by counterposing questions of securing historical justice and allowing freedom of information, on the one hand, with concerns about ascribing collective guilt and retroactive justice, on the other.

In the Polish case, the specific focus for this approach was the so-called "Fourth Republic" project, based on a radical critique of post-communist Poland as corrupt and requiring far-reaching moral and political reform. Originally an idea that enjoyed quite broad political support (including from figures linked to Civic Platform), the "Fourth Republic" came to be associated with the 2005–2007 Law and Justice-led governments.[35] Broadening the scope of lustration was seen as a key element of such a renewal. Specifically, as noted above, the notion that post-communist political life was manipulated by the former (still influential) communist security services, and more broadly the perceived ability of elites linked to the former regime to use their communist-era networks to turn their old political power into economic power,[36] prompted many Poles to question the virtues of the "thick line" approach toward transitional justice.

Building on the notion that "there is a collective sense that the past actively affects the political and economic present," Horne argues that countries like Poland adopted late lustration programs as an expression of the perceived need to deepen the democratization process.[37] These programs sought to expand the scope of lustration to include those in "positions of public trust" in both the public and private sectors including journalists, academics, and business leaders. As Horne puts it, "lustration is resonating with a symbolic and institutional sense that something about the democratic transitions is incomplete."[38] Horne rejects what she calls the "dominant explanation" that lustration is a tool of party politics and a "threat to democratic consolidation," and instead distinguishes "politically motivated" lustration laws (which, she argues, they all were) from "politically manipulated" laws ("elite driven" and "wielded against political parties for personal gain" leading to "personal advantaging of the party in power" rather than advancing a reform-agenda).[39] For her, the evidence of late lustration in Poland supported neither a strong "revenge hypothesis" nor a "limited hypothesis" that the laws were timed and designed for direct political party advantage.[40] Rather late lustration was both linked to and driven by legitimate social, economic, and political concerns. Post-communist governments – in Poland and other post-communist states such as Latvia, Macedonia, Slovakia, even the Czech Republic, that instituted transitional justice measures early in the transition – continued to grapple with the issue and, in some cases, used late lustration to further and correct some of the problems associated with post-communist transition by addressing public concerns about corruption, distrust and inequality.[41] The new lustration laws were thereby restructured and packaged with other reform measures, specifically anti-corruption programs.

The way calls for greater lustration and file access, and transitional justice more generally, have become bound up with other critiques of post-communist democratization as part of a broader policy package may also explain why the introduction of more radical lustration procedures may have been driven by "demand" (from Polish voters) and "supply" (largely from political elites), although some commentators have argued that the issue was of low salience to most voters in countries like Poland.[42] Certainly, polling on Polish public attitudes toward transitional justice suggests that lustration and file access did not, on their own, determine election outcomes. Throughout the post-communist period, there was no conclusive evidence of a linear relationship between voter demand and transitional justice supply. Again, surveys conducted during the last twenty-five years found that most Poles favored a radical approach, and there was popular support for making access to the SB files widely available and for radical lustration based on vetting those holding in a wide range of public offices. But they also did not consider transitional justice to be an important or salient issue.[43] However, looking at transitional justice through its apparent electoral salience among Polish voters may misleadingly underestimate the extent to which citizens might have considered questions of lustration and file access to be of much greater (even crucial) importance, when considered in conjunction with other and issues and policy packages. This argument, although a plausible basis for developing hypotheses for future research, obviously requires more rigorous analysis of Polish public attitudes.

HISTORICAL JUSTICE OR THE "POLITICS OF HISTORY"?

Finally, lustration and file access have also become embroiled in the "politics of history" as much as they have the "politics of historical justice." In Poland, the former concept was associated with a group of young conservative academics closely linked with the "Fourth Republic" project who were influential in the PiS governments and with the late President Lech Kaczyński. Most of them drifted out of the party's orbit after his death in 2010. The group's main objective was to present historical events and narrative in a way that both strengthened Poland's national unity and internal cohesion and ensured that its interpretation of history (on issues such as the expulsion of Germans from Polish territory after World War II) was widely accepted in international circles. One can also apply this concept of the "politics of history" to the way in which contemporary history, particularly the communist past, was used to legitimatize certain political actors and delegitimatize their opponents. This concept can be distinguished from the "politics of historical justice," which is more about the pros and cons of pursuing or not pursuing particular approaches to dealing with the (communist) past, rather than using debates and narratives about recent history as an element of inter-party debate and competition. Interestingly, this process was evident not just in debates between political figures linked to the former communist regime and the democratic opposition, but also between different groups of former anti-communist oppositionists and dissidents. A prime example of this dispute, which ran throughout the post-communist period, was seen in the different attitudes toward and interpretations of the spring 1989 roundtable negotiations preceding the semi-free elections that precipitated the end of the Polish communist regime. Critics of the roundtable agreements saw them as fatally flawed, allowing the former ruling elites to make a smooth transition into the new political and economic system and to entrench their power and influential positions within it.

We can see an example of the way in which the process of political self-legitimation and delegitimation of political opponents became entwined in debates about lustration in the divisions within the Solidarity-drawn post-communist elite over whether or not Wałęsa had collaborated with the SB as an informer in the early 1970s. These debates came to a head in June 2008 when, as noted above, amid huge public interest, the IPN published a book which, though bringing no new accusations, claimed to have found previously unknown SB files containing strong circumstantial evidence that linked Wałęsa to a very active collaborator codenamed "Bolek" who informed on his fellow Gdańsk shipyard workers in the early 1970s. The book also claimed that Wałęsa had accessed, tried to doctor, removed, and even destroyed some of the incriminating documents in his archived files while president in 1990–1995.

Wałęsa, who was involved in several court cases against former Solidarity colleagues who accused him of being "Bolek," denied accusations that he had ever been an agent and claimed that the documents incriminating him were forgeries. He cited as evidence the fact that he was cleared by a court of having submitted a false lustration declaration during the 2000 presidential election campaign and in 2005 was given access to his SB files by the IPN as someone who fell into the category of being persecuted under communism. The former president's reputation was defended by the PO, which argued that the book's publication was the latest move in a political war waged against Wałęsa by the PiS. Having helped to run his 1990 presidential election campaign and then worked in his presidential chancellery, Lech Kaczyński and his twin brother Jarosław, who went on to form and lead the PiS, had been in a bitter dispute with Wałęsa since the early 1990s and accused him of being an SB agent from the time that these allegations first emerged following the publication of the "Macierewicz list" in 1992. The PO argued that by attacking Wałęsa, whom they claimed symbolized Poland's international reputation as being in the forefront of a historical struggle for political freedom in the former Soviet bloc, the PiS was damaging an important Polish trade mark or "positive myth," and thus the country's international image. They avoided the issue of the allegation's veracity.

Wałęsa supported the PO against PiS in their bitter struggle, waged since they came to dominate the Polish political scene in 2005. The former president helped to legitimize the PO in the eyes of many Poles who identified with the Solidarity tradition. To the extent that he was discredited as a symbol of the anti-communist democratic opposition, he was less well able to help the party. Given the way Wałęsa thereby became an important element of the PO's "politics of history," his apparent "unmasking" by historians linked to the IPN ensured that lustration and file access once again became entwined in party political conflicts. As noted above, based on its claim that the book demonstrated that the IPN was being used by the PiS as a tool in its political battles, the PO-led government introduced legislation (passed in 2010) to reform the way that its leadership was selected in the hope of preventing further publications of this kind.

CONCLUSION

Poland is an archetypal case of late and recurring lustration. Although the country began the 1990s with a communist-forgiving approach and an initial avoidance of the issue, lustration and file access have remained on the political agenda well after many expected them to fade from public memory. The first decade of post-communism was punctuated by attempts to renew efforts at lustration with a belated mild lustration law and file access laws adopted and becoming operational at the end of the 1990s, and then the country moved on to more radical lustration and file access laws approved (although not enacted) in 2007. This significant delay – and the recurrence of the issue in political debates – is the most striking feature of Polish lustration and one that needs explanation and analysis. It thus provides us with an excellent basis for development frameworks to explain the phenomenon of "late" lustration.

Many scholarly attempts to tackle changes in lustration trajectory focus either on the political and electoral motives of the protagonists for transitional justice or on those who ascribe more ideological-programmatic motives to them. My own position on this question – set out in my writings co-authored with colleagues working on other countries (Williams and Fowler) – and those of other adopting the "politics of the present" approach was that the issue recurred because it had become instrumentalized as an element of the struggle or power tool in post-communist politics. However, on reflection this approach may need to be modified because it failed to fully grasp the extent to which the motives of those pushing for lustration and transitional justice were, in part at least, programmatically and ideologically driven and not motivated purely and simply by partisan interests and instrumental imperatives to gain a strategic advantage over their political competitors. The Polish case suggests at least the possibility that the driver for late lustration may have been the fact that political elites believed, or came to believe, that a more radical approach was both necessary and desirable from a normative perspective, or that some elites who always believed that lustration was necessary later found themselves able to implement it.

At the same, as this chapter shows, the lesson from the Polish case is that lustration and file access have become bundled up with other discourses and political developments in post-communist politics which one needs to understand in order to make sense of the issue. This chapter has identified two such areas that could form the basis for more detailed, grounded research both on the Polish case and on other cases of "late lustration." First, the need to push forward with more radical lustration and file access to improve the quality of post-communist democracy is linked to the anti-corruption fight and the public's "right to know" the background of its public officials and authority figures, including its political and cultural elites. In the Polish case, this has often been bound up with the notion that officials linked to the communist regime had taken advantage of communist-era networks to turn their old political power into economic power. This prompted many citizens and political elites to question the virtues of the "thick line," "amnesty but not amnesia" option. Lustration, therefore, became entwined with broader discourses on post-communist democratization and renewal, in the Polish case specifically the radical "Fourth Republic" critique of post-1989 Poland as corrupt and requiring far-reaching political and moral renewal. Second, lustration and file access also became embroiled in the "politics of history" as a means of questioning the legitimacy of political opponents. Prime examples of this phenomenon were different assessments of the 1989 roundtable agreement and the way that evaluations of the historical role of Wałęsa became entwined in party political struggles. This differs from the way that the existing literature posits the lustration issue as being used to gain strategic advantage through, for example, presenting political opponents as being insufficiently (or too) radical in terms of their approach to vetting or calculating that revealing or not revealing files about individual politicians is likely to support a particular party and/or damage its political opponents. It is more about using the contents of SB files, and the debates surrounding them, to locate that party within a particular historical narrative that it considers advantageous.

This chapter shows that if researchers are to make sense of late lustration they should adopt an expansive approach that considers the issue's relationship with both broader democratization discourses and the politicization of contemporary history. They also need to acknowledge and take greater account of the strong normative aspect underpinning calls for late lustration and the fact that it may often be ideologically rather than strategically driven. For policymakers and practitioners the lesson is that, even if one assumes that the initial avoidance of lustration and transitional justice is motivated by a desire for societal reconciliation and concerns about violating the rule of law rather than prevailing power arrangements, it can create future problems and fail to prevent the future resurfacing of troubling questions regarding public figures' links with the communist security services.

NOTES

1. Lavinia Stan, "Introduction: Post-Communist Transition, Justice, and Transitional Justice," in Lavinia Stan, ed., *Transitional Justice in Eastern Europe and the Former Soviet Union* (London: Routledge, 2009), 12.
2. Roman David, "Lustration Laws in Action: The Motives and Evaluation of Lustration Policy in the Czech Republic and Poland (1989–2001)," *Law and Social Inquiry* 28, no. 2 (April 2003): 388; and Stan, "Introduction," 1–14.
3. Aleks Szczerbiak, "Dealing with the Communist Past or the Politics of the Present? Lustration in Post-Communist Poland," *Europe-Asia Studies* 54, no. 4 (June 2002): 553.
4. Roman David, *Lustration and Transitional Justice: Personnel Systems in the Czech Republic, Hungary and Poland* (Philadelphia: University of Pennsylvania Press, 2011).
5. Monika Nalepa, "To Punish the Guilty and Protect the Innocent: Comparing Truth Revelation Procedures," *Journal of Theoretical Politics* 2, no. 2 (April 2008): 222.
6. Lavinia Stan, "Conclusion: Explaining Country Differences," in Lavinia Stan, ed, *Transitional Justice in Eastern Europe and the Former Soviet Union* (London: Routledge, 2009), 261–262.
7. David, "Lustration Laws in Action," 418.
8. Monika Nalepa, *Skeletons in Closet: Transitional Justice in Post-Communist Europe* (New York: Cambridge University Press, 2010), 15.
9. "Lista Maciererícza," Y-Elita Pl, no date, available at: http://yelita.pl/artykuly/art/lista-macierewicza (accessed December 16, 2013).
10. Jacek Kurski and Piotr Semka, *Lewy Czerwcowy* (Warsaw: Editions Spotkania, 1993).
11. Aleks Szczerbiak, "Dealing with the Communist Past," 553–572.
12. As clarified subsequently by the Constitutional Court, collaboration had to be conscious, secret and connected to the security services' operational activities. A declaration of intent was not enough, there had to be proof of actual activities undertaken in the form of information reports.
13. For example, he wanted it to exclude military intelligence and counter-intelligence, which were the communist-era security services that his erstwhile colleagues in the Democratic Left Alliance were most likely to have collaborated with.
14. Which critics argue that Kwaśniewski wanted to allow so that former security service operatives could view what had been retained about their activities in their files and, more generally, it would make the law unworkable.
15. "To nie jest lista agentów," *Rzeczpospolita*, January 31, 2005; Agnieszka Kublik and Wojciech Czuchnowski, "Wildstein wyniósł listę 240,000 nazwisk z IPN," Gazeta.pl, January 31, 2005, available at: http://serwisy.gazeta.pl/kraj/2029020,34317,2520547.html (accessed January 31, 2005).

16. Andrzej Kaczyński, Ewa K. Czaczkowska and Paweł Siennecki, "Donosił z Wiecznego Miasta," *Rzeczpospolita*, April 28, 2005.
17. Tomasz P. Terlikowski, "Arcybiskup Stanisław Wielgus byl agentem wywiadu PRL," *Rzeczpospolita*, January 4, 2007.
18. See: IPN, *Ustawa z dnia 18 października 2006r o ujawnianiu informacji o dokumentach organów bezpieczeństwa z lat 1944–1990 oraz treści tych dokumentów*, 2007, available at: http://ipn.gov.pl/__data/assets/pdf_file/0009/49284/1-7967.pdf (accessed May 3, 2012); and Jan Cienski, "Polish witch-hunt 'risks business chaos,'" *Financial Times*, March 14, 2007.
19. Secret collaborator was the operational name for those individual who collaborated consciously with the communist security services from 1957 to 1990. Operational link was a special category of collaborators with simplified recruitment procedures created in the 1970s when the security services stepped up its goal of infiltrating the dissident movement. Most of these were conscious collaborators but, due to simplified recruitment procedures, some of them (those drawn from the communist party and its satellites) may not have known about their secret collaboration. Monika Nalepa, "Institute of National Remembrance – Commission for the Prosecution of Crimes against the Polish Nation/Instytut Pamięci Narodowej – Komisja Scigania Zbrodni przeciwko Narodowi Polskiemu," in Lavinia Stan and Nadya Nedelsky, eds., *Encyclopedia of Transitional Justice* (New York: Cambridge University Press, 2013), Volume. 3, 202.
20. Nalepa, "Institute of National Remembrance," 202.
21. Sławomir Cenckiewicz and Piotr Gontarczyk, *SB a Lech Wałęsa. Przyczynek do biografii* (Warsaw: IPN, 2008).
22. Cezary Gmyz, "IPN wedlug Platformy," *Rzeczposolita*, March 19, 2010.
23. John Moran, "The Communist Torturers of Eastern Europe: Prosecute and Punish or Forgive and Forget?," *Communist and Post-Communist Studies* 27, no. 1 (March 1994): 95–109.
24. Samuel P. Huntington, *The Third Wave: Democratization in the Late Twentieth Century* (Norman: University of Oklahoma Press, 1991), 228.
25. Helga Welsh, "Dealing with the Communist Past: Central and East European Experiences after 1990," *Europe-Asia Studies* 48, no. 3 (May 1996), 413–428; Szczerbiak, "Dealing with the Communist Past"; and Kieran Williams, Brigid Fowler and Aleks Szczerbiak, "Explaining Lustration in Central Europe: A 'Post-Communist Politics' Approach," *Democratization* 12, no. 1 (February 2005): 22–43.
26. Nadya Nedelsky, "Divergent Responses to a Communist Past: Transitional Justice in the Czech Republic and Slovakia," *Theory and Society* 33, no. 1 (February 2004): 65–115; Eva Jaskovska and John P. Moran, "Justice or Politics? Criminal, Civil and Political Adjudication in the Newly Independent Baltics," *Journal of Communist Studies and Transition Politics* 22, no. 4 (December 2006): 485–506; and Stan, "Conclusion," 247–270.
27. Stan, "Conclusion," 269.
28. Williams, Fowler, and Szczerbiak, "Explaining Lustration in Central Europe," 22–43.
29. Welsh, "Dealing with the Communist Past," 413–428.
30. Nalepa, *Skeletons in Closet*.
31. Stan, "Conclusion," 269.

32. Stan, "Introduction," 4.
33. Noel Calhoun, "The Ideological Dilemma of Lustration in Poland," *East European Politics and Societies* 16, no. 2 (Spring 2002): 494–520; Noel Calhoun, *Dilemmas of Justice in Eastern Europe's Democratic Transitions* (Basingstoke: Palgrave Macmillan, 2004); and Hilary Appel, "Anti-Communist Justice and Founding the Post-Communist Order: Lustration and Restitution in Central Europe," *East European Politics and Societies* 19, no. 3 (Summer 2005): 379–405.
34. Cynthia Horne, "Late Lustration Programmes in Romania and Poland: Supporting or Undermining Democratic Transitions," *Democratization* 16, no. 2 (April 2009): 344–376.
35. For more on the Fourth Republic project see Paweł Śpiewak, "Pięć lat po czwartej," *Polityka*, June 26, 2010; and Ryszard Bugaj, "Osierocona idea IV RP," Rzeczpospolita, July 6, 2010.
36. Maria Los and Andrzej Zybertowicz, *Privatizing the Police-State: The Case of Poland* (Basingstoke: Palgrave Macmillan, 2000).
37. Horne, "Late lustration programmes in Romania and Poland," 357.
38. Horne, "Late lustration programmes in Romania and Poland," 366. She also argues that they lustration policies might have been a response to external cues from international audiences such as the EU, but largely rejects this explanation.
39. Horne, "Late lustration programmes in Romania and Poland," 351.
40. Horne, "Late lustration programmes in Romania and Poland," 366.
41. Horne, "Late lustration programmes in Romania and Poland," 366.
42. Nalepa, *Skeletons in Closet*, 28.
43. Szczerbiak, "Dealing with the Communist Past," 553–572.

PART II

The Impact of Transitional Justice

4

The Adoption and Impact of Transitional Justice

Moira Lynch and Bridget Marchesi

After the fall of communism, countries in Eastern Europe and the former Soviet Union implemented transitional justice mechanisms to reckon with the painful legacies of communist rule.[1] While much has been written on the use of lustration in the region, there has been less comparative analysis of other justice processes. While existing research has examined the impact of lustration on citizen trust in public institutions, few studies have analyzed the expected positive relationship between multiple transitional justice mechanisms and democracy and human rights protection in the region. Drawing on an original dataset from the Transitional Justice Research Collaborative, this chapter examines the implementation of prosecutions, amnesties, and lustration in post-communism and their impact on democracy and human rights.

The chapter proceeds in four parts. First, we explore current theoretical explanations on the impact of transitional justice mechanisms on democracy and human rights and the impact of lustration on citizen trust in public institutions. Second, we discuss testable hypotheses drawing on existing research concerning the effects of transitional justice. Third, using statistical analysis, we present our key findings. Finally, we conclude by discussing the implications of our findings.

THEORETICAL ARGUMENTS ON THE IMPACT OF TRANSITIONAL JUSTICE MECHANISMS

There are several arguments about how transitional justice mechanisms such as human rights prosecutions, truth commissions and amnesties can strengthen democracy and reduce human rights violations in a country. First, prosecutions are argued to improve the protection of human rights because they signal *enforcement* at the domestic level and thus may create a sense within the government apparatus that future violations are likely to be costly. Prosecutions are also argued to have *deterrence* effects – if the likelihood of punishment through a trial is high in a given society, in a similar manner to enforcement, government actors may perceive future engagement in human rights abuses as costly. These arguments have been confirmed by recent studies that assess the effects of prosecutions on improving human rights.[2]

Second, prosecutions and truth commissions are argued to positively impact human rights and democracy in that they communicate norms concerning rule of law and justice and *socialize* actors to accept and internalize those norms. This theory has been supported by recent cross-national studies on the effects of transitional justice mechanisms.[3] However, findings on the tendency of some truth commissions to entrench political attitudes, and on the dependence of a truth commission's impact on its scope, funding, and reputation, suggest that the socialization theory varies depending on the transitional justice mechanism.[4]

Third, trials can signal a strengthening in the rule of law by demonstrating that state actors do not benefit from impunity, domestic law is effectively enforced, and the judiciary is independent. A more robust rule of law, in turn, is expected to improve human rights and democracy. Finally, in addition to examining the independent effects of single transitional justice mechanisms, recent studies have evaluated whether combinations of mechanisms produce positive or negative results for human rights and democracy. For example, when implemented together, and particularly when amnesties precede trials, amnesties and trials produce positive outcomes because amnesties can provide the political and economic stability that allows judicial institutions to perform fairly and efficiently. Prosecutions are said to be destabilizing to new democratic regimes and thus protection to outgoing political leaders can prevent regime collapse and pave the way for subsequent justice processes. Truth commissions on their own are not found to lead to improved human rights and democracy outcomes, but when combined with trials and amnesties, they can strengthen accountability through their restorative nature and role in recommending reparations and institutional reforms.[5]

THEORETICAL ARGUMENTS ON THE IMPACT OF LUSTRATION IN POST-COMMUNIST COUNTRIES

Much of the literature on post-communist transitional justice has focused on the use of lustration, which is the dismissal, banning, or public identification of personnel in the public sector who are former members of or collaborators with the communist regime.[6] Lustration sanctions include banning such personnel from certain public sector positions or dismissing personnel from their current positions if individuals lie about the nature of their involvement or collaboration with the communist regime.[7]

The broader literature on the impact of transitional justice mechanisms has mainly focused on their effects on human rights and democracy, as discussed earlier. In contrast, research on the impact of lustration in post-communism has largely assessed the effects of such policies on *citizen trust* in public institutions and the national government. Lustration is argued to be a central ingredient in the formation of strong democratic norms and institutions. These policies can demarcate the new democratic system from the old regime by removing tainted officials from the public sector and shaping the moral conscience of a society that seeks to cleanse itself from the legacies of totalitarianism.[8]

Lustration is also viewed as severely undermining the public's trust in public institutions and the government when it involves violations of due process and retroactive justice, relies on secret police files for screening, and is manipulated by political actors.[9] Research that sought to respond to the debate concerning whether lustration erodes or builds citizen trust has mainly examined four key aspects of the lustration process to evaluate its effects on citizen trust: the extensiveness of lustration policies, their targets, their timing, and their impact when paired with other transitional justice mechanisms.

The Extensiveness of Lustration

Various studies on lustration have defined and operationalized it differently, but most have assessed lustration on a spectrum from weak to harsh, or insufficient to sufficient.[10] These categorizations seek to evaluate the nature of lustration policies (dismissals or bans) and whether their implementation was thorough and consistent. Was the lustration process *extensive* or *narrow*? Did a lustration law set the terms for widespread dismissals or were officials exposed through a public naming process but not removed from employment? Were lustration laws passed but actual removals or bans in the public sector remained minimal? The theory behind evaluating the extensiveness of lustration is that the more lustration policies root out personnel associated with repressive communist rule, the more citizens will trust public institutions and the government apparatus after transition.

There is evidence that more extensive policies are associated with increased citizen trust in public institutions such as political parties, parliament, the judiciary, army, police, the press, and unions.[11] In essence, lustration policies that produced thorough and sustained institutional change, as opposed to a narrow policy that is not actually implemented or that is inconsistently applied over time, was strongly associated with citizens' trust in the public sector.

The findings on the impact of lustration on citizen trust in *national government* are more mixed. When asking respondents about their trust in a hypothetical government ministry, David found that more extensive lustration policies, namely widespread dismissals, produced the largest positive effect on respondents' trust in government. Less extensive lustration policies that involved individual confession in exchange for job retention, or simply the exposure of a public official, also produced a positive effect on citizen trust in government but to a much lesser degree. Lustration, regardless of where it falls on the spectrum of extensive to narrow in nature and implementation, has a positive impact on citizen trust in government, but greater levels of trust are strongly associated with more extensive lustration laws.[12]

The Targets of Lustration

The scope of lustration policies also matters when considering whether policies target high-ranking or low-ranking positions in the public sector. The targets of such processes can have varying impacts on citizen perceptions of justice and trust in public institutions. For example, trials that focus on high-ranking military officers may satisfy some victims' quest for justice by bringing before the courts those who directed and sanctioned human rights abuses. Yet, an inattention to prosecuting the "small fry," which may include foot soldiers who carried out extra-judicial killings and massacres, can produce deep wells of resentment and an absence of social reconciliation, particularly when witnesses remember the faces, even the names, of those who murdered their loved ones.[13] Research has shown that post-communist lustration policies that target high-ranking positions in the public sector, such as a party leader or head of a security sector unit, are associated with higher levels of citizen trust in public institutions.[14]

The Timing of Lustration

Several studies have emphasized the importance of *when* mechanisms are implemented as a measure of their impact on stability and democracy. Early implementation of trials and truth commissions, for example, is argued to help establish robust rule of law institutions, which can foster trust in the public sector among citizens.[15] Delays in transitional justice may make the mechanisms susceptible to political manipulation and decrease citizen trust in public institutions that are created or reformed after the transition. Additionally, disenchantment with the new regime may result if justice mechanisms are put off for several years.

Similar arguments have been made in the research on lustration policies' effects. The earlier lustration is implemented in the transition period, the less likely it will be vulnerable to manipulation by political elites.[16] However, the timing of lustration matters less than previously thought. Though timing has been positively correlated with greater citizen trust in public institutions, even if implementation is critical early on, it reaches a tipping point followed by diminishing returns.[17]

Recent research has also demonstrated the importance of evaluating immediate and cumulative effects of transitional justice mechanisms in an effort to assess impacts on democracy and human rights.[18] For example, the immediate effect of domestic criminal prosecutions on government respect for physical integrity or political rights may be negative or minimal, while their cumulative effect might be positive.

The Impact of Lustration in Combination with Other Transitional Justice Measures

Finally, there is evidence that countries are more likely to achieve improvements in democracy and human rights if multiple transitional justice mechanisms are adopted during transitions from authoritarianism to democracy or from conflict to peace. Contrary to arguments that advocate for the use of one particular mechanism as a pathway to stability and improved human rights outcomes, recent findings suggest that a more holistic approach to transitional justice produces more positive and lasting impacts for societies. Two ideal combinations of transitional justice mechanisms have been identified as important for democracy and human rights outcomes as discussed above: prosecutions and amnesties, and prosecutions, truth commissions, and amnesties.[19]

However, when comparing the effects of lustration in isolation and in combination with other mechanisms, the notion of a holistic approach is somewhat less supported. Lustration implemented on its own has much more impact on citizen trust in public institutions than when combined with trials and access to secret archives for ordinary citizens.[20] Thus, while the latter combination positively and significantly improved citizen trust, the impact was significantly less than when lustration was implemented as the sole transitional justice mechanism.

THEORY AND HYPOTHESES

Here we examine the implementation of lustration, trials and amnesties in Eastern Europe and the former Soviet Union after 1989. We analyze the effects of these processes on two dependent variables: human rights and democracy, measured as physical integrity rights and political rights, respectively.[21] Building on the theoretical and empirical findings described above, we formulated the following hypotheses.

Regarding the importance of measuring the immediate and cumulative effects of transitional justice mechanisms on human rights and democracy, we expect lustration policies to have positive and significant cumulative effects.

> *H1: We expect a statistically significant difference between immediate and cumulative effects on both dependent variables and we expect that the cumulative effect of lustration over time will correspond to improvements in physical integrity rights and political rights.*

Given the findings that the more transitional justice mechanisms are implemented, the greater the trust among citizens in public institutions and the greater positive outcomes for democracy and human rights, we expect that when lustration and declassification are paired, significant and positive effects would result on the two dependent variables. Declassification is the process of making public secret files on citizens. During communist times, it was common for state security members to generate secret files on citizens and citizen informants. We code declassification as a type of lustration policy, alongside dismissals, bans, or a combination of the three in some form. Other analyses treat declassification as a separate transitional justice mechanism.[22] We aim to test whether a certain combination of sanctions within lustration policies (dismissal or bans or declassification, or a combination of two or three of these sanctions) leads to more positive outcomes than others. This is another means of analyzing the *extensiveness* of lustration.

> *H2: We expect that lustration policies with multiple sanctions or combinations of sanctions will correspond to improvements in physical integrity rights and political rights.*

Existing findings concerning the spectrum of lustration policies suggest that the more thoroughly and consistently lustration is implemented in a country, the more likely we will see democratic stability and respect for human rights.

> *H3: We expect that extensive lustration policies will correspond to improvements in physical integrity rights and political rights.*

Similarly, to capture the *extensiveness* of lustration policies, the positioning of those targeted may have important implications for the stability of democracy and respect for human rights.

H4: We expect that extensive policies that include high rank public employees will correspond to improvements in physical integrity rights and political rights.

Finally, we attempt to parse out whether there are positive outcomes in terms of physical integrity rights and political rights when lustration is combined with one or more transitional justice mechanism, including prosecutions and amnesties. We build on existing research that finds that trials consistently lead to improvements in government respect for rights and that multiple transitional justice measures are essential to rights protection.[23] Our analysis will elucidate whether current findings on certain combinations of mechanisms are generalizable across regions and whether lustration plays a role in improving or worsening respect for physical integrity rights and political rights.

H5: We expect the effects of prosecutions will correspond to improvements in physical integrity rights and political rights.

INTRODUCTION TO THE DATA

The Transitional Justice Research Collaborative (TJRC) has developed a large-N, cross-national database on transitional justice mechanisms.[24] Teams from Oxford University and the University of Minnesota have collected data on human rights-related criminal prosecutions, truth commissions, amnesties, and vetting spanning forty years and covering all regions of the world. The dataset allows researchers to study quantitatively or qualitatively the effect of specific mechanisms or combinations of mechanisms on political outcomes such as rights protection, democratic consolidation, and conflict recurrence. Data is collected from the United States State Department Annual Country Reports on Human Rights Practices, Keesing's World News Archive, Human Rights Watch country reports, International Center for Transitional Justice country reports, transitional justice laws and decrees, secondary literature on specific countries, and in-country media sources. Detailed information is collected and coded for each mechanism including information about procedure, timing, perpetrators and victims, implementation, media coverage, and outcomes.

The data used in the analysis are time-series cross-section (panel) data on twenty-nine European and former Soviet Union transitional countries.[25] Although our dataset includes data covering the years 1974–2010, our analysis effectively covers only the years 1981–2010 due to the availability of imported data from external data sources.[26] Because we are only interested in the impact of transitional justice mechanisms on political outcomes in countries that have undergone democratic transitions, we include only transitional democratic country-years and exclude all autocratic reversion country-years. We base our case selection on Polity IV's *Regime Transition Variable* (*Regtrans*), and include major and minor democratic transitions as defined by Polity IV.[27] The analysis is focused on three transitional justice mechanisms: domestic criminal prosecutions, amnesty policies, and lustration policies.[28] Our unit of observation is the country-year-policy: "Slovakia-2002-Law on National Memory."

The TJRC collects data on mechanisms that are coded if they meet the following criteria: the human rights harm must take place prior to democratic transition, and the mechanism must take place after democratic transition. Domestic criminal prosecutions are defined as all prosecutorial activity conducted in a single country for crimes committed in that country or anywhere by nationals of that country. Such prosecutions are further defined as the use of domestic courts of law to bring criminal procedures against state agent perpetrators of human rights violations. All international, foreign, and hybrid prosecutions are excluded from domestic criminal prosecution coding. Amnesty is defined as an official state declaration that individuals or groups accused or convicted of committing human rights violations will not be prosecuted, further prosecuted, and/or will be pardoned of their crimes and released from prison. Amnesty data includes *de jure* amnesties and *de facto* amnesties such as pardons. Self-amnesties passed by the *ancien régime* are included unless they have been legally revoked by the new democratic regime. Lustration is defined as an official state policy that deprives categories of perpetrators access to public sector employment on either a temporary or a permanent basis as the result of past human rights abuse. The TJRC operationalizes lustration as dismissal from existing employment, banning from future employment, or a combination of dismissal and banning. In addition to dismissal and banning, the TJRC codes declassification, understood as the process of making public secret files. Lustration policies are coded by country-policy-year, but are collapsed into a country-year format for analysis.[29] The TJRC collects detailed information about each policy including policy source, sanctions, targeting by position, legal and other official challenges, and implementation. When possible, policies that evaluate the individual integrity of public employees are differentiated from policies that automatically sanction individuals for group membership or affiliation (see Figure 4.1).[30]

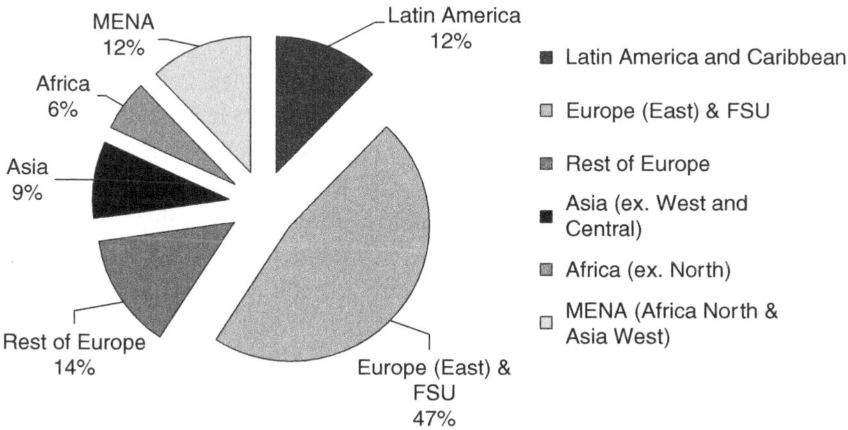

FIGURE 4.1: Vetting Policies – Includes Transitional Years Only

DEPENDENT VARIABLES

This study builds on earlier quantitative studies that use similar dependent variables and empirically tested controls recognized as determinants of state human rights behavior.[31] Two dependent variables measure the level of physical integrity in a given country-year (for example, Poland-2000). The first measure is the Political Terror Scale (PTS), the five-point coding scheme that measures the extent to which states violate their own citizens' personal integrity rights through political imprisonment, torture, killings, and disappearances. PTS level 1 represents countries under secure rule of law where physical integrity abuse is extremely rare. PTS level 5 represents countries where physical integrity abuse extends to the whole population.

The second measure is the Cingranelli-Richards physical integrity index (CIRI-PI), an additive index constructed from factor variables that measure torture, extrajudicial killing, political imprisonment, and disappearances. CIRI-PI is a nine-point scale ranging from 0 (no government respect for physical integrity rights) to 8 (full government respect for physical integrity rights). We invert the scale so that interpretation of coefficients is more intuitive and the CIRI scale matches the orientation of PTS. We test all statistical models that estimate the impact of transitional justice mechanisms on the level of physical integrity rights using PTS and CIRI-PI. However, we report results using CIRI-PI.[32]

We are also interested in estimating the impact of transitional justice mechanisms on democratic development. Scholars generally use two measures as stand-ins for regime authority, democratic consolidation, or political rights. The first measure is POLITY2 from the Polity IV project. Polity variables measure institutionalized authority traits that characterize distinct polities such as autocracies and consolidated democracies. Polity is a composite measure that evaluates authority traits of polities such as competitiveness of executive, independence of executive authority, and political competition and openness. The second measure is CIRI empowerment rights index (CIRI-EP), an additive index constructed from variables that measure a government's respect for political rights. It includes measures of freedom of foreign movement, freedom of domestic movement, freedom of speech, freedom of religion, worker's rights, and electoral self-determination. CIRI-EP is a fifteen-point scale that ranges from 0 (no government respect for political rights) to 14 (full government respect for political rights). To improve interpretability of results and to match the orientation of our physical integrity rights dependent variables, we invert CIRI-EP. Polity and CIRI-EP are overlapping, but they measure different aspects of democratic development. Whereas Polity measures only the institutional and governing characteristics of a regime, CIRI-EP measures electoral freedom and participation, and more directly individual political rights. Because we are interested in the impact of transitional justice on *rights*, we employ CIRI-EP as our measure of democratic development.[33]

SPECIFICATION AND METHODOLOGY

We are interested in estimating the effects of transitional justice mechanisms on civil and political rights. We estimate all ordered logit models using maximum likelihood estimation.[34] Our independent variables are domestic criminal prosecutions, amnesty policies, and lustration policies. We code each mechanism as a country-year binary variable (where values are 1 or 0), as a country-year count variable (where values are the total counts of a mechanism in a given country-year), and as cumulative counts or carry-forwards. The carry-forward coding convention adds the country-year count variable from the previous country-year observation *(t-1)* to the current country-year count variable *(t)* and then carries-forward the sum to the next country-year observation. The carry-forward begins with the second country-year observation and continues until the final country-year observation in the dataset. We code all primary transitional justice variables and associated attribute variables using the binary, count, and carry-forward coding conventions. The binary and count variables allow us to test the impact of mechanisms in the year of event or policy adoption. We conceptually think about this as the immediate effect. The carry-forward variables allow us to test the cumulative impact of mechanisms over time. We conceptually think about this as the cumulative effect. While many scholars do not distinguish between immediate and cumulative effects, recent empirical studies have used a similar approach.[35] Substantively, the carry-forward allows us to better understand the differences between immediate and cumulative effects, and enables us to see how the effects change over time and with each increase in event or policy. We report all results using the count and carry-forward independent variables.

We include several covariates in our analysis to control for potential confounders. Following much of the quantitative empirical literature, we include a lagged dependent variable. The level of civil and political rights in the previous time period *(t-1)* is theorized to have an effect on the level of rights in the current time period *(t)*. Using country-year data from the World Bank's development indicators, we control for the level of economic inequality and the level of population. The covariates annual GDP per capita and population are log-transformed. Using country-year data from Polity IV, we control for the level of institutional democracy using the Polity2 measure.[36] Additionally, we include a squared transformation of the Polity2 variable to reflect the quadratic relationship between Polity2 and our dependent variables. We lag all covariates *t-1* years to control for potential endogeneity and temporal dependence.

RESULTS[37]

We begin our analysis by testing the immediate and cumulative effects of lustration on CIRI-PI and CIRI-EP.[38] Our hypothesis is two-fold: we expect to find a statistically significant difference between immediate and cumulative effects on both dependent variables, and that the cumulative effect of lustration over time will correspond to improvements in physical integrity rights and political rights. Our first model tests the immediate and cumulative effects of lustration on physical integrity rights. We find no statistically significant relationship between the two in either time period.[39] Our second model tests the immediate and cumulative effects of lustration on political rights. In the immediate period, we find no statistically significant relationship. The cumulative effect of lustration on political rights is positive and significant. Holding all covariates at a fixed value, a 1-unit increase in lustration corresponds to a 25.3 percent increase in the odds of worsening political rights. Unless otherwise reported, all coefficients are significant at the 1 percent level.[40]

Next we test the impact of specific forms of lustration on CIRI-PI and CIRI-EP. We are still interested in the immediate and cumulative effects of lustration on physical integrity and political rights but want to explore how variation in sanctions might impact rights outcomes. We hypothesize that lustration with multiple sanctions or combinations of sanctions will correspond to improvements in physical integrity rights and political rights. Our first model tests the impact of lustration with combinations of sanctions on physical integrity rights in the immediate and cumulative periods. Our second model tests the impact of lustration with combinations of sanctions on political rights in both time periods. Both times we find no statistically significant relationship in either period.

Building on this analysis, we test the effect of lustration policies with declassification sanctions on physical integrity rights and political rights. Our hypotheses are the same as in the previous analysis except our independent variable of interest is declassification. We find no statistically significant effect of declassification on either physical integrity rights or political rights in either period.

Our next analysis tests the effect of "extensive" lustration on physical integrity rights and political rights. We hypothesize that extensive lustration will correspond to improvements in physical integrity rights and political rights. To test the extensiveness of lustration, we build an additive index comprised of independent variables that measure the number of sanctions, the number of positions targeted, and policy implementation. We do not collect or code detailed information about lustration policy implementation. Our implementation variable is a binary variable where implementation is coded 1 if any aspect of the policy is implemented and coded 0 otherwise.[41] The "extensive" index ranges between 0 and 4. We substantially interpret higher values of the index as more extensive lustration policies.

Our first model tests the immediate and cumulative effects of extensive lustration policies on physical integrity rights. We find no statistically significant relationship between the two in either period. Our second model tests the impact of extensive lustration policies on political rights in the immediate and cumulative periods. We find no statistically significant relationship in the immediate term, but the cumulative effect is statistically significant and negative. Holding all covariates at a fixed value, a 1-unit increase in extensive lustration corresponds to a 16.2 percent increase in the odds of improvements in political rights. Results are statistically significant at the 5 percent level.

Again, we are interested in exploring a subset of lustration policies that are both extensive and target high rank public employees (what we call "vertically extensive" lustration). We hypothesize that vertically extensive lustration will correspond to improvements in physical integrity rights and political rights. To measure this subset, we add independent rank variables to our previous index. We code any policy that targets high rank positions or high

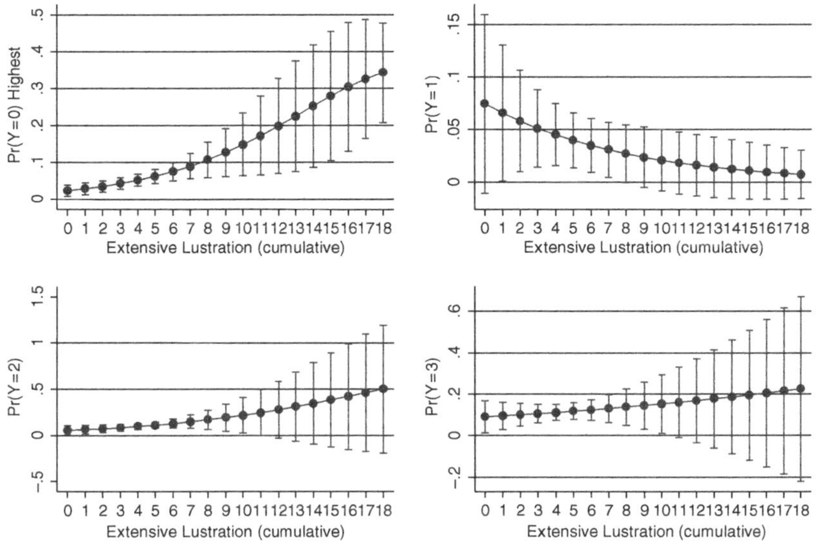

FIGURE 4.2: Predicted Probability by Response Level of CIRI-EP

and low rank with a value of 1, and policies that only target low rank positions with a value of 0. Again, we substantively interpret higher values of the index as more extensive lustration policies. Our first model tests the immediate and cumulative effects of vertically extensive lustration on physical integrity rights. We find no statistically significant relationship in either period. Our second model tests the immediate and cumulative impact of vertically extensive lustration on political rights. We find no statistically significant immediate effect. The cumulative effect is statistically significant and negative. Holding all covariates at a fixed value, a 1-unit increase in extensive lustration corresponds to an 18.7 percent increase in the odds of improvements in political rights.[42]

Figure 4.2 shows the results of an out of sample data simulation.[43] The chart shows the mean predicted probability of observing the dependent variable across the range of values for extensive lustration holding all covariates at their mean values. Because the dependent variable has many categories, we estimate the mean predicted probabilities for its specific levels. Although we cannot interpret them with a high degree of confidence, the results suggest that the mean predicted probability of observing the highest values of CIRI-EP (or the most government respect for political rights) increases as countries adopt more extensive lustration policies.

Our final analysis tests the immediate and cumulative impact of multiple transitional justice mechanisms on physical integrity and political rights. We hypothesize that the adoption of multiple mechanisms will correspond to improvements in physical integrity rights and political rights. We begin by estimating a fully specified model that includes domestic criminal prosecutions, lustration policies, and amnesty policies. We find no statistically significant relationships between any of the mechanisms and physical integrity rights in the immediate period. The cumulative effect of amnesty on physical integrity rights is positive and significant. Holding all covariates at a fixed value, a 1-unit increase in amnesty corresponds to a 72.2 percent increase in the odds of worsening physical integrity rights. Although our results are highly significant, we cautiously interpret them due to the small number of amnesty policies in our data sample.[44] We also test the immediate and cumulative effects of the three mechanisms on political rights. We find no statistically significant relationships between any of the mechanisms and political rights in the immediate term. The cumulative effect of lustration and domestic criminal prosecutions on political rights is statistically significant and positive. Holding all covariates at a fixed value, a 1-unit increase in lustration corresponds to a 22.6 percent increase in the odds of worsening political rights, while a 1-unit increase in domestic criminal prosecutions corresponds to a 6.4 percent increase in the odds of worsening political rights. The cumulative effect of amnesty on political rights is not statistically significant.

DISCUSSION

The Impact of Lustration on Physical Integrity Rights and Political Rights

Our analysis shows there are null results regarding lustration's impact on government respect for human rights. For the average country in our sample, lustration policies did not correspond to improvements in government respect for *physical integrity rights* (e.g., torture, extrajudicial killing, political imprisonment, and disappearance). This finding is significant, since other mechanisms, notably prosecutions, truth commissions, and amnesties, have been found to have clear positive or negative effects, on their own or in combination, on human rights outcomes.[45] We do find a statistically significant and negative cumulative effect on political rights. For the average country in our sample, lustration policies worsened government respect for political rights.

The null effect of lustration on human rights protection illuminates a few key distinctive historical and political conditions in the region. Government violations of physical integrity rights certainly occurred under communist regimes, but mostly during the first two decades of communist rule. After 1960, the rates of abuse or violence were not nearly as high as in regions such as Latin America, where disappearances, extrajudicial killings, and torture were often part of a strategic government policy to eliminate an internal threat. The potential for a change in the human rights landscape after the implementation of transitional justice in Latin America is thus significantly higher than in Eastern Europe and the former Soviet Union, and this is why we see clear positive improvements in human rights protections in Latin American countries that employed human rights prosecutions and very little effect on human rights in this region.[46]

In addition, what we know about citizen trust and lustration is relevant here. The literature suggests that lustration on the whole has positive effects on citizen trust in public institutions. Citizen trust is typically evaluated in terms of citizens' faith in certain public institutions. Thus, citizen trust is more likely to be an indicator of how the government respects freedoms related to speech, employment, movement, and political participation (*political rights*) than an indicator of whether or not the government engages in torture practices or extralegal violence against its own citizens (*physical integrity rights*).

Lustration differs from other transitional justice mechanisms. It is contentious because unlike prosecutions, truth commissions and amnesties, there is no evidence to date that it is linked to improvements in human rights and democracy through enforcement, deterrence, socialization, or the strengthening of rule of law. Lustration is often argued to cause social discord by stigmatizing and alienating some social segments.[47] It has also been strongly criticized for relying on secret police files for evidence. Its immediate and cumulative effects may be particularly important in that the worsening or strengthening of political rights may be dependent on the very nature of the process itself and its implementation (its *extensiveness*).

Unlike mechanisms with either a retributive or a restorative justice focus, the aims of lustration are largely institutional reform. We would expect lustration to have a more positive effect over time on the protection of political rights due to the institutional reforms it produces. Our finding that the opposite holds true could indicate two conditions. First, the implementation of lustration in post-communist countries was quite varied. Countries that adopted and maintained lustration laws some years after the regime change were often led by post-communist governments which initiated lustration as a preemptive move when they expected to lose power to young anti-communist parties.[48] Thus, lustration sometimes emerged not out of a motivation for institutional reform or from ideological and programmatic concerns (factors key in Aleks Szczerbiak's chapter in this volume), but rather from political actors' desire to gain electoral success. The absence of reforms and the strong presence of political partisanship in some of these cases signal a corresponding lack of government respect for political rights.[49]

Second, there is a tipping point in terms of the effects of lustration on government respect for political rights. While Horne's chapter in this volume examines early versus late adoption of lustration laws, and finds that late adoption does not necessarily indicate weaker democratic consolidation, we assess the immediate effect of lustration laws as opposed to the effect of cumulative laws enacted over time. In essence, we explore whether the sustained implementation of policies leads to improvements in political rights. Unlike existing findings on prosecutions in other parts of the world, where sustained legal action promotes and fosters a rights culture, we see no rights improvements when considering the cumulative count of post-communist lustration. Sustained implementation of one or more lustration policies might indicate the presence of government corruption[50] or political opportunism rather than the development of a rights culture. Finally, because we know that extensive lustration policies can have a strong and positive effect on citizen trust in public institutions, this finding also suggests that we need to know more about the lustration policies themselves, which we discuss next.

The Extensiveness of Lustration

For the average country in our sample, the cumulative effects of *extensive* lustration correspond to improvement in government respect for political rights. Our findings suggest that the extensiveness of lustration policies matters, and policies that specifically target high rank positions or target both high and low rank positions have important positive cumulative effects over time on government respect for political rights. This result parallels research showing that lustration policies have positive effects on citizen trust when they are extensive in nature and thoroughly implemented.[51] It also aligns with Horne's findings in this volume. In essence, both her and our findings suggest that the overall quality of the lustration process matters for democracy more than the simple adoption of the laws or the timing of their enactment. While lustration can worsen government respect for political rights over time, not all policies have these effects. Policies that target multiple sectors, are thorough in attempting to remove personnel from both high and low rank positions, and are at least partially implemented tend to produce an environment where

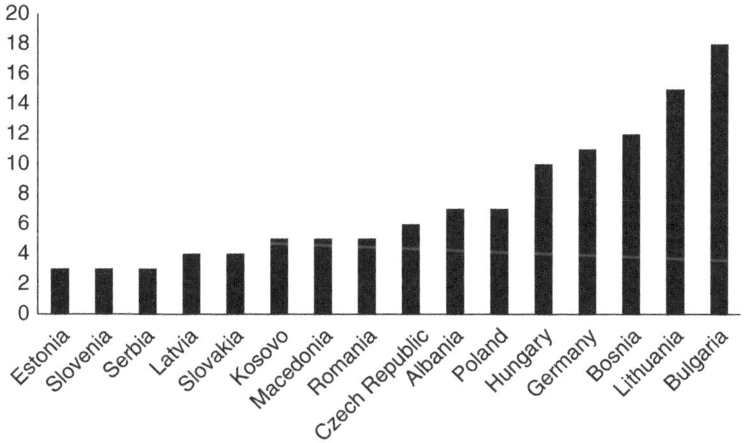

FIGURE 4.3: Cumulative Extensiveness Index Score

political rights are protected by the government.[52] Figure 4.3 presents a country ranking by index score.

The Impact of Lustration in Combination with Other Transitional Justice Mechanisms

We expected lustration to have stronger positive effects on physical integrity rights and political rights, if combined with prosecutions and amnesties. The worsening of political rights that results from the additive effects of prosecutions and lustration is a key finding since trials are the main driver in improving political rights when combined with other mechanisms.[53] There are several possible explanations for this result. First, of the ninety-nine prosecutions implemented in nineteen countries in this region, many were held very early in the transition period and in most cases each country only saw one or a handful of prosecutions. Thus, contrary to Latin America, where the number of prosecutions was significantly higher *and* often consistently implemented over several years after transition, post-communist prosecutions were minimal and far less systematic. This is important because the consistent implementation of prosecutions produces a "rights culture." Socialization within a society to human rights norms and rule of law after a transition is unlikely if prosecutions are held as one-time events and only in the immediate aftermath of the transition. Recent studies demonstrate that the immediate effects of prosecutions on physical integrity rights are null; the positive effects only appear in the long term.[54]

Second, much of the early timing and limited scale of post-communist prosecutions may result from the negotiated nature of most democratic transitions in the region. If communist officials were assured protection from judicial scrutiny or were invited to participate in the new regime alongside the opposition, prosecutions on a grander scale were highly unlikely. This points to their quality. We might see a slightly worsening effect on political rights where prosecutions and lustration were held because some of the trials held early on, particularly those held *before* lustration was enacted (in about half of the cases), were not conducted fairly and thus did not contribute to strengthen a rights culture and rule of law. Specifically, we may see a negative effect as a result of a few cases where prosecutions have been strongly criticized, namely Serbia, Croatia, and Bosnia, which make up 51 percent of the prosecutions in our dataset. We plan to further investigate this finding in future research.

Third, some of these trials may have not been conducted fairly and systematically because there was little judicial institutional reform after transition. Of the twenty-nine countries in the region, lustration policies targeted the judicial sector in only seven (Czech Republic, Poland, Romania, Albania, the former East Germany, Kosovo, and Slovenia). The absence of judicial reform in the remaining twenty-two cases may have produced low-quality prosecutions and this may have contributed to a worsening of political rights in the long term.

Finally, our finding on the additive effects of prosecutions, lustration, and amnesties is an important test of existing theories on the positive effects of prosecutions used in combination with other mechanisms. We expected to see improvements when prosecutions and lustration were used, but the varied nature and implementation of lustration and the political conditions in the region demonstrate that prosecutions and lustration do not reinforce one another. The use of both processes may have, in the long-term, fostered social discord if the judiciary was not reformed, prosecutions were seen as illegitimate, and lustration was partially implemented. Again, while the additive effect of prosecutions, lustration and amnesties tends to lead to a worsening of political rights, we find that *extensive* lustration policies can be a mitigating factor. Countries that implemented extensive lustration did not experience the same worsening of political rights as those with narrow policies.

Although we use the most advanced statistical techniques to control for potential confounding relationships such as reverse causality and spurious correlation, we cannot claim that our findings are unquestionably "causal." However, because we use the best available cross-national data on transitional justice mechanisms, we are confident that our results help explain a portion of the variation in political rights. There are, nonetheless, important limitations of our analysis. We find that extensive lustration corresponds with improvements in government respect for political rights, but our results are potentially biased due to selection bias or omitted variable bias.[55] We also do not explore the multiplicative or interactive effects of domestic criminal prosecutions and lustration. We will address both of these limitations in future research.

CONCLUSION

This chapter provides key lessons on the effects of post-communist transitional justice on physical integrity rights and political rights. First, the findings expand our understanding of the impact of lustration by moving beyond existing research that examines citizen trust in public institutions in a selection of cases in the region. We conduct a complete cross-national analysis that directly engages with some of the most important claims in the literature concerning the expected positive relationship between transitional justice mechanisms and human rights and democracy outcomes. We show that lustration had no real immediate or cumulative effects on government respect for physical integrity rights. This illustrates both the limits of this mechanism and the unique historical context of the post-communist world.

We also find that the extensiveness of lustration policies matters. While lustration can lead to a worsening of government respect for political rights, policies that are thoroughly implemented, include multiple sanctions, target more than one area of the public sector, and target high-ranking as well as low-ranking positions can curtail this effect. The immediate effects of lustration on government respect for political rights are null, but its cumulative effects can actually worsen respect for political rights *unless* the policies are extensive in their scope and implementation. In essence, if lustration cannot thoroughly remove tainted public officials and instigate robust institutional reforms, thereby creating a new culture of political rights protection, democratization will likely stagnate (as in Romania).[56]

Second, since most of the literature on transitional justice in this region focuses on lustration only, our examination of cross-national trends in prosecutions, amnesties, and lustration and our findings on how lustration can produce distinctive effects in combination with other mechanisms are significant. Our finding that the cumulative effects of lustration in combination with prosecutions over time lead to a worsening of political rights is a key insight. In contrast to Latin America, post-communist trials were not the driver of democracy and human rights improvements due to their limited number, quality and scope. It may also matter that many prosecutions were held before lustration got underway. Lustration targeted the public sector, but the judiciary was not its primary focus. The lack of reform in this sector may have prevented prosecutions from being widespread and from aiding in the establishment of a rights culture.

Finally, these findings provide us with valuable information about how scholars and practitioners should consider the design and implementation of vetting policies in the future. The quality of lustration matters; its scope – in terms of sanctions and targets – matters for improvements in political rights. Our findings also show the potential for vetting and trials to work together if the proper conditions exist. Vetting of the judicial sector, for example, may help to foster the use of free and fair prosecutions. This could, in turn, assist in establishing a rights culture that may prevent the creation of politically motivated vetting policies. Thus, future transitional societies may be wise to consider sequencing vetting *before* prosecutions.

Our findings serve as an important launching pad for assessing the impact of vetting on democracy and human rights globally. Lustration is clearly distinctive from other transitional justice mechanisms in that there are limits to what it can contribute to democratization in the long term. In future research, we plan to investigate if these findings are generalizable to other regions in the world.

NOTES

1. This chapter is based on work supported by the National Science Foundation and the Arts and Humanities Research Council under Grant No. 0961226. Research support was also provided by Prof. Kathryn Sikkink and the Regents Professorship at the University of Minnesota. Any opinions, findings, conclusions, or recommendations expressed here are those of the authors and do not reflect the views of their universities or those of the National Science Foundation or the Arts and Humanities Research Council. The authors wish to thank the members of the TJRC for their valuable help developing the coding manual and coding. The authors also wish to thank Kathryn Sikkink, James McAdams, Lisa Sundstrom, and Ben Bagozzi for their helpful comments.
2. Kathryn Sikkink, *The Justice Cascade: How Human Rights Prosecutions Are Changing World Politics* (New York: Norton, 2011); Tricia D. Olsen, Leigh A. Payne, and Andrew G. Reiter, *Transitional Justice in Balance: Comparing Processes, Weighing Efficacy* (Washington, D.C.: United States Institute of Peace Press, 2010).
3. Ibid.

4. Jelena Subotic, *Hijacked Justice: Dealing with the Past in the Balkans* (Ithaca, NY: Cornell University Press, 2009); Priscilla B. Hayner, *Unspeakable Truths: Transitional Justice and the Challenge of Truth Commissions* (New York: Routledge, 2010).
5. Tricia D. Olsen, Leigh A. Payne and Andrew G. Reiter, *Transitional Justice in Balance: Comparing Processes, Weighing Efficacy* (New York: United States Institute of Peace Press, 2010), 154–158.
6. Cynthia M. Horne, "Assessing the Impact of Lustration on Trust in Public Institutions and National Government in Central and Eastern Europe," *Comparative Political Studies* 45, no. 4 (2012): 412–446.
7. Horne, "Assessing the Impact of Lustration"; Lavinia Stan, ed., *Transitional Justice in Eastern Europe and the former Soviet Union: Reckoning with the Communist Past* (London: Routledge, 2009); Natalia Letki, "Lustration and Democratization in East-Central Europe," *East-Asia Studies* 54, no. 4 (2002): 529–552.
8. Horne, "Assessing the Impact of Lustration"; Roman David, *Lustration and Transitional Justice: Personnel Systems in the Czech Republic, Hungary and Poland* (Philadelphia: University of Pennsylvania Press, 2011).
9. Horne, "Assessing the Impact of Lustration," 415; Monika Nalepa, *Skeletons in the Closet: Transitional Justice in Post-Communist Europe* (New York: Cambridge University Press, 2010).
10. Letki, "Lustration and Democratization in East-Central Europe"; M. Kaminski and Monika Nalepa, "Judging Transitional Justice: A New Criterion for Evaluating Truth Revelation Procedures," *Journal of Conflict Resolution* 50, no. 3 (2006): 383–408; Stan, *Transitional Justice in Eastern Europe*; Horne, "Assessing the Impact of Lustration."
11. Horne, "Assessing the Impact of Lustration."
12. David, *Lustration and Transitional Justice*.
13. Sigall Horovitz, "Transitional Criminal Justice in Sierra Leone," in Naomi Roht-Arriaza and Javier Mariezcurrena, eds., *Transitional Justice in the Twenty-First Century: Beyond Truth Versus Justice* (New York: Cambridge University Press, 2006), 43–69; Eric Stover and Harvey Weinstein, eds., *My Neighbor, My Enemy: Justice and Community in the Aftermath of Mass Atrocity* (Cambridge: Cambridge University Press, 2004).
14. Horne, "Assessing the Impact of Lustration," and David, *Lustration and Transitional Justice*.
15. Hayner, *Unspeakable Truths*; Sikkink, *The Justice Cascade*.
16. Nalepa, *Skeletons in the Closet*.
17. Horne, "Assessing the Impact of Lustration," 435.
18. Geoff Dancy, Bridget Marchesi, Tricia Olsen, Leigh Payne, Andrew Reiter, and Kathryn Sikkink, "Stopping State Agents of Violence or Promoting Political Compromise? The Powerful Role of Transitional Justice Mechanisms," paper presented at the American Political Science Association annual meeting, Chicago, August 30, 2013.
19. Olsen, Payne and Reiter, *Transitional Justice in Balance*, 154.
20. Horne, "Assessing the Impact of Lustration," 439.

21. We do not examine the impact of lustration on citizen trust because there is limited panel data available in the Eurobarometer survey. Instead, we examine the impact of lustration alone, and in combination with amnesties and prosecutions on physical integrity rights and political rights.
22. Horne, "Assessing the Impact of Lustration."
23. Sikkink, *The Justice Cascade*; Olsen, Payne, and Reiter, *Transitional Justice in Balance*; Horne, "Assessing the Impact of Lustration."
24. The TJRC was made publicly available in 2014. Please contact the authors for more information.
25. We focus on Europe and the former Soviet Union for theoretical and statistical reasons. These countries share similar political and transitional pasts and thus should be studied together. By including all former Soviet countries, we increase our confidence in our statistical results and believe our results are more generalizable.
26. The availability of certain variables (CIRI) limits our years of analysis to 1981–2010. Our lustration "treatment" years begin in 1990.
27. Monty G. Marshall and Keith Jaggers, "Polity IV Project: Political Regime Characteristics and Transitions 1800–2012," 2012, available at: http://www.systemicpeace.org/polity/polity4.htm (accessed February 6, 2014).
28. Countries enter the TJRC database in the first year of major democratic transition. Once a country experiences a major democratic transition, it enters our database and does not exit. For some analysis, scholars may want to exclude country-years of autocratic reversion.
29. Our unit of observation is the country-year-policy. Some countries have more than one lustration policy in a given country-year. We collapse country-years with multiple policies into a single observation. This means that we increase the policy count and combine policy features such as sanctions and positions targeted.
30. Although not included in the analysis, there are four countries in the sample that have had truth commissions.
31. Steven C. Poe and C. Neal Tate, "Repression of Human Rights to Personal Integrity in the 1980s: A Global Analysis," *American Political Science Review* 88, no. 4 (1994): 853–872; Steven C. Poe, C. Neal Tate, and Linda Camp Keith, "Repression of the Human Right to Personal Integrity Revisited: A Global Cross-National Study Covering the Years 1976–1993," *International Studies Quarterly* 43, no. 2 (1999): 291–313.
32. There are trivial differences in results between PTS and CIRI-PI models. We follow standard practice and note when substantial differences between models arise.
33. Horne uses the Freedom House Nations in Transit measure of democratic consolidation. The Nations in Transit democratic measure is a seven-point index that measures a broad array of regime characteristics and political rights such as electoral process, civil society, independent media, corruption, judicial independence and governance. It operationalizes democratic consolidation by rating a country's political and socioeconomic reforms. Data are available for 29 former communist states in Europe and Eurasia from 1999–2013.
34. We test the fit of our model using AIC and BIC test statistics. We test the fully specific model – which includes all covariates and a lustration variable – against less complicated models with fewer covariates. The test statistics for the fully

specified model were always smaller than the more constrained model suggesting the fully specified model is the better model.

35. Hunjoon Kim and Kathryn Sikkink, "Explaining the Deterrence Effect of Human Rights Prosecutions for Transitional Countries," *International Studies Quarterly* 54, no. 4 (2010): 939–963; Geoff Dancy, "The Impact of Human Rights Law in Time," Ph.D. Dissertation. University of Minnesota, 2013; Dancy, Marchesi, Olsen, Payne, Reiter, and Sikkink, "Stopping State Agents of Violence or Promoting Political Compromise? The Powerful Role of Transitional Justice Mechanisms."
36. When analyzing the impact of transitional justice on political rights using the CIRI-EP measure, we include Polity2 as a control variable. Polity2 and CIRI-EP are highly correlated measures that do not have a perfectly colinear relationship. We include Polity2 to control for the institutional democracy level, which we believe is a predictor of the level of political rights. We also run all CIRI-EP models without Polity2 as a covariate and do not see substantial changes in terms of direction of signs or significance. We report all models that include Polity2 as a covariate.
37. The data set used here is in progress thus the results are preliminary. We are undertaking a global study of the impact of vetting which will help to correct some of the potential biases resulted from our small sample size.
38. We do not report results for covariates. Every model uses the same control variables: *dependent variable* $_{t-1}$; *log transformation of economic development* $_{t-1}$; *log transformation of population* $_{t-1}$; *democratic development* $_{t-1}$; *and democratic development*$^{2}_{t-1}$.
39. When testing the cumulative effect of lustration on physical integrity rights, we find a weakly significant (10 percent level) and positive relationship. As the confidence interval contains 0, we should not reject the null hypothesis.
40. All standard errors are estimated using a 95 percent confidence interval.
41. Thirty-one lustration policies in post-communist countries are coded "partially or fully implemented." We also collect data on legal and other official challenges to policies. Bulgaria 1992 is fully overturned.
42. The authors run a series of binary logit models to test if the effect of extensive lustration is consistent across the range of values for the dependent variable. This analysis suggests that the general model – which estimates a 19 percent increase in the odds of improving political rights – likely underestimates the effect of extensive lustration at some levels of the dependent variable. Please contact the authors for more information about this robustness check.
43. Predicted probabilities are estimated using the Margins data simulation program.
44. Countries with amnesty policies in our data sample are Albania (1997) and Romania (1994).
45. Olsen, Payne, and Reiter, *Transitional Justice in Balance*; Sikkink, *The Justice Cascade*.
46. Sikkink, *The Justice Cascade*.
47. David, *Lustration and Transitional Justice*.
48. Nalepa, *Skeletons in the Closet*.
49. See Szczerbiak's chapter in this volume on how Poland is a distinctive case in this regard.

50. As Szczerbiak notes in this volume, some of the late lustration laws in this region were created as elements of anti-corruption programs.
51. Horne, "Assessing the Impact of Lustration"; David, *Lustration and Transitional Justice*.
52. We do not code the degree of implementation. Instead, we have developed a crude binary measure that distinguishes between policies that are never implemented and policies that are either partially or fully implemented.
53. Olsen, Payne, and Reiter, *Transitional Justice in Balance*.
54. Dancy, Marchesi, Olsen, Payne, Reiter, and Sikkink, "Stopping State Agents of Violence or Promoting Political Compromise? The Powerful Role of Transitional Justice Mechanisms."
55. We include all transitional countries in Eastern Europe and the former Soviet Union to reduce selection bias.
56. Stan, *Transitional Justice in Eastern Europe and the Former Soviet Union*.

5

Transitional Justice Effects in the Czech Republic

Roman David

The Czech Republic has been a fascinating laboratory of dealing with the legacy of the communist past. Unlike in other countries in Central and Eastern Europe, the Communist Party has never returned to power since its defeat in the first democratic elections in 1990. Its dwindling influence led to a transitional justice process, the scale and variety of which is unprecedented in the region. The twenty-fifth anniversary of the demise of communism allows us to assess transitional justice in the light of popular expectations and the theoretical dilemmas postulated at its onset. This assessment can serve countries that have recently launched or are about to launch transitional justice, such as Libya, Egypt, Tunisia, Yemen, and Burma. Many other countries reflect back on their transitional justice policies, laggards try to draw level with their neighbors, and new conflicts create new injustices and lead to new calls for dealing with the past. What can be learned from the Czech experience with transitional justice?

There we see that a broad program of transitional justice is not a guarantee of its popular appreciation. The Czech Republic can boast ten transitional justice policies, which include a comprehensive program for the rehabilitation of former political prisoners and the thorough lustration of senior administrative and security personnel in the state apparatus. Two special government offices deal with the past. Nevertheless, the public view of the process of dealing with the past is lukewarm. Only 17 percent of respondents agreed that social divisions stemming from the past have been overcome, while 50.4 percent disagreed in the survey conducted in 2010.[1] How can we explain this paradox?

I suggest that the overwhelming emphasis on justice at the expense of reconciliation explains why the level of appreciation for how the past is dealt with does not correspond to the effort made in major areas of transitional justice. The imperatives of justice are important, but the expectations of justice have remained unrealistic in the Czech Republic. In the absence of reconciliation, justice has been viewed as an extension of power, and a legal seal of the communist defeat. The country's turbulent historical experiences and cultural patterns have strengthened the view of justice as victors' justice. Consequently, the Communist Party was sidelined, but it remains defiant about the past and has a stable electorate that assures its future. The Party was not eliminated from the democratic process, and its support surged in the parliamentary elections of 2013.[2]

This chapter theoretically develops and empirically examines this argument. To pursue the argument on the theoretical level, I first discuss the roles of justice and reconciliation as two paramount transitional justice objectives. I then empirically examine the transitional justice program, including the reparative, revelatory, and retributive measures, that is implemented in the Czech Republic in the absence of a reconciliation program. I show that this program has some potential to meet social expectations of justice, but a very limited potential to contribute to reconciliation.

The chapter draws on a nationwide 2010 survey about dealing with the past in the Czech Republic. I will first describe the public assessment of the major measures of transitional justice, then analyze their contribution to justice and reconciliation. I conclude by identifying three factors that account for the lackluster assessment of the broad transitional justice program in the Czech Republic: the inability to convey the message of reconciliation as a worthy objective, the absence of a reconciliation program, and the limited capacity of existing measures to contribute to reconciliation.

This chapter fills notable gaps in the literature. The prominence of transitional justice in the current political science, legal, and sociological scholarship contrasts with the persistent gap in empirical research on the effects of transitional justice. Although many studies have explained its origin,[3] we still crave answers to the plain bread-and-butter questions about its effects, most notably whether and which transitional justice measures can contribute to the promotion of historical justice and social reconciliation. Moreover, comparative studies that examine the utility of a *variety* of transitional justice measures are almost nonexistent.[4]

TRANSITIONAL JUSTICE WITHOUT RECONCILIATION

The preference for justice at the expense of reconciliation in the Czech Republic can be observed in three dimensions. First, reconciliation was seldom considered and pursued as an objective of transitional justice. Instead, statements by political leaders suggest that justice and the rectification of injustices were the major objectives. Second, reconciliatory measures are not part of the transitional justice program. Reconciliation is almost absent from the public discourse. Third, existing measures have only a limited capacity to foster reconciliation. This final argument is based on the assumption that all transitional justice measures, including measures of retribution and revelation, can be assessed with regard to their ability to deliver both justice and reconciliation. These three factors may provide us with a possible explanation of the poor assessment of transitional justice.

This chapter will not reiterate the objectives and nuances of each measure, rather explain their essential features in the light of the major theoretical debates on transitional justice. The description of transitional justice in the Czech Republic has been provided in several publications, most recently in the *Encyclopedia of Transitional Justice*.[5]

Justice as the Objective of Dealing with the Past in the Czech Republic

Owing to their strategic relevance and intellectual appeal, several themes have become prominent in the transitional justice literature. One of these is the dilemma of "justice or reconciliation" rooted in what Huntington called the torturer's problem: prosecute and punish, or forgive and forget.[6] Since it was formulated in 1991, the dilemma has lost much of its intellectual attractiveness because most countries have chosen to deal with the past and adopt transitional justice. Nevertheless, the question of justice and forgiveness has been included in the objectives that transitional countries (should) achieve. It is agreed that countries launch transitional justice to pursue backward-looking (accountability, justice, and punishment) and forward-looking (peace and democracy, including tolerance, a human rights culture, reconciliation, and forgiveness) objectives.[7] For Teitel, the focus of transitional justice is both backward-looking and forward-looking, retrospective and prospective.[8] Transitional justice is a response to the injustices and divisions of the past regime and an effort to build a new democracy. Situated between an authoritarian and a democratic regime, transitional justice must facilitate the transformation of political regimes, political cultures, and corresponding mindsets.[9]

At the same time, the very notion of a dilemma suggests that some of the objectives of transitional justice may be mutually exclusive, contradictory, and irreconcilable[10]: the pursuit of one objective may undermine another one. For example, some scholars argue that the pursuit of justice may jeopardize peace, as in Argentina where the prosecution of the military junta backfired and forced the adoption of the Full Stop Law that halted new investigations.[11] Likewise, measures to achieve justice by purging the state apparatus may put the nascent democracy at risk, with Libya a recent case in point. By purging Qaddafi's loyalists from the state apparatus via the Political Isolation Law, the state's capacity to provide security for its citizens and contain the armed militia was weakened, and the country risked becoming a failed state in 2013.[12] The promotion of reconciliation in turn may solidify the impunity of major perpetrators of crimes and revive past conflict, as in the fiasco of the amnesty process in Sierra Leone in 1999.[13]

I reject the black-and-white view of justice or reconciliation. Without considering a degree of reconciliation, justice in itself may not be a sufficient objective to guide the process of dealing with the past. Justice without reconciliation is emptied of its positive restorative content. Such naked or raw justice is merely a function of political power, an infliction of hardship and penalties upon offenders without considering the outcome. It is based on the victors' assumption that punishment of communist wrongdoers would make them compliant with the new system. It seems naïve to expect that punishment and lustration would turn communists and secret police informers into democrats. Indeed, research conducted in Central Europe suggests that exclusion augments historical divisions.[14]

The roots of this approach in the territory of the Czech Republic are historically and culturally typical. In trying to deal with different pasts, Czech decision-makers always placed a strong emphasis on justice. The Czechs experienced seven political regimes, or types of rules, in the twentieth century: the Austro-Hungarian Empire, the inter-war democratic Czechoslovakia (1918–1938), the Nazi Protectorate (1939–1945), the postwar democracy (1945–1948), the Stalinist communist regime (in the 1950s), the thawing of repression (in the mid-1960s) and the short intermezzo of the Prague Spring (1968), the normalization era (from the 1970s until 1989), and then democracy. Each political change was followed by efforts to negate the past, starting in 1918 with the spontaneous destruction in Prague's Old Town Square of the Mariensäule, a monument which allegedly symbolized the humiliation of the Czech nation by the Austro-Hungarian Empire. Each political change resulted in widespread purges, the shaming of the representatives of the old regime and the glorification of its victims. Following a brutal retributive wave after World War II, the most dramatic purges of the state apparatus occurred in the wake of the communist takeover in 1948 and in the aftermath of the Soviet-led military intervention of the Warsaw Pact armies in 1968.

It is thus unsurprising that, in dealing with the communist past, legislators often stated their determination to "temper" (*zmírnit*) or "condemn" (*odsoudit*) the injustices of the past, instead of including the need to overcome deep historical divisions in the society. Justice without reconciliation acquired a meaning of triumph and domination over the forces of the past. The cultural expectations of justice after transition signify the ritual conclusion of the past regime, a symbolic finale, in which anyone connected with that regime should be "finished" by being dismissed, punished, or excluded from the public eye. While demands for such raw justice may be legitimate with respect to communist torturers and apparatchiks, they are less justifiable for people who joined the party for career prospects or gave in to the secret police under duress. The new elites excluded these people too, making enemies out of those who may not have considered themselves enemies in the first place.[15]

Justice as the means of domination and retribution has become deeply entrenched in the value-normative system of the Czech political culture. The close connection between justice and power has been apparent after every post-communist election. Although elites might know that a change of government as a result of an election is not a change of political regime, the state administration is routinely cleansed of the supporters and appointees of the previous government.[16] The reason may be that the new government does not tolerate the presence of personnel loyal to the previous government and needs to distribute political posts to its supporters.[17] Electoral victory translates into power, power translates into purge.

Similarly to justice after elections, political revenge is a key feature of the Presidency of Miloš Zeman (elected in 2013). Those who criticized his actions have been subsequently "punished" by not being invited to a state function, not being given an award, or not being given an appointment.[18] Whether transitional justice has created the blueprint for this revengeful behavior or whether transitional justice and revenge are both expressions of a particular understanding of justice in the Czech political cultural landscape is irrelevant. The link between justice and power is entrenched in the Czech political culture.

The Absence of Reconciliation

The emphasis on "raw justice" has accompanied the absence of reconciliation. Because of the prominent role of justice in modern Czech history, the pursuit of reconciliation in post-communist times has been placed in its shadow. Reconciliation was completely sidelined as an objective of transitional justice. No explicit reconciliation program has been formulated, no truth commission was established, no reconciliatory forum was held, and no dialog about the past took place to help understand the individuals' motives in the past. Apologies issued by those responsible for the injustices of the communist regime have been rare.[19] Personal confessions, employed in South Africa and Poland as alternatives to trials and lustration,[20] have never been presented as a path of self-reflection and coming to terms with the past.

Reconciliation was explicitly prioritized only during the regime change in 1989, when Václav Havel coined the non-retributive phrase "we are not like them." In saying this, Havel was aware of the retributive tendencies of the Czech political culture, manifested most dramatically in the postwar expulsion of three million ethnic Germans from the Sudetenland. He tried to convey a message that would make ordinary Czechs feel that they stood on the moral high ground in contrast to their communist oppressors and their postwar ancestors. However, the post-1989 political elites, except Havel, have never considered reconciliatory measures as viable objectives for dealing with the past.[21] President Havel supported transitional justice but was unable to shape its direction after 1991, when he lost a significant battle in the Federal Assembly over his version of the lustration law.[22]

The Communist Party, which remains defiant in its stance on the past, may be partly to blame for the lack of reconciliation. The recognition of the human rights abuses committed under its rule was a reasonable precondition attached by many of the party's opponents to its acceptance to the political process. The lack of self-reflection was the main reason why Havel never invited the Party to any political consultation and why other formations have avoided any governing coalition with the communists. At the same time, after being politically isolated, it may be hard for the communist leadership to persuade its members of the need to abandon denial and apologize for the past.[23]

Gestures of reconciliation were rare and made on an individual basis. For instance, an heiress of prosecutor Karel Vaš, notorious orchestrator of the show trials of the 1950s, gave part of her inheritance to the daughters of former political prisoners.[24] Individual forgiveness, sometimes expressed unconditionally, was also reported among former political prisoners.[25] However, given the socio-cultural context, former political prisoners frequently mentioned an inimical response by those who had contributed to their ordeal as the major obstacle to their forgiveness.

Transitional Justice Measures in the Czech Republic

Transitional justice measures pursued in the Czech Republic include reparatory, retributive, and revelatory measures.[26] Although a reconciliatory program is absent, we cannot rule out the possibility that the existing transitional justice program can – at least marginally – contribute to reconciliation. To make this assessment credible, one needs to accept the counterintuitive arguments that different measures (including retribution, revelation, and reparation) may achieve the backward-looking objective of justice or the forward-looking objective of reconciliation, or both, or none of these.

Reparation laws, aimed at rectifying injustices experienced by victims, were among the first measures approved.[27] They included the compensation and rehabilitation of the victims of communism on the eve of the first democratic elections in 1990 and the restitution of nationalized or confiscated property in 1991. The restitution and rehabilitation measures, repeatedly amended afterwards, were extraordinary measures that affected hundreds of thousands of people.[28] Instead of an individual case-by-case judicial approach, wrongful punishments were annulled and properties were returned *ex lege*. Town halls, the presidency, schools, and other organizations further acknowledged victims' sacrifices by a variety of informal measures, such as invitations to speak, medals of honor, and awards.

The reparation program was, however, pursued in a one-dimensional and one-sided way: it was justice-oriented and purely victim-centered. Any reconciliatory forum between victims and perpetrators that would enable them to have a dialog about the past in a controlled environment was absent. Nevertheless, many victims encountered their oppressors in their daily life, and expressed dissatisfaction with the arrogance of the perpetrators. Moreover, the broader society was not engaged in the reparation process, which resulted in a feeling of continuing social isolation on the part of victims. Both the attitude of the perpetrators and the isolation undermined the reparation process and the resources spent.[29]

Retributive measures, which dealt with the perpetrators of human rights abuses and other wrongdoers, included the nationalization of the property of the Communist Party and the Socialist Youth Association in the autumn of 1990; the lustration law that purged senior communist officials, secret police members and their collaborators from the state administration in the autumn of 1991; and the 1993 law on the illegality of the communist regime, which lifted the statute of limitations, enabled the prosecution of communist crimes in the courts, and symbolically condemned the previous regime.[30] Common sense suggests that prosecuting, punishing, and sanctioning wrongdoers would lead to justice[31] and undermine reconciliation, because retribution leads to the persistence or deepening of past divisions.[32] However, scholars have argued that retributive measures may contribute to reconciliation if successful criminal trials produce a deterrent effect that impacts the entire society and prevents the recurrence of violations.[33] The delivery of justice can also relieve victims of their desire for retribution and provide them with closure.[34] Conversely, failure to punish, condemn, and dismiss wrongdoers means they retain their privileged positions in society.[35]

The absence of reconciliatory objectives affected the utility of other transitional justice measures, including retribution, since, under certain conditions, measures of retributive justice may serve the objectives of both justice and reconciliation. If reconciliation were articulated and considered as a goal of transitional justice, then the purpose of punishment and lustration would be restoration rather than retribution or both. Instead, in the absence of the reconciliatory discourse, punishment may not provide closure even if an offender has served his or her sentence.

Similarly, the success of lustration may be conditional on a degree of reconciliation. Although the lustration law was originally passed as an interim measure that was to be valid for five years until the new democracy had taken root, its validity was later extended to ten years, and it finally became a permanent feature of the democratization process. The initial lustration discourse suggested that certain persons should be removed from public positions because they had been unable to withstand pressure from the totalitarian regime. A degree of empathy with some low-key collaborators and an understanding of their plight intermingled with the security needs of the nascent democracy. But this discourse has largely disappeared, and lustration has become the end point for all secret collaborators. Its goal has thus been changed, with the conciliatory tone being replaced by a clearly retributive one. The lustration law valid for five years signaled that collaborators were unable to withstand the pressure of blackmail under the communist system. Once the transitional period passed and democracy was established, they were expected to come back and contribute to the new regime with their expertise. The message of indefinite lustration is different. Collaborators are unchangeable, intractable, and forever tainted.

The revelatory measures provide the most innovative avenue for transitional justice, as they aim at disclosing the truth about the past regime.[36] The expansion of truth commissions, the opening of secret archives, and the establishment of institutes of national memory have revived scholarly interest in the traditional value of truth. In the Czech Republic, revelation included the unofficial publication of the names of secret informers, from 1991 onwards, followed by their official publication in 2000; and the gradual opening of the secret police archives beginning in 1996. Since 1990, new history textbooks have become available, although many of them initially only deleted explicit references to the ideology of Marxism-Leninism.

The notion of truth epitomizes the ambiguity of transitional justice. Does truth lead to justice or reconciliation or both? It has been argued that measures of truth contribute to justice by establishing political and individual accountability for the past. People need to know who the perpetrators are and who gave the perpetrators the orders to carry out their wrongdoing. In contrast, the South African truth process was mandated to contribute to reconciliation by satisfying victims' demands for truth and exposing the illegitimate deeds of the previous regime to the whole society.[37] Empirical research confirmed that truth could contribute to reconciliation, at least among some social groups.[38] However, truth also undermines reconciliation by opening old wounds and reviving past hostilities.[39] Skeptics see the impact of truth on reconciliation as overstated and contentious.[40] Forensic and epistemological limitations prevent countries from establishing their "authoritative accounts" of the past.[41]

Moreover, the truth from secret archives has been hotly contested. According to Maria Łoś, post-communist Europe has seen a variety of "truth narratives," ranging from dystopian to affirmative discourses. While the former expected to see a negative impact of truth on democratic consolidation, the latter warned of the risks of continuing secrecy about the past.[42] We would expect that truth from the secret archives would have a negative effect in society. In the absence of a reconciliatory ethos, truth loses its reintegrative potential. In the presence of a justice ethos, truth serves as a means of shaming, which results in the social isolation of collaborators, decreasing their prospects of reintegration.[43]

Two special institutions have assisted in dealing with the past. The first is the Office for Documenting and Investigating the Crimes of Communism, established in 1995. The second is the Institute for the Study of Totalitarian Regimes. Founded in 2008, the Institute is a Czech version of the institutes of national memories that operate in many Eastern European countries.[44] While the former would conceptually fit into the retributive category, the latter was mandated to be the guardian of the secret archives.

POLITICS OF TRANSITIONAL JUSTICE

Although many transitional justice measures were approved more than twenty years ago in the Czech Republic, they are still being implemented, amended, or reviewed. Most measures, though initially controversial, have now been generally accepted as part of the Czech legal system. They do not stir up as much political controversy and media interest as when they first appeared. For instance, a search for the keyword "lustration" in two of the major online newspapers, *Aktuálně.cz* and *iHned.cz*, reveals a declining interest in the topic. After excluding matches that concerned types of lustration unrelated to transitional justice and lustration in other countries, the search in the business-oriented *iHned* returned forty-eight articles mentioning "lustration" in 2007, but only six articles in 2012. Likewise, in the investigative centrist newspaper *Aktuálně* there were twenty articles on lustration in 2007, but only five in 2012.[45] The number is expected to increase in 2013 and 2014 with the surge in the popularity of new political parties and the need for new politicians, previously unlustrated and suspected of collaboration, to provide lustration certificates.[46]

Is this silence a sign of reconciliation? Reduced media interest might signal that the past has become relatively settled at the macro-political level. Successive post-communist governments and parliamentary majorities have not repealed any major transitional justice law. Center-right formations have always advocated for transitional justice. The center-left Social Democratic Party (ČSSD), which contains both post-communists and dissidents, was never able to block transitional justice measures; when it led a coalition government in the early 2000s, it supported further reparation for the victims of communism. Havel's successor President Vaclav Klaus was never seriously interested in dealing with the past. For him, the process was a rearview mirror that could obstruct forward-looking objectives. While in office he most famously slammed former dissidents and political prisoners by saying that it was the ordinary people who had resisted communism by their inefficiency.[47]

Unsurprisingly, transitional justice remains on the agenda of the Communist Party of Bohemia and Moravia (KSČM), which nevertheless has failed to place the topic on the national agenda. Despite persistent support from voters, which increased to 14.91 percent in 2013, the absence of the Communist Party in any government coalition after 1990 reveals its diminishing political influence. The lack of coalition potential hinders any attempts to revoke policies dealing with the past. The party's last attempt to do so dates back to 2008 when it failed to repeal the lustration law.[48] Thus, if transitional justice is an extension of power, then the issue of the past remains "settled" as long as the party does not gain popularity.

The only two controversies about the past that still hit the headlines of the major newspapers and split public opinion concern the Institute for the Study of Totalitarian Regimes and the restitution of church property. As to the former, the controversies stem not from its activities but from the composition of its personnel and from infighting between different cliques of intellectuals with different personal and ideological trajectories. Its founding director, the anti-communist Pavel Žáček, was replaced in 2010, after a few interim appointments, by Daniel Herman, a laicized Catholic priest. In spite of support for him from the Confederation of Political Prisoners (KPV), Herman was sacked in 2013 and replaced by an unknown state official, Pavla Foglová. The abrupt change in the Institute leadership prompted commentators to call the process a "putsch" and a "purge." The new leadership is apparently more left-leaning ideologically, and less anti-communist, than the previous center-right leadership. Members of the current leadership have criticized their predecessors for lack of professionalism, while members of the previous leadership have criticized the lack of personal integrity in the new leaders vis-à-vis their pasts, especially the Communist Party membership of many board members.[49]

The second controversy surrounds the restitution of the property of the Catholic Church and other churches. Initially, the public was receptive to the needs of various groups for justice, including the property demands of churches. More recently, however, the traditionally atheist or anti-clerical Czechs have become less amenable to compromise about church restitution; the adverse economic environment created by the global economic crisis also negatively affected people's opinions. The law that enabled the restitution of the property to various churches was as unpopular as the center-right coalition that proposed it.[50] The bill was supported by 16 percent of Czechs and opposed by 65 percent.[51] The ruling coalition then forced the bill through the Chamber of Deputies in 2012, despite a veto by the Senate, which was dominated by Social Democrats (ČSSD), a veto by the center-right President Klaus, and a constitutional complaint by a group of Senators.[52] President Zeman suggested that parliament should amend the law to decrease the amount of compensation for the churches.[53] The division between people over the restitution issue may be caused less by past injustices than by present social, political, and economic problems, such as increasing unemployment, corruption and government instability.[54]

THE SEARCH FOR TRANSITIONAL JUSTICE ANSWERS

To empirically examine the effect of transitional justice on perceptions of justice and reconciliation, an opinion poll survey was conducted in the Czech Republic. The survey, supported by the British Academy and Newcastle University in the United Kingdom, was carried out on a nationwide representative sample of 1,079 citizens aged over 15 by the Center for Public Opinion Research in 2010. Respondents were asked to rate the success or failure of ten transitional justice measures and of the two government bodies that deal with the past. Emphasis was placed on the subjective assessment of transitional justice and reconciliation. The survey offers a unique glimpse into questions of transitional justice in a country that pursued a strong retributive policy with almost no emphasis on reconciliation.

The analytical strategy chosen to present the survey data is two-fold. First, in Chart 5.1 I present descriptive statistics about the popular views of the objectives of transitional justice. Table 5.1 and Chart 5.2 summarize the perception

TABLE 5.1: *Popular Assessment of Transitional Justice Measures in the Czech Republic*

The realization of the following measures was successful or unsuccessful	Successful (percent)	Unsuccessful (percent)
Financial compensation of former political prisoners.	40.9	20.6
Social acknowledgment of former political prisoners [social rehabilitation].	48.3	18.8
Return of nationalized property to original owners or their heirs [restitution].	50.9	14.1
Punishment of perpetrators of communist crimes.	22.0	42.8
Moral condemnation of communist crimes.	32.6	32.0
Confiscation of the property of the Communist Party.	28.2	36.8
Departure of people associated with the communist regime from leading posts in the state administration and the police [lustration].	23.1	43.5
Official publication of the names of secret collaborators with the secret police.	35.5	26.0
Opening the archives of the secret police to the public.	37.8	22.6
Publication of new history textbooks.	40.8	17.5
The following institutions contributed to dealing with the past:	*Agree (percent)*	*Disagree (percent)*
Office for the Documenting and Investigating the Crimes of Communism (ÚDV)	58.8	12.4
Institute for the Study of Totalitarian Regimes (ÚSTR)	56.2	13.1

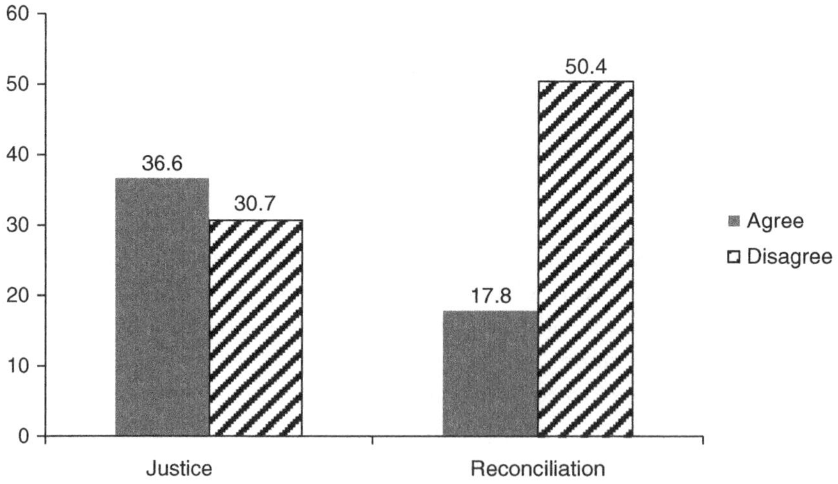

CHART 5.1: The Perception of the Objectives of Transitional Justice in the Czech Republic

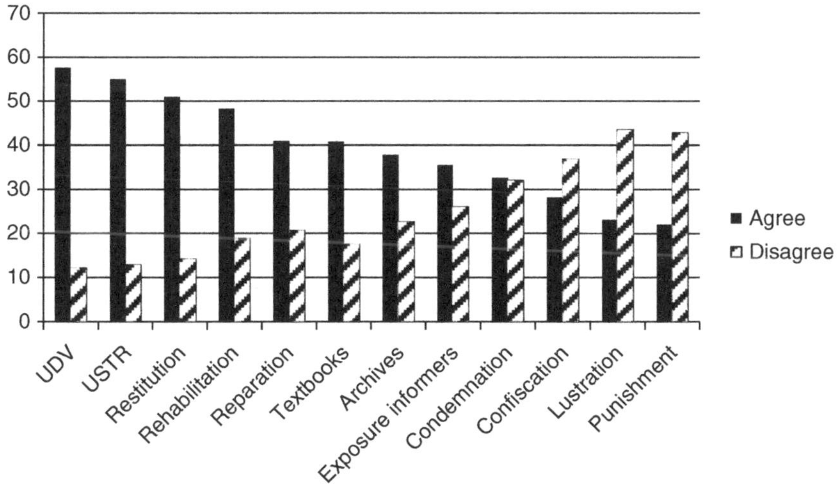

CHART 5.2: Popular Assessment of Transitional Justice Measures in the Czech Republic

of the ten transitional justice measures and the standing of the two special institutes for dealing with the past. Second, the chapter presents the results of an analysis in which justice and reconciliation are regressed on the ten measures and the two institutes, in Table 5.2. To make these findings easily comprehensible, Chart 5.3 plots the regression of the coefficients from the two regression models on justice and reconciliation axes.

The Perception of Transitional Justice

To enquire about justice, we asked respondents whether the greatest injustices of the previous regime have been undone. Some 36.6 percent of respondents agreed with the statement, while 30.7 percent disagreed. Given the absence of a positive reconciliation program in the Czech Republic, reconciliation was conceptualized in a negative form as the absence of reconciliation. Respondents were asked about the persistence of social divisions inherited from the past. Some 50.4 percent agreed that social divisions inherited from the previous regime have continued, indicating a lack of reconciliation. Only 17.8 percent had an opposite view. These preliminary results (Chart 5.1) indicate that the ambitious transitional justice program in the Czech Republic delivered some justice, but little reconciliation.

Chart 5.2 reveals a remarkable pattern in the public assessment of transitional justice in the Czech Republic. The assessment of individual measures

TABLE 5.2: *OLS Linear Regression Analyses of Justice and Reconciliation*

	Justice		Reconciliation	
	B	*SE*	*B*	*SE*
(Constant)	−.06	(.22)	1.16	(.24)
Age (5 categories)	.03	(.03)	−.07*	(.03)
Sex (Female)	.13*	(.06)	−.05	(.07)
Education (4 categories)	−.02	(.03)	.03	(.04)
Income (categories)	.02^	(.01)	.01	(.01)
Pre-1989 Communist Party member	.13	(.17)	.29	(.18)
Gray Zone	−.04	(.21)	−.10	(.24)
Financial compensation	.19***	(.05)	.00	(.05)
Social rehabilitation	.03	(.04)	.03	(.05)
Restitution of property	.08*	(.04)	−.12**	(.04)
Punishment of perpetrators	.14***	(.04)	.06	(.05)
Condemnation of the previous regime	.10*	(.04)	.00	(.05)
Expropriation of the Communist Party	.06	(.04)	−.01	(.04)
Lustration	.13***	(.04)	.13**	(.04)
Publication of names of informers	.10*	(.05)	.04	(.05)
Access to secret police archives	−.06	(.05)	.05	(.05)
Publication of new history textbooks	−.04	(.04)	−.02	(.04)
ÚDV	.14**	(.05)	.01	(.06)
ÚSTR	−.07	(.05)	.10^	(.06)
SEE	.897		.996	
R^2	.333		.073	
Adjusted R^2	.319		.054	
N	886		886	

B – unstandardized regression coefficient; *SE* – standard error
^ p <.1 * p <.05 ** p <.01 ** p <.001

follows their conceptual clusters: after an overwhelmingly positive appraisal of the two special government institutions, the most positively assessed category is reparation, followed by revelatory measures, and ending with retributive measures. The two institutions mandated to deal with the past received support from more than 50 percent of the public. The Office was viewed positively by 58.8 percent of respondents, while 12.4 percent viewed it negatively. The Institute was endorsed by 56.2 percent, while 13.1 percent disagreed with this. The strong support for these institutes suggests the extraordinary nature of transitional justice: new special institutions are seen as considerably more efficient in dealing with the past than the courts, which have only delivered a few dozen punishments to perpetrators of human rights violations.[55]

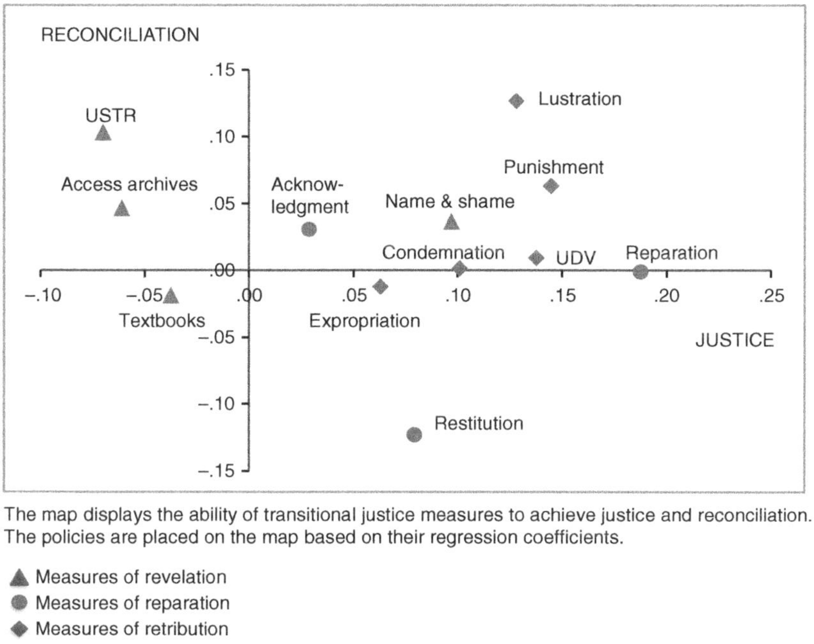

CHART 5.3: The Opinion Map of the Efficiency of Transitional Justice Measures
The map displays the ability of transitional justice measures to achieve justice and reconciliation. The policies are placed on the map based on their regression coefficients.

The positive assessment of reparation measures, which comprised the restitution of property and the rehabilitation/compensation of victims, ranges from over 40 percent to over 50 percent. The strong support for these measures may be an expression of natural sympathy with the victims.[56] It may also reflect the scale of the repression, which included over 100,000 political prisoners in the Czech Republic.[57] The restitution of property to their original owners and heirs was seen as successful by 50.9 percent of respondents, while 14.1 percent saw it as unsuccessful. This is one of the most surprising findings, because restitution has been seen as redressing old injustices and creating new social problems. For example, heirs could not freely deal with their returned property, while tenants faced an enormous uncertainty about their future in the booming housing market. The social acknowledgment of former political prisoners was seen as successful by 48.3 percent, while 18.8 percent viewed it as unsuccessful. In comparison, financial compensation was seen as successful by 40.9 percent, while 20.6 percent viewed it as unsuccessful. Although the difference between social acknowledgment and financial compensation is not large, it is surprising that financial compensation was not assessed in a more favorable light. Financial compensation for the victims of communism was amended several times, and the victims received compensation in the form of direct payments and an increase in their pensions.[58]

Revelation, which comprised the opening of secret archives, the exposure of secret informers and the publication of new history textbooks, was the third most positively assessed category, with support between 35 and 40 percent. The publication of new history textbooks was seen as successful by 40.8 percent of respondents and unsuccessful by 22.6 percent. The reasons for dissatisfaction among some parents were that the stereotypes of "class struggle" and other Marxist-Leninist concepts remained intact.[59] Opening the secret police archives was seen as successful by 37.8 percent of respondents and as unsuccessful by 22.6 percent. Today there are hardly any obstacles to public access to the secret archives. The official publication of the names of secret informers was seen as successful by 35.5 percent and unsuccessful by 26 percent. The narrowing gap between endorsement and disapproval of this measure suggests that this publication was not without controversy. Most notably, some celebrities demanded that their names be removed from the lists; some historians, however, saw such removal as a falsification of historical records.[60]

The policy that received the most negative assessment was that of retribution: the condemnation of the communist regime, the confiscation of the properties owned by the Communist Party and its youth league, and lustration were seen as successful by between 22 and over 32 percent of respondents, while between 32 and over 42 percent saw them as unsuccessful. Each measure in this cluster may have been assessed in that way for a different reason. The confiscation of communist property was a one-off measure that took place a long time ago; moral condemnation may be seen as pointless in face of the defiance of the Communist Party about the past. Lustration, although quite successful, was expected by the public to cleanse the entire state administration, which was not within its scope. The number of gross abusers of human rights who were punished was objectively low. Lustration and punishment were thus the worst assessed transitional justice measures: lustration was seen as successful by 23.1 percent of respondents, and as unsuccessful by 43.5 percent; punishment was seen as successful by 22.0 percent of respondents and as unsuccessful by 42.8 percent of them. The weak assessment of retributive measures may be understood in light of the popular preference for justice in the Czech political and cultural landscape. However, to get more conclusive evidence, I now turn to the multivariate analysis.

DOES TRANSITIONAL JUSTICE HELP TO ADVANCE JUSTICE AND RECONCILIATION?

In the second step, this analysis used linear regression analyses, in which justice and reconciliation were the dependent variables,[61] and the ten transitional justice measures and the two special institutes were the independent variables.[62] I control for basic socio-demographic variables, including age, sex, education, and income. Since this research was conducted in a divided society, I controlled for membership in the former Communist Party. Some 10.2 percent of respondents revealed that they were previously members of the Communist Party of Czechoslovakia. Finally, I also controlled for the so-called "gray zone communists," people who were party members for utilitarian reasons but were not politically identified with the party. The gray zone variable was given for pre-1989 party members who did not vote for the Communist Party in the most recent elections.

The comparison of R-square coefficients of the two regression models reveals an apparent association of transitional justice measures with justice rather than reconciliation (Table 5.2). Transitional justice and the other six independent variables predict 33.3 percent of the variance of justice but only 7.3 percent of the variance of reconciliation. Another manifestation of the association between transitional justice and justice as a goal is apparent from plotting the regression coefficients on the justice versus reconciliation axes (Chart 5.3). Eight of the twelve transitional justice measures are placed in the belt along the justice axis but do not go beyond the reconciliation axis by 0.05. Therefore, transitional justice can satisfy popular demands for justice but can hardly meet dissatisfaction with the lack of reconciliation.

The financial compensation of victims has by far the largest impact on justice. If policymakers were to amend transitional justice, increasing financial compensation would be the best way. Unlike the punishment of wrongdoers, which has the second largest effect on the perception of justice and is a matter of the independent criminal justice process, financial compensation is within the purview of government power. Financial compensation of victims would, however, have almost no impact on reconciliation, according to this model.

The negative impact of property restitution on reconciliation is surprising. Restitution was supposed to be the major mechanism for redressing inequalities created in the past, but it has left both supporters and opponents of the previous regime unhappy. Those who received their property back were also given the obligation to keep intact the tenancy contracts they inherited. While property owners lamented that they could not use their properties effectively, tenants experienced uncertainty about the future. Many of these relationships were strained, as owners frequently tried to force tenants to move out.

The effect of punishment on justice runs according to our expectations. The findings suggest a strong link between the punishment of perpetrators of wrongdoing and the perception of justice. However, justice is unable to contribute to the positive perception of reconciliation. The most counter-intuitive finding is the positive effect of lustration on both justice and reconciliation. The effect of this retributive measure on justice is obvious: lustration has been considered an effective means of administering justice. The effect of lustration on reconciliation is unexpected, but it makes sense in the light of the widely shared popular belief about the dominance of post-communist forces over the politics of the present. People suggest that there will be no reconciliation unless the social stratification stemming from the past is rectified. Lustration is undoubtedly one of the means of this rectification.

Chart 5.3 also shows that the role of truth revelation in the process of dealing with the past is partly in line with expectations. Although the Institute and the new history textbooks have no significant effect on justice, the revelation of the names of secret police informers has a significant positive effect on justice. This finding is in line with our expectations about the prominence of the justice perspective. Truth does not serve as a proxy for justice unless it names and shames secret collaborators. While the revelation of secret informers serves the objective of justice via the imposition of shaming penalties, the Institute has no retributive role. At the same time, measures of truth may lead to reconciliation. The assessment of the Institute is positively correlated with reconciliation, but it marginally fails to reach the accepted significance level.

CONCLUSION

The Czech Republic has implemented the most comprehensive transitional justice program in Central and Eastern Europe. This contrasts with the meager perceptions of the program's two paramount objectives: justice and reconciliation. I hypothesized that the paradox may have been caused by the overwhelming emphasis on justice at the expense of reconciliation. When only justice is accentuated as an objective of dealing with the past, a society risks pursuing reparation without closure, shaming without reintegration, and punishment without changing the offenders' behavior. Without reconciliation, transitional justice is just a power game with new actors in the same roles of exclusion.

The survey shows that Czechs are moderately satisfied with achieving justice but remain dissatisfied with the lack of reconciliation. This is because, apart from the notable exception of President Havel, reconciliation was never explicitly articulated as an objective of transitional justice by the political elites. Since the dominant discourse revolved around justice, respondents may seldom have been confronted with the continuation of inherited social divisions. Second, measures that could lead to reconciliation, such as a reconciliatory lustration system, were not approved. The measures adopted in the Czech Republic were largely designed to achieve the goals of justice and, in fact, have succeeded in shaping public perception that justice has been achieved.

The chapter shows that the financial compensation of victims and the restitution of property are major predictors of the perception of justice. Property restitution has been a divisive issue, negatively affecting social reconciliation. Restitution provides the strongest evidence for my argument about the preference for justice at the expense of reconciliation. The mere achievement of justice cannot help to overcome divisions inherited from the past.

In absolute terms, revelatory measures are assessed to lie between reparatory measures and retributive measures. The multivariate analysis suggests that truth is unable to contribute to justice, unless it names and shames wrongdoers. The publication of the names of secret informers, which produced a shaming effect in the Czech Republic, is associated with an increase in the perception of justice. "Truth" successfully served as a proxy for justice, but its potential contribution to reconciliation was never positively sanctioned by political elites.

Finally, in line with expectations, retributive measures are closely associated with justice. In the absence of reconciliation, lustration contributed to a perception that reconciliation has been achieved. The positive effect of lustration on the perception of reconciliation must be interpreted in the context of social stratification. Overcoming social divisions inherited from the past may signify both reconciliation and the redistribution of social positions after transition. Lustration is one of the means of this redistribution.

Clearly, these answers may be tentative and context dependent, since they rely on one survey in the Czech Republic. Note that the Czech Republic has entered a post-transitional justice stage. Although the existing transitional justice measures are amended, no new measures are proposed. Controversies over lustration, restitution, and the Illegitimacy of Communism Act are no longer apparent, while the remaining topics surrounding the personal infighting in the institutes for dealing with the past attract little public attention. The church property restitution was the last topic to divide society, but the argument was not between the redress of historical injustices and the creation of new ones, but between the unresolved issues of the past and the interests of contemporary society.

The major lesson of this case study concerns the importance of reconciliation. Societies dealing with the legacy of human rights violations committed under past regimes or in the contexts of postwar transformations have typically debated the imperatives of justice in their particular political and legal context. The calls for reconciliation only emerged when prosecutions and purges were impossible because of the balance of power in transition. Reconciliation, frequently pursued with the help of some truth-finding bodies, has thus been considered the second best option in dealing with the past. The case of the Czech Republic, which accentuated the imperatives of justice throughout its political transition, shows that justice itself may be insufficient in dealing with the past. To be accepted, justice requires a degree of reconciliation. Indeed, this survey finding echoes previous research conducted in the Czech Republic. A survey of former political prisoners showed that lack of reconciliation, manifested in the inimical attitudes by former adversaries and the response of the neighbors of former prisoners, is a significant inhibitor of political prisoners' self-assessment of their own rehabilitation.[63] Therefore, reconciliation is not an alternative to justice but its prerequisite. Without a clear reconciliatory program, victims would not achieve closure and society would remain divided, undermining the notion of justice. The statement that "reconciliation is not an option" may sound like moralizing kitsch, but empirical evidence suggests that reconciliation needs to be promoted regardless of whether justice or amnesty takes place.

NOTES

1. Roman David, The Utility of Transitional Justice in the Czech Republic, Grant SG-54378, 2009, funded by the British Academy.
2. Český Statistický Úřad, "Výsledky voleb a referend," no date, available at: http://volby.cz (accessed January 20, 2014).
3. Helga Welsh, "Dealing with the Communist Past: Central and East European Experiences after 1990," *Europe-Asia Studies* 48, no. 3 (1996): 413–428; Aleks Szczerbiak, "Dealing with the Communist Past or the Politics of the Present? Lustration in Post-communist Poland," *Europe-Asia Studies* 54, no. 4 (2002): 553–572; Lavinia Stan, ed., *Transitional Justice in Eastern Europe and the Former Soviet Union: Reckoning with the Communist Past* (London: Routledge, 2009); Nadya Nedelsky, "Divergent Responses to a Common Past: Transitional Justice in the Czech Republic and Slovakia," *Theory and Society* 33, no. 1 (2004): 65–115.
4. Some excellent studies have been conducted on the effects of the Truth and Reconciliation Commission in South Africa and the International Criminal Tribunal of Former Yugoslavia in Bosnia-Herzegovina. However, we still do not know how transitional justice measures compare to each other. For instance, are criminal trials viewed as more effective than lustration in satisfying the social needs

for justice and overcoming the divisions of the past? Are records originating from the secret archives more effective than the truth processed through government sponsored institutes of national memory, which spread in Eastern Europe in the last decade?

5. Lavinia Stan and Nadya Nedelsky, eds., *Encyclopedia of Transitional Justice* (New York: Cambridge University Press, 2013); Roman David and Susanne Y. P. Choi, "Victims on Transitional Justice: Lessons from the Reparation of Human Rights Abuses in the Czech Republic," *Human Rights Quarterly* 27, no. 2 (2005): 392–435; Nadya Nedelsky, "Czechoslovakia, and the Czech and Slovak Republics," in *Transitional Justice in Eastern Europe and the Former Soviet Union: Reckoning with the Communist Past*, ed. Lavinia Stan (London: Routledge, 2009), pp. 37–75; Roman David, "Twenty Years of Transitional Justice in the Czech Lands," *Europe-Asia Studies* 64, no. 4 (2012): 761–784.
6. Samuel Huntington, *The Third Wave: Democratization in the Late Twentieth Century* (Norman: University of Oklahoma Press, 1991).
7. The backward-looking objectives are typical of most of the legal scholarship. For forward-looking objectives, see Gibson, "Truth, Justice, and Reconciliation"; Roman David and Susanne Y. P. Choi, "Forgiveness and Transitional Justice in the Czech Republic," *Journal of Conflict Resolution* 50, no. 3 (2006): 339–367.
8. Ruti Teitel, *Transitional Justice* (New York: Oxford University Press, 2000).
9. Roman David, *Lustration and Transitional Justice: Personnel Systems in the Czech Republic, Hungary, and Poland* (Philadelphia: University of Pennsylvania Press, 2011).
10. Bronwyn A. Leebaw, "The Irreconcilable Goals of Transitional Justice," *Human Rights Quarterly* 30 (2008): 95–118.
11. Amnesty International, "Argentina: The Full Stop and Due Obedience Laws and International Law" (April 1, 2003), available at: http://www.refworld.org/docid/3f13d9d34.html (accessed November 15, 2013).
12. Roman David and Houda Mzioudet, "Personnel Change or Personal Change? Rethinking Libya's Political Isolation Law," *Brookings Doha Center – Stanford University Project on Arab Transitions Paper Series*, 4 (March 2014).
13. William Schabas, "The Relationship between Truth Commissions and International Courts: The Case of Sierra Leone," *Human Rights Quarterly* 25, no. 4 (2003): 1035–1066.
14. David, *Lustration and Transitional Justice*.
15. The typical responses by members of the gray zone to the revelation of their collaboration were denial and excuses, not defiance and inimical statements. Zdena Slaivorova-Skvorecka, *Osočení: pravdivé příběhy lidí z "Cibulkova seznamu"* (Brno: Host, 2000). Denial and excuses for one's involvement in the past regime indicate an effort of the individual to be accepted in the democratic society.
16. Michaela Nováková, "Ekonomové změřili, jak se po každých volbách opakuje hra o 'trafiky,'" *iDnes* (September 11, 2013), available at: http://zpravy.idnes.cz/ies-vydal-studii-o-propojeni-politiky-s-verejnym-sektorem-pan-/domaci.aspx?c=A130911_170759_domaci_ael (accessed October 13, 2013).
17. Naturally, the practice of the spoils system comes at considerable cost, manifested in the inability to submit professionally designed projects to access European Union subsidies.

18. This practice began under President Václav Klaus, but is a hallmark of the Presidency of Miloš Zeman.
19. David, *Lustration and Transitional Justice*.
20. Roman David, "In Exchange for Truth: The Polish Lustration and the South African Amnesty Process," *Politikon: South African Journal of Political Studies* 32, no. 1 (2006): 81–99.
21. David and Choi, "Victims on Transitional Justice."
22. David, *Lustration and Transitional Justice*.
23. Ibid.
24. ČTK[Czech Press Agency], "Dcera Rudého kata rozdala dědictví těm, kterým ublížil," *Aktualne.cz* (August 30, 2013), available at: http://aktualne.centrum.cz/domaci/spolecnost/clanek.phtml?id=789080&utm_source=email&utm_medium=email&utm_campaign=posli (accessed October 13, 2013).
25. David and Choi, "Forgiveness and Transitional Justice."
26. David, *Lustration and Transitional Justice*.
27. Transitional justice in the Czech Republic first emphasized the victims of communism, then turned against those responsible for communist crimes and finally pursued the policy of truth. Reparation led to retribution, followed by revelation. By contrast, in Latin America the truth phase, characterized by the rise of truth commissions, led to the justice phase with the overturning of many amnesty laws and the launch of key prosecutions. Aryeh Neier, "What Should Be Done about the Guilty?" *The New York Review of Books* (February 1, 1990).
28. David and Choi, "Victims on Transitional Justice."
29. Ibid.
30. David, "Twenty Years of Transitional Justice."
31. Lustration laws imposing sanctions on wrongdoers were passed to grant "minimal" justice. Maria Łoś, "Lustration and Truth Claims: Unfinished Revolutions in Central Europe," *Law and Social Inquiry* 20, no. 1 (1995): 117–161.
32. David, *Lustration and Transitional Justice*.
33. Deterrence is a common justification for criminal trials. Hunjoon Kim and Kathryn Sikkink, "Explaining the Deterrence Effect of Human Rights Prosecutions for Transitional Countries," *International Studies Quarterly* 54, no. 4 (2010): 939–963. Skeptics argue that the evidence of deterrence still needs to be produced. Julian Ku and Jide Nzelibe, "Do International Criminal Tribunals Deter or Exacerbate Humanitarian Atrocities?" *Washington University Law Review* 84 (2006): 777–833.
34. Roman David and Susanne Y. P. Choi, "Getting Even, or Getting Equal? Retributive Desires and Transitional Justice," *Political Psychology* 30, no. 2 (2009): 161–192.
35. Susanne Y. P. Choi and Roman David, "Lustration Systems and Trust: Evidence from Survey Experiments in the Czech Republic, Hungary, and Poland," *American Journal of Sociology* 117, no. 4 (2012): 1172–1201.
36. David, *Lustration and Transitional Justice*.
37. Priscilla Hayner, *Unspeakable Truths: Confronting State Terror and Atrocity* (New York: Routledge, 2001).
38. James L. Gibson, "Does Truth Lead to Reconciliation? Testing the Causal Assumptions of the South African Truth and Reconciliation Process," *American Journal of Political Science* 48, no. 2 (2004): 201–217.
39. David and Choi, "Victims on Transitional Justice."

40. David Mendeloff, "Truth-Seeking, Truth-Telling, and Postconflict Peacebuilding: Curb the Enthusiasm?" *International Studies Review* 6 (2004): 355–80.
41. Audrey Chapman and Patrick Ball, "The Truth of Truth Commissions: Comparative Lessons from Haiti, South Africa, and Guatemala," *Human Rights Quarterly* 23, no.1 (2001): 1–43.
42. Łoś, "Lustration and Truth Claims."
43. Lustration law concerned a limited number of positions, mainly in the state administration. However, since the lists of secret police informers were easily accessible, it was implemented beyond the scope of the law.
44. "Otevřel se Ústav pro studium totalitních režimů," *iHned* (February 1, 2008), available at: http://zpravy.ihned.cz/c1-22871540-otevrel-se-ustav-pro-studium-totalitnich-rezimu (accessed October 13, 2013).
45. The search was performed for the period of the calendar year. It included articles, news reports and articles written by bloggers attached to the newspapers.
46. For the case of Andrej Babiš, leader of new party Ano [Yes], see ČTK, "Babis Says He Need not Be in Czech Government, Will not Seek Lustration" (November 6, 2013), available at: http://www.ceskenoviny.cz/zpravy/babis-says-he-need-not-be-in-czech-govt-will-not-seek-lustration/1004873 (accessed November 14, 2013).
47. The Social Democrat proposal may have sought to dispel the growing mistrust over the comeback to government of people associated with the communist regime. People who could not work in the state apparatus due to the lustration laws worked as advisors to ministers. David, *Lustration and Transitional Justice*.
48. "Poslanci schválili, že diskriminovat bude trestné," *Aktualne.cz* (March 19, 2008), available at: http://aktualne.centrum.cz/domaci/politika/clanek.phtml?id=600192 (accessed October 13, 2013).
49. Tereza Krobová, "Rada ÚSTR rozhodla: Hermana nahradí Pavla Foglová," *Aktualne.cz* (April 10, 2013), available at: http://aktualne.centrum.cz/domaci/zivot-v-cesku/clanek.phtml?id=776543 (accessed October 13, 2013); "Čistka v ÚSTR: Nová šéfka se zbavuje lidí napojených na exředitele, nechtějí s ní mluvit," *iHned.cz* (April 18, 2013), available at: http://zpravy.ihned.cz/c1-59717020-sefka-ustr-foglova-zahajila-cistku (accessed October 13, 2013); Martin Fendrych, "Začíná rudý úklid, antikomunista Herman končí," *Aktualne.cz* (April 11, 2013), available at: http://aktualne.centrum.cz/blogy-a-nazory/komentare/clanek.phtml?id=776608 (accessed October 13, 2013); Martin Fendrych, "Gottwaldovec kádruje Čunase, *Aktualne.cz* (August 19, 2013), available at: http://aktualne.centrum.cz/blogy-a-nazory/komentare/clanek.phtml?id=788006 (accessed October 13, 2013).
50. Public support for the center-right coalition government of Prime Minister Petr Nečas was 17 percent in October 2012 when Act No. 428/2012 Sb., on the Property Settlement with Churches and Religious Communities was debated. "Nečasově vládě už věří jen necelá pětina lidí. Ztrácí i podporu stoupenců ODS," *iHned* (October 5, 2012), available at: http://zpravy.ihned.cz/c1-57779990-necasove-vlade-uz-veri-jen-necela-petina-lidi-ztraci-i-podporu-stoupencu-ods (accessed October 13, 2013).
51. Centrum pro Výzkum veřejného mínení, "Názor veřejnosti na roli církví ve společnosti a na navrácení církevního majetku" (October 23, 2012), available at: http://cvvm.soc.cas.cz/media/com_form2content/documents/c1/a6901/f3/pi121023b.pdf (accessed October 13, 2013).
52. The Constitutional Court refused the complaint in its decision Pl. ÚS 10/13 in 2013.

53. Josef Kopecký, "Zeman chce změnu restitucí, aby církve dostaly méně peněz," *iDnes* (September 1, 2013), available at: http://zpravy.idnes.cz/zeman-je-pro-zmenu-zakona-o-cirkevnich-restitucich-f8g-/domaci.aspx?c=A130901_112141_domaci_kop (accessed October 13, 2013).
54. The unemployment remains at 7 percent, above the 4.5 level of 2008. In 2013, the Czech Republic ranked 57 out of 175 countries in the Corruption Perception Index. In 2008, it ranked 45–46 out of 180. There have been nine governments in office between 2004 and 2014.
55. Stan and Nedelsky, *Encyclopedia of Transitional Justice.*
56. Charles Batson, *The Altruism Question: Toward a Social Psychological Answer* (Hillsdale, NJ: Erlbaum, 1991).
57. David and Choi, "Victims on Transitional Justice."
58. Ibid.
59. David, "Twenty Years of Transitional Justice."
60. For the notable case of Jirina Bohdalova, see Jiri Priban, "Oppressors and Their Victims: The Czech Lustration Law and the Rule of Law," in *Justice as Prevention: Vetting Public Employees in Transitional Societies*, eds. Alexander Mayer-Rieckh and Pablo De Grieff (New York: Social Science Research Council, 2007).
61. An OLS linear regression model was preferred to an ordinal logit because the former is easier to comprehend. The dependent variables were coded from the most negative (0) to the most positive (4).
62. The coding of transitional measures on the Likert scale ranged from the most negative (0) to the most positive (4).
63. David and Choi, "Victims on Transitional Justice."

PART III

Key Challenges

6

The Timing of Transitional Justice Measures

Cynthia M. Horne

Starting in 1989 with the fall of communism, countries in Central and Eastern Europe and the former Soviet Union began the process of transitional justice, with many continuing to engage in a variety of accountability mechanisms through the present. The direct and indirect effects of transitional justice on reform goals remain conditional and contended, reflecting both differences in the quality of reforms across countries and the causal ambiguity surrounding a process as complex as regime transformation.[1] As Lynch and Marchesi demonstrate in this volume, lustration demonstrates different effects when enacted separately or as part of multiple transitional justice measures, and lustration can have divergent effects on different transition goals, such as improving political rights but having limited impact on physical integrity rights. Nonetheless, there is evidence to suggest these measures have supported numerous post-communist transition goals, increasing trust in targeted public institutions at the national level, improving government effectiveness, supporting political rights, and contributing to the process of democratization in many but not all cases.[2] While the effects of lustration and supporting measures on reform goals may remain active first order impact assessment questions, this article engages with a related but different, second order question. With twenty-five years of experience with transitional justice in the post-communist region, does the timing of transitional justice affect relative efficacy? When is it too late to start transitional justice measures?

There is a widespread assumption that measures should be enacted as soon after a transition as possible for maximal benefit, and that if enacted too late could even be harmful.[3] The counterpoint to this assumption is a belief that there is no automatic expiration date on reforms and that delayed transitional justice is better than none at all.[4] This chapter explores the two sides of the debate, asking: Is there a time after which transitional justice is no longer constructive? Is there evidence that late programs undermine reform goals?

Using a cross-national comparison of lustration programs, file access policies, and public disclosures in ten post-communist countries, this chapter provides a retrospective on *if* and *how* the timing of these transitional justice reforms affected trust in government and democratization.

In particular, this chapter looks at variation both within and across countries over a 12–15 year time period, tracing whether timing has independent causal impact on two reform goals across the region. Timing might matter, but not very much in the larger reform picture. Using quantitative methods, we can estimate both how much timing matters, if at all, and model the relationship between timing and reform efficacy. The large-N research design (a large number of cases) and the time series nature of the analysis allow us to examine cross-national changes over time, thereby giving us traction on some causal relationships that would not be possible with small-N studies (a small number of cases) or with quantitative studies that looked at a single year or moment in time.

To preview the findings, first this chapter demonstrates that timing does affect final levels of trust in government and democracy, but the size of the overall effect is small. In the case of democracy it explains only 3 percent of the variation in level of democracy, although trust in government is more sensitive to timing with earlier reforms having a 5–9 percent trust premium on later reforms. Moreover, the magnitude of effect of measures enacted early in the transition was similar to measures enacted 15–16 years into the transition. This demonstrates the limited impact of the timing of reforms on overall efficacy. In other words, although timing matters, it is not the only or necessarily the most important determinant of democracy or trust; the quality of implementation most certainly counts for more than timing. Lynch and Marchesi reach similar conclusions in this volume, highlighting the importance of the quality and extensiveness of reforms for beneficial outcomes.

That said, timing does have an independent impact on outcomes. This chapter then models the timing of reforms across the region and demonstrates that delayed lustration measures were the most efficacious, with a decade or so after the transition being the peak moment for passing reforms. This is contrary to popular assumptions that delayed transitional justice measures are less efficacious or even harmful. There is evidence of declining efficacy several decades after the transition; starting reforms more than twenty years after the regime change could be counterproductive to certain reform goals. In sum, timing matters very little to the overall success of transitional justice reforms. These findings significantly elongate the window of opportunity for starting reforms, and qualify our understanding of the alleged drawbacks of *late reforms* in practice.

EARLY VERSUS LATE REFORMS

Although a variety of transitional justice measures have been used across the post-communist region, this chapter focuses on the timing of lustration or employment vetting, file access, and public disclosure reforms.[5] They are the dominant regional transitional justice choices and are often grouped together in reform packages. Lustration is broadly defined as a process that authorizes legally constrained government actions against individuals who were complicit with the previous communist regime, defined in terms of secret police affiliation, secret police collaboration, active abetting of the communist regime, and/or possible Communist Party affiliations.[6] The consequences for this involvement encompass a range of government actions, including disqualifying those individuals from public and semi-public positions of trust, publically disclosing information about those individuals, and outright employment bans. Some of the social and political reasons given to enact lustration include the pursuit of justice, forced bureaucratic cleansing and personnel changes, the securitization of the state, anti-corruption efforts, trust building, and democracy promotion.[7]

Lustration involves a mixture of backward and forward looking justice mechanisms, both redressing wrongs in the past and building an effective state and society for the future.[8] Because of the backward-looking elements, policymakers, and academics have assumed that reforms should be enacted as quickly after the regime change as possible to prevent a state from becoming mired in the past. There are several justifications for the early or not at all approach to lustration and public disclosures. First, lustration measures are framed as reform mechanisms possible, necessary, and maybe only beneficial during periods of *extraordinary politics* at the start of the transition.[9] Lustration entails legal compromises, in particular the prioritization of justice concerns over strict rule of law adherence.[10] These compromises are potentially appropriate for a short period early in the transition. Once that early extraordinary transitional environment has passed, the appropriateness and utility of lustration becomes questionable.

Second, policymakers argue that if lustration comes too late it is no longer a practical means of removing communist collaborators from positions of power, as there is a natural changing of the old guard of public office holders with time.[11] Third, in some countries lustration laws were caught in cycles of political manipulation, with political parties wielding the laws against rivals in order to improve their political standing.[12] There is fear that the danger of overt politicization of the laws increases as the time period from the transition stretches out.[13] In sum, there is a hypothesized inverse relationship between timing and efficacy, with early reforms assumed to be both the most efficacious and the most legally appropriate. As time from the transition increases, not only are reforms considered less legitimate but they could also undermine the goals of the transition.

This conceptualization of lustration as a policy for use early in the transition is evident in the short expiration dates included in the first laws. For example, the Czech law was originally designed to last for five years.[14] Similarly, the Hungarian lustration law was designed to expire after six years, and Latvia's Election Law was designed to expire after ten years.[15] Temporal constraints were also placed on the time period for which employment penalties would be in place. For example, Lithuania's law included employment bans for five years, and Albania's Verification Law barred individuals from serving in certain public positions for seven years.[16] In Poland, individuals who lied about their past during the lustration process were banned from positions for ten years.[17] In essence, the design of the laws focused on early lustration, implicitly suggesting that late reforms were either not necessary or not productive.

National and international legal authorities were more explicit in their arguments about the benefits of early reforms only. The European Court of Human Rights (ECHR) ruled that while lustration laws were acceptable rule of law compromises during periods of extraordinary politics early in the transition period, they lost their appropriateness, legality, and utility over time.[18] Rule of law derogations should be the exception, rather than the rule, and must be phased out when the transition was over.[19] Similarly, the Polish Constitutional Tribunal addressed the temporal limitations of lustration by arguing that "lustration measures should cease to take effect as soon as the system of a democratic state has been consolidated."[20]

At the same time, the focus on timing could minimize the cognitive and organizational importance of exposing collaborators and removing them from political life.[21] This perspective contends that the quality of reforms matters more than the speed of the measures. In particular, the presence of collaborators in positions of public trust demoralizes citizens and erodes the legitimacy of the new state. The low bureaucratic turnover and high penetration of former collaborators in positions of authority across many post-communist countries elevate the issue of timing politically, socially, and economically.[22] From this perspective, timing is less important than correcting the problems of the past that haunt the present and the future.

There is regional evidence to support this perspective, with many post-communist countries changing their views on the initial temporal limitations on lustration measures. The Czech Republic's original five-year expiration date was extended for an additional five years, and then indefinitely in 2000.[23] Hungary's lustration law was extended in 2000 for an additional four years, and file access in Hungary has remained active and even expanded in recent years.[24] Poland, Bulgaria, and Romania all reengaged actively with public disclosures late in the transition, with Poland and Bulgaria expanding the number of individuals subjected to employment vetting.[25] In this volume, Aleks Szczerbiak explores in detail the dynamics of late lustration programs. Despite the initial assumption that lustration and public disclosures should be enacted immediately after the regime change and only until democracy is established, countries continue to find utility in new and renewed policies. The next section turns to the issue of how to empirically and conceptually examine the conditions under which the timing of reforms affects efficacy.

CONCEPTUALIZING TEMPORAL DIMENSIONS

I examine ten post-communist countries that passed lustration, file access, and/or public disclosure policies: Albania, Bulgaria, the Czech Republic, Estonia, Hungary, Latvia, Lithuania, Poland, Romania, and Slovakia. The majority of these countries started to engage with transitional justice issues soon after the collapse of the communist regime and continued those policies over a period of two decades or more. The dominant approach can be most generally classified as protracted transitional justice, with noticeable variation in the start of reforms and the actual implementation of reforms.

To test the impact of timing, I use two different measures. First, timing can be most simplistically measured as a function of the years that pass between the collapse of the communist regime and the time when lustration policies are passed. For this measure the focus is on the start of reforms, understood as the moment when the first law is passed. Measuring timing as a function of the passage of the first major lustration or public disclosure policies takes into consideration the fact that lustration is a catalyst for both symbolic and institutional changes, even if there are problems or delays with later implementation.

For this measure, timing is recorded as the difference between the year of the first lustration policy and the earliest possible start of a lustration program, meaning the year of regime change.[26] Exact dates are presented in Table 6.1. Since lustration measures are assumed to have continued impact on the state and society even when they technically expire, once lustration is enacted it remains coded as "active" for the duration of the time period considered. The literature suggests a linear relationship between timing and efficacy, with efficacy declining over time. This assumption can be tested by including a variable for the timing of lustration and a variable for timing squared, in order to test for the possible presence of a nonlinear relationship between timing

TABLE 6.1: *Timing of First Lustration Laws*

Country (start of transition)	Year first law passed	First Lustration and/or Screening Policies Refers to the earliest effort to move forward with the process of lustration, which could be either citizen access to secret police files, employment vetting laws, and/or citizenship requirements.
Albania (1990)	1995	Law Nr. 8001 of September 22, 1995, on Genocide and Crimes Against Humanity Committed in Albania during the Communist Regime for Political, Ideological and Religious Reasons (The Genocide Law) Law Nr. 8043 of November 30, 1995, on the Control of the Moral Figure of Officials and Other Persons Connected with the Protection of the Democratic State (The Verification Law)
Bulgaria (1989)	1992	Law No. 25 of March 18, 1992, on Banks and Credit Activity Law of December 9, 1992, for Temporary Introduction of Some Additional Requirements for the Members of the Executive Bodies of Scientific Organizations and the Higher Certifying Commission (The Panev Law)
Czech Republic (1989)	1991	Czech and Slovak Federal Republic: Screening ("Lustration") Law, Act No. 451 of October 4, 1991, on Conditions for Holding Certain Positions in State Bodies and Organizations
Estonia (1991)	1992	Citizenship Law and Local Election Law of 1992, stipulating written oath of conscience (*süümevanne*) for civil service positions
Hungary (1989)	1994	Law No. 23 of March 8, 1994, on Background Checks to Be Conducted on Individuals Holding Certain Important Positions
Latvia (1991)	1994	Citizenship Law of 1994 Article 9 of the Election Law of January 25, 1994, on Cities and Town Councils, District and Pagasts Councils
Lithuania (1991)*	1991	Decree No. 418 of October 12, 1991, Banning KGB Employees and Informers from Government Positions Law No. I-2115 of December 17, 1991, on the Verification of Mandates of Those Deputies Accused of Consciously Collaborating with Special Services of Other States
Poland (1989)	1997	Law of April 11, 1997, on Disclosing Work for or Service in the State's Security Services or Collaboration with Them between 1944 and 1990 by Persons Exercising Public Functions (The Lustration Act)
Romania (1989)	1999	Law No. 187 of December 9, 1999, on Access to Personal Files and the Disclosure of the Securitate as a Political Police (The Ticu Law)

TABLE 6.1: (*cont.*)

Country (start of transition)	Year first law passed	First Lustration and/or Screening Policies Refers to the earliest effort to move forward with the process of lustration, which could be either citizen access to secret police files, employment vetting laws, and/or citizenship requirements.
Slovakia (1989)	2002	Act No. 553/2002 of August 19, 2002, on Disclosure of Documents Regarding the Activity of State Security Authorities in the Period 1939–1989 and on Founding the Nation's Memory Institute and on Amending Certain Acts (The Nation's Memory Act)**

Author compiled. For transition dates see: J.F. Brown, *Surge to Freedom: The End of Communist Rule in Eastern Europe* (Duke University Press, 1991); and Jan Zielonka, *Democratic Consolidation in Eastern Europe* (Oxford University Press, 2001). For additional country details see Lavinia Stan, "Conclusion," in *Transitional Justice in Eastern Europe and the Former Soviet Union* (New York: Routledge, 2009).

* Lithuania declared independence in March 1990, but was not recognized by the Soviet Union until September 1991.

** Slovakia renounced the Czechoslovak Lustration Law after independence. The year 2002 reflects its first efforts at lustration.

and efficacy. This variable is measured in years and will be called *timing* and *timing squared* in the quantitative analyses (see Appendix 1 for data details).

The date of the passage of laws does not always capture the period over which reforms were primarily implemented. Elster presents a simple categorization along three temporal dimensions capturing more broadly the concept of the timing of reforms. He suggests that *immediate transitional justice* takes place right after the start of the transition and lasts for five years, *protracted transitional justice* starts immediately and then lasts until the issues are resolved, and *postponed transitional justice* takes place ten or more years after the start of the transition.[27] Using this loose conceptual periodization of reforms, I developed a second timing variable to capture the regional waves of reforms. The lustration waves variable represents the period in which the bulk of a country's reform efforts took place, including lustration policies, file access measures, and public disclosures. While it is difficult to determine the exact moment of reform implementation in each country, there is a distinctive clustering effect observed in the implementation of measures. This resulted in overlapping but clearly discernible periods: First Wave (1989–1996), Second Wave (1997–2005), and Third Wave (2006–2014). Table 6.2 summarizes this variable called *lustration waves*, showing the ordinal categorizing of the three main time periods for reform.

TABLE 6.2: *The Timing of Reforms: Lustration Waves*

First Wave 1989–1996 (1)	Albania	1991 – Ruli Report-first trials of former regime on economic grounds
		1993 – first lustration attempts, focus on lawyers
		1995 – Genocide and Verification laws – limited implementation-expire 2001
		Current – 2008 renewed lustration declared unconstitutional – end process
	Czech Republic	1991 – Lustration Law passed; 1992 minor lustration law also passed
		1995 – lustration extended, some file accessibility
		1998 – more file declassification, and 2000 – lustration extended indefinitely
		2007 – increase file transparency, and 2008 — National Memory Institute created
		Current – On-going file access, no significant lustration
	Estonia	1992 – Citizenship and Local Elections Law
		1995 – Citizenship Law requires public disclosures for all civil positions
		1998 – Security Police Board releases names of those who gave false info
		Current – process not active
	Latvia	1991 – citizenship and language laws exclude Russians from public positions
		1994 – Citizenship Law and Election Law-employment bans for council positions
		1995 – former collaborators banned from parliamentary positions
		1999 – Police Act vets police
		2000 – State Civil Service Act
		Current – President vetoes attempts to open files – ends process
Second Wave 1997–2005 (2)	Hungary	1994 – Lustration Law passed but delayed implementation
		1995–96 – parts of lustration unconstitutional and narrowed to top political positions
		2000 – lustration extended for four years, screenings increase from 900 to 17,000
		2002 – Mécs Commission investigates public officials
		2003 – Historical Archives created – public file access
		Current – ongoing file access but lustration terminated
	Poland	1997 – Lustration law passed

		2000 – created Institute of National Remembrance to oversee file access 2001 – lustration implementation in earnest 2006 – expanded lustration program with creation of Vetting Office ***Current – active, on-going lustration process***
	Slovakia	1996 – Czechoslovak lustration law expires with no implementation 2002 – Memory Bill passed – ÚPN created 2004 – no official lustration but some public disclosures of collaboration 2007 – ÚPN increases file access and continues some limited public disclosures ***Current – weak public disclosure program, fading out***
Third Wave 2006–present/ on-going (3)	Bulgaria	1992 – Panev lustration law passed, only lustrated science and academics 2006 – Declassification of secret police archives 2006–present – Dossier Commission starts massive file reviews of public and semi-public officials, covering more than 100,000 files 2012 – continued public outing of collaborators across positions ***Current – active, on-going public disclosure process***
	Lithuania	1991 – Lustration law passed –but immediately halted so no implementation 1999 – New lustration law passed but immediately halted – no implementation 2005 – Lustration commission renews activities and reopens cases 2005–10 – renewed interest in lustration and expansion of voluntary lustration 2010 – lustration amended eliminating private sector positions ***Current – scheduled to terminate in 2012, but still actively debated in 2012***
	Romania	1999 – Ticu Law creates CNSAS and file oversight, but little implementation 2005 – 1 million files transferred to CNSAS, start more file access 2006 – renewed lustration and public disclosure program 2008 – present – CNSAS makes public disclosures of public and semi-public positions across thousands of positions ***Current – active, on-going public disclosure process***

This variable focuses less on the exact year of the passage of the lustration laws, and more on when the main discourse on transitional justice was translated into concrete policy actions. For example, Bulgaria's first Law on Banking was passed in 1992 but not really implemented, with actual public disclosures gearing up in the third wave period. Hungary passed its first lustration laws in 1994 but only engaged in a committed lustration and reform processes during the second wave period. Table 6.2 illustrates that all countries in the region have protracted reforms, spanning the past twenty-five years, with some overlap across the temporal categories. Poland continues to engage in lustration efforts, as does Bulgaria and Romania. However, the main periods of reform passage and implementation in each country are relatively concentrated and suggest discernible, if not discrete, regional waves of reforms.

In sum, both timing variables complement each other. One focuses on the moment the laws are passed, and the other focuses on the primary implementation period. Together and separately they serve as our primary independent variables, in order to assess *if* and *how* the timing of reforms affects efficacy. In other words, neither addresses the *quality* of reforms directly – both are timing variables. Other papers in this volume focus on implementation, therefore the findings here complement and qualify what we know about the conditions under which reforms are beneficial in a given country case.

TESTING THE IMPACT OF TIMING

Dependent variables

There are a variety of transition goals that lustration measures allegedly support, including building trust, promoting democracy, enhancing civil society, reducing corruption, and supporting good governance. There is evidence that lustration does promote some but not all of these goals.[28] If we believe the preliminary evidence that lustration supports *trust in government* and *democratization*, we can ask the second order question: To what extent is the efficacy of lustration, both to improve trust in government and support democratization, conditional on timing? If this preliminary assumption is not true, then we will see no relationship between the timing of reforms and outcomes in this study.

Trust in national government is a multi-variable composite, capturing a holistic assessment by citizens of the credibility, fairness, transparency, compliance, and effectiveness of the government. It spans both different agencies and various social, political, and economic issue areas.[29] Lustration is often framed as a way of increasing trust in government, both directly through changing perceptions of trust in public institutions and indirectly through demonstrations of the transparency and legitimacy of government. There is evidence to support the claims that lustration improves trust in targeted public institutions and by extension trust in government as well.[30] Using Eurobarometer public opinion surveys on trust in national government, it is possible to test if the timing of lustration affects citizen perceptions of trust in national government (see Appendix 1).

Democratization is an important transition goal for post-communist states. The use of lustration measures is framed as a means of protecting and supporting democracy. Using Freedom House's Nations in Transit measure of democracy, we can test for a relationship between the timing of reforms and democratization. This measure provides substantial nuance in evaluating changes in democratization both within and between countries in the same region. Again, if there is no relationship between lustration and democracy, we will see no effects from timing on outcomes in this study.

SOCIAL, ECONOMIC, AND POLITICAL CONTROLS

This study considers several control variables: economic growth, levels of inequality, perceptions of corruption, levels of democracy, and the strength of the political opposition. The data sources and transformations are described in Appendix 1. There is significant variation across these political, economic, and social variables within our country sample, as well as variation in country groupings and historical and current political alliances as well.

First, economic growth or decline could affect citizen perceptions of any of these dependent variables, particularly in the post-communist environment in which economic stability is often conflated with democracy and trust. Second, in terms of material conditions, inequality could negatively impact citizen perceptions of trust in government or the quality of democracy, especially given the noted increases in regional inequality since the fall of communism.[31] Third, corruption could undermine perceptions of democracy or trust in government, minimizing any possible benefits from transitional justice measures. Fourth, while democracy is a key dependent variable in this analysis, levels of democracy could systematically affect citizens' perceptions of trust in government. Since democracy could be so important an explanatory variable as to obviate any impact lustration has on reform goals, it is important to consider its independent effects in the trust analysis.

Fifth, one of the principal concerns of late transitional justice is the susceptibility of the measures to manipulation. The logic of the political manipulation hypothesis is that as the political landscape takes shape after the transition from communism to democracy, political parties will actively use lustration against potential rivals. If political opposition is low, there is little need for the messy politics of lustration. If political opposition is high, lustration could be employed as a tool for political advantage. Because of the real concern that late lustration policies will be instrumentally manipulated for narrow party politics reasons, it is especially important to consider this variable in our temporal analysis.

To test for the effects of the timing of reforms on transition goals, the next sections analyze the two dependent variables separately. First, I examine the extent to which *trust in government* is sensitive to the timing of reforms using the two independent variables for timing discussed above. Second, I examine how the timing of reforms affects *democratization*. I expect the findings with respect to this big picture goal of democratic consolidation to differ from the narrower trust goal both because of the complexity of democratization and the multiplicity of economic, social, and political factors that affect the process.

The regression analyses employed are cross-national time series models, in which the country experiences are treated individually (within country variation) and collectively (between country variation). This allows us to estimate how timing affects outcomes in each country and across the sample over time. In this way, we are able to see if there is independent causal weight attributed to the timing of reforms, and then we can estimate how strong the effect of timing is on overall reform efficacy. If lustration reforms do not support trust in government and democracy, we will see no relationship between the timing of reforms and outcomes. In this way a quantitative approach to timing sheds light on causal relationships that would be harder to isolate in a single or paired country study or a study that did not investigate changes over time.

TRUST IN GOVERNMENT

With respect to trust in government, are lustration's trust building effects conditional on the timing of reforms? This section examines the dependent variable trust in government, over the time period 2001–2012. Table 6.3 presents the results of a series of regression analyses across nine of the ten countries in our sample with trust in government as the dependent variable: Albania is not included due to lack of data.[32] The table shows that the lustration waves variable is significant in both Models 1 and 2. This means that the timing of reforms affected the level of trust in government. The coefficient is negatively signed, demonstrating that earlier programs are associated with more trust in national government than later programs. This means that timing does affect overall trust in government in the hypothesized manner – early reforms are associated with more trust in government.

TABLE 6.3: *Lustration and Transitional Justice Measures and Trust in Government*

	Trust in National Government (2001–2012, 9 countries)	
	Model 1 *Parabola model*	Model 2
Lustration Waves	−6.27**	−8.10***
	(2.07)	(2.42)
Timing Lustration	2.33*	3.08**
	(1.08)	(1.21)
Timing Lustration squared	−.13**	−.16**
	(.05)	(.06)
Corruption	−.53***	−.72***
	(.13)	(.17)
Democracy	−1.33***	−1.79***
	(.39)	(.44)
Economic growth	.23	−.61
	(.21)	(.48)
Inequality	–	−.41
		(12.63)
Strength of Pol Opposition	–	.001
		(.002)
Constant	78.94***	98.90***
N	108	79
Wald χ^2	36.68***	35.83***

Cross sectional time series FGLS regression analyses, clustered by country. All models test for heteroskedasticity and multicollinearity – no problems with reported models.
Unstandardized regression coefficients (b) reported, with standard errors in parentheses. 95% confidence interval, two tailed * p <.05, ** p <.01, *** p <.001

We know timing matters, but how much? I calculate the magnitude of the effect of the timing of reforms on trust in government using predicted value calculations. Because Model 1 is the simplest presentation of variables with the largest sample size covering the longest time period, I use this model specification to calculate the magnitude of the effect. First wave reform programs produce 4.5 percent more trust in government than second wave lustration programs, and the same is true for second wave programs compared to third wave programs. In total there is a 9 percent trust in government dividend that first wave programs get in comparison to third wave programs. These trust numbers suggest that as more time passes after the regime transition, the magnitude of the effect of reform programs on building trust in government goes down. Each wave of delayed reform forgoes trust in government by approximately 5 percent. While this is statistically significant it is a relatively moderate effect.

We can qualify these findings about lustration waves using the actual timing in years variables. With respect to the timing of lustration variable, both timing and timing squared are robust. Timing is positively signed and robust, and timing squared is negatively signed and robust. This suggests a nonlinear relationship between the timing of lustration and trust building. Put more simply, timing can be represented as an inverted parabola, or a modified inverted U-shape. The efficacy of lustration rises over time, reaches a critical tipping point, and then declines with time. Timing matters, but not in the hypothesized inverse relationship assumed in the literature. In fact, timing and efficacy show a more complex nonlinear relationship with later lustration yielding the biggest trust gains.

This relationship can be graphed using the quadratic functional form for a parabola[33]:

> *$y=ax^2 + bx + c$, where a and b represent two of the slope coefficients of the quadratic equation, x is timing and x^2 is timing squared, and c is the constant term.*

The coefficients for timing, timing squared, and the constant term are shown in Table 6.3 (Model 1), and can be plugged into the quadratic equation in order to derive the following equation:

$$\textit{Trust in Government}: \; y = -0.13x^2 + 2.33x + 78.94$$

Figure 6.1 models this relationship, with the inverted parabola representing the relationship between timing of lustration and trust in government. The vertex of the parabola is at point (9, 89.3), representing the apex of trust building in terms of timing. This means that delaying lustration for approximately a decade after the regime change has the biggest impact on trust building. Reforms enacted at the start of the transition are less efficacious than moderately delayed reforms. It is only after a decade that the expected negatively sloped line emerges, showing a decrease in the utility of measures over time. To be clear, the vertex point is just an estimate of optimal timing, as that point would vary according to country and circumstances. However, it shows that delaying reforms is most effective.

There are several observations to make from this figure. First, the overall magnitude of effect of timing on outcomes is moderate to weak. Timing matters but even late reforms only impact trust in government by less than 10 percent. Second, the optimal time to start lustration is nine to ten years after

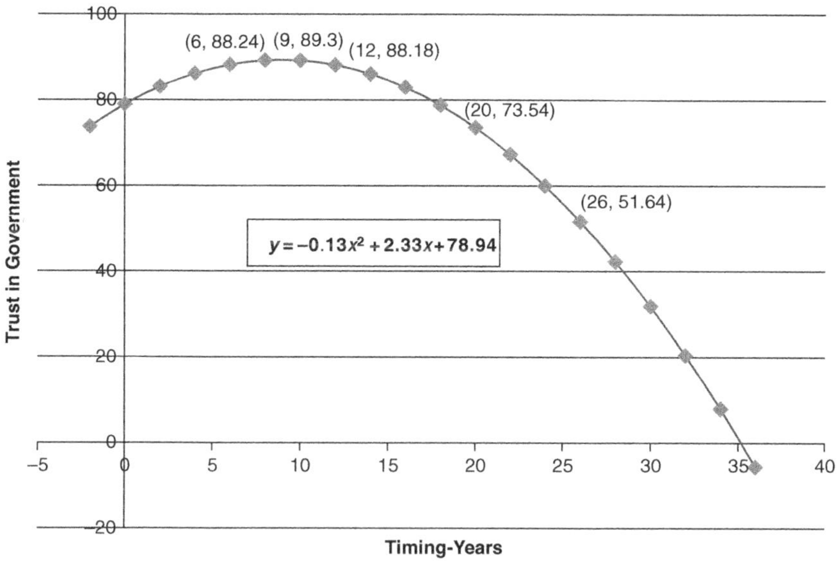

FIGURE 6.1: The Relationship between the Timing of Reforms and Trust in Government

the regime change.[34] Third, the effects from lustration measures on trust in government are similar over a period of six to twelve years after the regime change. Therefore, there is a window of opportunity for the passage of optimal lustration measures over which levels of trust differ by less than 1 percent. A much wider window for *optimal* reforms exists than hypothesized. Fourth, the benefits from policies continue even after that *optimal* window of opportunity, with the trust gains from reforms seventeen years after the transition looking very similar to reforms enacted two years after the transition.

In terms of the control variables, we see that as corruption goes down, trust in national government goes up, as per our expectations. Material conditions like economic growth and inequality do not affect the robustness of the timing of lustration and are not significant in their own right. We would also expect government polarization or a strong political opposition to affect perceptions of the trustworthiness of the national government. However, the strength of the political opposition does not undermine the robustness of lustration waves and is not a significant predictor of trust in national government. In general, the controls do not obviate the importance of timing on trust in national government and are not important explanatory variables in their own right.

In sum, our two timing variables demonstrate that, contrary to the assumption that only early lustration is positive, reforms do not have to take place immediately to be beneficial. While we see a trust boost from the first wave countries, the magnitude of the effect is small to moderate. This means timing is not an overwhelmingly important factor in determining trust in government. The timing of lustration variables measured in years (timing and timing squared) demonstrates that the efficacy of reform rises after the regime change for almost a decade. Delayed lustration is best, but early reforms and later reforms continue to be effective in improving trust in national government. However, the model presents cautionary evidence that 18–20 years after the regime change the start of lustration could negatively impact trust in government. There is a moment that is too late for the start of lustration reforms. The findings from the reform waves variable and the timing variables complement each other, introducing nuance in our understanding of the conditions under which timing affects reform efficacy. The next section turns to the effects of the timing of reforms on democratization.

LEVELS OF DEMOCRACY

Are the effects of lustration on democracy also conditional on the timing of reforms? To what extent does democracy evidence patterns similar to trust in government? Table 6.4 presents the results of a set of cross-national analyses of the impact of the timing of lustration measures on democracy across all countries in our sample over the period 1997–2012.

Models 1 and 2 demonstrate that lustration waves are significant predictors of democracy. The negative sign indicates that earlier programs are more efficacious than later programs in supporting democracy. Timing does matter, but how much? Using predicted value estimations, I calculate the magnitude of the effect of timing on democratization. For each successive reform wave there is a 1–2 percent change in democracy. Early lustration programs (the first wave) have a greater impact than later lustration programs (wave 2), but only by 1 percent. The difference in trust building between wave one and wave three lustration programs is only 3 percent. This suggests that while timing matters, it only weakly affects the efficacy of lustration programs on democratization. In other words, the timing of reforms has very little impact on overall levels of democracy in the region.

We see this confirmed with the timing of reforms and timing squared variables measured in years. Unlike the previous analysis of trust in government, the timing and timing squared variables are not even consistently significant. In Model 1, there is no statistically significant relationship between timing and democracy. In Model 2, with the truncated time period, there is the familiar inverted parabolic (inverted U-shaped) relationship between

TABLE 6.4: *Timing of Lustration and Democracy (1997–2012; 10 countries)*

	Democracy	
	Model 1 1997–2012	Model 2 1997–2008 *Parabola model*
Lustration Waves	-1.23^{**}	-2.37^{***}
	(.47)	(.55)
Timing Lustration	.39	$.79^{**}$
	(.27)	(.23)
Timing Lustration *Squared*	−.02 (.01)	$-.03^{**}$ (.009)
Corruption	$-.38^{***}$	$-.33^{***}$
	(.03)	(.04)
Economic growth	−.01	−.05
	(.07)	(.11)
Inequality	–	4.54
		(4.06)
Strength of Political Opp	–	.0002
		(.0005)
Constant	34.02^{***}	33.76^{***}
N	153	114
Wald χ^2	174.12^{***}	136.68^{***}

Cross sectional time series FGLS regression analyses, clustered by country. All models test for heteroskedasticity and multicollinearity – no problems with reported models.
Unstandardized regression coefficients (b) reported, with standard errors in parentheses. 95% confidence interval, two tailed * $p < .05$, ** $p < .01$, *** $p < .001$

timing and the efficacy of reforms. Earlier reforms are not the best. Efficacy rises for a period after the regime change, before reaching a vertex moment after which there is relatively declining efficacy. Using Model 2 in Table 6.4, the equation for this relationship can be algebraically represented by using the quadratic functional form for a parabola, and plugging in the x^2, x, and constant term coefficients:

$$\textit{Democratization}: y = -0.03x^2 + 0.79x + 33.76$$

Figure 6.2 graphs the parabolic relationship between democratization and the timing of reforms. There are two observations that can be drawn from these models. First, the timing for optimal policy measures is also delayed from the start of the transition. The vertex position is thirteen years after the start of the transition. This presents us with at least a decade or more of time after the regime change in which to pass lustration laws that could support

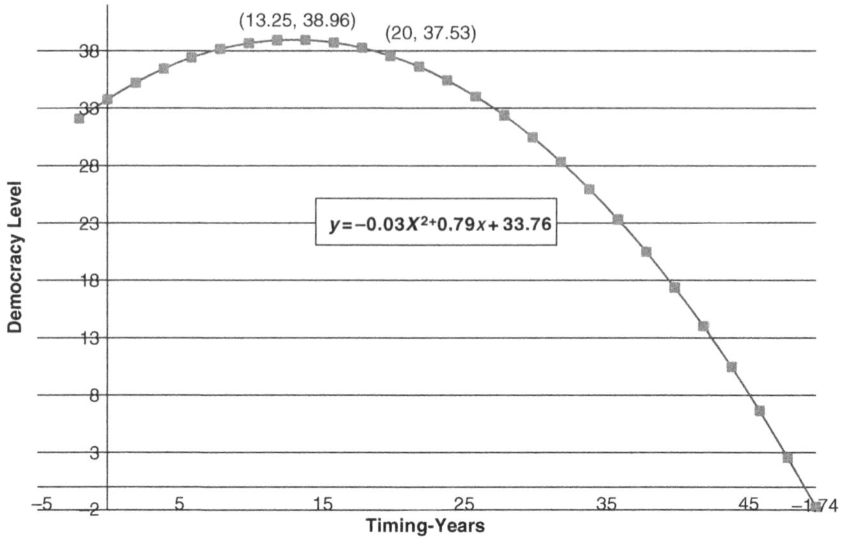

FIGURE 6.2: Democratization and the Timing of Reforms

democratization. Second, the widow of opportunity for policy measures is much wider than previously assumed. The slope of the parabola near the vertex, either plus or minus, is not steep ($m = -0.03$). There are actually large windows of time for hitting an "optimal" vertex point or a "peak policy moment." For example, even twenty years after the start of the transition, there is only a 3 percent change in the effect on democracy.[35]

In terms of our controls, corruption continues to be an important predictor of democracy, with higher levels of corruption undermining democratization. However, the additional controls fail to account for shifts in levels of democracy over time in the region. We see that democracy is affected by lustration because the lustration waves variable is significant. This means lustration does support democratization, however the effects are not sensitive to the timing of reforms.

In sum, the timing of reforms has a very small effect on their overall efficacy to support democracy. While early reform waves do show more gains in democracy over time, the utility gained from late lustration can be similar to early lustration programs – with marginal changes of 1–2 percent. The timing variables illustrate that the window of opportunity for enacting – not implementing fully but simply passing lustration measures – is much wider than the accepted folk wisdom about the need for early reforms or none at all. Passing lustration anywhere from 10 to 15 years or later after the start of the transition yields similarly optimal returns in terms of democracy levels.[36] Moreover, compared to the analyses of trust in national government, democracy can still be supported with reforms starting twenty or more years after the regime change.

LESSONS FROM THE POST-COMMUNIST EXPERIENCE

This chapter explored how the timing of transitional justice policies in the post-communist space affected efficacy with respect to two transition goals – trust in government and democratization. The chapter demonstrated that timing does matter but not very much and not in the way assumed in the transitional justice literature. First, while we do see greater efficacy in first wave reform countries, the boost in trust building or democracy promotion was moderate to weak. In other words, early reformers did not have an overwhelming advantage. In the case of democracy the boost for the earliest reforms compared to the latest reforms was approximately 3 percent. Overall, timing is less important than the quality of reforms. While there is much debate about the importance of timing on reform efficacy, the models do not support that assumption. Second, our timing variables illustrated that delayed transitional justice measures were the most efficacious, with a decade or so after the start of the transition being the peak moment for passing lustration measures. While there is evidence that significantly delaying the passage of measures could undermine reforms, in practice this means more than twenty years after the regime change. This is much longer than the assumed five- to ten-year post-transition window hypothesized in the literature.

There are several important messages to draw from this comparison of the impact of the timing of reforms on transition goals. First, although the peak moment to start reforms differed between the goals, in both cases delaying the passage of lustration measures was better than immediate reforms and in both cases reforms were associated with more trust and more democracy. Future research could examine whether other types of transitional justice in other regions evidence similar delayed reform tendencies. Additionally, neither timing variable captured the quality of implementation of measures. Further research is needed to explore how variation in the scope and implementation of reforms combined with timing considerations affect overall transition goals. Lynch and Marchesi's chapter incorporates a quality of lustration measure to assess how different types of programs affect outcomes. They find more extensive programs improve political rights significantly, although find little impact on democracy. This piece on the timing of lustration and Lynch and Marchesi's chapter on the impact of lustration complement each other and further our understanding of the conditions under which transitional justice supports regime goals.

Second, the magnitude of the effect of timing was small. Timing mattered, but not very much. While lustration affected both outcomes – trust and democracy – the timing of the reforms was less important than the reforms themselves. The magnitude of effect of timing on democratization was almost inconsequential, with each successive wave of reforms seeing a 1–2 percent change in effectiveness. In some cases earlier reforms have a bigger impact on reform goals, but the size of the dividend is neither uniform nor overwhelming. Post-transition states must make trade-offs and balance their many reform needs in the uncertain transition environment. Recognizing that the magnitude of foregone gains from delayed transitional justice measures could be relatively low is useful information for post-transition states juggling competing policy goals.

Third, the window of opportunity within which reform measures could be passed to positively contribute to transition goals was also much wider than originally believed. The window of opportunity for supporting trust in government with maximal efficacy was nine to twelve years after the regime change, while democratization was most efficaciously promoted in the ten–fifteen year time window. Although very delayed lustration measures could adversely impact transition goals, even fifteen years after the regime change a country still has optimal conditions to *initiate* measures. Of course, initiating reforms and implementing them well are separate but related issues. However, the findings give us some temporal context as to what it means to be *too late* to start reforms.

In sum, there are potential policy lessons for other countries to be derived from the post-communist experience. If early reforms are not always better and late reforms not always bad, this opens up policy options for countries post-transition. Knowing that transitional justice measures could remain effective reform tools for a decade or more after the regime change helps to reduce the burden of immediate reform placed on fledgling regimes. It also demonstrates that transitional justice measures might be most efficacious once institutions are in place to fairly and comprehensively implement reforms. While our findings come too late to benefit the post-communist countries studied here, the information remains important for more proximate and future cases of post-authoritarian transitions, such as those that swept the Middle East during the Arab Spring. It also resonates with the recent examples of late transitional justice measures in Cambodia, Spain, and Guatemala. For those countries the post-communist experiences could inform the structure and function of current and future vetting programs.[37]

APPENDIX 1: DATA SOURCES AND TRANSFORMATIONS

Corruption – Corruption Perceptions Index (CPI), *Transparency International*, 1997–2012. http://www.transparency.org/cpi2012.

- *Transformations include using inverse of CPI scores (10 is transformed to mean more corruption on a scale of 1–10), and square of inverse measure.*

Democracy – *Freedom House, Nations in Transit*. 2012 updates. http://www.freedomhouse.org/report-types/nations-transit

- *Transformations include using inverse of democracy measure (7 is now more democracy on scale of 1–7), and square of inverse measure.*

Economic Growth – GDP change. *International Monetary Fund, World Economic Outlook Database*, October 2012 updates. http://www.imf.org/external/pubs/ft/weo/2011/02/weodata/index.aspx

- *No transformations, two year lagged GDP change figures.*

Inequality – GINI coefficient. Branko Milanovic, *All the GINIS Dataset*, World Bank. Version summer 2012. (Measures between 0 and 1.) Accessed 4 October 2013. http://siteresources.worldbank.org/INTRES/Resources/469232-1107449512766/all_ginis_Description_dataset.pdf

- *Lagged two year absolute numbers.*

Lustration Waves – Ordinal categories. Wave 1 countries coded 1; Wave 2 countries coded 2; Wave 3 countries coded 3. A negative regression coefficient means earlier lustration is more effective.

Strength of Political Opposition – share of opposition vote. Thorsten Beck, George Clarke, Alberto Groff, Philip Keefer, and Patrick Walsh, "New tools in comparative political economy: The Database of Political Institutions." 15:1, 165–176 (September), *World Bank Economic Review*. http://go.worldbank.org/2EAGGLRZ40. updated December 2010. (2001)

- *Transformed into square of share of vote.*

Timing of Lustration – Timing is measured in years, as the difference between the year of the first lustration policy and the year of regime change. Before lustration is enacted, the absence of lustration is coded as the difference between 2012 and the year of regime change. After enactment, timing is coded as the difference between the year of the lustration policy and the year of regime change.

Timing of Lustration Squared – the timing variable is squared.

Trust in National Government – *Standard Eurobarometer Reports*, Public Opinion in the European Union, various reports covering period 2001–2012. Each trust measure is percentage of individuals polled who said they trusted the government. Last updated October 2012. http://ec.europa.eu/public_opinion/index_en.htm

NOTES

1. Thoms, Ron, and Paris's recent review of the state of the discipline concluded that given both the methodological problems with impact assessments and the contradictory findings thus far, we do not have sufficient knowledge to conclude definitely whether and under what conditions the impact of transitional justice is positive, negative or neutral. See Oskar Thoms, James Ron, and Roland Paris. *The Effects of Transitional Justice Mechanisms: A Summary of Empirical Research Findings and Implications for Analysts and Practitioners* (Ottawa: Centre for International Policy Studies, 2008).
2. International institutions, such as the United Nations, the European Court of Human Rights, and the Council of Europe, have supported a direct relationship between lustration and democracy promotion. See United Nations, *Rule of Law Tools for Post-Conflict States: Vetting: An Operational Framework*. Office of the UN High Commission on Human Rights, New York, United Nations HR/PUB/06/5 (2006); European Court of Human Rights, *Case of Ždanoka v. Latvia*, Judgment 58278/00, March 16, 2006 (Strasbourg: Council of Europe, 2006), 18§87; and Council of Europe, Measures to Dismantle the Heritage of Former Communist Totalitarian Systems. Resolution 1096 (1996), available at: http://assembly.coe.int/Documents/AdoptedText/ta96/ERES1096.HTM (accessed December 7, 2013).

   Academics have also demonstrated relationships between lustration, political trust, political rights, and governance. See Roman David, *Lustration and Transitional Justice* (Philadelphia: University of Pennsylvania Press, 2011); Cynthia M. Horne, "Assessing the Impact of Lustration on Trust in Public Institutions and National Government in Central and Eastern Europe," *Comparative Political Studies* 45, no. 4 (2012): 412–446; and Vladimíra Dvořáková and Anđelko Milardović, eds. *Lustration and Consolidation of Democracy and Rule of Law in Central and Eastern Europe* (Zagreb: Political Science Research Centre Zagreb, 2007).
3. László Sólyom, "The Role of Constitutional Courts in the Transition to Democracy: With Special Reference to Hungary," *International Sociology* 18, no. 1 (2003): 141.
4. Eric Posner and Adrian Vermeule, "Transitional Justice as Ordinary Justice," *Harvard Law Review* 117, no. 3 (2004): 761–825.
5. The *Encyclopedia of Transitional Justice* also reviews the use of trials, truth commissions, memorialization, reparations and rehabilitation of political prisoners as regional transitional justice measures. Lavinia Stan and Nadya Nedelsky, eds., *Encyclopedia of Transitional Justice* (New York: Cambridge University Press, 2013).
6. Stan provides a broad definition to capture the umbrella of lustration like reforms. Lavinia Stan, ed., *Transitional Justice in Eastern Europe and the Former Soviet Union: Reckoning with the Communist Past* (New York: Routledge, 2009).
7. Roman David, "Lustration Laws in Action: The Motives and Evaluation of Lustration Policy in the Czech Republic and Poland (1989–2001)," *Law and Social* Inquiry 28, no. 2 (2003): 387–489; and Alexander Mayer-Rieckh and Pablo De Greiff, eds., *Justice as Prevention: Vetting Public Employees in Transitional Societies* (New York: ICTJ and Social Science Research Council, 2007).
8. Claus Offe, *Varieties of Transition: The East European and East German Experience* (London: Cambridge University Press, 1996).

9. This phrase is often attributed to Leszek Balcerowicz. Leszek Balcerowicz, *Socialism, Capitalism, Transformation* (Budapest: Central European University Press, 1995).
10. Roman Boed, "An Evaluation of the Legality and Efficacy of Lustration as a Tool of Transitional Justice," *Columbia Journal of Transitional Law* 37, no. 2 (1999): 357–402.
11. Lavinia Stan, *Transitional Justice in Post-Communist Romania: The Politics of Memory* (New York: Cambridge University Press, 2013), 290.
12. Csilla Kiss, "The Misuses of Manipulation: The Failure of Transitional Justice in Post-Communist Hungary," *Europe-Asia Studies* 58, no. 6 (2006): 925–940; Robert C. Austin and Jonathan Ellison, "Post-Communist Transitional Justice in Albania," *East European Politics and Societies* 22, no. 2 (2008): 373–401.
13. This sentiment is widely held by scholars in Eastern Europe, and was often repeated in personal interviews with the author in Hungary, Bulgaria, Romania, and Poland during field research on the topic, 2012–2013. For example, interview with Dimitar Markov, Senior Analyst/Project Director Anti-corruption and Judicial Reform Unit, Center for the Study of Democracy, Sofia, Bulgaria, July 2, 2012; Interview with Dr. János Kornai, Professor Emeritus at the Corvinus University of Budapest, Budapest, Hungary, April 8, 2013; Interview with Dr. Gabriel Andreescu, Professor at Școala Națională de Studii Politice și Administrative, Bucharest, Romania, October 10, 2012.
14. Act No. 451/1991 on Conditions for Holding Certain Positions in State Bodies and Organizations (October 4, 1991), the Screening ("Lustration") Law, translated in Neil Kritz, ed., *Transitional Justice: How Emerging Democracies Reckon with Former Regimes* (Washington, D.C.: United States Institute of Peace Studies, 1995), vol. 3: 312–321.
15. Law on Background Checks to be Conducted on Individuals Holding Certain Important Positions, Law No. 23/1994 (March 9, 1994), translated in Kritz 1995, 3: 418–425; and Latvian Constitutional Court, Case No. 2004–13–0106, Judgment, 22 March 2005, available at: www.satv.tiesa.gov.lv/upload/2004–13–0106E.rtf (accessed December 21, 2013).
16. Lithuania: Decree Banning KGB Employees and Informers from Government Positions. Decree No. 418 (October 12, 1991), translated in Kritz 1995, 3: 427; and Law Nr. 8001 of September 22, 1995, "On Genocide and Crimes Against Humanity Committed in Albania during the Communist Regime for Political, Ideological and Religious Reasons" (the Genocide Law) and Law Nr. 8043 of November 30, 1995, "On the Control of the Moral Figure of Officials and Other Persons Connected with the Protection of the Democratic State" (The Verification Law), translated by Kathleen Imholz, available at: http://www.lustration.net/albania_documentation.pdf (accessed February 2, 2011).
17. Mark Ellis, "Purging the Past: The Current State of Lustration Laws in the Former Communist Bloc," *Law and Contemporary Problems* 59, no. 4 (1997): 193.
18. European Court of Human Rights, *Case of Ždanoka v. Latvia*, Judgment 58278/00, March 16, 2006 (Strasbourg: Council of Europe, 2006), 21§100.
19. European Court of Human Rights, *Case of Sidabras and Dziautas v. Lithuania*, Final 55480/00 and 59330/00, July 27, 2004 (Strasbourg: Council of Europe, 2004). §115; European Court of Human Rights, Case of Matyvek v. Poland. 38184/03, April 24, 2007 (Strasbourg: Council of Europe, 2007) § 69.

20. Polish Constitutional Tribunal; Judgment of 11th May 2007, file Ref. No. K 2/07 LUSTRATION (2007), available at: http://www.trybunal.gov.pl/eng/summaries/documents/K_2_07_GB.pdf (accessed December 23, 2013).
21. Posner and Vermeule, "Transitional Justice," 808.
22. Alexandru Grigorescu, "The Corruption Eruption in East-Central Europe: The Increased Salience of Corruption and the Role of Intergovernmental Organizations," *East European Politics and Societies* 20, no. 3 (2006): 516–549; Marian Tupy, "The Rise of Populist Parties in Central Europe: Big Government, Corruption, and the Threat to Liberalism," *Development Policy Analysis*, No. 1 (Washington, D.C.: Cato Institute: Center for Global Liberty & Prosperity, 2006).
23. See Act 254/1995 and Act No. 422/2000 and 424/2000.
24. Act 93/2000, interview with Dr. Georgö Bendegúz Cseh, Deputy Head of Department, Historical Archives of Hungarian State Security, Budapest, Hungary, April 4, 2013.
25. Cynthia M. Horne, "Late Lustration Programs in Romania and Poland: Supporting or Undermining Democratic Transitions?" *Democratization* 16, no. 2 (2009): 344–376.
26. For similar coding in policy models, see Mark Donovan, Carolyn Tolbert, and Daniel Smith, "Political Engagement, Mobilization, and Direct Democracy," *Public Opinion Quarterly* 73, no. 1 (2009): 98–118.
27. Jon Elster, *Closing the Books: Transitional Justice in Historical Perspective* (Cambridge: Cambridge University Press, 2004), 75–76.
28. Horne and David both show trust in public institutions and trust in government benefits from lustration. Horne "Assessing the Impact," and David *Lustration and Transitional Justice*. Mayer-Rieckh and De Greiff focus on the relationship between lustration, justice, security, and state-building, see *Justice as Prevention*. For a discussion of the relationship between lustration, rule of law and democracy, see Dvořáková and Milardović *Lustration and Consolidation of Democracy*.
29. János Kornai and Susan Rose-Ackerman, eds., *Building a Trustworthy State in Post-Socialist Transition* (New York: Palgrave/Macmillan Press, 2004).
30. Horne, "Assessing the Impact."
31. Agnieszka Paczynska, "Inequality, Political Participation, and Democratic Deepening in Poland," *East European Politics and Societies* 19, no. 4 (2005): 573–613; Bo Rothstein and Eric Uslaner, "All for All: Equality, Corruption, and Social Trust," *World Politics* 58, no. 1 (2005): 41–72.
32. Inequality data limits the time period to 2009 for Model 2.
33. Standardized coefficients were derived using STATA 12, xtgls statistical techniques, clustered by country. Figures graphed using meta-calculator's graphing calculator functions, http://www.meta-calculator.com/online/.
34. The coordinates for those dates and trust levels are (6.0, 88.24) and (12.0, 88.18). The x and y coordinates demonstrate a negligible trust effect over that time period. Author's calculations.
35. Coordinates (20, 37.56).
36. Coordinates (10, 38.66) and (15, 38.86). This is marginally different from the vertex point (13, 38.96).

37. See Mariano Castillo, "Guatemala confronts a dark chapter," *CNN*, April 11, 2013; and "Cambodia: Bringing the Khmers Rouges to Justice," *The Economist*, October 7, 2004. Both Libya and Tunisia advanced plans for vetting public offices. See "The Arab Uprisings: Democracy's Hard Spring," *The Economist*, March 10, 2011; "Libya's Government and the Militias: Is the Tide Turning?" *The Economist*, June 15, 2013.

7

The Challenge of Competing Pasts

Monica Ciobanu

Whether using case studies, regional comparisons, or cross-regional comparisons, the transitional justice literature has been prolific in addressing the question of reckoning with the past. But many challenges involving post-communist countries – including the impact of the timing of transitional justice on democratization and state building, the role of external factors, and the use of the communist past for a revived nationalist mobilization – have not been fully examined. The impact of multiple pasts on the types of choices that countries make when dealing with different forms of repression remains another understudied topic. Do countries address issues of accountability and guilt with respect to all former repressive regimes or only in relation to some? In dealing with the communist past do they address different periods of these regimes or only certain episodes and events within them? As the events of 1989 have become more distant in the collective memory and a new generation with no direct experience with communist dictatorship has emerged, the twenty-fifth anniversary of the collapse of European communist regimes represents an appropriate and timely occasion to reflect on these questions.

Unlike other countries in the region, the exit from communism in Romania was abrupt and violent. For this reason, that country represents an ideal case for comparative analysis. There, after the collapse of the communist regime in December 1989, the new political actors found themselves in the unique position of having to address three distinctive and controversial histories. These were: (1) the crimes of the Holocaust committed during Marshal Ion Antonescu's fascist government in World War II; (2) the large-scale Gulag-style repression that followed the establishment of the communist regime in 1945; and (3) the violent events surrounding the overthrow of communism in December 1989 that resulted in more than 1,000 deaths. In addition, if we take into account the transformation of Romanian communism into a dynastic-nationalist regime under the dictatorship of Nicolae Ceauşescu (1965–1989), we can argue for the existence of a fourth such traumatic past.

Previous research on the politics of memory in Romania has focused either on a specific past or on a limited comparative analysis of the crimes perpetrated during the Holocaust and communism.[1] The focus of this chapter is much broader in scope. It addresses the competing and often controversial attempts at understanding the significance of various historical events associated with these pasts by examining legal responses employed by state actors (criminal trials and restitution policies) and truth-telling mechanisms (truth commissions, opening of the secret files, memorializations, lustration, and rewriting history textbooks) and assessing their impact on building a liberal democratic state.

HISTORICAL CONTEXTS: MECHANISMS OF REPRESSION AND VICTIMS

After World War I and following the Treaty of Versailles Romania acquired three new territories: Bessarabia from Russia, and Bukovina and Transylvania from Austria-Hungary. As a result, its territory more than doubled from 137,000 to 295,049 square kilometers. While the Old Kingdom's population was predominantly ethnic Romanian, the demographic make-up of Great Romania had significantly changed. By 1930, the Romanian majority (representing 71.9 percent of a total population of 18,057,000) coexisted with ethnic minorities.[2] The Jewish minority (numbering 756,930) represented nearly half of the urban population in Bessarabia and Moldova. In these provinces Jews were viewed with suspicion for their alleged pro-Soviet and communist sympathies, and their loyalty to the state was questioned. Strong anti-Semitism emerged in the late 1920s in the city of Iaşi among a nationalist and Orthodox student movement named the Legion of Archangel Michael, that later became known as the Iron Guard. The Legion quickly evolved into a quasi-mystical organization seeking the creation of a new heroic man dedicated to the service of God and community.

Following the abdication of King Carol II in 1940, the Iron Guard forged an alliance with Marshal Ion Antonescu, who had assumed power. During their brief participation in Antonescu's fascist government (September 1940–January 1941), the Guard members embarked on a chaotic killing campaign and riots against Jewish communities. Eventually, with the consent of Nazi Germany, Romania's ally, Antonescu removed the Iron Guard from the government, imprisoned its leaders, and consolidated his fascist rule. The second stage of the Romanian Holocaust then began. Antonescu's military alliance with

Hitler against the Soviet Union, as a result of which Romania lost Bessarabia, Bukovina and the Hertza territories in summer 1940, contributed to the escalation of nationalist and anti-Semitic sentiments. From 1941 to 1944, Antonescu pursued a systematic campaign of ethnic homogenization based on a strict racial classification.[3] Anti-Semitic policies consisted of discriminatory legislation that confiscated and nationalized Jewish assets and properties, banned Jews from education and the medical profession, and forcibly evacuated and interned them in concentration camps. Parallel measures seeking their physical extermination were organized. The total number of Jewish victims reached 280,000 to 380,000 in the occupied Soviet territories, including 80,000 to 150,000 deported from Bessarabia and Bukovina to Transnistria, 100,000 massacred in Odessa, Bogdankova, and Akmecetka, and 10,000 killed in the June–July 1941 Iaşi pogrom. The victims also included some 25,000 Roma deported to Transnistria, of whom 11,000 lost their lives.[4] Antonescu was more flexible toward the Jews residing in Wallachia and Moldova, where a significant number survived, but that attitude was less the result of benevolence on his part and more of ambivalence, circumstance, and opportunism.

The military defeat suffered by the Axis at Stalingrad in 1943 and the significant losses Romanian troops sustained on the Eastern front weakened support for the alliance with Hitler. On August 23, 1944, King Michael (Carol II's son) orchestrated a coup d'état and pulled the country out of the Axis. Eight days later the Red Army moved in. In 1948 with direct interference from the Soviet Union, all pre-World War II democratic institutions were dissolved. The country embarked on an intensive process of communization and Sovietization by dismantling private property and destroying class enemies. Repressive legislation and structural changes in the Ministry of Internal Affairs accomplished these goals. Law 16 of 1949 introduced capital punishment for treason. In 1948, a special department was created within the Ministry: the General Directory of People's Security or the Securitate. Its head Gheorghe Pintilie and his two deputies were agents of the Soviet People's Commissariat for Internal Affairs, the NKVD, which helped to set up the Securitate.[5] During its first two decades the Securitate employed uneducated officers from newly privileged classes who regularly engaged in summary executions, illegal searches and arrests, and brutal interrogations.[6]

After the penitentiary system was transferred from the jurisdiction of the Ministry of Justice to the Ministry of Internal Affairs, in 1951 work colonies were created to reeducate dangerous elements. Prisoners and internees were subject to inhumane treatment, while prisons were filled with political prisoners accused as counterrevolutionaries, including former members and sympathizers of pre-communist parties (notably the National Liberal Party [PNL] and the National Peasant Party [PNŢ]) and the Iron Guard, members of the upper bourgeoisie and their families, middle classes, peasants, participants, or supporters of the armed resistance, and representatives of ethnic and religious minorities.[7] The Romanian gulag became known for the practice of "reeducation through torture" implemented in some prisons and work colonies.[8] The victims of this massive repression included 600,000 political detainees, administrative internees, and deportees, and more than a half-million young people in forced labor.[9] Some 80,000 peasants were arrested for opposing collectivization.[10] In 1964, when the last prisoners were released from the nightmare of incarceration the communist regime was already consolidated.

In 1964, the leader of the Communist Party Gheorghe Gheorghiu-Dej asserted the party's independence from Moscow. The emerging nationalist-communist doctrine reached its peak in the 1980s under the party leadership of Nicolae Ceauşescu, who promoted an extreme cult of personality based on anti-Soviet xenophobic nationalism and his own absolute dictatorship. The Securitate's methods and personnel changed significantly. Surveillance became subtler, and was based increasingly on blackmail, intimidation, and rumors. In contrast to the earlier period, officers were recruited from more educated and qualified strata.[11] Civilians recruited as informers or collaborators heavily augmented the work of those officers. By December 1989 the number of Securitate employees was only 15,312, but these were at least 400,000 informers.[12] In fact, it was because of these willing collaborators that the Securitate was able to exert such strict control over the population. Recruitment, no longer achieved by extreme means as in the 1950s, was effected by more refined ways in exchange for personal favors, financial or non-financial benefits, and blackmail.[13] Dissidents and those involved in the very few opposition movements were kept under systematic surveillance and subjected to physical torture and abusive psychiatric treatment.[14] The Securitate maintained extensive files on those who could pose a threat to the regime, including former political prisoners, artists, and writers, as well as some high-level officials and their own collaborators.[15] The number of those monitored reached 1,162,418 by 1989.[16] Given this state of affairs, it is unsurprising that opposition to the regime was sporadic and disorganized.

The international context, which was strongly defined by the liberalization policies initiated by Mikhail Gorbachev in the Soviet Union in the late 1980s and the rapid succession of regime changes in 1989 throughout Eastern Europe, coupled with ongoing deterioration in living standards in Romania preempted any possibility of support for the regime. The revolution that began in Timişoara (a large multiethnic city situated in the western part of the country) on December 15, 1989, was marked by violent encounters between the local population and the army. In defiance, Ceauşescu called a mass meeting in Bucharest on December 21 to rally support against what he called "hooligans" and "CIA spies." The meeting turned into an anti-Ceauşescu demonstration that forced him to flee the capital. Radio stations and television were taken over by demonstrators and in this chaos the National Salvation Front (NSF) emerged spontaneously as the future transitional government. Even after the execution of Ceauşescu and his wife Elena on December 24, street fights between demonstrators, the army and some Securitate elements continued in Bucharest, resulting in casualties. The new Salvation Front leader Ion Iliescu accused these counterrevolutionaries of being "foreign terrorists," albeit they were neither foreign nor terrorists. It was a period of intense chaos and confusion. Among the casualties were demonstrators, bystanders, as well as army and security officers and soldiers who mistakenly killed each other following orders from their superiors. Siani-Davies estimates that this "bloody bacchanalia" led to 1,142 deaths, 3,138 wounded, and 760 imprisoned.[17]

LEGAL RESPONSES TO PAST CRIMES

The crimes committed during the Holocaust and the Gheorghiu-Dej communist regime surpassed those perpetrated during Ceausescu's late communism and the 1989 revolution in terms of number of victims and cruelty of repression. Although compared to other post-communist countries, Romania had the highest number of trials and court proceedings, these criminal prosecutions chiefly addressed the events of 1989.[18] There was no single legal proceeding for acts committed during Antonescu's regime. Neither were there many indictments that led to convictions against those involved in the repression of the 1950s and 1960s. Only two trials were finalized for crimes and abuses committed during the 1980s. The first addressed the murder of dissident Gheorghe Ursu in 1985. The second ("Bus trial") referred to the killing in 1981 of three young people who sought to leave the country by taking hostages.

The paucity of court trials resulted from the immediate political context following the 1989 overthrow of the communist regime and the reproduction of communist elites after the revolution. The December 1989 revolution created a legal vacuum and the Salvation Front had no coherent political project. As the new provisional power, the Front initially included students, dissidents, street revolutionaries, and former second-rank communist officials, but this broad alliance broke quickly, and the Front became a political party claiming to be the direct heir to the revolution. This move allowed Iliescu and other former communists to scapegoat the Ceauşescu family and the top

Communist Party echelon and thus avoid any substantial discussion about the past abuses of the communist regime they served. The public was persuaded to avoid an open discussion about the past by the spectacle of the Ceauşescus brought to justice and the emergence of a stable government. In comparison, the crimes of the Holocaust and of the Stalinist period seemed distant and irrelevant.

In fact, the precipitous indictment of the Ceauşescus under an ambiguous accusation of genocide by an improvised military tribunal followed by their immediate execution without any due process amounted to a backwards-looking justice typical of revolutions. Moreover, the sentences handed down to those who had been directly responsible for repressing the revolution – that is, the twenty-four members of the Communist Party Political Executive Committee (CPEx) who approved Ceauşescu's decision to use force – were either shortened or annulled. Genuine prosecution of the crimes of the revolution was stalled by amnesty laws passed by Ceauşescu in 1988 and by another law issued in January 1990 that granted amnesty and pardon for those crimes. As a result, the Communist Party leaders and the army and security officers responsible for those deaths and injuries went unpunished. It was only after 1996, when the anti-communist opposition Democratic Convention came to power, that a turning point in the trials of the revolution occurred and for the first time a state institution, the Ministry of Defense, was held responsible and required to pay compensation to civilians.[19] Ultimately, because of procedural delays and political interference by the Communist Party successors that returned to power in 2000, only two top military commanders were held accountable for their role in the revolution.

Officials involved in other crimes committed under the communist regime escaped prosecution because after 1989 crimes against humanity fell under the statute of limitations established by the communist Penal Code in 1969. Thus, two legal proceedings initiated by the Association of Former Political Prisoners (AFDPR) against Alexandru Draghici (Minister of Interior in the 1950s) and his deputy Alexandru Nicolschi failed. In 2006 the Institute for the Investigation of Crimes of Communism for the first time initiated five judicial proceedings for crimes committed by Securitate and party officials. The Institute claimed that the statute of limitations was inadequate as understood in international treaties and human rights legislation precedents. None of the five proceedings resulted in legal redress. As of this writing the institute, renamed in 2009 as the Institute for the Investigation of Crimes of Communism and the Memory of the Romanian Exile, has launched another investigation against thirty-five people suspected of crimes committed during communism.[20]

In regard to compensatory measures, the main beneficiaries have been the victims of the revolution, those who participated, were injured, or lost their lives (in which case their families were compensated). These measures served both the short-term and long-term interests of the newly reconstructed elites with roots in the old regime. The immediate advantage they sought was to prevent a genuine investigation of the December 1989 casualties and of the responsibility for them of former party officials and of army and security officers represented in the new government. Long-term, the manipulation of compensation for participants in the 1989 revolution became a cover-up for shady deals by the new oligarchy. In 1990, the Salvation Front was quick to pass legislation that established and legitimized the category of heroes-martyrs of the revolution.[21] Very generous financial and social compensations were awarded to the heroes-martyrs and their relatives by the State Secretariat for the Problems of December 1989 Revolutionaries, a state agency set up in 1995 to establish the needs of the revolutionaries and to commemorate the December 1989 events. However, two senior officials, Bebe Ivanovici and Emilian Cutean, appointed by the Social Democratic Party (PSD) (heir to the Salvation Front) were soon indicted for alleged corruption and misuse of funds. After 2000, when Iliescu returned to the presidency and the former communists to government, the 1990 law was amended and the category of revolutionaries numerically enlarged. Opportunities for further abuses subsequently followed. Immediately after the revolution the certificate designating revolutionary status for given individuals entitled to accompanying benefits was awarded to 3,000 individuals. By 2001 there were over 21,000 full-fledged certified revolutionaries.[22]

The legal measures aimed at compensating the many (and some of them long-standing) victims of communism were far less generous and inconsistently applied. They excluded those who lost their Romanian citizenship. Emergency Decree 119 of 1990 aimed at providing a social safety net in the form of access to subsidized public transportation and medical care, but the government was subsequently unable to honor this pledge. While physically wounded participants in the revolution received minimal pensions of between 2,250 and 4,500 Lei in 1990, those persecuted before 1989 were given a monthly allowance of only 200 lei. Adding to this pension the period of political persecution as years spent in the workforce failed to correct this unfair discrepancy. Moreover, it was only in 2009, that is, twenty years after the revolution, that criminal records were erased when the Law on Politically Motivated Court Sentences and Their Related Administrative Measures from March 6, 1945, to December 22, 1989 (Law 221/2009) was passed. However, one year later the Supreme Court declared as unconstitutional the part of the law that provided material compensation, and as such ultimately Law 221 failed its potential beneficiaries. Instead of restoring their dignity, the law subjected them to further humiliations.[23] The AFDPR is still trying to work out a legal settlement with the legislature.

In the case of Holocaust victims, the legislation of the 1990s continued the communist-era pattern of only indirectly acknowledging the victimization of the Jews. Decree 118 of 1990 assimilated them into the broad category of World War II victims,[24] mostly because the 1990s were characterized by a virulently nationalist-xenophobic ideology, Holocaust denial, and an Antonescu cult of personality. The Greater Romania Party voiced these extremist views, but former communists and some elements of the newly re-merged historical parties often used ethnic nationalism as a propaganda tool. At the same time, the public discourse emphasizing the horrors of Ceauşescu's era shaped a public view of national suffering that downplayed or ignored the victimization of ethnic and religious minorities. The victims of the Holocaust were finally individualized in 2000 when Law 189 clearly specified the categories of persons executed for ethnic reasons by the two fascist regimes that governed between September 1940 and March 1945. This move was the result of external pressures exerted by the West in the context of the country's accession into the North Atlantic Treaty Organization (NATO). Quite relevant to this clash between competing pasts, which defined and situated the victims of different repressions in different ways, was the opposition expressed by representatives of the Jewish community to including former Iron Guard members among the beneficiaries of Law 221/2009.

TRUTH-TELLING MECHANISMS

If criminal prosecutions and restorative justice measures were initiated during the first decade of post-communist transition, truth-telling transitional justice mechanisms were more vigorously pursued only after 2003. A combination of external and internal factors facilitated these developments. Romania's accession into NATO in 2004 was followed that same year by elections won by President Traian Băsescu and his center-right Truth and Justice Alliance. Their electoral campaign was based on a strong anti-corruption commitment and the regeneration of the post-1989 political elites without ties to the old regime. Moreover, unlike his predecessors, Băsescu (a former navy captain turned astute politician with populist instincts) did not reject his old ties to the communist regime. During a tumultuous presidency characterized by a difficult cohabitation between two coalition partners (the Liberals and the Democratic Party, a splinter of the Salvation Front to which Băsescu belonged), Romania joined the European Union in 2007.

The establishment of the International Commission for Studying the Holocaust in Romania and of the Presidential Commission for the Analysis of Communist Dictatorship in Romania occurred within this new political context. Both commissions were set up to mark a symbolic break with both anti-democratic ideologies (fascism and communism) and the crimes of their regimes. The Holocaust Commission, known as the Wiesel Commission for its president Elie Wiesel (a Holocaust survivor and Nobel peace prize winner), was founded in 2003 by President Iliescu in response to growing international concerns regarding the ambivalence of the PSD government officials toward the Holocaust and their open promotion of the Antonescu cult. The Commission's final report was released in November 2004 (months after Romania's admission into NATO). The Tismăneanu Commission, named for its president Vladimir Tismăneanu, a recognized scholar of communist and post-communist studies, was created in 2006 following the appeal of civil society groups and other activists keen to condemn the communist regime. Băsescu's endorsement in parliament of the Tismăneanu Commission's report in December 2006 was timed to precede Romania's accession into the EU in January 2007 and to mark a new beginning toward genuine democracy. The two commissions' broad mandates defined their historical nature. The Wiesel Commission's main objective was to correct misconceptions and denials about the role of the Romanian state in the persecution of the Jews that were often expressed in public opinion and by some academics. The Tismăneanu Commission attempted to demonstrate the illegality, illegitimacy, and criminality of the communist regime. Both produced lengthy reports that analyzed the historical contexts leading to the installation of the anti-democratic regimes, and stressed their criminal nature by examining their repression apparatus. Each documented the victimization of targeted groups and individuals, naming perpetrators, and identifying various forms of collaborationism and resistance. Each report made legal and non-legal recommendations for the repudiation and condemnation of both regimes.[25]

The limited time within which the Tismăneanu Commission had to finalize its report (six months compared to a year for the Wiesel Commission) resulted in chapters uneven in terms of length and academic rigor on different aspects and stages of the communist regime. The victims' input in the writing of the two reports also differed. The AFDPR authored parts of the Tismăneanu Commission's report and insisted on using "genocide" to characterize the crimes of communism. The use of this concept was criticized as improper and was seen as an obstacle to later criminal prosecutions. In contrast, the contribution of victims and survivors of the Holocaust was limited to providing primary material for the Wiesel Commission based on their individual experience.[26] Both reports triggered sharp public criticism. However, the attack on the Tismăneanu report was much more virulent, voiced in a raucously uncivil manner during the official parliamentary meeting that condemned the communist regime. This verbal violence was partly provoked by the fact that the report singled out two post-communist political leaders, Ion Iliescu and Corneliu Vadim Tudor, as part of the communist repression apparatus and requested a judicial investigation into allegations that the Salvation Front suppressed anti-communist demonstrations during the December 1989 revolution and the April 1990 elections. The Wiesel report was attacked by xenophobic elements that continued to deny the Holocaust. Despite the legal provisions incorporated in the Emergency Ordinance 31/2002 that declared the public denial of the Holocaust a punishable crime, there have never been any legal repercussions for such acts. The open letter sent to President Basescu by Ion Coja, leader of the nationalist Romanian Homeland Union, at a public meeting in November 2006 and titled "In Romania There Was No Holocaust" illustrates this point. Relatedly, there has never been any legal indictment for acts involving the use of fascist symbols in a public place. Public spaces of memory continue to be characterized by tensions and contradictions between the memory of fascism and communism. When some civic associations promoted the memorialization of the lives of former political prisoners and members of the armed resistance with Iron Guard ties, the Wiesel Institute and the Jewish community have expressed indignation and outrage. It is not uncommon that such public commemorations have become a source of such continuing political controversy.

The two reports have had some significant truth-telling impact. Following the Wiesel report, in 2005 the government established the Elie Wiesel Institute, which has actively pursued research and archival documentation on the Holocaust, launched its own journal, published academic books and memoirs, and engaged in educational programs involving the teaching of history and civic values. Steps in this direction were taken before the release of the Wiesel report. In anticipation of its entrance into NATO, Romania signed the Agreement of November 12, 2002, of Collaboration between the National Archives of Romania and the United States Memorial Holocaust Museum. The government also endorsed public admission of the Holocaust in 2004, when it recognized October 9 as the National Day to Commemorate the Holocaust in Romania. A popular place of pilgrimage in Bucharest is the Holocaust Memorial, opened in June 2009, which consists of five elements that symbolize the Holocaust (the Memorial, the Star of David, Via Dolorosa, the Gypsy Wheel, and the Column). As the Jewish community has substantially declined (numbering only 3,271 in 2011) its contribution to Romania's history and culture is now little known to the public. As such, current efforts by the Federation of Jewish Communities in Romania (FEDROM) and the government to support the restoration of the Jewish Sacred Heritage, consisting of 88 synagogues, 821 cemeteries, and other ritual buildings, are salutary.[27] The Wiesel report also resulted in positive changes in the content of history textbooks. In 1998, the Ministry of Education established the Holocaust as an obligatory subject in the history curriculum, but in the absence of a strong official position a majority of history textbooks denied or minimized the repression of the Jewish population during World War II. Since 2004, the historical facts have been presented in a much more objective light. A standard textbook is also used for the teaching of an optional course on the Holocaust.[28]

The truth-telling effects of the Tismăneanu Commission seem promising as well. In April 2007 a follow-up commission, the Advisory Presidential Commission for the Analysis of Communist Dictatorship, was created to advise the president on the implementation of the report's recommendations. By granting its members unrestricted access to the archives, the Tismăneanu Commission established an important precedent. As a fortuitous result, on December 29, 2006, all Securitate files (except some 100,000 files touching on national security) were transferred from the Romanian Information Service to the National Council for the Study of Securitate Archives (CNSAS). This measure came after many years of delays and direct interference by elements of the communist regime that had inhibited the efforts of the former AFDPR President Ticu Dumitrescu to open communist secret police files to ordinary citizens and historians. Law 187 (known as the Ticu Law) represented a significantly altered version of what its original author had intended. It perpetuated the myth of a patriotic Securitate and continued to link the management of the files to the interests of various parties represented in the government. The National Archives also became more transparent in 2007 with the appointment of new management and a substantially enlarged collection of Communist Party documents. Previously, Law 16/1996 had limited access to documents more than thirty years old and placed them under the jurisdiction of the Ministry of Interior.

The work of the Advisory Commission was undermined by the lack of an initial consensus among political actors over the condemnation of the communist regime. In this context, after the Liberals left the governing coalition in 2008, the Social Democrats were co-opted by the Democrats into the government and then entrusted with the Minister of Interior portfolio. Access to the Securitate and Communist Party archives again came under threat. The mandate of CNSAS was sharply restricted when the Supreme Court ruled in January 2008 that CNSAS was unconstitutional. According to Emergency Ordinance 24/2008, the Council's role became purely administrative, but between 2008 and 2012 the Council initiated 797 judicial proceedings. These legal actions involved former Securitate and police officers accused of human rights violations, as well as cases of alleged collaboration with the Securitate of office holders, candidates in local and national elections, and participants in the 1989 revolution. Despite the CNSAS's reduced mandate, the increased availability of documents allowed the general public and some academics to learn considerably more about the communist past. Some of CNSAS's most recent activities include: national annual conferences on communist history; thematic exhibitions focused on a variety of subjects ranging from daily life under communism to repression and resistance; the creation of the Oral History Center in 2010; and the digitization of files concerning the functioning of the Ministry of Interior before 1989 and the nature of the work colonies in the gulag. Similar educational initiatives have been pursued by the National Archives. If the memorialization activities undertaken in the 1990s by civil society groups were principally focused on the Stalinist repression, today the period of late communism and issues of collaborationism and acquiescence are debated as well.

Equally important truth-telling work has been pursued by the Institute for the Investigation of Communist Crimes (IICCR), established in 2006 by the prime minister to document the crimes of communism, develop educational activities, and express public condemnation of the regime. By utilizing exhumation and forensic investigation, the Institute attempted to combine the quest for truth with the goal of bringing healing and closure to victims of communist repression and to their families. In 2007, it launched a campaign to identify the remains and exhume the bodies of former members of the anticommunist armed resistance movement who were summarily executed by Securitate between 1948 and 1952. This campaign allowed the descendants to give victims a Christian burial, a deeply important ritual for small rural communities. The exhumations also divided local communities between descendants of those who had sided with the partisans and those who collaborated with the Securitate. These conflicts are another powerful illustration of how memory sites (*lieux de memoire*) can become contested places of struggle for individual and group identity and recognition. Today, the Institute seeks to transform the former communist-era Râmnicu Sărat prison into a memorial.

Before the release of the Tismăneanu report, which was followed by more coordinated efforts at memorialization by official bodies, the task of preserving the memory of communist repression was undertaken by civic associations, activists, and former political prisoners. The most notable initiative was represented by the project launched by former dissident and poet Ana Blandiana and novelist Romulus Rusan that resulted in the creation of the Sighet Memorial as a national site in 1997. The Memorial, situated in a former Stalinist jail, was subsequently taken under the patronage of the European Union. The Memorial has been active in gathering documents and testimonies of repression. In parallel, a vast number of memoirs and autobiographical accounts published by former political prisoners have made the crimes of the gulag fully known to the public.[29]

This hesitant manner of addressing communist crimes was also present in history textbooks during the first decade of post-communism. Professional historians trained in the nationalist school dominant since the 1970s have continued to influence the teaching of national history (including the communist-nationalist period) in ideological terms of extreme patriotism. During the 1990s the topic of communism was barely incorporated in school curricula. When in 2010 at the recommendation of the European Union Council alternative history textbooks were introduced, Social Democrat legislators and some historians engaged in an angry attack on the new textbooks during a parliamentary session, condemning the texts as unpatriotic.[30] It was not until 2008 that this nationalist approach was officially challenged. That year the Ministry of Education endorsed the textbook edited by the Institute for the Investigation of Communist Crimes for teaching an optional course on communism in high schools. This textbook departs from the traditional chronological method and incorporates a variety of sources that allow students to critically assess the history of communism.[31]

While state-led actions to commemorate the victims of communism and of the Holocaust were initiated more than a decade after the overthrow of the communist regime, the immediate official response after December 1989 in respect to the politics of memory was geared toward legitimizing the new democratic regime as the heir to the revolution. Indeed, the myth of the whole country as a participant in the overthrow of the old regime was put forward at the time. The first transitional justice measures pursued by the Salvation Front were to erase communist symbols and erect new ones that celebrated the victors and heroes of the revolution. Even cities where no confrontations occurred in December 1989 found they had a Revolution Square, and many towns were celebrated as "martyr-towns." Interestingly, a growing number of public monuments and memorials installed in cemeteries present standardized images or symbols of the Orthodox trinity or the inscription "martyr-hero of the revolution" in place of specific personal episodes showing the individuals' involvement in the revolution.[32] One memorial that stands out consists of the twelve statues erected by the December 21, 1989, Association to represent the Memorial of the Timişoara Revolution. Each statue symbolizes some local events. By portraying death, these monuments emphasize martyrdom.[33] Other public memorials in the cities of Bucharest, Sibiu, and Cluj briefly acknowledge that the dead were "shot during the revolution" or "fell in December 1989" to indicate that some of the dead were simple casualties not elevated to heroic status. As Ruxandra Cesereanu points out, the revolution is fragmentarily represented in the collective imagination as a genuine revolution, a coup d'état, or a combination of both.[34]

To justify their particular agendas, political actors have manipulated their account of the revolution. For example, the anti-communist opposition and some elements of the communist regime embraced a revisionist theory that questions the genuine character of the revolt. While by doing so the former questioned the role of the Salvation Front as a true anticommunist formation, the latter claimed that the revisionist view was an argument against the involvement of the Securitate in quashing the revolution and perpetrating the crimes associated with it. Some former Securitate officers insisted that the real terrorists who blackmailed the Securitate and murdered peaceful protesters were part of the Army Information Directorate, a highly secretive branch.[35]

The significance of the December 1989 revolution and its starting point has remained a subject of post-communist political disputes. Iliescu and other former leaders and supporters of the Salvation Front have argued that the revolution was a genuine national and anti-communist popular uprising. For them, the founding document of the revolution is the official communiqué issued by the Salvation Front on December 24, 1989.[36] It is in these terms that the Institute of the Romanian Revolution, created in 2004 under President Iliescu's patronage, interprets December 1989. The opposite viewpoint is embraced by the anti-communist forces who have opposed the Salvation Front and its successor, the Social Democrat Party, during the past 25 years. These actors argue that former *nomenklatura* and Securitate members attempted to hijack the anti-communist course of the revolution. In their view, the true founding document was the Timişoara Declaration launched on March 12, 1990, and as such the real beginning of the revolution was marked by the anti-communist demonstration that took place in the University Square in Bucharest in spring 1990.[37] The Timişoara Declaration, a thirteen-point document endorsed by several anti-communist opposition groups and parties, articulated for the first time the need to enact lustration as a means to close the books on the past.

Since 1989, the Timişoara Society has become an important force in revealing the truth about the revolution. In 1998, the National Center for

Documentation, Research, and Public Information about the December 1989 revolution was set up by the Society under the leadership of Traian Orban, who had been wounded in the revolution. It features a museum representing the communist period and the revolution and it collects testimonials of the uprising in Timişoara. In 1998, the Society began to organize a pilgrimage of the relatives of those who died in the revolution at Popeşti-Leordeni, near Bucharest. This was the site where the bodies of the first forty-two people killed in Timişoara were secretly cremated by the communist authorities and their ashes thrown into a canal.[38]

After 1990, the successive Romanian governments have showed little interest in clarifying certain obscure aspects of the revolution, especially the role of the army and the Securitate in the repression, the death of the head of the armed forces General Vasile Milea in December 1989 (who allegedly committed suicide), the role played by the Salvation Front and its leaders, and the reasons for the heavy casualties registered after the execution of Nicolae and Elena Ceauşescus. Two Senate commissions were established to clarify these and other aspects of the revolution. Set up during the 1990–1992 legislative term, the first commission was headed by Salvation Front representative, actor, and director Sergiu Nicolaescu. The second commission, created during the 1992–1996 legislative term, was chaired by the Christian Democrat leader Valentin Gabrielescu. Both commissions failed to produce valid substantiated reports and reach an acceptable consensus. Representatives of the revolutionaries initiated legal action as early as 1992 (all such cases being grouped under the so-called Revolution File). However, until 2004 no case was prosecuted because the state legal authorities decided to stall judicial investigation. In 2008, General Dan Voinea was dismissed as chief military prosecutor for failing to finalize the cases related to the revolution. The statute of limitations for the crimes of the revolution lapsed in 2004, but the activism of civil society groups and the radical actions undertaken by the 21 December Association and its head Teodor Marieş prevented the cases from being sealed and the truth from being buried. After many interventions at the European Court of Human Rights, two hunger strikes involving Marieş, and many delays by the Romanian authorities, in 2011 the legal files pertaining to the crimes of the revolution were offered to the 21 December Association for safekeeping.[39]

The heirs to the Salvation Front and their allies stalled the passage of lustration laws. They have been successful in preventing any banning of former communist decision-makers and secret agents from public office and in supporting the reproduction of communist political elites in the post-communist period. The Timisoara Declaration has thus produced no consequences. After the 2004 elections lustration came back to the forefront of public debate, but the two attempts at initiating mild lustration bills in 2006 and 2010 were deemed unconstitutional by the Supreme Court. Ultimately, the absence of lustration has undermined reconciliation and the establishment of some degree of trust. As Lavinia Stan showed, it has "allowed the executive to engage in wild purges and prompted political parties and civil society groups to adopt unofficial vetting programs as alternative methods . . . based on untransparent criteria."[40] This, if nothing else, has further undermined the rule of law and the legitimacy of democratic institutions.

CONCLUSION

In the Romanian experience, when confronted with multiple pasts and an abrupt exit from dictatorship, the government's immediate responses to issues of accountability and guilt have tended to be influenced by two main factors. First, Romania's violent and sudden exit from authoritarian rule allowed the new rulers to scapegoat their political enemies. Second, the political context that immediately followed the regime change shaped the new national narrative. When the provisional revolutionary body assumed the country's leadership the need to make an immediate and irrevocable symbolic break with the communist past was imperative. Given the general public dissatisfaction with the old system and the violent repression that accompanied the December 1989 revolution, it was quite easy for the Salvation Front to narrowly limit responsibility for repression to the Ceauşescu family and a few top officials. This permitted the communist elites to deny their role in the repression both before and after 1989 and to claim legitimacy as the true heirs of the revolution. In addition, by promoting the idea of collective suffering under communism at the hands of a very few, the Salvation Front managed to avoid engaging in an uncomfortable discussion about collaborationism, passivity, and acquiescence. Instead, through lavish commemorations and by indiscriminately granting generous compensatory measures, the Front elevated the whole country to a heroic status as the progenitor of the December 1989 revolution. The idea that repression and suffering under communism were all-encompassing and extended to the whole country became deeply rooted in the collective imagination. Thus, any other claims of victimization and persecution targeting more specific segments of the population defined along religious, ethnic, or political lines were perceived as divisive and undermining national unity.

During the first twenty-five years of post-communist transition, this rhetoric indirectly allowed for the marginalization of victims of both the Holocaust and of the Stalinist gulag.

The initial exclusion of ethnic and religious minorities from transitional justice measures has inhibited the development of a civic and pluralist liberal democracy. At the same time, the parsimonious symbolic and material compensations awarded to former political prisoners have contributed to the persistence of a polarized political landscape divided between former communists and pro-democracy anti-communists. As the post-1989 political elites were largely recruited from unreformed elements of the communist regime, these elites felt a pressing need to re-construct their political legitimacy. This was accomplished with the myth of a cohesive nation subjected to a foreign and alien repression by the domination of a Soviet-style system. A more genuine attempt at a clear break with the fascist and communist pasts has occurred only since the mid-2000s mostly at the prompting of foreign actors in the context of Romania's NATO and European Union integration. At the same time, as this chapter shows, the impact of the Wiesel and Tismăneanu commissions has been rather limited. The legal mechanisms of criminalizing Holocaust denial continue to remain ineffective. Restitution laws for former political prisoners or legal proceedings brought against officials of the communist regime have been stalled by a sluggish and incompletely reformed judicial system. Perhaps these failures demonstrate that when initial memory policies favor one traumatic event over another, subsequent attempts at addressing multiple pasts simultaneously may be condemned to have only limited results. In the long term, such unresolved questions may resurface in old animosities and tensions, and generate renewing social and political divisions in the country.

In light of this analysis, when considering multiple pasts future academic studies should take into account the interaction between four distinctive but interrelated factors. First, the exit mode from the dictatorship will set up the terms of political debate between opposing actors. When the exit is abrupt, political competition can become extremely confrontational and intolerant. Second, the degree of continuity and/or change of political elites will impact the nature of official responses toward past abuses. Third, the creation of a hegemonic nationalist rhetoric will result in compensatory measures favoring ethnic or political majorities, whereas a more pluralistic and liberal rhetoric seems a preferable alternative, as it will likely lead to more inclusive restitution policies. Finally, the timing of external factors during the democratic transition is crucial for the effectiveness of transitional justice, as late legal responses to past violations may have only limited results.

NOTES

1. James Mark, *The Unfinished Revolution* (New Haven: Yale University Press, 2010), and Ruxandra Cesereanu, "The Final Report on the Holocaust and the Final Report on the Communist Dictatorship in Romania," *East European Politics and Societies*, 22, no. 2 (2008): 240–281.
2. Vlad Georgescu, *The Romanians: A History* (Ohio: Ohio State University Press, 1991), 189.
3. Lya Benyamin, "Politica antievreiască a regimului Antonescu 1940–1944," *Holocaust Studii şi Cercetări* 1 (2011): 1–9.
4. Radu Ioanid, *The Holocaust in Romania: the Destruction of Jews and Gypsies under the Antonescu Regime, 1940–1944* (Chicago: Ivan R. Dee, 2000).
5. Andrei Muraru, *Dicţionarul Penitenciarelor in România Comunista (1945–1967)* (Iaşi: Polirom, 2008).
6. Marius Oprea, *Banalitatea răului. O istore a Securitaţii în documente* (Iaşi: Polirom, 2002).
7. Ion Bălan, *Regimul Concentraţionar din România: 1945–1964* (Bucharest: Civic Academy Foundation, 2000).
8. Mircea Stănescu, *Reeducarea in România Comunistă (1945–1952). Aiud, Suceava, Piteşti, Braşov* (Iaşi: Polirom, 2010).
9. Romulus Rusan, *Chronology and Geography of Communist Repression in Romania* (Bucharest: Civic Academy Foundation, 2007).
10. Dobrincu, Dorin, and Constantin Iordachi, eds., *Ţărănimea şi puterea. Procesul de Colectivizare a agriculturii în România (1949–1962)* (Bucharest: Polirom, 2005).
11. Dennis Deletant, *Ceauşescu and the Securitate: Coercion and Dissent in Romania, 1965–1989* (Armonk, NY: M.E. Sharpe, 1995).
12. Oprea, *Banalitatea răului*, 48.
13. Mihai Albu, *Informatorul: studiu asupra colaborării cu Securitatea* (Iaşi: Polirom, 2008).
14. Deletant, *Ceauşescu and the Securitate.*
15. Stelian Tănase, *Acasă se vorbeşte in şoaptă. Dosar si jurnal din anii tirzii ai dictarurii* (Bucharest: Compania, 2002).
16. Lavinia Stan, *Transitional Justice in Post-Communist Romania: The Politics of Memory* (New York: Cambridge University Press, 2013), 69.
17. Peter Siani-Davis, *The Romanian Revolution of December 1989* (Ithaca, NY: Cornell University Press, 2006).
18. Stan, *Transitional Justice in Post-Communist Romania*, 30.
19. Raluca Grosescu and Raluca Ursachi, *Justiţia penală de tranziţie. De la Nuremberg la Postcomunimul românesc* (Bucharest: Institutul de Investigare a Crimelor Comunismului din România, 2009), 180.
20. "IICCMER is investigating 35 people under suspicion of having committed war crimes during the communist regime," *Jurnalul National*, April 11, 2013, available at: http://jurnalul.ro/stiri/observator/iiccmer-investigheaza-35-de-persoane-suspectate-ca-au-comis-crime-in-timpul-regimului-comunist-641060.html (accessed February 19, 2013).
21. "Decretul 40 din 9 ianuarie 1990 privind comemorarea eroilor revoluţiei," *Monitorul Oficial*, January 6, 1990.

22. Rodica Palade, "Profitorii Revoluţiei," 22 (August 1, 2011).
23. Monica Ciobanu, "Recent Restorative Justice Measures in Romania (2006–2010)," *Problems of Post-Communism* 60, no. 5 (2013): 45–57.
24. Alexandru Florian, "The Treatment of the Jews in Romanian Legislation," *Holocaust: Studii şi Cercetări*, 1 (2011), 45.
25. Vladimir Tismaneanu, Dorin Dobrincu and Cristian Vasile, eds., *Raport Final: Comisia Prezidenţială pentru Analiza Dictaturii Comuniste din România* (Bucharest: Humanitas, 2007), and Friling Tuvia, Radu Ioanid, and Mihail E. Ionescu, eds., *Raport Final: Comisia Internaţională pentru Studierea Holocaustului în România* (Bucharest: Polirom, 2005).
26. Personal communication with Adrian Cioflâncă in Bucharest on March 23, 2013
27. Lucia Apostol and Rudy Marcovici, "The Romanian Heritage: Rehabilitation, Restoration and Options for Preservation," *Studia Hebraica* IX-X (2011): 199–211.
28. Felicia Waldman, "Holocaustul în manualele şcolare postcomuniste din România," in *Holocaustul la periferie*, eds. Wolfgang Benz and Brigitte Mihok (Bucharest: Cartier, 2010), 320–335.
29. The Sighet Memorial website, available at: http://www.sighet.memorial.ro (accessed October 20, 2013).
30. Irina Culic, "Re-writing the History of Romania after the Fall of Communism," *History Compass* 1, no. 3 (2005): 1–21.
31. Dorin Dobrincu, Mihai Stamatescu, Raluca Grosescu, Liviu Pleşa, Sorin Andresscu, and Andrei Muraru, *O istorie a comunismului din România. Manual pentru liceu* (Bucharest: Polirom, 2008).
32. Mihaela Grancea, "Retorica morţii eroice în epitaful revoluţionarilor din decembrie'89," in *Revoluţia Română din Decembrie 1989: Istorie şi Memorie*, ed. Bogdan Murgescu (Iaşi: Polirom, 2007), 47–50.
33. Maria Ştoicuţa and Flavia Biianu, *Monumente memoriale ale Revoluţiei din Timişoara. Ghidul oraşului*, (Timişoara: Artpress, 2009).
34. Ruxandra Cesereanu, *Decembrie '89. Deconstrucţia unei revoluţii* (Iaşi: Polirom, 2004).
35. Richard Andrew Hall, "The Uses of Absurdity: The Staged War Theory and the Romanian Revolution of December 1989," *East European Politics and Societies* 13, no. 3 (1999): 501–542.
36. Ion Iliescu, *După 20 de ani: 1989 an de cotitură în istoria naţională şi în viaţa internaţională* (Bucharest: Semne, 2004), 218–223.
37. Cristina Tudor and Cornel Seracin, "Proclamaţia de la Timişoara: document al Revoluţiei Române din decembrie 1989," *Memorial 1989* 1, no. 6 (2010): 24–37.
38. Simona Mociolca, "Pelerinaj la Bucureşti, Popeşi-Leordeni şi Slatina-Olt pentru comemorarea victimelor Revoluţiei," *Memorial 1989* 1, no. 6 (2010): 191–194.
39. Teodor Marieş, "Despre dosarele revoluţiei," in *Şcoala Memoriei 2011*, ed. Călin Uba (Bucharest: Civic Academy Foundation, 2012), 390–412.
40. Stan, *Transitional Justice in Post-Communist Romania*, 110.

8

Beyond the National: Pathways of Diffusion*

Helga A. Welsh

Ideally, in the aftermath of dictatorial rule, victims' concerns are addressed and their oppressors punished, the truth about the structures and incidence of human rights violations is unearthed, and bridges are built between opposing camps to secure a democratic future. However, we have no expedient prescriptions for the best combination of preferred measures or the best way to implement them or the best way to translate them across locales. For some, coming to terms with the past is necessarily conditioned by a specific history, politics, and society. What fits one country may not fit another.[1]

In practice, the spread of transitional justice norms and processes exerts external influence on policies.[2] Brigitte Weiffen speaks of a "global phase" and divides international impact into two main categories: transnational networks, in particular non-governmental organizations ("bottom-up variant") and direct intervention ("top-down variant").[3] More specific international and transnational actors also agitate for accountability measures.[4] Ellen Lutz and Kathryn Sikkink coined the term "justice cascade" to describe the process by which one transnational advocacy network – activist lawyers – contributed to the proliferation of human rights trials in Latin America.[5] Independent of the particular form of influence, international transitional justice advocacy has increased and become more professionalized.[6]

When the countries in Central and Eastern Europe, defined here as those nominally sovereign during communist rule and now members of the European Union (EU) and NATO,[7] exited communism in 1989–1990, dealing with the abuses of the previous regime was an urgent and immediate task. Discourses were heated, policies contested, and the timing, methods, and scope of responses differed considerably, exposing a continuum of action from leaders to laggards. Surprisingly, then, in comparison to other parts of the world, external influence on transitional justice policies here has received scant attention. Once the EU became a major actor, John Gledhill highlighted the largely unintended consequences of regional integration on "historical reckoning" but concluded that the influence was "partial and variable."[8] A second strand of literature analyzed how international courts set standards for transitional justice policies.[9]

Twenty-five years after the newly established democratic governments first openly confronted the human rights legacies of communist regimes, I revisit the question,[10] asking to what extent the salience and form of international organizations and transnational interactions have evolved and to what effect. This approach is warranted by the view of Europe as an ideal laboratory for diffusion studies due to the Europeanization of policies and Central and Eastern Europe as an ideal demonstration of the significance of transnational actors during the transition years.[11] I also want to examine the imputation that geographic diffusion effects reinforce regional patterns – what would drive such convergence?[12]

I use the term *diffusion* to encompass indirect, exogenous effects on framing debates, setting standards, and institutionalizing transnational networks. In its most basic form, it refers to the local effects of policies and practices that originated in other countries or with international organizations. It privileges processes over outcomes, which can vary greatly; scholars emphasize the conditions that favor it, the mechanism used, the actors that promote it, and its function.[13] Diffusion mechanisms can be used to advance certain policies, mobilize support, gain legitimacy, and validate often divergent policy approaches. I differentiate between some form of learning as part of cross-national demonstration effects, norm promotion, passive leverage, and spillover. These categories serve as an analytical road map; they may be distinct in theory, but in practice, their borders are fluid.

I begin with a synopsis of transitional justice in Central and Eastern Europe, highlighting convergence amid differentiation. The main section describes relevant diffusion mechanisms, their effects on receiving countries, and the agents involved (see Figure 8.1). I pay special attention to the variety of expressions of Europeanization processes.[14] The discussion traces the evolution of transmission channels from mostly bilateral contacts to interactions with international organizations and the establishment of structured networking. The conclusion summarizes how diffusion played out in Central and Eastern Europe, the barriers it encountered, and suggestions for future research.

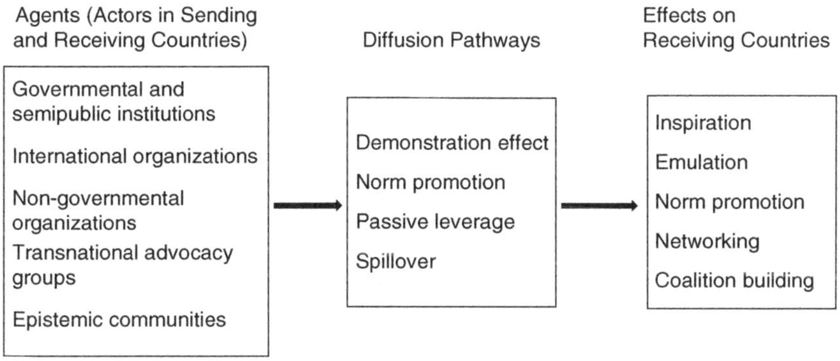

FIGURE 8.1: Agents, Diffusion Pathways, and Effects

TRANSITIONAL JUSTICE IN CENTRAL AND EASTERN EUROPE: AN OVERVIEW

Choosing a starting point for any study of regional diffusion processes at once raises important methodological questions: How to establish a certain degree of commonality among a set of countries without downplaying or misrepresenting their policy diversity? Can commonality be explained by path-dependent domestic processes or international trajectories? When both are involved, what is their individual weight? The few extant cross-national, longitudinal studies illustrate the problems of delineating causality. Tricia D. Olsen, Leigh A. Payne, and Andrew G. Reiter, covering the period from 1970 to 2007, suggest regional patterns: "Trials, lustration policies, and reparations occur most often in Europe. Non-European countries more frequently adopt truth commissions and amnesties than do their European counterparts, with a particularly high number of amnesties granted in Latin America."[15] Another study by the same authors, examining court trials from 1970 to 2004, challenges the assumption of regional contagion effects per se; advocacy networks and membership in international organizations and/or international nongovernmental organizations are crucial.[16]

Although transitional justice, under different names, has a long tradition,[17] the post-communist challenges were unique with few precedents to draw from. Rights abuses were convoluted; in targeting large groups, they took the form of expropriation and surveillance, and subjected alleged and real political dissenters to a wide range of measures, including imprisonment. The most brutal forms of terror and repression were exercised in the late 1940s and the 1950s. The "softer" forms that gradually replaced them still relied on intimidation and harassment and tolerated no opposition.

In reaction, a distinct, shared preoccupation with the legacy of state security agents and access to their files became the prime mode of revelation. In contrast to lustration procedures, court trials of deposed communist officials were mostly symbolic; they were old and ill, and their sentences were lenient. Restorative measures were widely seen as the material and immaterial redress that victims were owed, but although restitution of confiscated private property was deemed central to economic justice, it was politically charged. Excluding Romania, where property restitution remains unresolved,[18] the other countries acted relatively swiftly but policies differed in who was entitled, what time frame was applied, and what form restitution (in-kind restitution versus material compensation) would take. Each of these decisions raised questions about exclusion and potential discrimination. While state-sponsored truth commissions to achieve historical reckoning have spread around the world, regionally, their role and impact have been muted and restricted to Germany and Romania.[19] Memorialization strategies abounded everywhere, ranging from renaming a street to the construction of museums.

Some path development was expected, and similarities in approach, but not scope and timing, can be explained by common contexts – the countries' geographic and systemic proximity and the roughly forty-year span of communist rule. Nonetheless, scholars have been preoccupied with the degree of variation in these countries' transitional justice policies. (East) Germany and the Czech Republic were forerunners with prompt, extensive policies. After slow starts, Poland and Slovakia became more engaged but not Bulgaria and Romania. Hungary has occupied a special position, as its policy repertoire mirrored those of other countries, but was particularly constrained by constitutional jurisdiction.[20]

Broadly speaking, explanations for these variations focus on legacy and present politics, but the proper mix remains disputed.[21] Recurring variables are: (1) the different degrees of legitimacy of the communist regimes; (2) distinctive paths away from communism toward democracy that produced variations in accommodation with and influence of the previous communist elites; and (3) strategic elite calculations.[22] Transitional justice is generally portrayed as a struggle among political elites, neglecting not only civil society groups and the media but also external factors that played important roles in the discourse and kept it alive, particularly where legislation and/or implementation were delayed or weak.[23]

The following sections explore divergent diffusion channels and outcomes across the region.

DEMONSTRATION EFFECTS AND CROSS-NATIONAL COMMUNICATION

Czechoslovakia and Germany were the first to enact lustration, the aspect of transitional justice most distinct to Central and Eastern Europe and the most disputed.[24] Germany pioneered public access to state security files, and both countries have been vigilant in enacting transitional justice policies. Consequently, their acts have been frequent reference points in the neighboring countries' discourse, although best practices were also drawn from other sources. For example, in the lustration debates at the beginning of the 1990s, Spain's and Portugal's "drawing a thick line" and advocating "forgive and forget" countered the Czech and German emphasis on disclosure and potential employment bans.[25]

Lustration laws required screening public officials, a task most often handled by special committees. In all settings, it was soon intimately linked with public access to the files of the former secret police. Proponents advocated file access as an important step in the decommunization process and the main vehicle of "truth finding."[26] Naming secret service agents and collaborators was also perceived as an important corollary to the few criminal trials. Arguments against reliance on the files and public access to them have run the gamut: the files are incomplete and inaccurate; opening them will expose and undermine secret police methods, spark revenge and hatred, and violate laws to protect personal information and other laws.[27]

Despite these concerns, in summer 1990, the freely elected parliament of the German Democratic Republic (GDR) voted unanimously to open the files of the hated state security, commonly called the Stasi, and in August it passed by a wide majority a law securing Stasi files as one of its last acts. Following unification with West Germany in 1990, the Stasi Records Act passed in December 1991,[28] and public access started in 1992. A separate agency, the Federal Commissioner for the Records of the State Security Service of the former German Democratic Republic (BStU), was created to house the files, to organize the modalities of public access, and to conduct research on them. This institutional innovation proved too important to ignore, and by 2002, all countries in the region had opened special state security archives and made files accessible to the public.

Important country-specific differences remain. They include the number of files made public or destroyed in the aftermath of the communist collapse and privacy stipulations. The archives themselves differ in terms of organizational structure, staff, and public availability. Some include documents from World

War II. Several institutions copied the BStU in building substantial research departments, while others are solely archives. Public response to file access has also differed; applications remain highest in Germany. Explanations for this variation include the availability of files, bureaucratic obstacles to access, and the passage of time, which may have dampened interest.

Disparities notwithstanding, the spread of file access begs for an explanation. Domestic factors, such as shifting political coalitions and policy goals, may have pushed neglected demands for file access to the top of the agenda. Council of Europe Resolution 1096 (1996) recommended opening secret service files, but its impact was marginal at best. More likely is the power of the demonstration effects from neighboring countries. As in other areas of transitional justice, observers cited German file access as either a model or unsuitable for other countries in the region. Although skepticism about the practice, seen as "typically German," prevailed initially, the debate continued.[29] When the perceived negative side effects did not materialize, the German model became attractive: it helped to prevent the illegal release of files and subsequent media leaks that rocked politics everywhere.[30] As Georges Mink contends, "the model that won all countries' admiration was the one designed by the Germans of the former GDR," referring to the BStU, whose sheer existence spurred emulation, however delayed and controversial.[31]

In Poland, public file access was rejected at first because creating an archive would have delayed lustration, but the BStU example turned opinion. The Polish Institute of National Remembrance (IPN), founded in 1998, is hardly imaginable without the BStU.[32] IPN member Antoni Dudek explains: "The example of the BStU was very important for authors of the act on the IPN, but the IPN is not a copy." Among other novel features, it has a prosecution department, and the Polish lustration model is quite different from Germany's.[33]

In the Czech Republic, the idea of public file access was discussed from the beginning of lustration: "the fact that it was possible to do it in Germany was one of the arguments for the opening of the archives."[34] Slovak reporters used legislation in neighboring countries to support similar measures: "it was therefore 'high time' for the country to do the same."[35] In similar fashion, Archivist Lászlo Varga refers to the important role that the BStU played in debates about founding the Historical Archive in Hungary.[36] Paweł Machcewicz speaks of a "chain reaction with the most important countries, Germany and Poland, showing the way."[37]

In countries where public file access ran into strong resistance, the German approach was particularly attractive. The first head of the BStU, Joachim Gauck, writes that in Bulgaria and Romania, "the few who advocated dealing with the past praised our solution almost effusively," while others clearly disassociated themselves from it.[38] He visited Romania in 1992, 1994, and 1997. In 1992, he was invited by the Association of Former Political Prisoners (AFDPR), an important civil society actor with over 100,000 members; according to Petrescu and Petrescu, "[i]t was the first time . . . the problem of dealing with the files of the secret police was discussed in a professional manner."[39] As part of his 1997 visit, Gauck reported to the Romanian parliament. As early as 1993, Constantin Ticu Dumitrescu, Senator for the National Peasant Party and a founder of the AFDPR, proposed a bill that would allow citizens access to Securitate files, but he was criticized even by his own party. Gauck allegedly encouraged him: "Don't think in Germany it was easier."[40] Defeated several times, the 1999 "Ticu law" allowed limited access to the Securitate files; it was revised in 2006, but the Romanian Constitutional Court declared it unconstitutional by unanimous vote in 2008. To this day, file access is disputed.[41]

Initially, the post-communist countries were preoccupied with how they would tackle their past; information about neighboring practices was communicated mostly through the media. Often these accounts lacked detail about limitations and weaknesses of particular approaches but they were still expedient as they invited comparison with the situation at home. The practice of file access spread by example and soft means – information visits, conferences, and workshops. The BStU mattered, but emulation was reinforced by cross-cultural communication that raised awareness and inspired others.

Inquiries from abroad arrived at the BStU; its employees were invited to visit, and Gauck traveled widely, often supported by funds from German political foundations and government ministries. How the agency should respond to these requests was a matter of debate. Promoting the German example was rejected, but disseminating ideas and information about the agency's work, which was intended to dispel objections to creating similar agencies in other settings and to support domestic stakeholders in the German model, was deemed acceptable. BStU researchers could accept invitations to engage in such activities, while they could not travel on official business.[42]

At times, German political foundations acted as brokers between sending and receiving countries. All major German political parties have such foundations that provide "assistance for democratization and political cooperation" at home and abroad; after the fall of communism, they quickly established themselves in Central and Eastern Europe.[43] These foundations pursued political education on transitional justice by establishing contacts among politicians, civil society groups, and media representatives in the host countries, on the one hand, and the BStU and other German transitional justice agencies, on the other. They mediated the diffusion of ideas by arranging study trips and political consultations, and acted as "norm entrepreneurs" or "agents of projection" when they organized national and international seminars and conferences.[44] For example, just before the parliamentary debates in 1999, Romanian members of parliament, journalists, and historians visited the BStU, and the media reported on its activities, highlighting the substantial differences between the German and Romanian experiences in dealing with the communist state security services.[45] Ekaterina Boncheva, board member of the Committee for Access and Disclosure of Documents and Announcing Affiliation of Bulgarian Citizens to the State Security and the Intelligence Services of the Bulgarian National Armed Services, used her journalistic credentials to interview Gauck when he visited Bulgaria and, in 1999, wrote about the work of the BStU after a visit to Berlin funded by the Konrad Adenauer Foundation.[46]

Journalists played important roles in informing the public of practices in other countries, and became active in their own right. Inspired by Bulgarian efforts, in 2006, Romanian journalists launched a Clean Voices campaign to identify secret agents among television reporters, press contributors, and talk show hosts.[47] Before the law enabling access to communist secret documents was adopted in December 2006, non-governmental organizations and journalists organized an international conference with representatives from Poland, the Czech Republic, Germany, Slovakia, and Romania and collected the laws of these countries to influence Bulgarian legislation based on "European best practices."[48] Evocation of European standards was a powerful device used in all countries.

NORM PROMOTION AND PASSIVE LEVERAGE: THE ROLE OF EUROPEAN INSTITUTIONS

The "return to Europe" and entry into the international community of democratic states figured prominently in the policy objectives of all Central and East European countries. Due to the special circumstance of German unification, the former East Germany joined European institutions in 1990. For the others, membership in the Council of Europe was expedited in the first half of the 1990s; accession to the EU followed in 2004 and 2007.

For the EU, transitional justice is an evolving activity that focuses on international criminal justice and support for victims; in other domains, its support is more muted and limited to funding. Most initiatives to promote criminal prosecutions, truth commissions, victim reparation programs, and security system reform, including, but not limited to, vetting the police, army, and judiciary,[49] have come too late to affect Central and East European countries in concrete ways. Nevertheless, the prospect of joining European institutions influenced discourse and practices.

Norm Promotion. The Copenhagen criteria, passed in 1993, demanded democracy and rule of law, among other things, as preconditions for EU accession, but their link to reckoning with the past was vague at best and never a benchmark in negotiations. However, the pursuit of democracy and rule of law was not without utility in enabling policy entrepreneurs to assert soft influence, albeit to different ends. Noel Calhoun argues, for example, that in Poland, lustration was initially restrained by a political debate about its compatibility with liberal democratic principles. With time, the "debates grew more nuanced," as policy entrepreneurs learned from their own experiences, those of neighboring countries, and parameters set by international organizations.[50]

The rule-of-law criteria are indispensable but open-ended when applied to the pursuit of transitional justice. They focus on Europeanization channels through the legal community, in particular the Council of Europe and its Court, the European Court of Human Rights (ECHR). Although the newly established courts in post-communist Central and Eastern Europe became important in framing transitional justice policies, they became embroiled in legal disputes over the constitutionality of criminal trials, lustration, and restitution rulings. Domestic courts entered largely uncharted waters to find answers to such vexing problems as retrospective justice, statutes of limitations, fairness, and the right to privacy versus the public good. In lustration cases, for example, Maran Safjan, former Polish Constitutional Tribunal judge and now member of the EU Court of Justice, summarized the dilemma: "two opposite sides can present serious arguments based directly on constitutional values and principles."[51]

Divergent approaches have been explained by procedural versus substantive applications of the law. The history of the communist regime in question and its legal and political reasoning heavily influenced transition modes. The jurisdiction of the Hungarian and Czech constitutional courts stood at opposite ends, while the Polish constitution took a compromise approach.[52] As in other areas of transitional justice, the rationales for avenues taken stem from national conditions.

However, domestic courts did not act in isolation: they borrowed laws, applied comparative frameworks, and received advice from international courts. European institutions and national non-governmental organizations from Europe and the United States trained public officials, including legal personnel, aiming for both knowledge transfer and socialization. References to the practices of neighboring countries were common,[53] but access to international legal bodies, such as the ECHR and the International Labour Organization (ILO), subjected affairs once considered solely in the domestic domain to advisement, if not scrutiny. "An intervention from Strasbourg," where the ECHR is located, "was seen as an important and highly appreciated guarantee of the correct path and irreversibility of the democratic transition, which included a 'human rights approach' to transition."[54] Together with the Venice Commission, an advisory body of the Council of Europe and the ECHR, standards were set by scrutinizing and fine-tuning national legislation. In her account of the ECHR case law, Eva Brems attests to the court's restraint in dealing with transitional justice yet demonstrates its importance in setting criteria for resolving disputes and addressing individual complaints.[55] In a similar vein, Hamilton and Buyse laud the "nuanced approach" of the court, whose adjudications stressed the timing of certain policies, individual assessment of collective guilt, and the context and implementation of transitional justice measures.[56]

The court has been most active in property restitution, and Central and Eastern European claimants have used this avenue repeatedly; it reviewed far fewer questions about lustration. Overall, the court was limited by temporal jurisdiction – adjudication can only happen in matters that occur after a country has ratified its membership in the court. The effects of these debates on the adjudication of transitional justice are open to discussion. Wojciech Sadurski, a legal scholar, attributed the "by-and-large lukewarm attitudes of many constitutional courts" partly to "external influences that, on balance, inclined the legal systems . . . against rather than in favour of lustration."[57] For Jiří Přibán, referring to rule of law became a "power technique."[58] Others emphasize how lustration debates helped to define citizens' rights, state duties, and judicial restraint.[59] So far, the notion of Europeanization has been distinguished from the EU framework whose impact on transitional justice through passive leverage was fleeting.

Passive leverage: Milada Vaduchova introduced the term *passive leverage* to highlight the indirect influence that prospective membership can have on EU applicant countries, as opposed to *active leverage*, which sets out concrete goals that have to be met. It shows the "traction that the EU has on the domestic politics of credible candidate states by virtue of its existence and its usual conduct."[60] In the absence of active leverage, both advocates and opponents jiggled the possibility of EU membership to legitimize their own agendas. The coup attempt in the Soviet Union may have accelerated passage of the Czech lustration law in 1991, but in the long run, the attraction of EU membership proved more important.[61] When Bulgaria and Romania were excluded in the 2004 round of accession, lustration and file access became tools to advance membership. File transfer to the National Council for the Study of Security Archives picked up remarkable speed between 2005 and 2007.[62] In the May 2006 Romanian parliamentary debates, some "[l]egislators believed that lustration had helped other post-communist countries to gain early acceptance into the EU."[63]

Counterarguments were raised on the same premise. Lustration was sidestepped by pointing out that Romania had not remedied corruption to gain accession; others referenced European values and ECHR rulings to defend their opposition to lustration.[64] Romania passed a new ordinance in 2006 to expand lustration, but in 2008, one year after it joined the EU, the law on file access was declared unconstitutional. With a dose of sarcasm, Iancu points to the "impeccable sense of timing"; efforts to show the cleansing of society were no longer necessary.[65] In Bulgaria in 2006–2007, the revived discussion about secret service file disclosure mingled endogenous pressure with desire for EU entry.[66]

This section explored the ways that different diffusion mechanisms framed debates and set standards. The topic of transitional justice could be broached when democracy and rule of law were at stake, although domestic policy stakeholders absorbed messages selectively to further their cause. In the absence of active leverage, politicians and citizens used at times contradictory references to European institutions to further their goals or, in the case of the ECHR, to seek legal redress.[67] References to Europe and Europeanization, noticeably accelerating by the end of the 1990s, also encouraged spillover in the form of networking, making Central and Eastern Europeans players in their own right.

SPILLOVER: INSTITUTIONALIZATION OF TRANSNATIONAL NETWORKS

Cross-border academic exchange and cooperation on joint projects disseminate ideas and build community. In the 1990s, the diffusion of ideas and practices was mostly limited to bilateral contacts or meetings of epistemic communities.[68] Structured transnational ties were slow to evolve,[69] but when membership in the EU was around the corner, the scope of transitional justice advocacy changed. Three organizations owe their creation to indirect spillover effects from Europeanization processes, supported by research institutes, many associated with state security service archives, that sprang up in Central and Eastern Europe. In chronological order, the European Network of Official Authorities in Charge of the Secret Police Files, the

Platform of European Memory and Conscience, and the European Network Remembrance and Solidarity. A brief discussion of their origins and missions shows how the focus of transitional justice shifted from legal-administrative measures with limited time frames to broader issues of memory politics, which is open-ended.

European Network of Official Authorities in Charge of Secret Police Files. In reaction to international inquiries and anticipation of the accession of Central and East European countries, the BStU promoted international cooperation and added a liaison section for international affairs in 2002. It was also crucial in setting up the European Network of Official Authorities in Charge of Secret Police Files, which connects the diverse Central and East European institutions and engages scholars and practitioners in the exchange of ideas.[70] The network first met in Berlin in 2008; founding members were Germany, Bulgaria, the Czech Republic, Hungary, Poland, Romania, and Slovakia. Recently, the Baltic States and Slovenia joined as observers, taking part in activities without voting rights. Leadership rotates among the member countries, with the chair institution hosting a meeting that generally takes advantage of a relevant anniversary rather than adhering to an annual cycle. The conference language is English. So far, most of its work has focused on exchanging information, providing exogenous support when particular institutions are under attack by domestic political actors, organizing a traveling exhibition and conferences, and publishing a reader.[71] Several working groups are engaged in joint projects; a coordinating group facilitates networking. The network endorses national approaches to the legacy of state security files and the benefits of exchanging views and mutual support; its work is closely circumscribed by its focus on the archives of the state security services.[72]

Platform of European Memory and Conscience. The Central and East European states that joined the EU in 2004 and 2007 have challenged its prevailing memory strands – centrality of the Holocaust – to incorporate the communist past. The conference that led to the Prague Declaration (June 3, 2008) and the resulting European Parliament resolution (April 2, 2009) called for addressing communism and Nazism as shared European historical legacies, and August 23 has since been dedicated as European Day of Remembrance. During the rotating EU presidency in 2009, the Czech Republic instituted the Platform of European Memory and Conscience, which places the crimes of the communist regimes alongside those of the National Socialist regime in European memory discourse. Headquartered in Prague, it was officially founded in 2011. Its activities have focused on conferences and exhibits; it recently published a reader, "Lest We Forget Memory of

Totalitarianism in Europe."[73] Its members are selected institutions from Central and Eastern Europe, the Baltic States, Slovenia, and Ukraine, with "Western" membership limited to Germany and Sweden. Its scope has been hampered by the indifference of Western European countries, the selection criteria for inclusion, and staunch anti-communist rhetoric.

European Network of Remembrance and Solidarity. Scholars have interacted on transitional justice since the fall of communism, but cross-border academic exchange and cooperation on joint projects to disseminate ideas and build community have evolved considerably from occasional seminars to more organized collaboration, and research institutes have sprung up across the region.

The European Network, headquartered in Warsaw, is the somewhat unlikely result of German-Polish disputes connected with a planned Center against Expulsions in Berlin. In 2003, faced with accusations of a German-centered approach to ethnic expulsions in twentieth-century Europe, the ruling coalition of the Social Democratic Party and the Alliance 90/The Greens in Germany sought to ease tensions that threatened cross-border reconciliation. The imminent enlargement of the EU into Central and Eastern Europe motivated continuation of the project, which was broadened to include the Visegrad countries (Poland, Czech Republic, and Hungary) along with Germany and Austria. In 2005, the Czech Republic and Austria distanced themselves, but the European Network was born nevertheless. In Poland, with a new conservative government, interest dwindled; in 2009, after another government turnover, the initiative was institutionalized.[74] Ministers of culture in Germany, Hungary, Poland, and Slovakia signed the agreement. This "difficult birth" of a politically sensitive project owes much to political actors in Germany and Poland and the cooperation of regional historians, who, according to one member, developed a "tear-proof net of professional and personal contacts."[75] Scientific, educational, and promotional projects involve the study and documentation of the dictatorial experiences in twentieth-century Europe. Activities ranging from international conferences and funding of media projects to the organization of youth seminars aim to promote cross-national understanding through discussions and knowledge transfer.

Pending EU membership and subsequent accession advanced the organization of transnational advocacy networks with clear missions, supplementing, but not abrogating, earlier activities. Pay-off is indirect, long-term, and part of a vision of Europeanization that includes memory culture. With EU membership, Central and East European countries moved from receiving Europeanization processes to participating in agenda-setting and coalition-building, although their reach remains limited.

CONCLUSION

This chapter suggests both the promise of and limits to diffusion of transitional justice in Central and Eastern Europe. It draws attention to external factors in the pursuit of transitional justice and encourages further studies on particular mechanisms and the role of actors in the spread of ideas and policies. The following findings should be of interest to scholars and practitioners alike.

First, although domestic actors drove the process of transitional justice, their policies did not simply evolve from past legacies or political power constellations; they were also shaped by exogenous influence. This study confirms that diffusion falls on fertile ground when actors in sender and receiving countries share similar values and goals; the policy model is sufficiently flexible so that it can be transplanted; and transnational diffusion channels exist.[76] The case study on public file access and the institutionalization of archives that house them illustrates the intersection of these factors. However, even if conditions are favorable, outcomes are not automatic or predetermined. Diffusion effects have been scattered; in no case was the "foreign" model copied directly.

Second, reflecting the heterogeneity of settings across the region, the openness to diffusion varied; the extent to which exogenous influence mattered depended on the policy measure under consideration, the receptivity of national actors, and their place in the national power hierarchy. (East) Germany and Czechoslovakia (later the Czech Republic) primarily exported, rather than received, diffusion practices; together with Poland, they emerged as the core "shapers" of transnational activities to advance transitional justice agendas in the region. Domestic pressure coupled with diffusion effects kept discourses alive in countries such as Bulgaria and Romania where transitional justice stalled; references to and practices from abroad reopened windows of opportunities for action but with mixed results.

Third, flows of information from abroad can assist in validating, supporting, defending, or defeating certain policy proposals. Political actors applied advice or responded to soft pressure selectively to strengthen divergent policy positions, often using them rhetorically and symbolically rather than proscriptively. Transitional justice actors also could choose from a repertoire of actions, each with advantages and drawbacks, although the reception of foreign models often lacked detail regarding its implementation in the sending countries. If the multiplicity of actors brought novel and diverse viewpoints or strategies, lack of coordinated efforts weakened their influence. Politicians could resist domestic and international pressure, but cross-border linkages made it increasingly difficult to ignore demands for action.[77]

Fourth, time matters: transnational and international ties have moved from the margins to assume greater scope and significance. Initially, policies that inspired and/or legitimized similar efforts in other settings were the predominant form of influence. Bilateral contacts to spread these ideas emerged slowly. Europeanization agendas existed from the beginning, but only gained influence toward the end of the 1990s when working toward entry and later membership in the EU promoted cross-national interaction. Ambiguous in their outcomes, references to European processes influenced discursive frames and tactical methods.[78]

Finally, the diffusion of transitional justice processes raises normative and empirical issues about the desirability and feasibility of external involvement. My findings emphasize the promotion of ideas and practices not by coercion, but by dialogue and assistance. The different pathways, ranging from inspiration to spillover, respect the domestic character of transitional justice processes, yet give credence to the importance of transnational and international channels. Such cross-border views and interactions are salient even if their outcomes are open-ended.

NOTES

* I am grateful for the research assistance of Sara Olsen and Thomas Walker. Special thanks to Dr. Sara Dahill-Brown for her critical reading of an earlier version of this chapter.

1. For example, Susanne Buckley-Zistel, "Vergangenes Unrecht aufarbeiten. Eine globale Perspektive," *Aus Politik und Zeitgeschichte* 63, no. 25–26 (June 17, 2013): 36–37.
2. The term *transitional justice* entered academic work in the mid-1990s; it has spread, but in day-to-day parlance, other terms often prevail. I use it to denote both legal-administrative measures and memorialization strategies.
3. Brigitte Weiffen, "From Domestic to International Instruments for Dealing with a Violent Past: Causes, Concomitants and Consequences for Democratic Transitions," in *Memory and Political Change*, eds. Aleida Assmann and Linda Shortt (Houndmills, Basingstoke: Palgrave Macmillan, 2012), 89–111.
4. Margaret E. Keck and Kathryn Sikkink, *Activists Beyond Borders. Advocacy Networks in International Politics* (Ithaca, NY: Cornell University Press, 1998), and Martha Finnemore and Kathryn Sikkink, "International Norm Dynamics and Political Change," *International Organization* 52 (1998): 887–917.
5. Ellen Lutz and Kathryn Sikkink, "The Justice Cascade: The Evolution and Impact of Foreign Human Rights Trials in Latin America," *Chicago Journal of International Law* 2 (2001): 1–33.
6. Jelena Subotić, "Transformation of International Justice Agency," *International Journal of Transitional Justice* 6 (2012): 106–125.

7. It excludes countries that broke off from the former Soviet Union or Yugoslavia but includes East Germany due to its role in shaping discourses and advocacy networks in the transitional justice policy domain.
8. John Gledhill, "Integrating the Past: Regional Integration and Historical Reckoning in Central and Eastern Europe," *Nationalities Paper* 39 (2011): 501. Ursachi identified external factors as a missing piece of the transitional justice puzzle; see Raluca Ursachi, "In Search of a Theoretical Model of Transitional Justice," in *Lustration and Consolidation of Democracy and the Rule of Law in CEE*, eds. Vladimira Dvořáková and Anđelko Milardović (Zagreb: Political Science Research Centre, 2007), 78.
9. Eva Brems, "Transitional Justice in the Case of the European Court of Human Rights," *International Journal of Transitional Justice* 5 (2011): 282–303, Cynthia Horne, "International Legal Rulings on Lustration Policies in Central and Eastern Europe: Rule of Law in Historical Context," *Law and Social Inquiry* 34 (2009): 713–744. From the large body of legal literature see Daniela Piana, *Judicial Accountabilities in New Europe: From Rule of Law to Quality of Justice* (Farnham: Ashgate, 2009).
10. In the mid-1990s, I asserted that cross-national contagion effects were one factor that could explain transitional justice actions but did not elaborate them. Helga Welsh, "Dealing with the Communist Past: Central and East European Experiences," *Europe-Asia Studies* 48 (1996): 413–438.
11. Mitchell Orenstein, Stephen Bloom, and Nicole Lindstrom, "A Fourth Dimension of Transition," in *Transnational Actors in Central and East European Transitions*, eds. Mitchell A. Orenstein, Stephen Bloom, and Nicole Lindstrom (Pittsburgh: University of Pittsburgh Press, 2008), 1–18; Valerie Bunce and Sharon Wolchik, "Transnational Networks, Diffusion Dynamics, and Electoral Change in the Postcommunist World," in *The Diffusion of Social Movements. Actors, Mechanisms, and Political Effects*, eds. Rebecca Kolins Givan, Kenneth M. Roberts, and Sarah A. Soule (Cambridge: Cambridge University Press, 2010), 141.
12. Tricia D. Olsen, Leigh A. Payne, and Andrew G. Reiter, "Transitional Justice in the World, 1970–2007: Insights from a New Dataset," *Journal of Peace Research* 47 (2010): 803–809.
13. David Marsh, and J. C. Sharman, "Policy Diffusion and Policy Transfer," *Policy Studies* 30 (2009): 274–275; Svein Eriksen, "Institution Building in Central and Eastern Europe: Foreign Influences and Domestic Responses, *Review of Central and East European Law* 32 (2007): 333–369; Christoph Knill, "Introduction: Cross-national Policy Convergence: Concepts, Approaches and Explanatory Factors," *Journal of European Public Policy* 12 (2005): 764–774; Jacint Jordana, David Levi-Faur, and Xavier Fernández Marin, "The Global Diffusion of Regulatory Agencies: Channels of Transfer and Stages of Diffusion," *Comparative Political Studies* 44 (2011): 1346; Wade Jacoby, "Inspiration, Coalition, and Substitution: External Influences on Post-communist Transformations," *World Politics* 58 (2006): 628, 625.
14. Robert Harmsen and Thomas M. Wilson, "Introduction: Approaches to Europeanization," *Yearbook of European Studies* 14 (2000): 13–26; Kevin Featherstone and Claudio M. Radaelli, eds., *The Politics of Europeanization* (Oxford: Oxford University Press, 2003).

15. Olsen, Payne, and Reiter, "Transitional Justice," 803.
16. Tricia D. Olsen, Leigh A. Payne, and Andrew G. Reiter, *Transitional Justice in Balance. Comparing Processes, Weighing Efficacy* (Washington, D.C.: United States Institute of Peace Press, 2010), ch. 5.
17. Jon Elster, *Closing the Books. Transitional Justice in Historical Perspective* (Cambridge: Cambridge University Press, 2004).
18. Monica Ciobanu, "Recent Restorative Justice Measures in Romania (2006–2010), *Problems of Post-Communism* 60 (2013): 45–57.
19. Lavinia Stan, "Truth Commissions in Post-Communism: The Overlooked Solution?" *Open Political Science Journal* 2 (2009): 1–13. Truth commissions were also instituted in the Baltic States.
20. For overviews of transitional policies in different countries, see Lavinia Stan and Nadya Nedelsky, eds., *Encyclopedia of Transitional Justice* (New York: Cambridge University Press, 2013).
21. Matt Killingsworth, "Lustration and Legitimacy," *Global Society* 24 (2010): 71–90; Lavinia Stan, ed., *Transitional Justice in Eastern Europe and the Former Soviet Union. Reckoning with the Communist Past* (London: Routledge, 2009); Kieran Williams, Brigid Fowler, and Aleks Szcerbiak, "Explaining Lustration in Central Europe: A 'Post-communist Politics' Approach," *Democratization* 12 (2005): 22–43; Aleks Szczerbiak, "Dealing with the Communist Past or the Politics of the Present? Lustration in Post-Communist Poland," *Europe-Asia Studies* 54 (2002): 553–572.
22. For the first explanation, see Nedelsky, "Divergent Responses to a Common Past: Transitional Justice in the Czech Republic and Slovakia," *Theory and Society* 33 (2004): 65–115; strategic elite choices are at the core of Monika Nalepa, *Skeletons in the Closet. Transitional Justice in Post-Communist Europe* (New York: Cambridge University Press, 2010).
23. Csilla Kiss, "Transitional Justice and the Reconstruction of Identity in Post-Communist Countries," in *Diktaturüberwindung in Europa. Neue nationale und transnationale Perspektiven*, eds. Birgit Hofmann, Katja Wezel, Katrin Hammerstein, Regina Fritz, and Julie Trappe (Heidelberg: Universitätsverlag, 2010), 69–83.
24. Defining the term lustration is fraught with difficulty as it has been used differently in different countries. For an authoritative account, see Monika Nalepa, "Lustration," in *Encyclopedia of Transitional Justice*, Volume 1: 46–51; and Brian K. Grodsky, *The Costs of Justice. How New Leaders Respond to Previous Rights Abuses* (Notre Dame, IN: University of Notre Dame Press, 2010), 58.
25. Noel Calhoun, *Dilemmas of Justice in Eastern Europe's Democratic Transitions* (New York: Palgrave Macmillan, 2004), 127; Paulina Gulińska-Jurgiel, "Transnational References in Times of Radical Changes. 'Europe' as a Function of Coming to Terms with the Past," paper presented at the 18th Conference of the Council of European Studies, Barcelona, Spain, June 20–22, 2010; Andrzej Walicki, "Transitional Justice and the Political Struggles of Post-Communist Poland," in *Transitional Justice and the Rule of Law in New Democracies*, ed. A. James McAdams (Notre Dame: University of Notre Dame Press, 1997), 185–237. Carlos Closa reminds us that civil society efforts challenged the Spanish model after 2000 with important consequences. See Carlos Closa, "Spain," in Stan and Nedelsky, *Encyclopedia of Transitional Justice*, Volume 2: 459–464.

26. Monika Nalepa, "To Punish the Guilty and Protect the Innocent: Comparing Truth Revelation Procedures," *Journal of Theoretical Politics* 20 (2008): 221–245. Czech President Vaclav Havel reluctantly signed legislation in 2002, saying, "the importance of truth is higher" than the arguments against opening the files. Cited in Nedelsky, "Divergent Responses," 95.
27. For a critical view, see the article by two prominent communist dissidents, Adam Michnik and Vaclav Havel, "Justice as Revenge?" *Journal of Democracy* 4 (1993): 20–27.
28. The law has been updated and annexed eight times since then; the major provisions from the original law still hold.
29. Csilla Kiss, "The Misuses of Manipulation: The Failure of Transitional Justice in Post-Communist Hungary," *Europe-Asia Studies* 58 (2006): 930; and Charles Bertschi, "Lustration and the Transition to Democracy: The Cases of Poland and Bulgaria," *East European Quarterly* 28 (1995): 441.
30. Lavinia Stan, "Vigilante Justice in Post-communist Europe," *Communist and Post-Communist Studies* 44 (2011): 319–327; and Calhoun, *Dilemmas of Justice*, 131.
31. George Mink, "Institutions of National Memory in Post-Communist Europe: From Transitional Justice to Political Uses of Biographies (1989–2010)," in *History, Memory and Politics in Central and Eastern Europe*, eds. George Mink and Laure Neumayer (Houndmills: Palgrave Macmillan, 2013); and James Mark, *The Unfinished Revolution. Making Sense of the Communist Past in Central-Eastern Europe* (New Haven, CT: Yale University Press, 2010), 28.
32. Włodzimierz Borodziej, "Der Kommunismus in der deutschen Erinnerungskultur. Kommentar aus polnischer Sicht," in *Woran erinnern? Der Kommunismus in der deutschen Erinnerungskultur*, eds. Peter März and Hans-Joachim Veen (Cologne: Böhlau Verlag, 2006), 209; Paweł Machcewicz, "The Institute of National Remembrance and the Legacy of Communism in Poland," *Politics, History and Collective Memory in East Central Europe*, eds. Zdzisław Krasnodębski, Stefan Garsztecki, and Rüdiger Ritter (Hamburg: Reinhold Krämer Verlag, 2012), 82.
33. Email correspondence, translated and transmitted by Katarzyna Holopiak, Division of International Relations, Office of the President of the Institute of National Remembrance, April 24, 2012.
34. Email correspondence with Roman David, February 15, 2012; Muriel Blaive, "Einige Etappen der Bewältigung der kommunistischen Vergangenheit seit 1989 in der Republik Tschechien," in *Die Überlieferung der Diktaturen*, 121–122.
35. Nadya Nedelsky, "Divergent Responses to a Common Past: Transitional Justice in the Czech Republic and Slovakia," *Theory and Society* 33 (2004): 98.
36. László Varga, "Vom Erbe des kommunistischen Staatssicherheitsdienstes in Ungarn," in *Lustration, Aktenöffnung, demokratischer Umbruch in Polen, Tschechien, der Slowakei und Ungarn. Referate der Tagung des BStU und der Akademie für politische Bildung Tutzing vom 26.-28. 10. 1998*, ed. Dagmar Unverhau with the assistance of Roland Lucht (Münster: LIT Verlag, 2005), 161–176.
37. Cited in Mink, "Institutions of National Memory," 160.
38. Gauck, in collaboration with Helga Hirsch, *Winter im Sommer – Frühling im Herbst. Erinnerungen* (Munich: Siedler, 2009), 319, my translation.

39. Cristina Petrescu and Dragoş Petrescu, "Retribution, Remembering, Representation: On Romania's Incomplete Break with the Communist Past," in *Geschichtsbilder in den postdiktatorischen Ländern Europas. Auf der Suche nach historisch-politischen Identitäten*, eds. Gerhard Besier and Katarzyna Stokłosa (Berlin: LIT Verlag, 2009), 161, and n26.
40. Lavinia Stan, "Access to Securitate Files: The Trials and Tribulations of a Romanian Law," *East European Politics and Societies* 16 (2002): 155.
41. Bogdan Iancu, "Post-Accession Constitutionalism with a Human Face: Judicial Reform and Lustration in Romania," *European Constitutional Law Review* 6 (2010): 28–29.
42. Helmut Müller-Enbergs, "Aufarbeitung der Vergangenheit in Mittel- und Osteuropa – Dimension der Staatssicherheiten," *Der allmächtige Geheimdienst. Ein Relikt der Vergangenheit. Zur Transformation der Geheimdienste Mittel- und Osteuropas nach 1990*, eds. Wolbert K. Smidt, Irina Mohr, and Helmut Müller-Enbergs (Berlin: LIT Verlag, 2012), 43.
43. This statement does not include the Rosa Luxemburg Foundation of the Left Party (formerly Party of Democratic Socialism) as it started work in Central and Eastern Europe later and has not targeted transitional justice. The other political foundations have cast their net of activities related to coming to terms with the past widely, with topics ranging from the Holocaust, the expulsion of Germans, to the more recent past.
44. From the substantial body of literature on the role of the German foundations abroad, see Ann L. Phillips, *Power and Influence after the Cold War. Germany in East-Central Europe* (Lanham, MD: Rowman and Littlefield Publishers, 2000); Dorota Dakowska, "German Political Foundations: Transnational Party Go-betweens in the Process of EU Enlargement," *Transnational European Union*, eds. Wolfram Kaiser and Peter Starie (London: Routledge, 2005). On the role of the Konrad-Adenauer-Foundation, see Gabriele Baumann and Nina Müller, "Vergangenheitsbewältigung und Erinnerungskultur in den Ländern Mittelost- und Südosteuropas," Konrad-Adenauer-Stiftung Working Paper no. 164 (2006).
45. Email correspondence with Claudiu Secaşiu, CNSAS board member since 1999 and, for a brief time in 2006, its head, February 22, 2012.
46. Email correspondence with Ekaterina Boncheva, facilitated and translated by Antoinette Primatarova, March 7, 2012.
47. Lavinia Stan, "Witch-hunt or Moral Rebirth? Romanian Parliamentary Debates on Lustration," *East European Politics and Societies* 26 (2012): 275.
48. Email correspondence with Hristo Hristov, Bulgarian journalist, January 19, 2013.
49. Laura Davis, "The European Union and Transitional Justice," International Center for Transitional Justice – Initiative for Peace Building (June 2010), available at: http://www.initativeforpeacebuilding.eu (accessed January 10, 2014; Thomas Unger, "The European Union and Transitional Justice," Center for the Law of EU External Relations (CLEER) Working Paper no. 1 (2010); and María Avello, "European Efforts in Transitional Justice," FRIDE Working Paper no. 58 (June 2008).
50. Noel Calhoun, "The Ideological Dilemma of Lustration in Poland," *East European Politics and Societies* 16 (2002): 497–498; Magdalena Zolkos, "The Conceptual Nexus of Human Rights and Democracy in the Polish Lustration

Debates 1989–97," *Journal of Communist Studies and Transition Politics* 22 (2006): 228–248.

51. Marek Safjan, "Transitional Justice: The Polish Example, the Case of Lustration," *European Journal of Legal Studies* 1 (2007): 8, available at: http://www.ejls.eu/2/29UK.htm (accessed October 15, 2013).
52. András Sajó, "Militant Democracy and Transition towards Democracy," in *Militant Democracy*, ed. András Sajó (The Hague: Eleven International Publishing, 2004), 218–220.
53. Wojciech Sadurski, *Rights Before Courts. A Study of Constitutional Courts in Postcommunist States of CEE* (Dordrecht: Springer, 2005), 249.
54. Michael Hamilton and Antoine Buyse, "Introduction," in *Transitional Jurisprudence and the ECHR. Justice, Politics and Rights*, eds. Antoine Buyse and Michael Hamilton (Cambridge: Cambridge University Press, 2011), 16.
55. Brems, "Transitional Justice in the Case of the European Court."
56. Hamilton and Buyse, "Introduction," 14.
57. Sadurski, *Rights Before Courts*, 232.
58. Jiri Přibán, "From 'Which Rule of Law?' to 'The Rule of Which Law?' Post-Communist Experiences of European Legal Integration," *Hague Journal on the Rule of Law* 1 (2009): 337–358.
59. Adam Czarnota, "Lustration, Decommunisation and the Rule of Law," *Hague Journal on the Rule of Law*, 1(2009): 335.
60. Milada Vaduchova, *Europe Undivided: Leverage and Integration after Communism* (Oxford: Oxford University Press, 2005), 65.
61. Blaive, "Einige Etappen," 120.
62. Lavinia Stan, *Transitional Justice in Post-Communist Romania: The Politics of Memory* (New York: Cambridge University Press, 2013), 73.
63. Stan, "Witch-hunt or Moral Rebirth," 286.
64. Ibid.
65. Iancu, "Post-accession Constitutionalism, 57; Stan, *Transitional Justice in Post-Communist Romania*, 95.
66. Email correspondence with Ekaterina Boncheva, March 7, 2012; Hristo Hristov and Alexander Kashumov, "Justice and Accountability Mechanisms in Bulgaria in the Transition Period (1989–2008)," in *After Oppression: Transitional Justice in Latin America and Eastern Europe*, eds. Vesselin Popovski and Mónica Serrano (Tokyo: United Nations University Press, 2012), 292.
67. Gledhill, "Integrating the Past," 481–506.
68. Lutz, and Sikkink, "Justice Cascade," 1.
69. A partial exception is the International Association of Former Political Prisoners – Victims of Communism (Inter-Asso), founded in 1991. Its members meet on an annual basis to discuss practices in their countries, but its effectiveness and visibility have been hampered from the beginning by in-fighting about who should be represented in the organization, language barriers, and, in particular, financial problems.
70. Senate of the Parliament of the Czech Republic, Prague Declaration on European Conscience and Communism, June 3, 2008, available at: http://www.praguedeclaration.eu/ (accessed February 23, 2012).

71. *The "European Network of Official Authorities in Charge of the Secret-Police Files." A Reader on Their Legal Foundations, Structures and Activities* (Berlin: Der Bundesbeauftragte für die Unterlagen des Staatssicherheitsdienstes der ehemaligen Deutschen Demokratischen Republik, December 2009), available at: http://www.bstu.bund.de/DE/Wissen/Publikationen/Publikationen/E_netzwerkreader_englisch.html (accessed January 14, 2014).
72. I am grateful to Bert Rosenthal (BStU) for information on the work of the network. The interviews were conducted on January 19, 2012, and March 1, 2013.
73. The target group is clearly spelled out in the subtitle: *A Reader for Older Secondary School Students Anywhere in Europe*, ed. Gillian Purves (Prague: Institute for the Study of Totalitarian Regimes, 2013).
74. The historical evolution is analyzed by Stefan Troebst, "Wiederbelebung einer 'Totgeburt'? Das Europäische Netzwerk Erinnerung und Solidarität," *Polen-Analysen* 33, no. 20 (May 2008): 2–7; Matthias Weber, "Gemeinsam Erinnern. Das Europäische Netzwerk 'Erinnerung und Solidarität,'" available at: http://www.bundesregierung.de/Content/DE/_Anlagen/BKM/2010-02-18-weber-zum-eruopaeischen-netzwerk-erinnerung-solidaritaet.pdf?__blob=publicationFile (accessed August 12, 2013); Stephan Raabe with Denny Schlüter, "Auf den Spuren des 'Europäischen Netzwerks Erinnerung und Solidarität,'" *Länderbericht*, Konrad-Adenauer-Stiftung: Auslandsbüro Polen (January 6, 2011), available at: http://www.kas.de/polen/de/publications/21555/ (accessed June 20, 2013).
75. Stefan Troebst, *Vertreibungsdiskurs und europäische Erinnerungskultur. Deutsch-polnische Initiativen zur Institutionalisierung. Eine Dokumentation*. Veröffentlichungen der Deutsch-Polnischen Gesellschaft Bundesverband e.V. vol. 11 (Osnabrück: Fibre, 2006), 22–23.
76. These findings support those of Valerie Bunce and Sharon Wolchik, "International Diffusion and Democratic Change," *The Dynamics of Democratization. Dictatorship, Development, and Diffusion*, ed. Nathan J. Brown (Baltimore: Johns Hopkins University Press, 2011), 286–287.
77. Iosif Kovras, "Explaining Prolonged Silences in Transitional Justice: The Disappeared in Cyprus and Spain," *Comparative Political Studies* 46 (2013): 730–756.
78. EU impact on member states may be patchy, uneven but not spurious. Tanja A. Börzel and Thomas Risse, "When Europeanisation Meets Diffusion: Exploring New Territory," *West European Politics* 35 (2012): 193–207.

9

The Mythologizing of Communist Violence*

Jelena Subotic

Yugoslav communism was unique in many ways, most significantly in its departure from Stalinist orthodoxy, political semi-liberalization, and profound ideological focus on supranational Yugoslav identity. The communist regime, however, carried out numerous human rights violations, including political purges, detention of dissidents, extrajudicial assassinations, and confiscation of property.[1] In much of the rest of the post-communist region, the decisions on how to properly deal with communist violence were made as part of the larger democratic "transition" and as a declared break with the communist past. In the former Yugoslavia, by contrast, the communist past morphed into ongoing nationalist debates over control of the federal state and the nature of post-Yugoslav succession. The year 1989 in Yugoslavia, therefore, was a transition not to democracy, but to nationalism, war, and violence. Because of this unique feature of Yugoslav post-communism, instead of dealing with legacies of communist crimes as part of democratic reform, these crimes became further mythologized, fueling new cycles of violence and injustice.

This chapter analyzes this mythologizing process by looking at the way in which communist violence was used for nationalist mobilization in Serbia and Croatia since the mid-1980s, and especially after 1989. This analysis points not only to the great variety in transitional justice experience since 1989 across Eastern Europe but also to a particularly pernicious way in which the memory of communist crimes colors memory projects of the future, making some topics worthy of remembrance and ignoring others.

The chapter proceeds as follows. I first place the transition from communism in the former Yugoslavia in the context of broader regional transitions and explain its unique character. I then describe particular practices of memory of specific communist crimes in Serbia and Croatia and trace their political use for nationalist mobilization in the region. I conclude by offering some lessons learned from the public memory of communist crimes in the former Yugoslavia and ways in which the abuses of this memory can be avoided.

THE CHALLENGE OF MULTIPLE TRANSITIONS

The cross-disciplinary field of transitional justice – the study of ways in which societies deal with legacies of past violence and human rights abuses – has developed almost beyond recognition since the early 1990s.[2] From the very beginning, the field was mostly focused on post-violence experiences of "democracies in transition" – primarily in Latin America, and then in Eastern Europe.[3] Comparisons were made quickly and predictions for post-conflict resolution and "reconciliation" offered with much confidence.[4] The Eastern European experience proved, unsurprisingly, to be quite different from other post-conflict societies transitional justice scholarship examined. The principal difference – and a unique analytical advantage of the Eastern European perspective – was the existence of multilayered and overlapping transitions in the region: from peace to war to unstable peace (in the Balkans and the Caucasus), from multiethnic federal to ethnic nation-states (Yugoslavia, Czechoslovakia, the Soviet Union), from centrally planned economy to some hybrid free market, and from authoritarianism to some type of democracy (across the broader region). These multiple transitions developed in different directions, were more consistent in some countries and more contradictory in others.

This richness of the East European experience complicated much of the transitional justice scholarship. It injected much more skepticism about post-conflict reconciliation into the literature that grew out of and used the perceived successes of the South African and Latin American transitions as a model to be emulated across the world.[5] The paradox of multiple transitions occurring simultaneously, with social forces pulling countries in many different directions, opened up much more space for analytical questioning of the concepts of social healing, post-conflict resolution, or political forgiveness.[6] The great reluctance across much of the region to engage systematically in addressing the legacies of both communist and post-communist violence has also challenged some major assumptions from the transitional justice literature, which predicted strong social demand for justice after conflicts end.[7]

The Yugoslav experience complicates the transitional justice landscape even further. As most of Eastern Europe entered the 1990s with hope and excitement about the prospects of democracy, liberalism, and human rights after half a century of communist totalitarianism, former Yugoslavia entered the decade under heavy clouds of looming war and total political and human insecurity. As the country broke apart along its seams, communism gave way to something much worse – protracted civil war, grim levels of violence, and ultimately genocide. Given this lived experience across Yugoslav successor states, 1989 was not something to be celebrated. The transition from communism was a transition to nationalism and then to war. Overnight, the "working Yugoslav people" of socialist Yugoslavia became the "Serbian people" of Milošević's Serbia or the "Croatian people" of Tudjman's Croatia. This was not a transition to democracy but to pernicious ethnic politics.

It was not just the oncoming war that sullied the post-communist experience for much of ex-Yugoslavs. The interesting thing about Yugoslav communism was that it did not register as a particularly bad era for much of the Yugoslav population. Certainly in comparison to communisms elsewhere, Josip Broz Tito's version was significantly more overtly liberal, while of course engaging in strict political discipline and not allowing much dissent. The standard of living was much higher than in other communist countries. Most Yugoslavs had few travel restrictions so they did not feel like they lived in a cage, and ever since Tito broke off with Stalin in 1948, he refocused Yugoslav communism from a primarily economic doctrine to one about multiculturalism and ethnic "brotherhood and unity." Much of the communist effort was put in the construction of a durable supranational Yugoslav identity, with overt expressions of ethnic nationalism, including explicit religiosity, consistently suppressed.[8] This anti-Stalinist turn endeared Tito's Yugoslavia both to Western governments and to many Western academics who became enthusiastic about the Yugoslav "third way," which included the economic experiment of "workers' self-management," the non-aligned movement, and other innovative features of Yugoslav socialism. This friendliness toward Tito's model also contributed to the reluctance of some Western liberals to dig deeper into the country's human rights record.[9]

The breakup of the federation in 1991 was in part specifically about destroying this multinational Yugoslav identity and reasserting atomized, exclusionary ethnic identities across the Yugoslav political space. In fact, the idea of "brotherhood and unity" had to be eradicated completely and replaced with a new construction, this time of a "fatal and eternal historical conflict of the nations of Yugoslavia."[10] Much of the dominating Serbian and Croatian nationalist discourse in the 1990s was explicitly about rejecting communist multinational identities, and about "rescuing" Serbian or Croatian identity from the perceived threat of the other. As part of this process, human rights abuses of the communist period were presented as evidence of a sustained communist conspiracy against Serbs by Croats, or vice versa, depending on who was writing the historical transcript.

Communist crimes, in other words, were never analyzed in a political vacuum. They were utilized for nationalist mobilization from the 1990s onward and were selectively activated for very specific nationalist purposes: to further solidify the victimization narrative of one's own nation, to justify civil war as a break from communist oppression, and to build the post-communist state on a profound rejection of the communist ideology by elevating previously suppressed expressions of identity, such as nationalism and religion. Communist remembrance became in effect "confiscated" by the new post-communist regimes.[11]

In the early years after Tito's death in 1980, there was some isolated but noted discussion of communist abuses, mostly in the work of writers such as Antonije Isaković, whose 1983 novel *Tren 2* dealt with the abuses at the communist detention camp in Goli Otok. Work by the noted Yugoslav historian Vladimir Dedijer also began to briefly touch on the nature of the communist regime.[12] These early proto-transitional justice efforts were modest and remained within a limited circle of historians and writers, without much broader public impact.

This political use of communist era crimes continued after the 1990s wars. The postwar legitimacy of the newly established former Yugoslav states rested on a rejection of communism and a reconnection with the pre-communist, more purely "national" character of statehood. This is why in both Serbia and Croatia, the post 1990s elites, even in the aftermath of Milošević's ousting in 2000 and Tudjman's death in 1999, insisted on rehabilitating many anticommunist public figures, including many anticommunists who were also profascist allies, as I will demonstrate later in the chapter. The purpose of this agenda was to bypass the communist past and reaffirm the historical connection with pre-communist Serbia and pre-communist Croatia, as proto-states that serve as inspiration for the contemporary manifestation of ethnic statehood.

Lastly, these mnemonic projects were led by very specific and clearly delineated political coalitions. In both Croatia and Serbia after the collapse of the communist regime the winning coalitions consisted of former communists turned virulent nationalists. Their political opponents, anti-nationalist liberals, saw as their principal political struggle the fight against nationalism and ethnic war. They were interested in exposing the crimes of the 1990s, whose perpetrators mostly got away with impunity or even enjoyed high positions in the postwar governments. The liberals had very little interest in revisiting the crimes of the communist era when much more recent and, by some measure, more brutal crimes of the recent past were left unexamined and unpunished. Significantly, many of the Yugoslav post-communist liberals had a communist background, a fact that shaped their view of this era. This lack of urgency by liberals in the Yugoslav successor states to revisit communist crimes is strategically understandable, since exposing recent crimes of perpetrators still in power seems like a clear priority. This reluctance is also understandable in context – Yugoslavia was destroyed by individual nationalisms, and the war that followed the death of the federation made the old Yugoslavia seem much better than the new alternatives.[13] The consequence of this decision, however, was that investigation of communist crimes was left to the nationalist bloc. This peculiar twist on the "red/black"[14] political cleavage meant that most of the examination of communist violence was conducted by nationalist authors and institutions, who approached this historical project with a clear political agenda: to demonstrate that communist crimes were just as bad, if not even worse than the crimes of the 1990s. If this can be demonstrated, then the transitional justice effort for accountability for 1990s crimes can be delegitimized, demoralized, and ultimately defeated.

Transitional justice for communist crimes was, therefore, politicized from the very beginning – ignored for political reasons by liberals and pushed for political reasons by nationalists. It reflected contemporary political divisions. It is only within this context that any analysis of transitional justice in the former Yugoslavia since 1989 can be carried out with any scholarly credibility.

In what follows, I describe the practices of communist remembrance in Serbia and Croatia. I focus on two paradigmatic cases: the memory of the communist massacre of Ustasha militiamen at the end of World War II in Croatia and the remembrance of communist assassinations of Chetnik collaborators after World War II in Serbia. These cases are significant because they have entered the public imagination in the two countries as narratives of ethnic injustice, suffering, and victimization at the hands of communist henchmen. These narratives have since solidified and have greatly contributed to the understanding and misunderstanding of both the communist regime in the former Yugoslavia as well as the character of the armed anticommunist opposition.

MEMORY OF COMMUNIST VIOLENCE IN CROATIA

Croatia emerged from the violent war of the 1990s an independent state, for the first time in its history. Croatian national desire for statehood was so fundamental to Croatian national consciousness that former Croatian President Franjo Tudjman famously proclaimed that, after becoming an independent state in 1991, Croatia had finally fulfilled its "thousand-year-old dream."[15] Croatian longing for sovereignty is also rooted in a problematic historical memory of the earlier Croatian "state," a Nazi puppet entity that existed during World War II and that carried out numerous atrocities against non-Croats and other political enemies, including a systematic persecution and extermination of Croatian Jews.[16] The Croatian homegrown fascist militia, the Ustasha, who modeled themselves after German and especially Italian fascists, were the enthusiastic executors of fascist rule throughout wartime Croatia.

The unfortunate complication with remembering communism in contemporary Croatia is that it was exactly the Ustasha and their apologists and sympathizers who were the strongest organized anticommunist forces in twentieth-century Croatia. This contested past and unsettling history of the twentieth century in Croatia delineates the memory and narrative fault lines that define much of contemporary Croatian transitional justice efforts.

After 1991, an important piece of Croatia's identity construction was its complete rejection of the communist past and conflation of this past with Serbian hegemony. Communism, in other words, was interpreted as an early project of Greater Serbian domination (ironically, Serbian nationalists interpreted communism as exactly the opposite – the domination of Serbia by Croatian and Slovenian interests). The "true" Croatia of the twentieth century was represented by the anticommunist forces. As in Serbia, Croatia was transformed overnight from the state of the "working people" to the state of the "Croatian people."

This transformation is nowhere clearer than in the personal transformation of Croatian leaders. Tudjman, the "father" of the newly independent Croatia, was a highly ranked communist official (and former partisan general), who grew disillusioned with communism during the Croatian "Liberal Spring" in the 1960s. He became convinced that the crimes of the Ustasha were greatly exaggerated, and over time became a virulent Croatian nationalist who incorporated much of the Ustasha's iconography into his nationalist movement of the 1990s.[17] Stjepan Mesić, Tudjman's nemesis and Croatia's president after Tudjman's death, was similarly a prominent communist, the last president of the socialist Yugoslavia, prior to its bloody collapse. Over time, Mesić moved from communism to nationalism (he was a high official in Tudjman's Croatian Democratic Union) to ultimately progressive anti-fascism. As president of Croatia (2000–2010), Mesić made it a priority to cleanse Croatia from its fascist legacy, by using his presidential addresses to the nation to advocate for a European Croatia, a modern state that rejects fascist symbols, narratives, and myths.[18]

Back in the 1990s, however, with Tudjman still in power, the central piece of his ideology was the "all-Croatian reconciliation," which presupposed the unification of all Croatian people everywhere (Croatian communists, anticommunists, Ustasha sympathizers, and a vast Croatian diaspora), a joint nationalist effort in pursuit of Croatian statehood.[19] This reconciliation project views World War II as an unfortunate civil war among Croats, where Croatian partisans and Croatian nationalists both struggled for their version of a Croatian state. As part of this process, Croatian transitional justice efforts since 1991 focused mostly on dealing with the violence of the most recent war, and especially on prosecuting members of the Serb rebel militia. Most of these trials were done in absentia, and almost all suffered from clear ethnic bias and lack of adherence to basic due process.[20] In line with "all-Croatian reconciliation," war crimes committed by the Croatian army against either Serbs or Bosniacs remained virtually unpunished.[21] As Grodsky demonstrates in his contribution to this volume, after much international pressure, Croatia agreed to cooperate with the International Criminal Tribunal for the Former Yugoslavia (ICTY), by arresting and transferring Croatian war crimes suspects, but against much domestic political opposition and without almost any attempt at national soul-searching.[22]

As a consequence of these priorities, much of remembrance of communist crimes became the domain of Croatia's right wing and fascist apologists. Croatian liberals were focused on advocating for justice for victims of crimes committed by Croatian troops in the 1990s, and the Croatian state was focused on avoiding much of this process and unifying the nation. This left the Ustasha apologists to take on this piece of the transitional justice landscape. Many communist crimes remained completely ignored, such as postwar repression against German and Italian minorities – an issue that is rarely discussed even today.[23]

The first changes in the way in which Croatia remembers the communist past occurred in the early 1990s, when streets, schools, and public buildings that carried the names of famous partisans or communist leaders – as was the practice across communist Eastern Europe – were overnight changed into names of famous pre-communist Croatian public figures. For example, in September 1990, the Square of the Victims of Fascism (Trg žrtava fašizma) in Zagreb was renamed the Square of Croatian Great Men (Trg hrvatskh velikana).[24] Other streets were renamed after officials of the fascist-era Independent State of Croatia [Nezavisna država Hrvatska-NDH] (1941–1945). Public monuments suffered the same fate. Communist era monuments were replaced with statues of pre-communist or anticommunist Croatian heroes, including public figures associated with the Ustasha regime, while thousands of communist era monuments were vandalized, or completely destroyed. A thorough analysis of the types of communist monuments destroyed revealed that most of them commemorated fascist massacres of Serbs and Jews.[25] This destruction of monuments continues in Croatia to this day, although with decreasing intensity and frequency. Today's targets are monuments to Serb victims of Croatia's war in the 1990s.[26]

The changing public remembrance of communism is perhaps best manifested in numerous public commemorations of communist crimes, a paradigmatic example of which is the introduction to the public memory of the events at Bleiburg (in today's Austria) in 1945, where Croatian militiamen, who fought on the side of Nazi Germany as enthusiastic collaborators, gained renewed historical acceptance as innocent victims, even martyrs of the nation, slaughtered by Serbian communists. The Bleiburg massacre also began to be referred to in Croatia as "The Way of the Cross," a name that invokes clear Christian and martyrdom sentiments.

The truth about what actually happened at Bleiburg is murky, but beyond much dispute is the fact that a few thousand remnants of Ustasha forces, other Croatian militiamen, and many Croatian civilians were captured by the Yugoslav communist partisan army at the very end of the war in May 1945, as they were retreating near the Austrian town of Bleiburg. While the number of victims has been hotly disputed over the years, with many Croatian nationalists inflating the number killed to as many as half a million, most scholarly consensus puts the number of killed somewhere near 70,000.[27]

Throughout the communist era, the events at Bleiburg were not publicly discussed, and the only commemorations at the site were organized and attended by the Croatian diaspora. After the end of communism and with the resurgence of Croatian nationalism in the 1990s the commemorations at Bleiburg became one of the central sites of Croatian nationalist mobilization. The attractiveness of the Bleiburg remembrance to the anticommunist right is based, first, on the fact that Tito's regime suppressed any information on the massacre, and it therefore entered the realm of myths, half-truths, and legends. The Bleiburg story remained alive in the Croatian (often pro-Ustasha) diaspora, which over time developed its own version of the event and prepared it for public consumption in post-1991 Croatia, with great assistance and involvement from the Croatian Catholic Church.[28]

Unlike its past commemoration as the site of the communist army's massacre of Croatian (primarily Ustasha) soldiers, Bleiburg in the Croatian public consciousness since 1990 began to be seen and commemorated as a communist assault on the entire Croatian nation.[29] At the fiftieth anniversary of the Bleiburg massacre in 1995, the speaker of the Croatian Parliament addressed the assembly calling Bleiburg "the Holocaust of Croatian martyrs."[30] The Parliament also instituted the Sunday closest to May 15 the day of

Bleiburg commemoration, as a day of memory of Croatian victims in the struggle for freedom and independence. This historical mythmaking was used to differentiate present-day ideological cleavages by constructing narrative continuity between Croatian anticommunism, Ustasha nationalism, and the 1990s war of independence. Croatian nationalists therefore built a seamless narrative connecting the events of World War II and those of the war of the 1990s, making the recent war seem historically predetermined and inevitable, and using tenuous historical analogies to provide a particular interpretation of the most recent past. For example, at annual commemorations of the Bleiburg executions, a frequent chant of "Ante, Ante!" was heard – not in memory of Ante Pavelić, the leader of the Independent State of Croatia, but instead of Ante Gotovina, the Croatian general indicted for war crimes against the Croatian Serb population in 1995.[31]

Over time, the commemorations at Bleiburg became hotly politically contested. The first sitting Croatian prime minister to attend the Bleiburg commemoration was Ivica Račan, a Social Democrat, in 2002. Croatian President Stjepan Mesić, however, refused to attend for the duration of his ten years in office, insisting that the accurate count of civilians and military personnel be carried out first to avoid manipulation of facts.[32]

As Croatia began receiving more clear signals about its European future from the European Union, the government embarked on a "re-memorialization" campaign to affirm Croatia's antifascist and pro-European heritage. Monuments and statutes of Croatian fascists glorified in the 1990s were removed and Parliament passed declarations affirming Croatia's antifascist past. In this same period, however, Parliament also passed a law extending the commemorations at Bleiburg to two days (Saturday and Sunday) to allow for greater participation of the Catholic Church. Andrija Hebrang, a member of Croatian Parliament (and son of one of the highest profile communist victims, discussed later in the chapter), stated at the 2011 Bleiburg commemoration, "Bleiburg is the biggest symbol of Croatian suffering that equates fascism and communism. Communism becomes worse than fascism, it becomes the world's biggest evil, because it turns into the system of killing everyone who thought differently."[33] Equating communism with fascism became a common trope in Croatian nationalist mobilization. Prime Minister Ivo Sanader on numerous occasions insisted on condemnation of "both totalitarianisms" – the "red one" and the "black one."[34]

This equation of communism and fascism is not an indigenous Croatian invention. This process has occurred throughout Eastern Europe, with much historical revisionism resulting from the attempts of Eastern European countries to deny or cloud their participation in fascist crimes, including the

Holocaust, by elevating communist crimes to the same level. The remarkably revisionist Hungarian House of Terror, which replaces fascist with communist crimes as the definition of "twentieth-century terror" is one of the most obvious cases in point.[35]

Croatian re-memorialization equates not only different types of crimes and ideologies, but also different victims. Many public monuments to "war victims" across Croatia do not differentiate between victims of Croatian fascists, communists, and victims of the most recent war (1991–1995), or even between military and civilian victims, but instead make generic homage to victims who gave lives for the independence and sovereignty of Croatia.[36] This political choice of memory denies victims the acknowledgment of their individual suffering, and hides the identity/political affiliation and motivation of perpetrators, making any effective transitional justice impossible.

Post-communist Croatia also began to show interest in uncovering evidence behind political assassinations of Croatian dissidents and radical émigrés by the Yugoslav secret intelligence service. The actual communist violence – extrajudicial assassinations of dissidents, often in exile, by the State Security Service (Uprava državne bezbednosti, UDBA)[37] were known but not widely discussed, and remained in the domain of scary legends and an ever-present feeling of insecurity and abundance of political caution by the population. By some estimates, the UDBA attempted about a hundred political assassinations.[38] Many of these assassinations also included cold-blooded murder of the primary victims' wives or children.[39] There has been renewed historical interest in the postwar period in Croatia recently, where new volumes of documents about communist crimes in Croatia in the early postwar years have been recently published.[40]

While UDBA violence was known and became a fabric of political life under communism, post-communist elites had no interest in uncovering these crimes mostly because UDBA seamlessly morphed into the new independent states' security and intelligence apparatus, and any attempt at lustration would cause significant embarrassment and political disturbance for the new governments. For example, in 2005 Germany indicted Croatian national and former UDBA operative Josip Perković for his role in the murder of Stjepan Djureković in Germany in 1983. The Croatian government viciously fought the extradition, even changing the extradition law to prevent Perković from being extradited – all because Perković was an important ally of former President Tudjman and had connections with the family of President Mesić.[41] Only after Croatia was accepted into the EU in 2013 did it relent under European pressure and threat of sanctions and changed the law, allowing for Perković's extradition.[42] More recently, in October 2013, a Zagreb court confirmed the indictment of Josip Boljkovac, Croatia's first interior minister after the 1991 independence, for allegedly ordering the killing of Croatian civilians accused of collaborating with the Ustasha in 1945, while he was a communist partisan officer.[43]

The political environment in Serbia, even after Milošević's ousting, was perhaps even worse for communist lustration as former state security operatives remained an integral part of President Koštunica's security and intelligence apparatus. Many observers have pointed fingers at these very unsavory connections in looking for the culprit behind the assassination of Serbian Prime Minister Zoran Djindjić in 2003.[44]

As the official state policy remains largely reluctant to open these files and find out the truth about UDBA operations, this space was left to the Croatian right-wing to continue to mythologize the past. For example, *Slobodna Dalmacija*, a right-wing and often openly nationalistic newspaper, published a series of articles about UDBA assassinations of Croatian émigrés, but focused exclusively on their Croatian identity as the reason for their targeting, ignoring the Ustasha or fascist sympathies of quite a number of these targets. In this interpretation, communist crimes were crimes of ethnic chauvinism against the Croats and further evidence of the fundamental anti-Croat bias of communist Yugoslavia.[45] Revising the communist violence was colored through a specific political nationalist lens, and involved one wing of the Croatian political spectrum.

A recent analysis of Croatian history textbooks, for example, uncovered a politicized pattern of education about communist violence. Bleiburg in contemporary Croatian textbooks is discussed at length, listing a wide range of victims from tens of thousands to as many as 300,000 in one textbook. One text places the "Bleiburg tragedy" in the contemporary setting by noting, "even though it has only been in recent times that Bleiburg and the Way of the Cross have begun to be spoken and written about, there is still resistance to the clarification of the circumstances and punishment of the perpetrators."[46] Interestingly, while the contemporary Serbian textbooks mention that the partisans captured 300,000 people at the end of the war, they describe them as "German and quisling soldiers from the NDH and Slovenia, as well as some Chetniks."[47] No civilians are mentioned, and there is no discussion of the fate of these prisoners of war.

Croatian textbooks mention communist crimes after the war, and mostly focus on communist repression of political liberties, such as limiting private ownership, oppressing religious communities, especially the Croatian Catholic Church, and eliminating freedom of the press and elections. Croatian texts also mention political purges, involving show trials of political opponents that in many cases resulted in long imprisonment, forced labor, and even death.[48] In many cases, however, much of this discussion is presented without a broader context of the communist regime, and with an emphasis of the Serbian domination of the communist Yugoslavia, which again makes a politically useful bridge to contemporary Croatian independence and emancipation from the communist past.

A more promising local memory effort is the "Croatian Memories: Unveiling Personal Memories on War and Detention" project, which presents oral histories from traditionally marginalized groups in Croatia (women and minorities) from 1941 to 1995. The project is run by the leading Croatian transitional justice nongovernmental organization Documenta, which has collected 450 video interviews that are available to the general public. While the majority of the interviews deal with the violence in the most recent Croatian war, a significant number of stories discuss communist violence, including stories from former detainees in the notorious Goli Otok detention camp for political prisoners and dissidents.[49] This project, while getting wider human rights acclaim, has been very controversial in Croatia, and has received funding from the Netherlands as the Croatian government refused to fund it.[50]

The memory of communism in Croatia, therefore, has been extremely contentious. The past is unsettled and the meaning of communism is a changing, moving target. Transitional justice for communist violence has been haphazard, unsystematic, and completely hijacked by fractious political factions. As I demonstrate in the next section, the lack of any serious addressing of the communist past is a political condition that Croatia shares with Serbia.

MEMORY OF COMMUNIST VIOLENCE IN SERBIA

Serbian politics in the 1990s underwent a profound transformation, when the former communist ideology of the struggle of the "working people" seamlessly morphed into the nationalist struggle of the "Serbian people." The nationalist mythmaking carried out by Serbian political and cultural elites, including the Serbian Orthodox Church, advocated the idea that Serbia is a victim of vast outside conspiracies that want to conquer or destroy it.[51] At the same time, the new Serbian history portrayed Serbs as fighting on the right side of conflicts around the world (unlike their enemies) and abstaining from doing any harm to their multiple and ever more vicious enemies.[52] This particular state narrative of injustice, victimization, and collective grief provided a cognitive window through which the Serbian society and its elites began to see and interpret the world around them. It portrayed political action by perceived adversaries (Slovenes, Croats, Bosniacs, Kosovo Albanians) as perpetually threatening.[53] A politicized memory of Serbian history was used to conflate the past – including the communist past – with the present, in order to interpret contemporary national problems as part of an ahistorical, eternal struggle of the Serbian people for survival.

A critical element of Serbian post-communist national identity construction was not so much the wholesale repudiation of communism but more a subsuming of communism into the larger Serbian national story. The ethnic identity of various communist leaders became much more important than their communist ideology. The fact that Tito was of Croatian origin factored greatly into this narrative of age-old, ahistorical Croatian oppression of Serbs. Tito's purges of his once-close allies, Milovan Djilas in 1954 and Aleksandar Ranković in 1966, were broadly interpreted as evidence of Tito's anti-Serbian bias. Amusingly, Croatian post-communist narrative also focuses on communists' ethnic identity, but only to point out the majority Serbian leadership of the party. The paradigmatic case of this "anti-Croatian" sentiment during the communist period was the high-profile disappearance and assassination of Andrija Hebrang, a high Communist Party official whom Tito perceived as a threat and disposed of, most likely around 1949. In fact, throughout the early 1990s, much of the Croatian media and political elite commonly used the newly coined phrase "Serbo-communists" to describe Milošević and his minions.

During Milošević's rule in the 1990s, communism was neither the target of any serious evaluation, nor were any crimes of communism systematically investigated. This is hardly surprising considering that Milošević came to power as the leader of the Serbian Communist Party in 1987 (the party morphed into the Socialist Party of Serbia in 1990), and his wife Mirjana Marković was the leader of the rump Communist Party renamed the Yugoslav Left from 1994 until the party's dissolution in 2003.

After Milošević was ousted in October 2000, a new coalition came to power led by the conservative Vojislav Koštunica. Only since 2000 has communism become a topic of great public interest in Serbia, with increasing numbers of newspaper articles, public exhibitions, and books dedicated to communist violence. This renewed interest was not an organic development. It was part of a larger national project of linking contemporary Serbia with its "golden era," the mythical pre-communist period when Serbia had full state sovereignty and was true to its core national identity.[54] The new government presented itself as an embodiment of these "classical" Serbian values and as the force that got rid of Milošević, the personification of communism.[55] An important element of this project was the rehabilitation of Serbia's wartime army and militia, the Chetniks, portrayed as pro-fascist Nazi collaborators throughout the communist period. As a consequence of this political agenda, almost the entire discussion of communist violence in Serbia became a discussion of communist violence against the Chetniks, who are no longer depicted as quislings but as alternative, anticommunist resisters to the Nazi regime.[56]

The Chetnik rehabilitation project has been particularly evident in education. Building on the early Chetnik rehabilitation efforts in Serbian historiography from the mid-1980s, contemporary Serbian history textbooks today describe Chetniks as "national patriots," even an "anti-fascist movement from the right."[57] Chetniks are today favorably portrayed as "traditional" and as "protecting the interests of the Serbian people."[58] A recent comprehensive analysis of the currently used textbooks in Serbia finds only one book that mentions Chetnik crimes, but even this text only discusses Chetnik crimes against other Serbs, while Chetnik massacres against Bosnian Muslims and Croats (abundantly covered in Croatian and Bosniac contemporary textbooks) are completely ignored.[59] Perhaps most egregious is the discussion of the government of Milan Nedić, the fascist collaborator under whose reign Serbia was declared Judenrein ("clean of Jews") in 1942, whom the current Serbian textbooks describe as "saving the biological essence of the Serbian nation," while his collaboration is explained as: "he thought that Germany was too powerful and that collaboration with the occupier was necessary to prevent the suffering of the Serbian people."[60] Members of another fascist group, the Volunteer Corps of Dimitrije Ljotić, close collaborators of Gestapo and SS units, are mentioned once as being "more ideologically fanatical than even the communists."[61]

The fight for Chetnik rehabilitation moved from textbooks into the legal realm in 2004, when the Serbian Parliament passed a law equating the rights of partisan and Chetnik World War II fighters. In 2006, Parliament adopted a law on rehabilitation, which allows "the rehabilitation of all individuals who were killed or denied rights in an extrajudicial manner, for political or ideological reasons since April 6, 1941 [the beginning of the German occupation of Serbia] until the day the current law comes into effect."[62] The main purpose of the law was to effectively rehabilitate Chetnik and quisling forces, which were for the duration of the communist period declared enemies of the state.[63] In 2009, a state commission was formed to investigate the circumstances of the execution of the Chetnik leader General Dragoslav "Draža" Mihailović, who was sentenced to death as an enemy of the Yugoslav state in 1946. Also in 2009, another commission was established to discover and memorialize all secret mass graves where individuals – mostly Chetniks and other quislings, but also many "bourgeois" civilians, shot by the partisans immediately after the partisan liberation of Belgrade in October 1944, are buried. In September 2010, a group of Serbian academics and lawyers initiated a lawsuit in the Serbian courts to legally rehabilitate the Chetnik leader Mihailović. This lawsuit has received much more extensive publicity in the Serbian media than any of the trials of Serb war criminals accused of violence during the 1990s and has been interpreted by much of the media as a case of overdue justice.[64] Since 2000, three monuments to Mihailović were erected in Serbia, and in 2005 the government even sponsored a commemoration to Mihailović in Ravna Gora, the mythical birthplace of the Serbian Chetnik movement.[65] As a further sign of how incredibly contentious the Mihailović rehabilitation process has been, the Helsinki Committee for Human Rights in Serbia, a leading Serbian human rights nongovernmental organization, filed a lawsuit against two historians who served as expert witnesses in favor of Mihailović's rehabilitation, for perjury during the trial proceedings.[66]

In October 2012, the Serbian government transported with great aplomb from Switzerland to Serbia the remains of Prince Pavle Karadjordjević and members of his family. Prince Pavle was the Serbian regent who presided over the signing of the pact with Hitler's Germany. He was expelled from Yugoslavia after the military coup of March 27, 1941, and later declared enemy of the state by the communist regime. The government organized a new official burial of Prince Pavle in Serbia, with all the pomp and circumstance of a state funeral. The role of Prince Pavle in Serbia's interwar history is complex and contradictory, but the current Serbian intellectual and political elites have used this case to link contemporary Serbia with its "golden era" of anticommunism and monarchism, even placing Serbia in the family of other interwar monarchies as one of the great European powers of the time.[67]

In fact, almost the entire effort to uncover communist crimes in post-Milošević Serbia was reduced to the rehabilitation of Chetniks and fascist collaborators as full-fledged patriots who fought the good fight against the onslaught of communist totalitarianism and for the preservation of the Serbian "golden era." This is also manifest in the extraordinarily expansive effort to rename Serbian streets and squares. Since the early 1990s, in Belgrade alone more than 1,500 street and square names – one-fifth of all named transit veins of the city – have been replaced. In almost all cases, the formerly communist themed names were replaced with new more desirable Serbian national symbols and figures.[68]

The rehabilitation of the Chetnik movement and its leading figures has been fully accepted in Serbia and is even institutionalized through official state efforts. However, this process has caused great alarm in Croatia, as the Chetniks carried out numerous atrocities against Croatian civilians during

World War II, and even directly collaborated with the fascist Italian forces in killings and deportations. The fact that they are now celebrated as "antifascists from the right" has led to an official rebuke from the Croatian government, which the Serbian government ignored.[69]

While most of the communist remembrance in Serbia has been focused on the rehabilitation of the Chetnik movement, there has also been a more recent effort to explore more systematically the crimes of the communist regime. In 2008, the Serbian Security-Information Service (the heir to the Yugoslav secret intelligence service) handed over 64,000 formerly classified personal files to the Serbian Archives for safekeeping. However, after a very brief initial period of openness in 2001, none of the personal files can be accessed since there is no law regulating the access to or treatment of these sensitive documents.[70]

In 2012, the Museum for the History of Yugoslavia in Belgrade put up an exhibition "Yugoslavia: From the Beginning to the End," which included a short treatment of the communist period and the crimes carried out by the communist regime.[71] This pilot exhibition was to represent the basis for the future permanent collection of the Museum. A more recent project is a series of books and a multimedia exhibition planned for March 2014 at the Serbian Historical Museum by Serbian historian Srdjan Cvetković, who put together new historical documents and evidence of crimes the communist regime committed against some 52,000 people, mostly in the early, most brutal, years of the regime (1945–1953). The crimes range from assassinations, kidnappings, detentions in camps, collectivization, political trials, and repression. This ambitious exhibition includes reenactments of communist torture chambers, short movies depicting show trials, mock election ballots boxes modeled after the actual communist fraudulent ballots, model prison cells and secret service offices, and troves of documents demonstrating the long reach of communist violence.[72] While this is the first effort of its kind and could show great promise in filling the huge gap in transitional justice projects in the region, some aspects of the project have raised red flags. For example, most of the materials for this project came out of the work of the highly controversial commission on discovering and memorializing communist mass graves, as discussed above. The project author claimed that most of the people killed by the communist regime were ordinary citizens, not Chetniks or quislings[73] – a claim that goes against much of conventional wisdom about this period, but is certainly a plausible one, especially later in the postwar period. However, the author's other claim, that the Chetnik movement was antifascist and pro-European,[74] is much more alarming, and indicates that even this promising new effort will possibly be hijacked by the revisionist forces, interested more in rehabilitating the Chetniks than in finding out the truth about communist crimes.

CONCLUSION AND LESSONS LEARNED

The uniqueness of the memory of Yugoslav communism in Serbia and Croatia lies in the almost complete absence of a systematic addressing of the communist past. This stands in stark contrast with many of the other former communist countries in Eastern Europe where much effort – and with varying degrees of success – was placed on lustration or historical examination of communist crimes. The Yugoslav experience was different in many other ways, as discussed above, from the somewhat more benign character of the Yugoslav communist regime to the absence of a post-communist democratic transition in 1989. The fact that former Yugoslavia left communism and replaced it immediately with war and nationalism made a serious and depoliticized evaluation of the communist past that much more difficult.

In both Serbia and Croatia, communist remembrance was mobilized for very specific political projects, on the Left and especially on the political Right. While Grodsky (this volume) focuses on ways in which political leaders were motivated by a pragmatic political calculus, my chapter demonstrates that Serbian and Croatian liberals fully gave ground to conservative anticommunist forces in the transitional justice project, choosing instead to focus on the more recent and obviously violent post-communist crimes. Many on the liberal left had past communist connections, and there was no constituency within this segment of the polity in favor of revisiting the old regime. This abandonment of the search for truth and justice for communist crimes opened the door for a complete takeover of this project by the anticommunist right, which approached this endeavor with renewed zeal and ambition. Most anticommunist forces, including many fascists and fascist collaborators, were rehabilitated under the banner of anticommunism and the struggle for freedom. This revisionist process in both countries connected the contemporary states of Serbia and Croatia with their mythical pre-communist selves, and in the course of this narrative shift contributed to a renewed cycle of mythologizing and nationalist mobilization.

The way in which communist violence is discussed in today's Serbia and Croatia is problematic for a number of reasons. The ideological commitment to "national reconciliation" of both fascist and antifascist forces of the twentieth century clearly equates fascism and communism as two sides of the same totalitarian coin, an ideological equivalency that has been promoted by the highest offices of the EU.[75] This focus on national reconciliation, shows Aida Hozić, "promotes national homogenization and, frequently, externalizes responsibility for crimes (to the Germans or the Soviets); by equating Nazi and fascist collaborators and antifascists, it erases the memory of resistance (and sometimes criminalizes it); by individualizing victimhood ... it institutionalizes forgetting of crimes committed against particular groups (e.g. Roma, homosexuals, Slavs, communists), and precludes possible discomforting comparisons with the present treatment of minorities. Mostly, by emphasizing World War II and communist crimes, it deals with the communist past parenthetically, limiting serious and critical inquiry of everyday practices that sustained and undermined communist regimes for over fifty years."[76]

As a consequence of this political mythologizing of communist remembrance, serious examination of this important era is yet to be accomplished. If there is one lesson to be learned from the Yugoslav experience, it is for the transitional justice scholars and practitioners not to give up this historical ground so easily to others, but to insist on a careful and systematic evaluation of the communist past. It is also important to carefully conceive of this research as a comparative endeavor, to avoid these pitfalls of national consensus and ideological bias.[77] Twenty-five years after the collapse of the communist regimes, there is much yet to be learned, understood, and interpreted about the layers of violence in the twentieth century in Eastern Europe.

NOTES

* I thank Marko Atilla Hoare, Aida Hozić, Maria Malksoo, Tamara Pavasović Trošt, Sabrina Ramet, and Dubravka Stojanović for sharing their work on this topic, the two volume editors for helpful comments and suggestions, Bogdan Ivanišević, Vladimir Petrović and Irina Subotić for detailed comments on earlier drafts of the chapter.

1. The extremely thin scholarly literature on communist crimes includes Latinka Perović, *Zatvaranje kruga: Ishod političkog rascepa u SKJ 1971/1972* (Sarajevo: Svjetlost, 1991); Srdjan Cvetković, *Izmedju srpa i čekića: Politička represija u Srbiji* (Belgrade: Institut za savremenu istoriju, 2011); Rajko Danilović, *Upotreba neprijatelja: Politička suđenja 1945–1991 u Jugoslaviji* (Belgrade: Zavod za udžbenike, 2010); and Branka Magaš, *The Destruction of Yugoslavia: Tracking the Break-up 1980–92* (London: Verso, 1993). An early artistic account of communist crimes, especially the abuses at the Goli Otok detention camp, was rendered in the theater play *Kad su cvetale tikve* by Dragoslav Mihailović in 1968. The government banned the play soon after the opening show.
2. Paige Arthur, "How 'Transitions' Reshaped Human Rights: A Conceptual History of Transitional Justice," *Human Rights Quarterly* 31, no. 2 (2009): 321–367.
3. Neil Kritz, *Transitional Justice: How Emerging Democracies Reckon with Former Regimes* (Washington, D.C.: United States Institute of Peace Press, 1995), 3 vols.
4. Payam Akhavan, "Beyond Impunity: Can International Criminal Justice Prevent Atrocities?," *American Journal of International Law* 95, no. 1 (2001): 7–31; Diane Orentlicher, "Settling Accounts: The Duty to Prosecute Human Rights Violations of a Prior Regime," *Yale Law Journal* 100 (1991): 2539–2568.

5. Kathryn Sikkink, *The Justice Cascade: How Human Rights Prosecutions Are Changing World Politics* (New York: Norton, 2011).
6. Fionnuala Ní Aoláin and Colm Campbell, "The Paradox of Transition in Conflicted Democracies," *Human Rights Quarterly* 27, no. 1 (2005): 172–213.
7. Thomas Risse, Steven Ropp, and Kathryn Sikkink, *The Power of Human Rights: International Norms and Domestic Change* (Cambridge: Cambridge University Press, 1999).
8. The literature on Yugoslavia is vast. Some excellent surveys are Sabrina P. Ramet, *The Three Yugoslavias: State-building and Legitimation, 1918–2005* (Washington, D.C.: Woodrow Wilson Center Press, 2006); John B. Allcock, *Explaining Yugoslavia* (New York: Columbia University Press, 2000); and John R. Lampe, *Yugoslavia as History: Twice There Was a Country* (Cambridge: Cambridge University Press, 1996).
9. I thank Vladimir Petrović for this insightful comment.
10. Nataša Govedarica, "Zemlja nesigurne prošlosti," in *Re:vizija prošlosti: Politike sjećanja u Bosni i Hercegovini, Hrvatskoj i Srbiji od 1990. godine*, eds. Tamara Banjeglav, Nataša Govedarica, and Darko Karačić (Sarajevo: ACIPS, 2012), 172.
11. Dubravka Ugrešić, "The Confiscation of Memory," *New Left Review* I, no. 218 (1996): 26–39.
12. Vladimir Petrović, "Modeli zaštite javnog sećanja u borbi protiv poricanja zločina," *Forum za tranzicionu pravdu*, no. April (2007): 131–139.
13. Mitja Velikonja, "Lost in Transition Nostalgia for Socialism in Post-socialist Countries," *East European Politics and Societies* 23, no. 4 (2009): 535–551.
14. The "red/black" cleavage refers to the historical animosity between "red" (communist) and "black" (fascist) forces.
15. Franjo Tudjman, *Address of the President of the Republic of Croatia on the State of the Nation* (Zagreb: 1998).
16. Ivo Goldstein and Slavko Goldstein, *Holokaust u Zagrebu* (Zagreb: Novi liber, 2001).
17. Ian Traynor, "Franjo Tudjman," *Guardian*, December 12, 1999.
18. Ivica Djikić, *Domovinski obrat: Politička biografija Stipe Mesića* (Zagreb: VBZ, 2004).
19. Tamara Banjeglav, "Sjećanje na rat ili rat sjećanja?" in *Re:vizija prošlosti: Politike sjećanja u Bosni i Hercegovini, Hrvatskoj i Srbiji od 1990. godine*, eds. Tamara Banjeglav, Nataša Govedarica, and Darko Karačić (Sarajevo: ACIPS, 2012), pp. 91–126.
20. Jelena Subotić, *Hijacked Justice: Dealing with the Past in the Balkans* (Ithaca, NY: Cornell University Press, 2009).
21. Human Rights Watch, *Justice at Risk: War Crimes Trials in Croatia, Bosnia and Herzegovina, and Serbia and Montenegro* (New York: Human Rights Watch, October 13, 2004).
22. Victor Peskin, *International Justice in Rwanda and the Balkans: Virtual Trials and the Struggle for State Cooperation* (Cambridge: Cambridge University Press, 2008); and Christopher K. Lamont, *International Criminal Justice and the Politics of Compliance* (Burlington, VT: Ashgate, 2009).
23. Zoran Janjetović, *Between Hitler and Tito: The Disappearance of the Vojvodina Germans* (Belgrade: s.n., 2000); and Vladimir Geiger, *Nestanak folksdojčera* (Zagreb: Nova stvarnost, 1997).

24. In 2000, after Tudjman's death and his replacement by Stjepan Mesić, the city of Zagreb returned the original name to the square after vigorous public protests.
25. Banjeglav, "Sjećanje na rat ili rat sjećanja?"
26. One of the few memorials to Serb civilians killed during the Croatian Army's Operation Storm in 1995 was vandalized in the village of Golubić, Croatia, in September 2013. Boris Pavelić, "Croatia Monument to Serb War Victims Vandalised," *Balkan Insight* (September 16, 2013), available at: http://www.balkanin sight.com/en/article/croatia-monument-to-serb-victims-vandalised/1460/5 (accessed January 13, 2014).
27. Pal Kolsto, "Bleiburg: The Creation of a National Martyrology," *Europe-Asia Studies* 62, no. 7 (2010): 1153–1174.
28. Ibid.
29. Ibid.
30. Banjeglav, "Sjećanje na rat ili rat sjećanja?" 109.
31. Kolsto, "Bleiburg," 1163.
32. Banjeglav, "Sjećanje na rat ili rat sjećanja?"
33. Ibidem, 115–116.
34. Ljiljana Radonić, "Standards of Evasion: Croatia and the Europeanization of Memory," *Eurozine* (April 6, 2012), available at: http://www.eurozine.com/ articles/2012-04-06-radonic-en.html (accessed January 13, 2014).
35. Ljiljana Radonić, "Croatia – Exhibiting Memory and History at the 'Shores of Europe,'" *Culture Unbound* 3 (2011): 355–367. On memory wars in Eastern Europe and Europeanization of memory see Maria Malksoo, "The Memory Politics of Becoming European: The East European Subalterns and the Collective Memory of Europe," *European Journal of International Relations* 15, no. 4 (2009): 653–680.
36. Banjeglav, "Sjećanje na rat ili rat sjećanja?"
37. UDBA was part of the reorganization of the earlier department of national security OZNA (Odeljenje za zaštitu naroda) and was later reorganized again into state security agency SDB (Služba državne bezbednosti).
38. The highest profile cases were the assassinations of Croatian dissidents Bruno Busić in Paris in 1978 and Stjepan Djureković in 1983, as well as of notorious Ustasha Jasenovac camp commander Maks Luburić in 1969.
39. John Schindler, professor at the United States Naval War College, in interview to *Studia Croatica*, February 11, 2010, available at http://studiacroatica.blogspot.com/ 2010/02/dr-john-r-schindler-agents-provocateurs.html (accessed January 13, 2014).
40. The first in a series of published document collections is Vladimir Geiger, Mate Rupić, Mario Kevo, Egon Kraljević, and Zvonimir Despot, eds., *Partizanska i komunistička represija i zločini u Hrvatskoj 1944–1946* (Slavonski brod: Hrvatski institut za povijest, 2005).
41. Schindler, interview (see note 39).
42. Boris Pavelić, "Croatia Changes Controversial Extradition Law," *Balkan Insight* (October 7, 2013), available at: http://www.balkaninsight.com/en/article/croatia-changes-lex-perkovic (accessed January 13, 2014).
43. Boris Pavelić, "Croatia Confirms Ex-Minister's WWII Killing Charges," *Balkan Insight* (October 29, 2013), available at: http://www.balkaninsight.com/en/article/ croatian-ex-minister-wwii-crimes-indictment-confirmed (accessed January 13, 2014).
44. Miloš Vasić, *Atentat na Zorana Đinđića* (Belgrade: Politika, 2005).

45. Josip Jović, "Državni terorizam: UDBA ubila 69 emigranata," *Slobodna Dalmacija*, June 18, 2010. *Slobodna Dalmacija* has continued to publish a series about UDBA crimes of Croatian nationals throughout September 2013.
46. Jovana Mihajlović Trbovc and Tamara Pavasović Trošt, "Who Were the Anti-Fascists? Multiple Interpretations of WWII in Post-Yugoslav Textbooks," in *The Use and Abuse of Memory: Interpreting World War Two in Contemporary European Politics*, eds. Christian Karner and Bram Mertens (New Brunswick, NJ: Transaction Publishers, 2013), 173–192.
47. Ibid.
48. Ibid.
49. Oral histories are available on the project website at http://www.croatianmemories.org/en.
50. Boris Pavelić, "Exploring the Power of Memory in Croatia," *Balkan Insight* (October 4, 2013), available at: http://www.balkaninsight.com/en/article/croatia-personal-war-memories-collection-presented (accessed January 13, 2014).
51. Sabrina P. Ramet, "The Denial Syndrome and Its Consequences: Serbian Political Culture since 2000," *Communist and Post-Communist Studies* 40, no. 1 (2007): 41–58.
52. Dubravka Stojanović, "U ogledalu 'drugih,'" in *Novosti iz prošlosti: Znanje, neznanje, upotreba i zloupotreba istorije*, eds. Dubravka Stojanović, Radina Vučetić, Sanja Petrović Todosijević, Olga Manojlović Pintar, and Radmila Radić (Belgrade: Beogradski centar za ljudska prava, 2010), 13–32.
53. Jelena Subotić, "Stories States Tell: Identity, Narrative, and Human Rights in the Balkans," *Slavic Review* 72, no. 2 (2013): 306–326.
54. Olivera Milosavljević, *Savremenici fašizma* (Belgrade: Helsinški komitet za ljudska prava, 2010).
55. Govedarica, "Zemlja nesigurne prošlosti."
56. The precise qualification of the Chetnik movement is difficult because the movement itself has gone through multiple transformations since its inception in 1904. It was originally established as a monarchist anti-occupation movement but during the course of World War II it took on exclusively anticommunist and increasingly Serbian nationalist character and perpetrated numerous atrocities against non-Serb civilians in Croatia and Bosnia. By the end of the war, the Chetnik movement worked closely with German occupation and Serbian collaboration forces. Throughout the war Chetnik forces perpetrated numerous atrocities against non-Serb civilians in Croatia and Bosnia. Sabrina Ramet and Ola Listhaug, eds., *Serbia and the Serbs in World War Two* (New York: Palgrave Macmillan, 2011).
57. Helsinki Committee for Human Rights in Serbia, *Human Rights Reflect Institutional Impotence* (Belgrade: HCHRS, 2011), 27.
58. Mihajlović Trbovc and Pavasović Trošt, "Who Were the Anti-Fascists?"
59. Ibid.
60. In Dubravka Stojanović, "Vinovnici i žrtve u srpskim udžbenicima istorije," *Peščanik* (September 19, 2013), available at: http://pescanik.net/2013/09/vinovnici-i-zrtve-u-srpskim-udzbenicima-istorije (accessed January 13, 2014).
61. Ibid.
62. "Rehabilitation Law, 25 April 2006," *Službeni glasnik Republike Srbije* 33/2006.
63. Govedarica, "Zemlja nesigurne prošlosti."
64. Helsinki Committee for Human Rights in Serbia, *Human Rights*.

65. Milan Radanović, "Istorijska politika u Srbiji nakom 2000. godine: Primeri manifestovanja sprege između akademskog istorijskog revizionizma i državne revizije prošlosti," in *Izgubljeno u tranziciji: Kritička analiza procesa društvene transformacije*, eds. Ana Veselinović, Petar Atanacković, and Željko Klarić (Belgrade: Rosa Luxemburg Stiftung, 2011), 258–305.
66. The text of the complaint is available on Helsinki Committee's website at http://www.helsinki.org.rs/serbian/doc/krivicna%20prijava%20hos%20sept_17_2013.pdf.
67. Srdjan Milošević, "Rehabilitacija kneza Pavla: Zbir netačnih podataka i pogrešnih tumačenja," *Novi magazin*, October 4, 2012.
68. Govedarica, "Zemlja nesigurne prošlosti."
69. AA, "Draža, Srbi i Hrvati," *Novi magazin*, March 31, 2012.
70. Aleksandar Roknić, "Iz podruma Udbe u podrum Arhiva," *Danas*, October 9, 2008.
71. More information about the exhibition is available on the Museum website, http://mij.rs/poseta/izlozbe/66/jugoslavija-od-pocetka-do-kraja.html.
72. Marko Lopušina, "Srđan Cvetković: Osvetljavamo mračne godine Srbije," *Večernje novosti*, October 13, 2013.
73. Marija Ristić, "Exposing the Secret Crimes of Communism in Serbia," *Balkan Insight* (September 9, 2013), available at: http://www.balkaninsight.com/en/article/serbia-still-unaware-of-communist-era-crimes (accessed January 13, 2014).
74. In AA, "Draža, Srbi i Hrvati."
75. Maria Malksoo, "Criminalizing Communism: Transnational Mnemopolitics in Europe," *International Political Sociology* 8, no. 1 (2014): 82–99.
76. Hozić, "It Happened Elsewhere."
77. A promising example is the special issue of the journal *Hereticus*, with participation of historians from several Yugoslav successor states. "Communist Repression at the End of the Second World War," *Hereticus* 9, nos. 1–2 (2011), available at: http://www.hereticus.org/wp-content/uploads/2011/Hereticus%201-2%202011.pdf (accessed January 13, 2014).

PART IV

History, Justice, and Public Memory

10

Post-Communist Truth Commissions: Between Transitional Justice and the Politics of History

Andrew H. Beattie

Although truth commissions are central to the study and practice of transitional justice globally, it is widely believed that they played almost no role in the European post-communist context. Indeed, for a long time, lustration dominated understandings and accounts of post-communist transitional justice, to the neglect of other features.[1] Yet in a number of post-communist countries, transitional justice has gone beyond lustration, and truth-revelation processes have gone beyond granting access to secret-police files to include official investigative commissions. This phenomenon has not received much systematic scholarly attention. Until recently, the growing literature on truth commissions largely failed to consider whether examples of the phenomenon could be found in post-communist Europe, or simply asserted that they could not.[2] Even experts on post-communist transitional justice initially overlooked examples or possible contenders or declared that truth commissions did not exist there.[3]

Closer inspection and the passage of time have brought to light a number of bodies that share at least important characteristics with truth commissions, and might even qualify as such. Examples have been identified in Estonia, Germany, Latvia, Lithuania, Moldova, Poland, Romania, Serbia, Slovenia, Uzbekistan, and Yugoslavia.[4] These bodies all differed considerably from one another, as do truth commissions. Given their not insignificant number, understanding these commissions is arguably more crucial for comprehending the first twenty-five years of post-communist transitional justice than either asserting their non-conformity to particular truth-commission models or seeking to explain the putative complete or relative absence of truth commissions from post-communist Europe.

This chapter examines the cases of Germany and the three Baltic states. Specifically, it considers Germany's commission of inquiry Working through the History and Consequences of the SED Dictatorship in Germany (1992–1994), Estonia's International Commission for Investigation of Crimes against Humanity (1998–2008), the Commission of the Historians of Latvia (1998–present), and the International Commission for the Evaluation of the Crimes of the Nazi and Soviet Occupation Regimes in Lithuania (1998–present). These commissions are among the best understood in Europe, but to date there has been little systematic effort to compare them with one another or with truth commissions more broadly, or to discuss their place within the broader transitional justice context, in Europe and beyond.[5] In part this is because numerous authors approach the commissions less as instruments of transitional justice than as exemplars of the politics of history or memory in the sponsoring states.[6] The transitional justice literature has yet to take a detailed comparative look at these commissions. In particular, as Eva-Clarita Onken noted in 2007, "There is no study to date that puts the Baltic commissions in a wider context of truth commissions worldwide ... a broader comparative study as to the impact of such commissions on the establishment of justice in transitional societies might provide interesting new perspectives."[7]

This chapter aims to do just that by offering a more systematic discussion of the extent to which these four post-communist commissions comply with various understandings of truth commissions and of the reasons for the widely diverging views on their status. It argues that the Estonian and German commissions clearly meet standard definitions of truth commissions and that the Latvian and Lithuanian commissions fail to do so only on relatively insignificant criteria. Nevertheless, all four commissions appear to lack certain features often associated with truth commissions and to share certain characteristics with one another that are not normally associated with such commissions elsewhere. They are intimately related to truth commissions, but it remains debatable whether they are better seen as a subset of truth commission or as first cousins within the family of investigative commissions, of which truth commissions are the most famous members.[8] Beyond such taxonomic questions, the chapter suggests that post-communist commissions need to be understood primarily in their own contexts, rather than as deviant or deficient variations of truth-commission models derived from other contexts. However, it also argues that they need to be approached critically, and that their claims about their aims, role, or motivation should not just be accepted on their own terms. Ultimately, these commissions need to be understood as instruments of both transitional justice and the politics of history.

POST-COMMUNIST TRUTH COMMISSIONS?

Views diverge on whether the investigative commissions established by post-communist European states qualify as truth commissions. On the one hand, numerous authors assert that the Baltic and German commissions should not be considered truth commissions. Meike Wulff states that the Estonian commission was not, and was "not intended to be a fully-fledged 'truth commission.'"[9] Similarly, Dovile Budryte states that the Lithuanian commission is not a truth commission because it is a permanent institution.[10] Meanwhile, the German commission has been dismissed for its insufficiently victim-centered approach and for the breadth of its mandate, which went well beyond human-rights abuses.[11] On the other hand, other authors assert that they do constitute truth commissions. Onken argues that "with the political mandate to investigate crimes against humanity committed in the past on its own territory, the Baltic commissions do qualify as 'truth commissions.'"[12] Similarly, numerous commentators intuitively perceive the German body as a truth commission.[13] Neither side of this debate goes beyond asserting its view. The deniers tend to operate with a rather narrow, often implicit understanding of a truth commission, and do not indicate how the post-communist commissions *should* be seen and what significance should be attached to their supposed differences from truth commissions. Meanwhile, the affirmers tend to overlook or minimize important differences and fail to consider their significance.

Whether one classifies the post-communist commissions as truth commissions or not depends primarily on one's understanding of the latter, and as Priscilla Hayner notes, "There is still no single, broadly accepted definition of what constitutes a truth commission."[14] A 2010 report by Amnesty International defined them as "commissions of inquiry tasked with the investigation of patterns of past crimes."[15] On this minimal definition, the Baltic commissions surely count, and the German commission arguably does too, despite crimes not being at the core of its mandate; in fact, all four went beyond investigating only crimes or human rights abuses to explore broader historical questions, a point explored below. Ironically, the Amnesty International report included the German commission but not the Baltic ones among its survey of truth commissions.[16] This is not the only instance in which cases are included that arguably do not fully meet the author's own definition, while other cases that do (or do so to the same extent) are overlooked.

Other, more complex definitions pose greater but hardly absolute challenges to classifying the post-communist inquiries as truth commissions. Previously, Amnesty International had used a 2005 United Nations definition, according to which truth commissions are "official, temporary, non-judicial fact-finding bodies that investigate a pattern of abuses of human rights or humanitarian law, usually committed over a number of years."[17] In the *Encyclopedia of Transitional Justice*, Nokukhanya Mncwabe defines them as "temporary state-sanctioned bodies investigating large-scale human rights violations committed over a specific period."[18] According to Hayner's influential 1994 definition, a truth commission is: (1) focused on the past; (2) set up to investigate a pattern of abuses over a period of time, rather than a specific event; (3) a temporary body, with the intention to conclude with a public report; and (4) officially authorized or empowered by the state.[19] All four commissions under consideration were certainly non-judicial bodies. They were also officially authorized by the state, in the Baltic cases by the state presidents and in the German case by the federal parliament. The German and Estonian commissions were also temporary bodies and concluded their work with a report; in the Estonian case, there were in fact three separate reports on different phases of the commission's work.

Whether the Latvian and Lithuanian commissions can be considered truth commissions on these definitions is debatable. It has been argued that the Lithuanian commission is not a truth commission because it is a permanent body. However, it is conceivable that it might be dissolved, or at least its investigative tasks largely wound up and/or its role altered further in the direction of education, if its "work plan" were completed; this might well already have happened had its meetings not been suspended in 2008, after which several years passed before the commission was reconstituted in 2012–2013.[20] Meanwhile, the Latvian commission has effectively been dormant since 2009–2010. Furthermore, neither the Latvian nor the Lithuanian commission has produced – or appears likely to produce – a concluding public report (the second aspect of Hayner's third criterion). Instead, they have published a series of books documenting their work and findings and, in the Lithuanian case, also a series of conclusions on a range of topics.[21]

Therefore, all that is necessary for both the Latvian and Lithuanian commissions to meet Mncwabe's and the UN's definitions is their dissolution, while a final report is also required to meet Hayner's definition. That neither has (yet) eventuated hardly seems a sufficiently significant reason to exclude them from a discussion of truth commissions. Indeed, some definitions such as that of Mark Freeman mention neither temporariness nor a final report.[22] The emphasis on temporariness in most definitions serves primarily to distinguish truth commissions from permanent human rights monitoring bodies, with which the Baltic commissions are unlikely to be confused.[23] Moreover, it is possible to argue that the Latvian and Lithuanian commissions constitute cases of what was initially conceived as a temporary body morphing into a semi-permanent entity with somewhat changed character. In this respect the continuation of their work, to the extent that it does continue, can be compared with the establishment in 1998 in Germany of the Federal

Foundation for the Reappraisal of the SED Dictatorship on the recommendation of the Bundestag commission, or with the 2008 creation of the Estonian Institute of Historical Memory, albeit without the clean institutional break of these cases, where the commissions ceased to exist and were succeeded by new, permanent bodies that pursue a similar agenda through somewhat different means.[24]

If the German and Estonian commissions fulfill the definitions discussed and the Latvian and Lithuanian commissions appear to fail to do so only in relatively insignificant respects, they do not meet the requirement proposed by Freeman that truth commissions not only meet the objective definition thereof, but also, subjectively, have to be widely or consensually viewed as such.[25] Clearly, as the foregoing discussion has suggested, there is no consensus in favor of viewing the four commissions under consideration as truth commissions. In part, this is due simply to their widespread neglect in the literature. In part, too, it is due to the lack of consensus about the objective criteria. However, it is mainly due to the fact that the relatively basic definitions discussed thus far do not capture the essence of what, on common understandings, truth commissions are and do.

APPROACH AND METHODS

Indeed, in the 2011 second edition of her global study of truth commissions Hayner added a fifth criterion to her definition: that a truth commission "engages directly and broadly with the affected population, gathering information on their experiences."[26] She thus made explicit what had not previously been part of her definition, but had nevertheless been a key component of her understanding of truth commissions: a "victim-centered" approach (a term also used in Freeman's definition), by which she primarily meant the collection of "thousands of victim testimonies."[27] This previously implicit dimension helps to explain the common view that the post-communist commissions were not truth commissions and that post-communist Europe has not utilized the latter instrument. As noted above, the German commission's apparent lack of attention to victims and particularly of mass victim testimony has disqualified it as a truth commission in the view of some commentators. A similar argument could be made in relation to the Baltic commissions, as they, even more than the German commission, relied primarily on archival evidence in their investigations and did not hold hearings with victims or other witnesses even to the limited extent that the German commission did.[28] Indeed, the four commissions under consideration were highly "academic" in nature, as every commentator agrees.[29]

However, as I have argued elsewhere in relation to the German commission, "a victim-centered examination and discussion of the past and its legacy is possible without large-scale testimony collection."[30] The German inquiry was thoroughly informed by victims' perspectives and sought to provide victims with a sense of symbolic and historical justice through its work.[31] This observation does not so much "challenge the assumed *role* of a truth commission," as Hayner suggests, as its assumed *method* of research.[32] To return to Hayner's fifth definitional criterion above, the German and Baltic commissions certainly can be said to have "gather[ed] information on [victims'] experiences," but they did not do so by "engag[ing] directly and broadly with the affected population."[33] Instead, they did so largely through archival research, with a degree of oral testimony in the German case. Thus, the more prescriptive a definition is in regard to methods, the less likely the post-communist cases considered here are likely to meet it. If one assumes that truth commissions must rely primarily or exclusively on oral sources and "statement-taking," then the availability and heavy reliance in post-communist settings on written records of the former regimes does indeed provide a plausible explanation for the lack of truth commissions (so defined) in post-communist Europe, as some commentators have suggested.[34] However, that assumption is contingent, rather than essential.

At first glance, the Baltic commissions appear (even) less focused on victims than their German counterpart. They certainly did less to gather information directly from victims. Moreover, in the Estonian case, the word "victim" is entirely absent from key documents, including President Lennart Meri's "Word of Welcome" and the International Commission's "Statement" in response, which together outlined the commission's tasks and self-understanding in January 1999. Instead, the focus lay more on the question of who was responsible for crimes against humanity, as well as for the country's occupation. The commission's three reports each began by citing President Meri's initial letter of August 14, 1998, to the commissioners: "It is my hope that the Commission can help my country to move confidently into the future after having identified all the individuals and groups responsible for the many tragedies visited on her half a century ago."[35]

The emphasis was on the crimes and those responsible for them, rather than on those who suffered from them, although establishing that there had been such crimes entailed establishing who and how many were their victims. The term "victim" was also absent from the commission's reports on the two periods of Soviet occupation in 1940–1941 and after 1944.[36] Only the report on the German occupation of 1941–1944 refers to Estonia's status and Estonians' self-understanding as a "victim nation" and insists that being a victim does not preclude one from possibly also being a perpetrator.[37]

This reference to Estonia as a "victim nation" is revealing, as it helps to explain and qualify the apparent lack of "victim-centeredness" that appears to characterize the Baltic commissions, relative to truth commissions elsewhere and even to the German commission. As Vello Pettai argues, "post-communist Estonia's approach to transitional justice has been heavily predicated on its view of the Soviet period as an illegal foreign occupation and annexation, thus casting transition [sic] justice as the process of dealing with the repression committed by a foreign power, and not by Estonia itself."[38] If the whole (titular) nation is a victim, as Meri's words quoted above also imply, then to explore the victims' experiences of repression requires studying the repression of the nation, and vice versa: if the whole nation is a victim, to study the history of the nation is, inherently, to address the experiences of victims. Therefore, while they may not seem "victim-centered" compared to or in the same ways as other truth commissions, in addressing the history of occupation and manifold persecutory policies the post-communist commissions were addressing and gathering information on the experiences of victims. To suggest that they were not truth commissions because they did not display the requisite interest in victims is therefore to ignore the specific understanding of victimhood that was operative in their particular contexts (and the methods of research required to operationalize it).

THE PAST UNDER INVESTIGATION

Indeed, the post-communist commissions under consideration operated with a two-fold understanding of victimhood (even if the term itself was not necessarily used): on the one hand, that of specific individuals and groups of victims, such as political leaders who were persecuted, or groups who suffered mass deportation to the USSR; on the other hand, that of the whole nation, which in the Baltic cases (from the commissions' perspective) suffered from three-fold occupation. In the terms of the Estonian commission, in effect, the whole country was viewed as a victim of forced "annexation" into the Soviet Union in 1940, of German occupation from 1941 to 1944, and of postwar Sovietization, while thousands of individuals were victims of specific "criminal events in Estonia."[39] A similar tendency was evident in the German commission. It viewed *all* East Germans (or at least those who were not themselves responsible for or willing accomplices of the SED regime) as victims, to some extent of Soviet occupation, but more so of the denial of basic rights and freedoms by the East German regime, and especially of the "large-scale deprivation of liberty by the border regime that culminated in the construction of the [Berlin] Wall"; meanwhile, a smaller number were regarded as outright victims of more specific repressive measures and arbitrary acts by the regime.[40] This two-fold conceptualization of victimhood has not been recognized in the literature to date, which instead has been content with asserting that distinguishing between victims and perpetrators in post-communist contexts has been harder than in post-authoritarian settings, if not impossible, and that this helps to explain the unpopularity of truth commissions in post-communist Europe.

Yet the two-fold conceptualization of victimhood reflected gradated experiences and understandings of oppression and repression, which ranged from the universal oppression experienced by all who lived under communist rule through to the severe and even lethal persecution of particular real or perceived enemies of the communist party leadership. Such a spectrum indicates the problematic nature of the well-known distinction drawn by Tina Rosenberg between the "deep" repression of Latin American dictatorships and the "wide" repression of Eastern-bloc communist dictatorships.[41] While this distinction contains an element of truth, particularly for the post-Stalin decades, there was of course considerable "deep" repression to be addressed in post-communist Europe, even if most of it had occurred during the Stalinist era. Unsurprisingly, the Baltic commissions in particular were especially and initially most interested in investigating that deep early repression. Despite its more open mandate and the expansive nature of the title of its final report and publication, which spoke of Estonia *since* or *from* 1944, the Estonian commission hardly looked beyond the mid-1950s.[42] The initial focus of the Lithuanian and Latvian commissions was also on the period(s) from 1940 through to the mid-1950s; only in 2005 did the former adopt a research plan for the period 1953 to 1990, and only in 2006 did the latter create a sub-commission to research the years 1956 to 1991.[43] Whereas the Baltic commissions thus focused on periods and aspects of "deep" repression, their German counterpart made a more concerted effort to examine virtually the entire workings of the East German regime and in particular to capture precisely the "wide" repression of ordinary East Germans in everyday life. Its attention was also more evenly spread across all four decades of communist rule, rather than focusing on the 1940s and the 1950s; yet throughout it sought to identify those who had suffered most amidst the many who had suffered.[44] To return briefly to the questions of victim-centeredness and methods discussed above, the focus on events over four decades in the past helps to explain the archival, academic and historical nature of the investigation and the relative or complete absence of oral testimony in the Baltic commissions and to a lesser extent in the German case.[45]

Recognizing that repression in communist Europe had been both wide *and* deep and that the post-communist commissions sought to address both types helps to qualify a substantial perceived difference and to explain the actual less radical difference from truth commissions elsewhere: the unusual breadth of the post-communist investigations. As mentioned above, the fact that the German commission's mandate went well beyond human rights abuses and acts of repression is well known and has provided grounds for some commentators to argue that it was not a truth commission. Similar arguments could be made, albeit with even less justification, about the Baltic commissions. They focused more directly and more explicitly than the German commission on crimes and human rights abuses, as was expressed in two of their titles: Estonia's International Commission for Investigation of Crimes against Humanity and the International Commission for the Evaluation of the Crimes of the Nazi and Soviet Occupation Regimes in Lithuania. The Latvian investigation similarly also foregrounded "Crimes against Humanity Committed in the Territory of Latvia under Two Occupations, 1940–1956."[46] Yet none of them focused exclusively on crimes against humanity or rights violations. As Pettai argues in relation to the Latvian commission, "although the Commission is mandated to investigate crimes against humanity, the studies it has published to date have taken a far broader approach."[47] The commissions also investigated the broader historical contexts, providing accounts of key events, developments, policies, institutions, and related issues. Of the four commissions, the Lithuanian commission has had the narrowest focus on crimes and the German commission pursued the broadest range of topics, such that crimes and rights abuses constituted only a small component of its expansive investigation. If truth commissions are deemed to focus exclusively on acts of violence or on the most severe human rights abuses while neglecting their larger historical context or subtler or more pervasive forms of repression, then one could exclude the post-communist commissions and especially the German one on that basis. However, it is increasingly recognized that more flexible and encompassing understandings of repression can and often should be considered, and that truth commissions also can and should not merely be concerned "with sorting out the facts of individual cases but also with providing an account of the broad causes and consequences."[48] In this regard, the post-communist commissions were arguably exemplary, even if providing complex accounts of context, causes and consequences inevitably had implications for their methods, mode of operation and ultimately their public reception and impact. As Lavinia Stan argues, "The diffused guilt penetrating the fabric of Eastern European societies ... explains the tendency of post-communist truth commissions to be academic in nature."[49] However, as mentioned, the commissions were interested not only in diffused guilt and suffering but also in specific responsibility, in wide, as well as deep repression.

A more genuinely distinctive feature of the Baltic commissions is their dual focus on the periods of Soviet and Nazi rule. Indeed, the significance of the German occupation of 1941–1944 for the Baltic commissions has not been fully recognized by commentators who approach them merely as instruments of post-*communist* transitional justice and seek to explain them (or the lack of truth commissions in other post-communist countries) primarily or exclusively through that lens. The creation of the three Baltic commissions in 1998 cannot be understood merely in terms of the development of post-communist transitional justice. Instead, it was due above all to international pressure on the Baltic states in relation to their seemingly deficient handling of the history of the Holocaust on their territories. As Pettai argues, "When convening the international commission to fill this gap and compile a historical record of past atrocities, [Estonian] President Meri decided to include within its mandate all of the crimes against humanity committed by both the Nazi and Soviet regimes on Estonian territory. Together with his two colleagues from Latvia and Lithuania he thus made a point that both totalitarian regimes needed to be equally thoroughly investigated in the Baltic context."[50] Addressing both regimes was by no means easy. Various participants and stakeholders had particular interests in one or other of the regimes, and cooperation was often difficult.[51] However, the move to create commissions devoted to both totalitarian regimes was of central symbolic significance.

In Germany, in contrast, for various reasons, but particularly due to the more advanced process of facing up to the Nazi past and greater sensitivity about being seen to treat Nazism and communism as equivalent, having a single commission devoted to the two totalitarianisms was never seriously considered. Nevertheless there, too, equal condemnation of the two totalitarianisms found strong advocacy from the political center-right and some on the moderate left, and in the Bundestag commission in particular.[52] Moreover, there too perceived inadequacies in facing up to the Nazi past served to promote efforts to address the communist past and motivated the establishment of the Bundestag commission, and in numerous other ways it proved impossible to talk about communism without also talking about Nazism (and vice versa).[53] Thus in the German and in the Baltic cases, the Nazi past was instrumental in fostering debate about the communist past, and comparison of the two totalitarianisms was more than just a rhetorical strategy to demonize communism, as it has sometimes been portrayed.[54] Indeed it is impossible to understand these commissions, and much more about post-communist transitional justice besides, without addressing that other, Nazi and fascist layer of the region's twentieth-century history.

MEMBERS AND FUNCTION

Perhaps the most distinctive feature of the four commissions under consideration is the prominent involvement of historians. Although the roles played by and the origins of the historians involved differed slightly, all three Baltic commissions relied almost exclusively on historical research. In the Latvian case, the international and local commissioners were overwhelmingly historians; in Lithuania the commissioners, who were both foreign and local, included historians as well as politicians and human rights activists; in Estonia, the International Commission's members were not active historians, but politicians, diplomats, and representatives of non-governmental organizations. Beyond the commissioners themselves, all three commissions employed large teams of primarily local historians to conduct the research.[55] Therefore, although only the Latvian commission was officially designated a "commission of historians" (given its staffing) it is hardly surprising that all three are informally called "historical" or "history" commissions. This was not the case with the German commission, whose methods were more diverse and whose character and reception were influenced by its parliamentary origin and location. However, it also contained a large number of historians and historically minded social scientists, both among the members of the Bundestag and the external experts among its members; it also invited a large number of additional historians and other scholars to conduct research or present their findings at hearings. Nevertheless, most of the Bundestag members and some of the external expert members were not historians, and the mixed membership of professional politicians and scholars, former dissidents, and former office-bearers was an interesting feature of the German commission.[56]

As is often the case in studies of transitional justice, there are tendencies in the literature on the post-communist commissions simply to accept at face value actors' claims about their laudable goals or motivation or the sensible nature of their activities, or simply to reject them as a smokescreen for political interests and ambition – or to be inconsistent in applying either of these approaches to differing contexts and actors. In relation to the Baltic commissions, it is sometimes observed that the presidents who established them did so to gain political capital relative to the state parliaments, but it is rarely suggested that the German Bundestag may also have sought to assert itself through the German commission.[57] Moreover, it is often assumed that political leaders have relatively base motives and merely instrumentalize the past to their own ends. According to Grodsky, they "follow a simple three-point methodology: rediscovery of significant historical events, politically advantageous reinterpretation of those events, and mobilization of the masses around these newly defined events. New elites use history as a tool to inspire and rally their publics, stressing the periods and events that most contribute to their end goals."[58] In contrast, it is sometimes assumed that historians are or should be dispassionately interested in the truth, the facts, and academic dialogue and exchange. As some authors see historians as being under an obligation to adopt "a critical stance in discussions on the role of historical knowledge in society," they see those who assume an "active political role" (like in a historical commission) as "blurr[ing] the image of the historical profession."[59] If historians appear to become too engaged in official memory work and too close to political actors, they sully themselves and their guild.[60]

More importantly, a degree of naiveté is evident in many characterizations of the Baltic and German commissions' functions. Observing the participation of historians and the historical subject matter, and accepting uncritically the actors' own statements, the Baltic commissions' roles are characterized in terms of "filling many of the existing gaps in the historical record" or of compiling "a complete historical record," "reconciling different previous assessments," and "raising awareness," while the German commission is described as seeking "to piece together a comprehensive account of SED abuses."[61] To be sure, it is recognized that "truth commissions are declared political tools producing political results at politically defined times," and that the histories they produce possess a particular quality as they amount to "official acknowledgement of regime abuses."[62] However, there is a tendency toward uncritical readings that rely on highly positivist understandings of what historians and historical commissions do. History does not wait "out there" to be discovered by historians, but is a construct of the present. However unbiased, objective, and professional its historian members may be, an official historical investigation or truth commission is inherently political. Far from being an objective exploration of East German history, for instance, the Bundestag commission was both a site and an instrument of a complex, multilayered struggle over the power to interpret the past (what the Germans call *Deutungshoheit*), in which competing political actors and traditions sought to legitimize themselves and delegitimize their rivals with reference to history.[63]

Even before analysis, evaluation, and narration begin, choices are made about defining the topic and scope of the investigation and the approach to be used. Indeed, the mere establishment of an investigative commission is a symbolic and political act of the highest order. As already mentioned, the Baltic commissions were a defensive measure to counter criticism from abroad about the states' reluctance to face up to difficult questions about local collaboration in the Holocaust. At the same time, the decision to investigate communist as well as Nazi-era criminality was an attempt to regain the initiative and assert the dominant Baltic perspective that communism was equally if not more criminal and had inflicted greater suffering on the Estonian, Lithuanian, and Latvian nations. Fundamentally, the ultimate issue here, too, was *Deutungshoheit*.

However, the stakes involved differed between the Baltic commissions and the German commission. In the latter, there was awareness that the international community was observing how Germany was handling its difficult twentieth-century history, but the stakes were primarily domestic. Of course a distinction needs to be made between the national level of debate which involved East and West Germans and a more intra-East German discourse. On the one hand, the commission claimed to want to promote reconciliation among East Germans, i.e. among victims, bystanders, and "perpetrators"; on the other, it sought to bring East and West Germans together. Similarly, some debates primarily concerned the history of East German opposition to the SED, such as the question of whether fleeing to the West should be considered an act of opposition or a detraction from the opposition movement; others primarily concerned the West German political parties and their relationship with East Berlin. As the last example suggests, the nature of disputes on and around the German commission was often moral, but more commonly ideological and partisan. Ultimately, the commission amounted to an instrument to legitimize German unification and the Federal Republic of Germany and to delegitimize the German Democratic Republic and all past, present, and future socialist alternatives.[64]

In the Baltic contexts, in contrast, the stakes were more international, and competing perspectives were more ethnic and national than ideological or partisan. For all the talk of filling in historical gaps and promoting understanding among the domestic publics, the audience of much of the commissions' work was abroad. This was particularly evident in the Estonian case, where the commission had an exclusively international membership, the commission made little effort to engage the domestic public, and its findings were published first in English rather than Estonian. Therefore, as Onken notes, "this commission mainly served the function of explaining Estonian history and clarifying still open questions to the outside world."[65] While the Latvian commission is credited with engaging more with the domestic public and promoting a more discursive engagement with historical questions, not least because it prioritized publishing in Latvian, there too its main purpose was similar: in the words of its German member Erwin Oberländer, "above all, to inform other states" about its finding on the crimes of both the Nazi and Soviet occupying powers in Latvia.[66] Meanwhile, the Lithuanian commission developed a split personality, with a high degree of international collaboration on the Holocaust, but a more domestic approach to the history of communism.[67] The international audience being targeted was the West, specifically the European Union, the United States, and Israel, whence Holocaust-related criticism emanated. The Baltic States' efforts to join the EU and NATO obviously played a motivating role here.[68] In contrast, they only belatedly, if at all, sought to engage in a dialogue with Russia, or their ethnic Russian populations.[69] Ultimately, the commissions served to underline the identity of the Baltic States as victim nations, to legitimize their still relatively recent independence by demonstrating the criminality of the Soviet occupations, and to promote their integration into the European and North Atlantic communities.

CONCLUSION

How does all of this help us understand transitional justice in post-communist Europe? First of all, it confirms Grodsky's observation: "The historical framing of the post-communist world as a special case of transitional justice may have been natural, but casting aside assumptions and reframing post-communism as a 'normal' environment for transitional justice is bound to be more illuminating."[70] In particular, the chapter has demonstrated that a particular framing of the post-communist world, coupled with a particular understanding of truth commissions, has led to inaccurate claims that such bodies did not exist in post-communist Europe. Abandoning that assumption and looking closer reveals that there have been a number of truth commissions in post-communist Europe, at least according to the more minimal definitions of truth commissions. A basic lesson here is that scholars of transitional justice can benefit from being more open-minded and more careful, as well from more comparative research.

However, such comparative research inevitably demonstrates not only similarities, but also differences. While they may share certain characteristics with truth commissions and meet various definitions thereof, the post-communist commissions all diverge from prevalent models of truth commissions. Moreover, the truth-commission frame is not necessarily the only one through which the Baltic and German commissions can be viewed. They also have much in common and can be compared with numerous historical institutes across the region, or with historical commissions established in non-transitional settings.[71] Therefore, while it is possible to argue that the post-communist commissions examined here do, more or less, meet various definitions of truth commissions, it may be more beneficial to acknowledge basic similarities but to insist on crucial differences, and thus to see the post-communist commissions as a set apart, rather than a subset of truth commissions. Whichever approach is taken, it should be explicit, consistent, and evidence-based. I favor the former position, not least because treating the post-communist investigations as truth commissions can help to broaden the horizons and sharpen the focus of the global study of the latter.

A further frame through which post-communist transitional justice has been viewed is Rosenberg's distinction between deep and wide repression. However, its significance for understanding (the use of) truth commissions in post-communist Europe is ambivalent. To be sure, as Stan argues, "the mild nature of communist repression explains [or perhaps helps to explain, AHB] why the overwhelming majority of post-communist countries were uninterested in employing truth commissions in their quest to overcome the past"; yet, as Stan also points out, it cannot explain why some countries did choose this method.[72] Moreover, ascribing deep repression to Latin America and wide, mild, or broad repression to communist Europe overlooks the deep, and often specifically targeted, nature of much early communist repression (not to mention the terrible "depth" of Nazi persecution and genocide that the Baltic commissions also addressed). It thus obscures crucial differences *within* the history of communist repression and among its victims. Reapplying this frame and using it to think about distinctions between deep and wide repression *within* communist Europe helps to illuminate the reasons not only for the establishment of truth commissions in particular countries, but also for the specific focus of their investigations, as well as for their methods and mode of operation.

Numerous authors have been highly critical of the German and the Baltic commissions, particularly for their "academic" nature and their lack of popular resonance. According to Pettai, the Latvian and Estonian commissions serve "as examples of how not to succeed in generating a conversation about a difficult past that involves equal partners and a process of mutual give and take, listening and being listened to."[73] In this vein, one could seek to draw lessons about how more meaningful and balanced conversations might be fostered. However, this is to accept that promoting such a conversation was or should have been the aim.

In contrast, the lesson that emerges from the preceding discussion is that both a greater degree of generosity and a greater degree of cynicism are needed in analyzing truth-revelation and transitional justice processes. On the one hand, we should be prepared to acknowledge and give credit for the interest the commissions demonstrated in victims' experiences, even if they do not measure up to standards of "victim-centeredness" derived from other contexts and did not even talk prominently about "victims." On the other hand, we need to do more to read between the lines in order to recognize that much talk about positive goals like reconciliation and the pursuit of truth serves to legitimize and can distract us from other, more directly political goals and functions, from self-promotion to state legitimization. Indeed, the commissions examined here demonstrate that affirming the illegitimacy of the old state and the legitimacy of the new one is a fundamental function of truth commissions and transitional justice that is often either overlooked or taken for granted. There is considerable overlap between transitional justice and the politics of history, and the post-communist "truth commissions" clearly straddled both fields.

NOTES

1. Brian Grodsky, "Beyond Lustration: Truth-Seeking Efforts in the Post-Communist Space," *Taiwan Journal of Democracy* 5, no. 2 (2009): 21–43.
2. Mark Freeman, *Truth Commissions and Procedural Fairness* (New York: Cambridge University Press, 2006), 11; Priscilla B. Hayner, *Unspeakable Truths: Transitional Justice and the Challenge of Truth Commissions*, 2nd ed. (New York: Routledge, 2011).
3. Gábor Halmai, "Lustration and Access to the Files in Central Europe," in *Lustration and Consolidation of Democracy and the Rule of Law in Central and Eastern Europe*, eds. Vladimíra Dvořáková and Anđelko Milardović (Zagreb: Political Science Research Centre, 2007), 23–24; Lavinia Stan, "Introduction: Post-Communist Transition, Justice, and Transitional Justice," in *Transitional Justice in Eastern Europe and the Former Soviet Union: Reckoning with the Communist Past*, ed. Lavinia Stan (New York: Routledge, 2008), 10; Georges Mink, "Institutions of National Memory in Post-Communist Europe: From Transitional Justice to Political Uses of Biographies (1989–2010)," in *History, Memory and Politics in Central and Eastern Europe: Memory Games*, eds. Georges Mink and Laure Neumayer (New York: Palgrave Macmillan, 2013), 158.
4. Grodsky, "Beyond Lustration"; Lavinia Stan, "Truth Commissions in Post-Communism: The Overlooked Solution?" *Open Political Science Journal* 2 (2009): 1–13; Andrew H. Beattie, "An Evolutionary Process: Contributions of the Bundestag's Inquiries into East Germany to an Understanding of the Role of Truth Commissions," *International Journal of Transitional Justice* 3, no. 2 (2009): 229–249.
5. For brief accounts of each of the commissions, see the entries in Lavinia Stan and Nadya Nedelsky, eds., *Encyclopedia of Transitional Justice*, Volume 3 (New York: Cambridge University Press, 2013): Thomas Großbölting, "Commission of Inquiry for the Assessment of History and Consequences of the SED Dictatorship in Germany," 57–61; Eva-Clarita Pettai, "Commission of Latvia's Historians," 74–78; Pettai, "Estonian International Commission for the Investigation of Crimes against Humanity," 117–121; Dovile Budryte, "International Commission for the Evaluation of the Crimes of the Nazi and Soviet Occupation Regimes in

Lithuania," 218–222. The German commission was followed by a second inquiry "Overcoming the Consequences of the SED Dictatorship in the Process of German Unity" (1995–1998), which is not considered here as to do so would add little to the analysis. See Beattie, "Evolutionary Process."

6. Meike Wulff, "Politics of History in Estonia: Changing Memory Regimes 1987–2009," *History of Communism in Europe* 1 (2010), 245–267; Eva-Clara Pettai, "Establishing 'Holocaust Memory': A Comparison of Estonia and Latvia," in *Geschichtspolitik im erweiterten Ostseeraum und ihre aktuellen Symptome – Historical Memory Culture in the Enlarged Baltic Sea Region and Its Symptoms Today*, eds. Oliver Rathkolb and Imbi Sooman (Göttingen: V&R Unipress, 2011), 159–173.
7. Eva-Clarita Onken, "The Politics of Finding Historical Truth: Reviewing Baltic History Commissions and Their Work," *Journal of Baltic Studies* 38, no. 1 (2007): 115, note 2.
8. Mälksoo describes the Estonian commission and similar "history" commissions as "one kind of" truth commission but then distinguishes the former from the latter. Lauri Mälksoo, "Soviet Genocide? Communist Mass Deportations in the Baltic States and International Law," *Leiden Journal of International Law* 14, no. 4 (2001): 769.
9. Wulff, "Politics of History," 254, 257.
10. Budryte, "International Commission," 218.
11. Anne Sa'adah, *Germany's Second Chance: Trust, Justice and Democratization* (Cambridge, MA: Harvard University Press, 1998), 184–185; Charles S. Maier, "Doing History, Doing Justice: The Narrative of the Historian and of the Truth Commission," in *Truth v. Justice: The Morality of Truth Commissions*, eds. Robert I. Rotberg and Dennis Thompson (Princeton, NJ: Princeton University Press, 2000), 276, note 1. For more discussion, see Beattie, "Evolutionary Process."
12. Onken, "Politics of Finding Historical Truth," 115, Footnote 2.
13. Tina Rosenberg, "Overcoming the Legacies of Dictatorship," *Foreign Affairs* 74, no. 3 (1995): 148; Timothy Garton Ash, *History of the Present: Essays, Sketches and Despatches from Europe in the 1990s* (London: Penguin, 2000), 308; Noel Calhoun, *Dilemmas of Justice in Eastern Europe's Democratic Transitions* (New York: Palgrave Macmillan, 2004), 87.
14. Hayner, *Unspeakable Truths*, 10.
15. Amnesty International, *Commissioning Justice: Truth Commissions and Criminal Justice* (London: Amnesty International Publications, 2010), 5.
16. Ibid., 8–9.
17. Amnesty International, *Truth, Justice and Reparation: Establishing an Effective Truth Commission* (London: AI International Secretariat, 2007), 1.
18. Nokukhanya Mncwabe, "Truth Commissions," in Stan and Nedelsky, eds., *Encyclopedia of Transitional Justice*, Volume 3, 99.
19. Hayner, *Unspeakable Truths*, 11.
20. International Commission for the Evaluation of the Crimes of the Nazi and Soviet Occupation Regimes in Lithuania (hereafter International Commission Lithuania), "Outline of Work Plan," August 29, 1999, available at: http://www.komisija.lt/en/body.php?&m=1173548714 (accessed December 4, 2013); President of the Republic of Lithuania, "Decree on the International Commission for the Evaluation of the

Crimes of the Nazi and Soviet Occupation Regimes in Lithuania," No. 1K-1245 Vilnius, October 16, 2012, available at: http://www.komisija.lt/Files/www.komisija.lt/File/Decree%2020121016%20-Unofficial%20translation.pdf (accessed December 4, 2013). Cf. Joachim Tauber, "Vergangenheitsbewältigung in Litauen: Politik, Gesellschaft und der Holocaust nach 1945," in *Geschichtspolitik im erweiterten Ostseeraum*, eds. Rathkolb and Sooman, 191–192; Budryte, "International Commission," 219–220; Stan, "Truth Commissions," 6.

21. The Latvian commission has published 26 volumes of the proceedings of its symposia. See the list available at President of Latvia, "Commission of Historians," no, date, available at: http://www.president.lv/pk/content/?cat_id=2766&lng=en (accessed December 4, 2013). The Lithuanian commission has published eight volumes in separate series on the Nazi and Soviet occupations of the country. See International Commission Lithuania, "Publishing," no date, http://www.komisija.lt/en/body.php?&m=1150461059 (accessed on December 4, 2013). See also International Commission Lithuania, "Conclusions of the Commission (List)," no date, available at: http://www.komisija.lt/en/naujiena.php?id=1187780828 (accessed December 4, 2013).
22. Freeman, *Truth Commissions*, 21.
23. Amnesty International, *Truth, Justice and Reparation*, 1; Eric Brahm, "What Is a Truth Commission and Why Does It Matter," *Peace and Conflict Review* 3, no. 2 (2009): 1–14.
24. See Bundesstiftung Aufarbeitung, available at: http://www.bundesstiftung-aufarbeitung.de (accessed December 4, 2013).
25. Freeman, *Truth Commissions*, 21–22.
26. Hayner, *Unspeakable Truths*, 12.
27. Hayner, *Unspeakable Truths*, 16; Freeman, *Truth Commissions*, 21.
28. Pettai, "Commission of Latvia's Historians," 78; Pettai, "Estonian International Commission," 117.
29. Pettai, "Commission of Latvia's Historians," 74; Stan, "Truth Commissions," 4.
30. Beattie, "Evolutionary Process," 247.
31. Ibid., 237–239.
32. Hayner, *Unspeakable Truths*, 53.
33. Ibid., 12.
34. Office of the United Nations High Commissioner for Human Rights, *Rule of Law Tools for Post-Conflict States: Truth Commissions* (New York: United Nations, 2006), 1.
35. *Estonia 1940–1945: Reports of the Estonian International Commission for the Investigation of Crimes against Humanity*, eds. Toomas Hiio, Meelis Maripuu, and Indrek Paavle (Tallinn: Estonian Foundation for the Investigation of Crimes against Humanity, 2006), vii.
36. Ibid., i-xvi, and *Estonia since 1944: Reports of the Estonian International Commission for the Investigation of Crimes against Humanity*, eds. Hiio, Maripuu, and Paavle (Tallinn: Estonian Foundation for the Investigation of Crimes against Humanity, 2009), xvii–xxvi.
37. *Estonia 1940–1945*, xxiii.
38. Vello Pettai, "Estonia," in Stan and Nedelsky, eds., *Encyclopedia of Transitional Justice*, Volume 2, 161.

39. *Estonia 1940–1945*, x, xi.
40. *Materialien der Enquete-Kommission "Aufarbeitung von Geschichte und Folgen der SED-Diktatur in Deutschland" (12. Wahlperiode des Deutschen Bundestages)*, Volume 1, ed. Deutscher Bundestag (Frankfurt am Main: Suhrkamp, 1995), 639–640. Cf. Andrew H. Beattie, *Playing Politics with History: The Bundestag Inquiries into East Germany* (New York: Berghahn Books, 2009), 38 and 73–77.
41. Rosenberg, "Overcoming the Legacies," 136.
42. Only a couple of the research papers in *Estonia since 1944* go beyond the mid-1950s.
43. International Commission Lithuania, "Sessions: 8th Meeting of the Commission, 18–20 April 2005," available at: http://www.komisija.lt/en/naujiena.php?id=1175272773 (accessed December 4, 2013), and Pettai, "Commission of Latvia's Historians," 77.
44. Beattie, "Evolutionary Concept," 234–235, 239–242.
45. Stan, "Truth Commissions," 11–12.
46. President of Latvia, "Commission of Historians," available at: http://www.president.lv/pk/content/?cat_id=7 (accessed December 4, 2013).
47. Pettai, "Commission of Latvia's Historians," 77.
48. Freeman, *Truth Commissions*, 15.
49. Stan, "Truth Commissions," 10.
50. Pettai "Estonian International Commission," 118. Cf. Pettai, "Commission of Latvia's Historians," 76; Grodsky, "Beyond Lustration," 31–32, 42; Andrejs Plakans, A *Concise History of the Baltic Sates* (Cambridge: Cambridge University Press, 2011), 440; Eva-Clarita Onken, *Demokratisierung der Geschichte in Lettland: Staatsbürgerliches Bewußtsein und Geschichtspolitik im ersten Jahrzehnt der Unabhängigkeit* (Hamburg: Krämer, 2003), 194–199; and Pettai, "Establishing Holocaust Memory," 168.
51. Budryte, "International Commission," 219.
52. Andrew H. Beattie, "Ein neuer Historikerstreit? Kommunismus und Nationalsozialismus in der deutschen Erinnerungs- und Geschichtspolitik seit 1990," in *Ein Kampf um Deutungshoheit: Politik, Opferinteressen und historische Forschung: Die Auseinandersetzung um die Gedenk- und Begegnungsstätte Leistikowstraße Potsdam*, ed. Wolfgang Benz (Berlin: Metropol Verlag, 2013).
53. Ibid., and Beattie, *Playing Politics*, 2, 12.
54. Muriel Blaive, "The Memory of the Holocaust and of Communist Repression in a Comparative Perspective: The Cases of Hungary, Poland and Czechoslovakia/the Czech Republic," in *Clashes in European Memory: The Case of Communist Repression and the Holocaust*, eds. Muriel Blaive, Christian Gerbel, and Thomas Lindenberger (Innsbruck: Studien Verlag, 2011), 157.
55. Pettai, "Estonian International Commission," 117; Pettai, "Establishing Holocaust Memory," 166. In the Lithuanian case the commission also appointed expert panels of mixed origin as a form of advisory board or peer review panel. See International Commission Lithuania, "Sessions: 4th Meeting of the Commission, 1–2 June 2000," available at: http://www.komisija.lt/en/naujiena.php?id=61 (accessed December 4, 2013).
56. Beattie, *Playing Politics*, 41–44, 241.
57. Stan, "Truth Commissions," 4, 12; Beattie, *Playing Politics*, 27, 32.
58. Brian Grodsky, "Producing Truth: The Politics of Investigating Past Human Rights Violations in Post-Communist States," *World Affairs* 169, no. 3 (2007): 126.

59. Meike Wulf and Pertti Grnholm, "Generating Meaning Across Generations: The Role of Historians in the Codification of History in Soviet and Post-Soviet Estonia," *Journal of Baltic Studies* 41, no. 3 (2010), 376. Cf. Marek Tamm, "History as Cultural Memory: Mnemohistory and the Construction of the Estonian Nation," in *Contested and Shared Places of Memory: History and Politics in North Eastern Europe*, eds. Jörg Hackmann and Marko Lehti (New York: Routledge, 2013), 116–133.
60. See Mink, "Institutions of National Memory."
61. Eva-Clarita Onken, "The Baltic States and Moscow's 9 May Commemoration: Analysing Memory Politics in Europe," *Europe-Asia Studies* 59, no. 1 (2007): 34; Pettai, "Establishing Holocaust Memory," 166–167; Stan, "Truth Commissions," 12. Cf. Eva-Clarita Pettai, "The Convergence of Two Worlds: Historians and Emerging Histories in the Baltic States," in *Forgotten Pages in Baltic History: Diversity and Inclusion*, eds. Martyn Housden and David J. Smith (Amsterdam: Rodopi, 2011), 266.
62. Stan, "Truth Commissions," 2.
63. Beattie, *Playing Politics*, 62–63.
64. Ibid., 125, 228.
65. Onken, "Baltic States," 35.
66. Erwin Oberländer, "Soviet Genocide in Latvia? Conflicting Cultures of Remembrance of Stalin's Policy, 1940–1953," in *Forgotten Pages in Baltic History: Diversity and Inclusion*, eds. Martyn Housden and David J. Smith (Amsterdam: Rodopi, 2011), 246. Cf. Pettai, "Establishing Holocaust Memory," 169.
67. International Commission Lithuania, "Partners," available at: http://www.komisija.lt/en/body.php?&m=1182947575 (accessed December 4, 2013).
68. For a discussion of the use of history in Baltic foreign policy through to the mid-1990s, see Philippe Pertoch, "History as a Tool for Foreign Policy in the Baltic States after Independence," in *Geschichtspolitik im erweiterten Ostseeraum und ihre aktuellen Symptome – Historical Memory Culture in the Enlarged Baltic Sea Region and Its Symptoms Today*, eds. Oliver Rathkolb and Imbi Sooman (Göttingen: V&R unipress, 2011).
69. Onken, *Demokratisierung*, 213. See President of Latvia, "Former Presidents of Latvia, Valdis Zatlers, Commission of Historians, Events 2010," available at: http://www.president.lv/pk/content/?cat_id=9055&lng=en (accessed December 4, 2013).
70. Grodsky "Beyond Lustration," 43.
71. Hayner, *Unspeakable Truths*, 2nd ed., 10–17; Mink, "Institutions."
72. Stan, "Truth Commissions," 10.
73. Pettai, "Two Worlds," 267.

11

Public Memory, Commemoration, and Transitional Justice: Reconfiguring the Past in Public Space

Duncan Light and Craig Young

Transitional justice is usually addressed through institutional processes such as lustration, restitution, prosecution, and truth commissions, around which a comprehensive academic literature has developed. However, this chapter explores a relatively neglected symbolic dimension of transitional justice,[1] namely practices of memorialization and commemoration that are represented, played out, and contested in urban space. There is widespread acknowledgment within the transitional justice literature that memorialization – in the form of monuments, statues, and museums – has a key role to play in healing the wounds of the communist past. Such memorials "represent a critical terrain where the past is confronted and conflict can be addressed."[2] Memorialization is a means of giving recognition to those who suffered hardship, repression, exile, or death under communist regimes. The practice makes a visible statement about what (and who) a political order considers worthy of remembrance and is a means of reaching large numbers of people over an extended time period.

This chapter focuses on the ways in which transitional justice for the victims of communist regimes is expressed in the highly complex entanglement of urban cultural landscapes, public memory, and commemorative sites and practices. We contend that attempts to shape public memory through practices of commemoration and memorialization are important (if neglected) aspects of transitional justice, that have much to tell us about how post-communist societies choose to remember and forget the period of Communist Party rule. Following a review of the relationships between public memory and urban space, we begin by examining efforts to erase the commemorative landscape produced by communist regimes. We then look at the variety of initiatives (by diverse elites and publics) to commemorate the victims of communist regimes, with particular reference to monuments, memorials, and museums. We also highlight the importance of both domestic and international tourism to these sites of memory as central to the way in which they "work."

PUBLIC MEMORY, COMMEMORATION, AND URBAN SPACE

Public memory can be defined as "a body of beliefs and ideas about the past that help a public or society understand both its past, present, and by implication, its future."[3] It is not only a society's collective understanding of the past, but also the ways that this past is represented in the present.[4] Since memory is integral to the formation of identities, collective (or public) memory has long been important in the construction of collective identities.[5] In particular, nation-states construct and promote a particular understanding of the past within nation-building projects that are intended to foster social cohesion and allegiance to a particular "imagined community."[6] The formation of such a collective memory involves choices about what a society wishes to remember. Nevertheless, while states may play a leading role in the construction of collective memory they do not enjoy a monopoly over this process. Instead, various elites and publics both within and without the state (each of which may be fractured by competing and contesting agendas) participate in the process[7] so that the formation of public memory is a fluid process of negotiation.[8] Public memory "emerges from the intersection of official and vernacular cultural expressions"[9] and, for this reason, it is best regarded as an activity or process, rather than an outcome.[10]

Public memory is a process which is worked out in the public arena. This is achieved through various practices of remembrance and commemoration intended to reify public memory by turning it into visual spectacle. In particular, human geographers argue that urban space – or landscape – is essential to the "working" of public memory.[11] All political orders seek to create an "official public landscape"[12] intended as a rhetorical statement of specific political values. Remembrance and commemoration are central aspects of such landscapes: Edensor[13] has coined the term "memoryscape" for those parts of the urban landscape that are given over to collective remembrance. The urban environment can be the setting for a range of temporary (if cyclical) commemorative practices including ceremonies, parades, festivals, and rituals. However, most forms of commemoration are permanent and include statues, monuments, memorials, and other public buildings, along with commemorative names attached to streets, buildings, and other urban landmarks. Such commemorative practices concretize "official" conceptions of public memory, rendering it immutable in the public arena. They can also be sites for the expression of opposition to and contestation of this official public memory.

Since public memory is produced in a particular political context it is vulnerable to political change. In particular, all shifts of political power "generate a reconfiguration of the 'known past.'"[14] This issue is of particular relevance in post-communist societies which have sought to build political identities based on an emphatic rejection of communism (a strategy which generally enjoyed widespread popular support). Such societies faced the need for a new, appropriate, and "usable" past to replace now discredited communist-era constructions of the collective past. The most readily available exemplar was that of the period before communist rule.[15] Therefore, Central and Eastern Europe has focused on the pre-communist past as the model for a post-communist future. As Katherine Verdery argued, this is about effectively excising the communist period from the historical time line and connecting the post-communist present with the period before World War II.[16] This enabled post-communist societies to "resume" the historical trajectory that they would have followed had it not been for the "aberration" of four decades of communist rule. Clearly in post-communist contexts, the past is fluid and flexible, with different state and non-state groups competing to establish a new historical narrative (see Chapter 7 in this volume).

Similarly, public memory is also in a state of reformation.[17] Within the political transformation from totalitarianism to democracy, post-communist societies face new choices about what (and who) they want to remember, and how (and where) this remembrance will be enacted. At the same time as seeking to forget communism, the new societies want to remember the repression and violence of the former regime and to honor the victims of state persecution. There may also desire to remember the events that brought about the collapse of communist regimes (even if, in some cases, these events did not in themselves bring about a clear break with those regimes). Moreover, given that the urban landscape is central to the expression of public memory these debates will, in some way, be worked out in urban space. In particular, there will be a significant remaking of the commemorative landscape. People and events honored by the previous regime will be de-commemorated and their memorials removed from the public arena. New acts of commemoration will subsequently follow in a way that accords with the political values and public memory of the new regime.

In this way, practices of commemoration and memorialization within the urban landscape can be important (if often overlooked) elements of transitional justice projects in post-communist states. Indeed, memorialization and collective remembrance are fundamental processes in societies recovering from traumatic pasts.[18] Barsalou and Baxter argue that memorialization has a number of roles in such projects: it offers symbolic reparations to the victims of violence; it can promote reconciliation; it can encourage engagement with education programs about the recent past; and it creates specific sites that can be the focus both of individual mourning and official ceremonies of remembrance.[19] Of particular relevance to this chapter is that memorialization makes a highly visible statement in the public arena about a post-communist society's commitment to a new set of political values. In fact, of all the forms of transitional justice, memorialization is the most visible and can have an impact on the everyday lives of the greatest number of people. However, to date, there has been only sporadic attention in the transitional justice literature to the role of memorialization projects within the urban landscape. This reflects a broader context in which political scientists have paid relatively little attention to the role of monuments and memorials as political symbols.[20] In the following sections we explore changing practices of memorialization in post-communist Central and Eastern Europe, focusing first on the removal of the commemorative landscapes created by communist regimes, and then on efforts to create new memorial sites and landscapes within transitional justice projects.

ERASING THE COMMEMORATIVE LANDSCAPE OF COMMUNISM

When communist regimes came to power in the late 1940s they immediately set about remaking public memory. This was principally achieved through a comprehensive rewriting of history and total control over the education system. It also included a comprehensive remaking of the urban landscape to decommemorate the historical narrative associated with the discredited former regime. Since communist regimes attached special importance to the transformative power of public space for creating a new socialist consciousness,[21] the public arena effectively became an instrument of state propaganda. An entirely new commemorative landscape was produced which was saturated with a variety of symbols (including statues, memorials, monuments, plaques, murals, banners, and slogans) that were intended to shape the ways that people thought about their individual and collective pasts.[22]

As communist regimes collapsed in 1989 their official commemorative landscapes swiftly became the targets of protest, resulting in the familiar process of "landscape cleansing."[23] This activity was initiated by the populace during the euphoria that accompanied the collapse of communist rule and was continued by the new post-communist administrations. This process satisfied the demand to see evidence of political change.[24] Czepczyński identifies a number of strategies for landscape cleansing: removal, renaming, rededication, and reuse.[25] The most visible strategy is removal, where monuments placed by the communist states were directly expunged from the urban arena. By far the most iconic images of the collapse of communist regimes were the removal of statues of Soviet figures such as Lenin. These events required considerable organization and resources and so were usually orchestrated by the state.[26] They provided a dramatic and highly visible proclamation that political order was changing. However, in most cases the eradication of communist statuary was both less spectacular and less immediate, with most removals taking place quietly during the early years of post-communism.[27] Only in a few instances were communist monuments destroyed in situ, the dynamiting of Georgi Dimitrov's mausoleum in Sofia in 1999 being the best example.[28]

In most instances communist monuments and statues were not destroyed but instead they were simply moved to new locations. For example, in Hungary, the Budapest city authority made the decision in 1991 to remove over forty communist-era statues and monuments and relocate them in an open-air museum on the edge of the city, named "Statuepark," which opened to visitors in 1993. This strategy allowed the monuments to be retained both as historical artifacts and as reminders of a traumatic past but in a way that emasculated their symbolic power within the urban landscape.[29] In other cases, the removal of communist statues was vigorously contested. The best example is the "Bronze Soldier" in Tallinn, Estonia, which commemorated Soviet soldiers who had fallen in the liberation of the city at the end of World War II. As an obviously Soviet symbol, its presence in the city centre was unwelcome for the post-communist Estonian government, which, in 2007, made the decision to move the memorial to a military cemetery on the edge of the city. This provoked violent protest by Estonia's Russian minority, who interpreted the removal of the statue as an attack on their heritage and identity.[30]

A less dramatic strategy was the renaming of streets, buildings, and other urban landmarks to de-commemorate events and personalities from communist-era historiography. This practice has been termed "toponymic cleansing."[31] Such renaming is "an act of political propaganda with immense proclamative value and public resonance"[32]: it makes an immediate statement that public memory is changing and is relatively quick and simple to implement. Renaming was intended to decommemorate the communist past and place a new narrative of national history and memory into public space. However, renaming urban streets and buildings was relatively limited in scale and was most prominent in the central areas of towns and cities. Since many toponyms allocated during the communist era had no ideological connotations, they did not need to be renamed. For example, in Bucharest only 6.6 percent of the city's streets were renamed after 1989.[33] In other post-communist cities, the proportion was lower.

Strategies of rededication and reuse were applied mostly to museums. Communist regimes attached considerable importance to museums[34] as a means of socialist propaganda so that hundreds of new museums were established in communist Central and Eastern Europe. Most countries had at least one museum dedicated entirely to the history and activities of that country's Communist Party. These were complemented by a network of regional and local museums, all of which interpreted local history through the lens of Marxism-Leninism. With the fall of communism, the museums dedicated to Party history were swiftly closed. Some reopened as different museums (for example, in Bucharest the former History Museum of the Communist Party and of the Revolutionary and Democratic Movement of Romania reopened in 1990 as the Museum of the Romanian Peasant[35]), while in other cases the buildings were put to entirely new uses. As the formerly communist states were gripped by "collective amnesia" about the recent past almost all museums simply closed any galleries which dealt with the communist period: the displays remained in place but in locked rooms with no public access. Bădica[36] describes this as the "black hole paradigm" where the historical narrative presented in museums simply ended in 1945.

Overall, the efforts to neutralize the commemorative symbols of communism (and the public memory that they represented) was a crude first step in achieving redress for the abuses and hardship of the communist era. However, the process of landscape cleansing was always partial. It was applied most thoroughly to the central parts of cities (particularly capitals) and to a lesser extent (sometimes hardly at all) in more peripheral districts. Its target was the most visible and iconic symbols of the communist regime, while smaller or more inconspicuous symbols were often ignored or overlooked. Removing or reconfiguring the commemorative landscape of communism effectively cleared space in the urban arena for an entirely new set of commemorative practices specifically intended to remember the victims and abuses of communism. These are discussed in the following section.

COMMEMORATING THE VICTIMS OF AND RESISTANCE TO COMMUNIST REGIMES

Within strategies to redefine public memory there have been two broad strands to the remaking of commemorative landscapes. First, in the effort to (re)establish a "normal" past post-communist societies have attempted to correct the distortions of communist-era historiography. In addition to de-commemorating key figures from the communist version of history there has been a focus on reinstating and re-commemorating those people (politicians and monarchs) who were excised from public memory by communist historians. This, in turn, resulted in new practices of memorialization in the public arena and, once the official public landscape had been decommunized, it could be repopulated with new monuments, statues, memorials, and toponyms. The most straightforward way to do this was by returning streets to their pre-communist commemorative names. For example, in central Bucharest fourteen streets commemorating pre-communist politicians that had been renamed by the communist regime returned to their former names, as did four streets that commemorated the Romanian monarchy.[37] Over time, new statues and monuments were commissioned to commemorate those figures who had been disavowed during the communist period. For example, a statue of Tomáš Masaryk was erected in Prague in 2000, and a statue of King Carol I (based on an earlier statue destroyed by the communist regime) was unveiled in Bucharest in 2010. Such practices represent a symbolic correction of a form of historical injustice, although they are not usually considered as part of transitional justice projects.

Second, post-communist societies faced the challenge of how to remember the communist period and how to commemorate its victims. Although in many countries there was an initial desire to forget the communist past completely, at a later stage there was general agreement that the abuses of communism should be memorialized. The construction of memorials, monuments, and museums is a means of acknowledging the abuses of the communist era, giving recognition to the victims, and promoting a sense of social cohesion and belonging that is rooted in a traumatic recent past.[38] A range of actors both within and outside the state participate in such memorialization. In some countries, governments have been very active in promoting remembrance of the abuses of communist regimes as a form of transitional justice that compliments other legal and institutional measures.[39] States can also use practices of memorialization to affirm and legitimate (to both domestic and international audiences) their commitment to political values that are the antithesis of communism.[40] Civil society groups and non-governmental organizations have also been active in memorializing the communist past, particularly in those countries where former communist officials have remained in power and have been more unwilling to condemn the communist era.[41] In addition, ordinary individuals can also be involved in the process of remembrance through creating and placing their own, informal memorials in the urban landscape. The commemorative landscape is therefore characterized by a bricolage of memorial forms, dedicated to different subjects and groups, in a wide range of locations, and with a wide range of sponsors. In what follows, we focus on two broad categories of memorialization: (1) monuments and memorials and (2) museums (with associated practices of tourism).

Monuments and Memorials

For states engaged in enacting transitional justice, the erection of monuments and statues in the public arena has provided one means of recognition of communist-era injustices. As a result, there are many examples of such commemoration, although it is by no means a thorough, consistent, and comprehensive practice. Indeed, what is perhaps surprising is the relative paucity of such memorials combined with the controversy that they sometimes generate. Representing the condemnation of the communist past and its injustices through memorialization is not, therefore, a straightforward process.

The memorials that have been erected differ widely in terms of their form, the subject that they commemorate, and the sponsoring organization behind them. Some memorials commemorate the actions and death of a specific individual. While they focus on the sacrifice of the individual they implicitly draw attention to the broader injustices of the regimes responsible. Examples here include the monument in Prague to Jan Palach, the student who committed suicide in January 1969 in protest against the Soviet repression of the Prague Spring. A bronze cross is now embedded into the spot outside the national museum where he died. Palach is also commemorated through the naming of a square in Prague, several other memorials throughout Europe, and even the naming (by a Czech astronomer) of an asteroid after him. Other memorials are dedicated to groups of individuals who died in specific sites. A key example is the memorials to those killed trying to cross the Berlin Wall. The White Crosses memorial features seven crosses inscribed with the names of thirteen people who were killed in this way. First erected by a private group in 1971 in West Berlin, it has always been associated with key symbolic parts of the urban landscape, initially being located near the Reichstag and now beside the offices of the new unified German government. Deaths associated with the Berlin Wall are also commemorated generically at the Gedenkstätte Berliner Mauer (Berlin Wall Memorial).

Some memorials acknowledge deaths associated with specific events or more broadly with specific aspects of totalitarian oppression. These include a series of memorials to victims of the KGB in Tartu, Vilnius, Riga, and Potsdam, and memorials to the Katyn massacre. In Moldova a stone cross at Răzeni commemorates the ten victims of the Soviet-led massacre of 1941, while in Chişinău there is a Memorial to the Victims of Stalinist Repression. A plaque in a square just off Rustavelli Avenue in Tbilisi, Georgia, commemorates those killed by Soviet forces during protests in 1956 (protests partly motivated by the denouncement of Stalin). In Gdańsk (Poland) the Monument to the Fallen Shipyard Workers of 1970 memorial was unusually erected during the communist period itself (in 1980). Other memorial sites are aimed more broadly at remembering the national experience of communism. For example, the Memorial to the Victims of Communism in Prague, erected in 2002, seeks to shape the collective memory of those who died under Czechoslovak communism. Supported by the local authority and the Confederation of Political Prisoners (KPV) it seeks to commemorate those who suffered politically and personally, detailing the numbers shot or who died in prison, were arrested or exiled. A bronze plaque reads: "The memorial to the victims of communism is dedicated to all victims not only those who were jailed or executed but also those whose lives were ruined by totalitarian despotism." This memorial has attracted some criticism for its gendered nature (no female figures are represented) and for its aesthetic qualities, raising the issue of the public reception of such forms of commemoration.

Finally, some monuments commemorate collective suffering under communism and are intended to denounce the period as a whole. Such monuments sometimes prove to be controversial. The Gloria Victis Memorial is located on the outskirts of Budapest, Hungary, and seeks to honor "the 100 million victims of communism."[42] This memorial, the first to commemorate all the victims of communist repression, was erected in 2006 (the fiftieth anniversary of the 1956 Hungarian Revolution). This memorial is more complex than those commemorating individuals or specific groups, and incorporates local, national, and international representations of the victimization of citizens. It includes a world map of victims; memorials to the Ukrainian minority in Hungary; tablets commemorating the Molotov-Ribbentrop Pact, Jewish and Roma victims of communism, and the Katyn massacre; and the text of Resolution 1481 (2006) of the Council of Europe on The Necessity of International Condemnation of the Crimes Committed by Totalitarian Communist Regimes. Clearly such a memorialization process becomes significantly more complex when trying to represent the suffering of all the victims of communism, compared to the memory of an individual.

In addition to memorializing the abuses of communist regimes, various monuments commemorate the events that brought about the overthrow of communist regimes in 1989. Pearce suggests that some post-communist states have encountered problems in trying to establish official commemorative practices around the events of 1989 (such as which key dates or events should form the basis of state-sponsored commemoration).[43] In some cases, the official narrative of events is strongly contested. For example, in 2005 Romania erected a *Memorial of Rebirth* in Bucharest to symbolize the struggle against the Nicolae Ceausescu regime and to commemorate those who died in the violent "revolution" of 1989. It is the official site of remembrance and the setting for state-led performances and rituals which attempt to shape post-communist visions of Romania's past and future. However, the monument has been roundly criticized on aesthetic and architectural grounds. Moreover, the site holds little resonance for many Romanians who interpret the events of December 1989 more as a coup d'état than a genuine popular revolution. Consequently, the *Memorial of Rebirth* has failed to become the focus of popular allegiance and its role in shaping public memory among Romanians is unclear.

This overview of the use of monuments, plaques, statues, and memorials is not intended to be exhaustive, but instead seeks to demonstrate the range of types of demoralization practices which attempt to place transitional justice into the public arena. There is not space here to discuss in detail the design and symbolism of each of these sites (although this is an important subject for further research). Moreover, we know relatively little about the public reaction to and reception of such commemorative landscapes. However, the examples above give hints of how even what might appear to be a straightforward process – condemning communism and commemorating its victims in public space – can be contested and subject to debate. The example of the Memorial of Rebirth illustrates that while political elites may seek to shape transitional justice projects and the remembrance of the victims of communism, they may not always succeed. Instead, projects to shape commemoration and public memory can sometimes be contested and challenged by the populace. The public reception of sites and practices of demoralization remains a neglected aspect of transitional justice.

Museums and Tourism

To fully appreciate the role of museums in transitional justice projects it is important to recognize that museums are not simply collections of objects put on public display for the education and entertainment of visitors. Instead, museums have always had a broader ideological purpose. They are a form of public culture through which political elites tell a society about itself and where it has come from. In particular, museums that are sponsored by the state have an important role in "telling the national story." They are institutions that are intended to be visited by the citizenry and which have a clearly articulated educational mission. They aim to communicate a particular understanding of the past and thus play a significant role in the making (and remaking) of public memory. More broadly, as a means of "staging" the nation[44] museums contribute to the formation of collective identities and their importance within nation-building projects is widely acknowledged.[45] As the earlier discussion noted, communist regimes were fully aware of the educative and propagandist role of museums in communicating their political agenda (and the associated narrative of national history) to a broad public.

In the post-communist context, museums are important "vehicles of memory"[46] within projects to memorialize the communist past. In particular, museums can tell the story of the oppression, human rights abuses, and suffering inflicted by communist regimes. This, obviously, is a story that has not been formally told before (since it was not something that communist regimes were likely to draw attention to). Moreover, museums can interpret the communist period from the perspective of the people who lived through it. This is a bottom-up narrative of history that focuses on everyday lives of ordinary people, rather than the macro-political agenda of the communist state and its leading party. Memorial museums also interpret communist rule for future generations who did not experience it themselves in order to help them understand the experiences that shaped their parents' and grandparents' generation. Museums can also be locations for ceremonies and rituals intended to commemorate the victims of communist rule. Overall, memorial museums that are established as part of transitional justice projects are institutions intended to encourage remembrance, reflection, and civic engagement.[47] However, they are not just about the communist past: museums can also be used to make an unambiguous statement about a state's post-communist political identity and aspirations. In this context, they are sites for "performances of democracy, not static representations of national identity."[48] The use of museums in this way is as ideological as anything seen during the communist period but for entirely different ends.

What is important, but frequently overlooked, is the role of tourism in this process. Memorial museums are intended to be visited (and as such they function as visitor "attractions" even if their subject matter is far from attractive). Some of the visitors to memorial museums will be children and young people, studying the communist period as part of their educational curriculum. However, most people will be visiting during their leisure time. Furthermore, many of these people will be tourists (conventionally defined as people staying away from their home area for at least 24 hours) who can be both domestic (citizens of a country traveling within that country) and international (visitors from other countries). Although political scientists may be inclined to dismiss tourism as trivial and with little to offer in understanding politics, there is growing interest within the discipline of tourism studies in the ways that tourism can contribute to broader political projects and objectives.[49] For example, visiting historic buildings and monuments is a means of "connecting" with the broader community of the nation.[50] As such, tourism can be identified as one form of banal nationalism.[51] Tourism can also be used to project political identities to an external audience. For example, recent studies have explored how the Central and Eastern European countries have used their state-sponsored tourism promotional materials to project a distinctly *post*-communist political identity to the wider world.[52]

In the context of transitional justice projects, tourism at memorials and museums can be used to communicate a message about the communist past and the post-communist future. Moreover, many of the visitors to such places will be heritage tourists who are interested in and receptive to learning during their leisure time.[53] For domestic tourists, the visit to a memorial museum performs the same role as other monuments and memorials: it is a reminder of the traumas of the recent past, a recognition of the victims of that past, a warning to future generations, an affirmation of the rejection of communism, and a commitment to broader "European" values. However, international tourists are an equally important (and sometimes numerically dominant) audience (and for this reason most memorial museums make extensive use of displays and interpretation in the English language and often in a range of other European languages). Most international visitors will have no direct experience of living under communist rule (and often little background knowledge or understanding of communism). Therefore, museums are a way of telling such visitors the story of "what we lived through" and "the events that shaped us." This is also a way of affirming and legitimating a commitment to the same political and economic agendas that have underpinned European integration since World War II.

There are an increasing number of museums in the Central and Eastern European countries that explicitly address the communist era. Most countries have a national museum (usually a monumental building located in the capital city) and these frequently include a gallery dedicated to the recent past (although such galleries are fairly neutral historical accounts of the communist period). There are also museums specifically dedicated to interpreting the nature of life in a communist state. Some (such as the Museum of Communism in Prague or the DDR Museum in Berlin) have been set up by private entrepreneurs to cater to the interest of Western visitors, rather than being intended to contribute to transitional justice projects. However, many other museums have been established with the direct or indirect support of the state authorities specifically to remember the abuses and victims of communist rule. Perhaps the best examples are Estonia's Museum of Occupations (which opened in 2003 in a purpose-built structure), the Museum of the Occupation of Latvia (opened 1993), and Lithuania's Museum of Genocide Victims (established 1992 in the former headquarters of the Soviet Security service). Each is located in the respective capital city. All are run by foundations with state support. The motto of Latvia's museum, "Remembering, Commemorating, Reminding,"[54] clearly indicates the place of the museum within the broader project of achieving transitional justice. The displays of these museums focus on the nature of totalitarian rule; its impact on politics, economy, and domestic life; the nature of domestic repression and human rights abuses; the activities of resistance groups; and the struggle for and achievement of independence in the early 1990s. All receive large numbers of foreign tourists and are included in the itineraries of visiting politicians and dignitaries.

Other museums have been opened in buildings that were formerly prisons or were associated in other ways with the repressive apparatus of communist regimes. The conversion of such buildings into memorial museums is a form of symbolic "re-inscription" that is intended to give them a new use for memorializing the practices that they formerly hosted. The best example is the Memorial to the Victims of Communism and to the Resistance in Sighet, Romania. This opened in 1998 in a building that had formerly been used as a prison and in which the majority of the pre-World War II Romanian political, military, social, and academic elite had been imprisoned after the communist regime took power. The museum was developed by the Civic Academy Foundation (a non-governmental organization) with the financial support of the Council of Europe. It hosts summer schools for young Romanians and publishes regular volumes of academic study about the communist era.[55] Its significance as a site of public remembrance of the human rights abuses of the communist regime was recognized by the Romanian government, which declared it a site of national interest in 1997.

Another celebrated example is the former headquarters of the East German security service (the Stasi) in Berlin, which opened as a memorial and research centre in November 1990. The site was managed by a non-governmental civil rights organization, although with the support of the German government. The complex includes a museum with displays about the history and activities of the Stasi. Elsewhere in Berlin, a former Stasi prison and interrogation centre opened in 1994 as a museum and memorial (the Berlin-Hohenschönhausen Memorial). It is run by a private foundation with government support and aims to encourage "a critical awareness of the methods and consequences of political persecution and suppression in the communist dictatorship."[56] Another example is Budapest's House of Terror, again established by a public foundation with government backing. It is housed in the former headquarters of the Hungarian security police (ÁVH). This site is intended as a memorial to those Hungarians who were interrogated and tortured by the communist regime, an interpretation of life in communist Hungary, and an account of the struggle against the communist regime which ended in 1989.[57] Significantly, it is also one of Budapest's most popular tourist attractions. Elsewhere throughout post-communist Central and Eastern Europe there are numerous smaller prisons and interrogation centers that have been turned into museums, intended for both domestic and international visitors.

Memorial museums are not without their critics. Although tourism is one of the principal means through which memorial sites are encountered, there has long been a tendency to dismiss the practices of visitors to such places as trivial or insignificant. At best, tourists who visit places associated with trauma or tragedy are regarded as passive and unquestioning consumers incapable of fully appreciating the significance of the story presented to them and, at worst, as shallow thrill-seekers motivated by "a morbid and senseless curiosity."[58] However, recent research in the disciplines of tourism studies and anthropology has demonstrated that the behavior of visitors to memorial places is far more purposeful and significant than is often appreciated and that visitors can undertake highly meaningful acts of remembrance and engagement with the subject matter they encounter.[59] Other authors accept that visits to memorial museums may be associated with short-term learning, understanding, and changed attitudes but they question the longer-term impacts of such visits in bringing about deeper learning and a broader engagement with the issues of transitional justice.[60] Overall, the consumption of memorial museums by their visitors is clearly a subject which merits much fuller research.

CONCLUSION

Issues of memorialization and the reformulation of public memory are often considered to be "soft" aspects of transitional justice, and consequently they have not received as much academic attention as the "hard" politics of truth commissions, lustration, or restitution. However, we argue that the issue of shaping public memory through commemorative practices and landscapes is an integral element of transitional justice projects which merits much fuller investigation. In concluding, we highlight the importance of considering the cultural politics of transitional justice and we identify the lessons of accepting such a perspective.

One lesson that emerges from considering public memory and its expression in the urban landscape is that transitional justice is not only played out in the spaces of courtrooms, legislatures, and administrations. It is also worked out in public squares, memorial landscapes, and museums. We need to recognize the vast range of sites and spaces in which multiple practices of transitional justice works, through the initiatives of both elites and publics. In this context, it is important to acknowledge that the past itself (and ways that it is represented and memorialized) is fluid, multifaceted, and contested. While states are active players in the commemoration of the communist past and in broader efforts to shape public memory, they do not have a monopoly on the process. Instead, there are a range of other organizations and individuals involved in such commemoration, and consequently there is a diverse range of monuments, memorials, and museums dedicated to the abuses and victims of communist regimes. These are sites where individual and personal negotiations of transitional justice occur, alongside the official memorials, ceremonies, and rituals sponsored by the state.

Another key issue is the reach of these spaces of transitional justice. While processes such as lustration and even restitution symbolically show that post-communist states are acting to address past injustices, in societal terms their impact may be relatively limited. Not everyone in society was able to reclaim property or necessarily had a personal connection to key figures who were placed on trial. Hence, such practices arguably may have a limited impact on the everyday lives and practices of the majority of the population. However, monuments and commemorative landscapes can reach far more people in the course of their daily lives and to address their wish for justice in a much more immediate and visible way. For most people, commemoration in the public arena is a form of public recognition that is important in coming to terms with past injustices.

Furthermore, there are important temporal aspects to transitional justice that should be considered. The largest waves of restitution have been completed and there is probably considerably less scope for lustration (since those who could be tried either already have been, or are too old, or have died). Memorialization in the public arena has a potentially much longer impact with the possibility of shaping public memory across generations. Twenty-five years have now elapsed since 1989 and perhaps the forms of transitional justice projects must reflect this. Shaping public memory through commemorative landscapes may well assume a greater importance as other processes decrease in frequency and effectiveness. If the purpose of such memorialization is to help society to move on (without forgetting) then public commemorative landscapes perhaps hold the key. The construction of memorial landscapes may follow on from other, more contentious, processes of transitional justice (which, in turn, may shape the nature of commemorative practices). If such commemoration becomes a more long-term form of transitional justice which persists in public space for decades to come, then it will require careful consideration and management.

The final lesson from our chapter is that there is a need to explore public reception of landscapes and memorialization. This is the area in which the literature is most weakly developed. As Barsalou and Baxter suggest, "The impact of *all* transitional justice processes – memorialization among them – remains under-researched."[61] They note the difficulty in determining what memorialization actually contributes to reconciliation and justice. Thus, we need to explore questions such as: How do people relate to memorials and landscapes linked to transitional justice projects in their everyday lives? Do memorials work effectively as vehicles of transitional justice? Are they sites of remembrance or contestation, or do they simply become a backdrop to the everyday use of space in the city? Are they even regarded with apathy or simply ignored? Again, these issues have temporal and generational dimensions, and will vary across multiple publics and elites. For example, some authors are skeptical about the long-term impact of museums on the public consciousness.[62] Furthermore, as Clark suggests, there is a danger that too much memorialization may inhibit societies' ability to move on.[63] Moreover, different generations may have very different responses to the ways in which commemorative landscapes function as part of transitional justice, responses shaped by interactions between the generations mediated through the family and representations of history. An important issue for further research is the public reception of memorialization aimed at righting the wrongs of the communist era in order to help support the longer-term achievement of transitional justice and its expression in public space.

NOTES

1. Janine N. Clark, "Reconciliation through Remembrance? War Memorials and the Victims of Vukovar," *International Journal of Transitional Justice* 7, no. 1 (2013): 117.
2. Brendon Hamber, Liz Ševčenko, and Ereshnee Naidu, "Utopian Dreams or Practical Possibilities? The Challenges of Evaluating the Impact of Memorialization in Societies in Transition," *International Journal of Transitional Justice* 4, no. 3 (2010): 397.
3. John Bodnar, *Remaking America: Public Memory, Commemoration, and Patriotism in the Twentieth Century* (Princeton, NJ: Princeton University Press, 1992): 15.
4. Kenneth E. Foote and Maoz Azaryahu, "Towards a Geography of Memory: Geographical Dimensions of Public Memory and Commemoration," *Journal of Political and Military Sociology* 35, no. 1 (2007): 127.

5. John R. Gillis, "Memory and Identity: The History of a Eelationship," in *Commemorations: The Politics of National Identity*, ed. John R. Gillis (Princeton, NJ: Princeton University Press, 1994), 24; and Cristiane Wilke, "Remembering Complexity? Memorials for Nazi Victims in Berlin," *International Journal of Transitional Justice* 7, no. 1 (2013): 141.
6. Benedict Anderson, *Imagined Communities: Reflections on the Origin and Spread of Nationalism*, 2nd ed. (London: Verso, 2006).
7. Benjamin Forest, Juliet Johnson and Karen Till, "Post-totalitarian National Identity: Public Memory in Germany and Russia," *Social and Cultural Geography* 5, no. 3 (2004): 358, 362.
8. Karen Till, "Staging the Past: Landscape Designs, Cultural Identity and Erinnerungspolitik at Berlin's Neue Wache," *Ecumene* 6, no. 3 (1999): 254.
9. John Bodnar, "Public Memory in an American City: Commemoration in Cleveland," in *Commemorations: The Politics of National Identity*, ed. John R. Gillis (Princeton, NJ: Princeton University Press, 1994), 75.
10. Forest, Johnson and Till, "Post-totalitarian," 358.
11. Derek H. Alderman, "Memory and Place: Geographies of a Critical Relationship," *Social and Cultural Geographies* 5, no.3 (2004): 347–355; Nuala Johnson, "Public Memory" in *A Companion to Cultural Geography*, eds. James S. Duncan, Nuala C. Johnson, and Richard H. Schein (Oxford: Blackwell, 2004), 316–327; Karen Till, *The New Berlin: Memory, Politics, Place* (Minneapolis: University of Minnesota Press, 2005).
12. James Bell, "Redefining National Identity in Uzbekistan: Symbolic Tensions in Tashkent's Official Public Landscape," *Ecumene* 6, no. 2 (1999): 186.
13. Tim Edensor, "National Identity and the Politics of Memory: Remembering Bruce and Wallace in Symbolic Space," *Environment and Planning D* 15, no. 2 (1997): 178.
14. Gail Kligman and Katherine Verdery, *Peasants Under Siege: The Collectivization of Romanian Agriculture, 1949–1962* (Princeton: Princeton University Press, 2011), 9.
15. Katherine Verdery, *What Was Socialism and What Comes Next?* (Princeton: Princeton University Press, 1996), 136.
16. Katherine Verdery, *The Political Lives of Dead Bodies: Reburial and Postsocialist Change* (New York: Columbia University Press, 1999), 116, 124.
17. Forest, Johnson, and Till, "Post-totalitarian," 358–363.
18. Hamber, Ševčenko, and Naidu, "Utopian Dreams," 398.
19. Judy Barsalou and Victoria Baxter, *The Urge to Remember: The Role of Memorials in Social Reconstruction and Transitional Justice* (Washington, D.C.: United States Institute of Peace, 2007), 4, available at: http://www.usip.org/publications/the-urge-remember-the-role-of-memorials-in-social-reconstruction-and-transitional (accessed on October 3, 2013).
20. Benjamin Forest and Juliet Johnson, "Unravelling the Threads of History: Soviet-Era Monuments and Post-Soviet National Identity in Moscow," *Annals of the Association of American Geographers* 92, no. 3 (2002): 271.
21. David Crowley and Susan E. Reid, "Socialist Spaces: Sites of Everyday Life in the Eastern Bloc," in *Socialist Spaces: Sites of Everyday Life in the Eastern Bloc*, eds. David Crowley and Susan E. Reid (Oxford: Berg, 2002), 11.
22. Gordon Church, "Bucharest: Revolution in the Townscape Art," in *The Socialist City: Spatial Structure and Urban Policy*, eds. R. A. French and F. E. I. Hamilton

(Chichester: Wiley, 1979), 502–503; and Robert Argenbright, "Remaking Moscow: New Places, New Selves," *The Geographical Review* 89, no. 1 (1999): 6.
23. Marius Czepczyński, *Cultural Landscapes of Post-Socialist Cities: Representations of Powers and Needs* (Aldershot: Ashgate, 2008), 116–125.
24. Deborah Schultz and Alina Serban, "Public Memory and National Identity under Construction: The Trajectory of Monuments in Romania in the Communist and Post-Communist Periods," *Centropa* 10, no. 1 (2010): 64.
25. Czepczyński, *Cultural Landscapes*, 115.
26. Schultz and Serban, "Public Memory," 63.
27. Kenneth E. Foote, Atilla Tóth, and Annet Árvay, "Hungary after 1989: Inscribing a New Past on Place," *Geographical Review* 90, no. 3 (2000): 310–311.
28. Maria Todorova, "The mausoleum of Georgi Dimitrov as *lieu de mémoire*," *Journal of Modern History* 78, no. 2 (2006): 388.
29. Beverly James, "Fencing in the Past: Budapest's Statue Park Museum," *Media, Culture and Society* 21, no. 3 (1999): 303.
30. Marko Lehti, Matti Jutila, and Markku Jokisipilä, "Never-Ending Second World War: Public Performances of National Dignity and the Drama of the Bronze Soldier," *Journal of Baltic Studies* 39, no. 4 (2008): 393–418.
31. Reuban Rose-Redwood, Derek Alderman, and Maoz Azaryahu, "Geographies of Toponymic Inscription: New Directions in Critical Place-Name Studies," *Progress in Human Geography* 34, no. 4 (2010): 460.
32. Maoz Azaryahu, "The Power of Commemorative Street Names," *Environment and Planning D: Society and Space* 14, no. 3 (1996): 318.
33. Duncan Light, "Street Names in Bucharest, 1990–1997: Exploring the Modern Historical Geographies of Post-Socialist Change," *Journal of Historical Geography* 30, no. 1 (2004): 160.
34. Zbynek Z. Stransky, "Museums in Post-Communist Countries," in *Museums and Europe 1992*, ed. Susan Pearce (London: Athlone Press, 1992): 174–176.
35. Simina Bădica, "The Black Hole Paradigm: Exhibiting Communism in Post-Communist Romania," in *History of Communism in Europe*: Volume 1: *Politics of Memory in Post-Communist Europe* (Bucharest: Zeta Books, 2010), 88–89.
36. Bădica, "Black Hole."
37. Light, "Street Names," 163–164.
38. Elizabeth Jelin, "Public Memorialization in Perspective: Truth, Justice and the Memory of Past Repression in the Southern Cone of South America," *International Journal of Transitional Justice* 1, no. 1 (2007): 147.
39. Czepczyński, *Cultural Landscapes*, 138, in the case of Poland.
40. Forest and Johnson, "Unravelling the Threads," 270.
41. Lavinia Stan, "Reckoning with the Communist Past in Romania: A Scorecard," *Europe-Asia Studies* 65, no.1 (2013): 142.
42. "The memorial," available at: http://gloriavictis.hu/en/memorial.html (accessed on January 6, 2014).
43. Susan C. Pearce, "Delete, Restart or Rewind? Post-1989 Public Memory Work in East-Central Europe," *Sociology Compass* 5, no. 4 (2011): 256–257.
44. Tim Edensor, *National Identity, Popular Culture and Everyday Life* (Oxford: Berg, 2002), 85.

45. Donald Horne, *The Great Museum: The Re-presentation of History* (London: Pluto, 1984), 165–179; and Fiona McLean, "Museums and the Construction of National Identity: A Review," *International Journal of Heritage Studies* 3, no. 1 (1998): 244–252.
46. Jelin, "Public Memorialization," 141.
47. Barsalou and Baxter, *Urge to Remember*, 14.
48. Liz Sevcenko, cited in Barsalou and Baxter, *Urge to Remember*, 14.
49. Michael C. Hall, *Tourism and Politics: Policy, Power and Place* (Chichester: Wiley, 1994); Nigel Morgan and Annette Pritchard, *Tourism, Promotion and Power: Creating Images, Creating Identities* (Chichester: Wiley, 1998); and Michael C. Hall, *Tourism: Rethinking the Social Science of Mobility* (London: Routledge, 2005).
50. Catherine Palmer, "An Ethnography of Englishness: Experiencing Identity through Tourism," *Annals of Tourism Research* 32, no. 1 (2005): 11.
51. Michael Billig, *Banal Nationalism* (London: Sage, 1995).
52. Morgan and Pritchard, Tourism Promotion; Derek Hall, "Destination Branding, Niche Marketing and National Image Projection in Central and Eastern Europe," *Journal of Vacation Marketing* 5, no. 3 (1999): 227–237; Derek Hall, "Brand Development, Tourism and National Identity: The Re-imaging of Former Yugoslavia," *Brand Management* 9, no. 4–5 (2001): 323–334; Duncan Light, "Romania: National Identity, Tourism Promotion and European Integration," in *Tourism in the New Europe: The Challenges and Opportunities of EU Enlargement*, eds. Derek Hall, Melanie Smith, and Barbara Marciszewska (Wallingford: CABI, 2006), 256–269.
53. Duncan Light, "Heritage as Informal Education," in *Heritage, Tourism and Society*, ed. David T. Herbert (London: Mansell, 1995): 117–145.
54. "Museum of the Occupation of Latvia 1940–91," available at: http://okupacijasmuzejs.lv/en/about-museum/mission-and-history (accessed on 18 October 2013).
55. Bădica, "Black Hole," 96–101; "Memorialul Victimelor comunismului şi al Rezistenţei," available at: http://www.memorialsighet.ro/ (accessed 18 October 2013).
56. "The Berlin-Hohenschönhausen Memorial," available at: http://en.stiftung-hsh.de/document.php?cat_id=CAT_231&special=0 (accessed October 19, 2013).
57. "Terror," available at: http://www.terrorhaza.hu/ (accessed October 19, 2013).
58. Joy Sather-Wagstaff, *Heritage that Hurts: Tourists in the Memoryscapes of September 11* (Walnut Creek, CA: Left Coast Press, 2011), 77.
59. Sather-Wagstaff, *Heritage*, 115–170; Laurajane Smith, "The Cultural 'Work' of Tourism," in *The Cultural Moment in Tourism*, eds. Laurajane Smith, Emma Waterton, and Steve Watson (London: Routledge, 2012), 219–229; Andrea Witcombe, "Using Immersive and Interactive Approaches to Interpreting Traumatic Experiences for Tourists," in *Heritage and Tourism: Place, Encounter, Engagement*, eds. Russell Staiff, Robyn Bushell, and Steve Watson (London: Routledge, 2013), 152–170.
60. Hamber, Ševčenko, and Naidu, "Utopian Dreams," 145–148.
61. Barsalou and Baxter, *Urge to Remember*, 3.
62. Hamber, Ševčenko, and Naidu, "Utopian Dreams," 415–418.
63. Clark, "Reconciliation through Remembrance?" 133–134.

12

Stories We Tell: Documentary Theater, Performance, and Justice in Transition

Olivera Simić

> Perhaps we believe the horror we have lived through will not be repeated. Or perhaps we think it has all been a nightmare, an error, a bad dream better quickly forgotten. What has overtaken us that we forget so easily? Perhaps some blind faith that history cannot repeat itself?
>
> Dah Theater[1]

> A present without memory condemns us to a poor future. To believe that today owes nothing to yesterday allows us to think that we have no responsibility to tomorrow. On the contrary, memory and imagination complement each other since they allow us to represent what has already passed and what one day might occur.
>
> Miguel Rubio[2]

DOCUMENTARY THEATER AS A TRANSITIONAL JUSTICE MECHANISM

Although it has been twenty years since Yugoslavia's violent disillusion, the painful past, unresolved grievances, and social trauma are still very much present in the region. The Yugoslav successor states are experiencing three simultaneous transitions: from war to peace, from single party rule to pluralist democracy, and from a communist planned economy to liberal market economy. Bosnia and Herzegovina (BiH) is no exception. Since the end of war in 1995, the country has undergone a post-conflict transitional process involving immense economic, political, and social-cultural reconstruction. Today, BiH is an ethnically divided country, and national, ethnic and religious divisions represent an obstacle to its political, economic and social development. Likewise, Serbia is a country that suffers from its "indirect" involvement in the wars and appalling socioeconomic and political conditions.[3] Similar to BiH, it is going through a process of dealing with the past with no formal transitional justice mechanisms established. Over the past twenty years and under these circumstances, many grassroots arts-based projects have been developed. One of these innovative, informal, or "unofficial projects,"[4] has been documentary theater, which serves to artistically express issues often repressed by the governments. These projects can help form social bonds between people by bringing to the fore commonly shared experiences, spreading awareness about the suffering of the families of victims and of the communities that grieve for them, and inviting communities to engage with each other.[5]

According to Robin Soans, "documentary play" describes theater where the audience expects the play to be political, where the format is unconventional, while the material is contentious and challenges their opinions.[6] It is also a theater that uses documentary materials as the basis for plays, which is a rather new and increasingly popular trend among young theater directors in the former Yugoslavia.[7] It has been suggested that the reason why documentary theater is on the rise across the globe is because "it seems better suited to dealing with serious subject matter."[8] An upsurge in such theater has been seen not only in the Balkans, but across the globe recently. However, while attracting a considerable amount of coverage in the arts pages of newspapers, theater journals and websites, scholarly engagement has been limited thus far.[9] Local projects involving documentary theater have largely remained neglected, although civil society and community initiatives have been recognized as important facilitators of transitional justice.[10]

The plays analyzed in this chapter have been directed by prominent theater directors, all informed by the recent war and political events experienced by the people who survived both of them. The theater in this way has become a tool of social change that addresses underlying but often ignored social problems lingering within the community. It brings on stage voices and experiences of marginalized people. Documentary theater enlightens public opinion and often engages the audience in after-show discussions where they are able to express their opinions about the shortcomings of government, human rights issues, and emotional suffering that has not experienced closure despite prosecutions being made against people who committed the war crimes. Such theater invites the audience to participate in the witnessing of events and of suffering often denied or neglected by government. It reveals guilt and pain experienced by common people and leads to acknowledgment, if not healing and closure. As Nataša Govedarica notes, these plays have a "commemorative function" and represent some sort of "temporary monuments" because they "acknowledge that something has happened and [they] have testimonial value and [offer] symbolic reparation."[11]

Although transitional justice scholars, such as Ruti Teitel, argue that punishment of former perpetrators provides victims with legal redress and may even reconcile victims and their abusers while unveiling truth about the past,[12] trials should not be considered the only valid mechanism to achieve these aims. As Jacqueline O'Connor notes, the justice system often fails to achieve closure, or to resolve private or public discord, and ought not be the only resource that we employ for settling disputes or healing individual and collective trauma.[13] Indeed, trauma often remains long after a crime has been committed, a verdict has been rendered, and court has adjourned.[14] Retributive justice is, according to Teitel, essentially "backward-looking" and "crime-focused,"[15] unable to place a priority on preventative measures, such as the rehabilitation of offenders, or to serve as a venue for forgiveness and clemency.[16] Clearly, they may not be the best forums to accomplish this goal.[17] As Martha Minow argues, if the goal is to establish consensus and memorialize "controversial complex events," then "trials are not ideal."[18] They fail to grapple with the complexity of trauma, especially the collective trauma of a nation.[19]

The need to memorialize, dramatize, and document crimes against humanity is enormous, and as trials alone cannot satisfy this need, they need to be supplemented with alternative justice mechanisms and non-judicial methods that may help societies come to terms with past human rights violations.[20] Documentary theater provides a space to question assumptions and create new fresh ideas and views about issues raised upon the stage. It has become a means of communication; a political platform through which artists informally reveal, convey, and question injustices in the communities in which they live.[21] It serves as a new means of redress, a mechanism that can promote a positive collective memory while giving victims a place of respect, agency, and dignity in the process.[22] Documentary theater raises awareness about topical issues often left unspoken and discussed; issues that the common person may be afraid to ask about or comment on. Through narrative and performative strategies, documentary theater calls attention to its factual content and to its creation from existing documents, archival sources, authentic testimonies, and in that way challenges divisions between reality and how it has been represented by the media and government.[23] According to Peter Rush, the divergences between different transitional justice methods can "only be mediated by history and by visceral notions of personal and collective responsibility."[24]

The subjective, authentic, and emotional truth promulgated on stage gives visibility to people who have remained voiceless and unnoticeable in volumes of official documents about recent wars.[25] Documentary theater aims to reconstruct the public's memory, and to reverse silence and forgetting by bringing fact-based stories to light. The idea here is to create disequilibrium within the spectator, in order not only to empathize with the protagonist on stage, but also to prepare the way for concrete actions to address injustices and bring about transformation.[26] Emily Mann, a distinguished director and documentary playwright, explains her form of documentary theater thus: "I usually ask [people] if they have seen any documentary films. Almost everyone has. I say, well that's what I do. I go out and I find the event. I go to the place. I do a lot of work on it. I do a lot of research on it. I interview a whole lot of people. I find documents that have to do with that. Then I construct a play out of it. I'm working from life, and it's very personal."[27]

This chapter critically analyzes the use of documentary theater in BiH and Serbia. As a qualitative case study, the chapter draws from multiple sources including direct observation, documentary materials, and fieldwork undertaken during the summer of 2013, and analysis of texts and documents produced by the theater groups. The chapter also draws on interviews with directors of two plays *Prisustvo odsustva/Presence of Absence* (Dijana Milošević, Serbia) and *Sedam uzdaha/Seven Breaths* (Tanja Miletić Oručević, BiH), and with a dramaturg and playwright of *Hipermenzija/Hypermnesia* (Nataša Govedarica, BiH). All three plays are based on authentic testimonies about past wrongdoings and the effects on the lives of survivors. Common across the three case studies is the use of performance as a strategy for resistance and intervention. With permission and consent from the interviewees, the analysis draws on email correspondence between the author and the interviewees, photographs produced by the theater groups, internal theater documents on aims and objectives of performances, and secondary media sources in the Serbo-Croatian-Bosnian language.[28]

The chapter opens with a brief overview of documentary theater in Serbia and BiH. It then analyzes three plays currently on stage in those countries. The chapter concludes that documentary theater provides an important space to create meaning out of often unspeakable events from a shared past. It is an alternative and innovative tool of transitional justice that should be utilized as a way to create space for remembrance and reflection and to open discussion about a common, recent painful past.

WORKING IN THE DOCUMENTARY TRADITION

> Story is the way we remember, the way we make judgments – and perhaps, because they touch the heart – stories point the way to forgiveness and understanding. By means of story, we can experience the terrible and noble

> dimensions of what happened, we can put names to faces, meaning to places and events, gain a sense of the humanity of the victims and the victimizers, relive the events of history in their fearsome detail.[29]

Before the 1990s communist Yugoslavia did not have a tradition of independent professional groups, no cultural understanding of what these groups were about, and no financial support to enable their existence.[30] In regions lacking a tradition of civil society, such as the former Yugoslavia, that have also been saturated by violence and destruction, the arts and in particular the dramatic arts are an indispensable part of a comprehensive critical approach to the legacy of violence.[31] The Balkans, as a region known for its violent past, is seeing a mushrooming of innovative arts-based approaches to discuss the 1990s war in the former Yugoslavia and also transitional justice issues at the grassroots level. Selma Spahić, a Bosnian theater director, noted that there is a new generation of artists who feel they need to review the past in order to deal with the present: "The region has seen a new wave of documentary theater plays as artists wrestle with their own pasts as well as with the present ... documentary theater is alive in a special way, precisely because of its authenticity and the actuality of the theme at the moment when it occurs."[32]

Spahić was only six years old when war started in BiH, and now at the age of twenty-six she has become one of the most significant documentary theater directors in the region. The desire to look at the past with one's eyes wide open, and speak about it openly and without shame and censure, is what inspires this young director. Spahić and her colleagues are all aware that ignoring the past and lacking the will to deal with it can reopen the wounds that never properly healed. They recognize that memory of the past provides the roots of a culture's collective identity, and that the past always animates the present and compromises the future.[33] The stage then becomes the site where these multiple temporalities are embodied and dramatized.[34] In countries such as BiH, where perpetrators of gross human rights violations still walk free and some victims must encounter them on a daily basis, traumatic events are ever present. Spahić opted for documentary theater partly to deal with herself, which is why she put on the show *Hypermnesia*: "Documentary theater concerned me, as a member of the audience, in a completely new way, often causing intense emotion. I was faced with my own self, honestly and painfully. That prompted me to put on my own documentary show."[35]

According to Govedarica, a dramaturg and playwright of *Hypermnesia*, documentary theater is a "socially engaged or political theater"[36] which provides a space for people to connect with one another and recognize their experiences. Artists use theater and other arts-based critical interventions, such as street performance, photo exhibitions, and movie screenings, to discuss the recent wars. As Laura McLeod, Jovana Dimitrijević, and Biliana Rakočević argue, it is of paramount importance to create space for the consideration of alternative approaches to transitional justice that takes into account the social and political context.[37] These alternative approaches can be viewed through artistic practices, as artistic engagement disrupts the linear narrative often presented about transitional justice, thereby opening possibilities for alternative ways of thinking about ways to deal with the past.[38] In the former Yugoslavia, documentary theater is linked to experiences of the recent war and is seen as a space for resisting amnesia. Oliver Frljić, a prominent Croatian theater director, sees theater "as a space in which I can form my own opinion against the mainstream social norms. I can speak about things which everyone knows but don't talk about. For example, in theater, I can say that the war was not unavoidable and that the independence of Croatia, in comparison with how many people died in the war and poverty in which people live today, was not worth it."[39]

Official processes such as judicial proceedings, truth commissions, museums, or monuments share the goal of forging national consensus and consolidating a shared understanding of the past in order to create a particular vision for a nation's political future. As such, official processes rarely, if ever, dominate popular understandings of the past.[40] Or if they do, it is in such a way that national leaders and politics are effectively dictating the past to be remembered. However, in Serbia and BiH, in the absence of any formal, national processes for justice and truth, except retributive justice pursued via trials for war crimes, communities seek their own means for remembering past violations. This context is enriched by the new forms of theater that seek to "address victim's 'justice' needs, including an acknowledgment of wrongdoing."[41] Arts-based initiatives are coming from people affected by the conflict who "repudiate past violence ... demand remembrance ... and insist that violence not be repeated."[42]

Storytelling on stage can possess more power than the often fragmented official record, since it is raw and real and helps individuals to make sense of their past. But arts should be more than a mere tool for helping survivors to heal. As Vikki Bell suggests, artworks tend to be "poorly understood as facilitative or therapeutic visual accompaniment," where artistic engagement is thought to be "merely illustrative or a witnessing of social and political issues."[43] In both Serbia and BiH, documentary theater is used not only for healing and reconciliation purposes, but also to open space for reflection, consideration, and public debates about the best way to achieve transitional justice. As Dijana Milošević argues in the context of former Yugoslavia, "the 'creative power' of art and theater transforms difficult experiences, creates a safe ground where people can meet in all their differences, and thus contributes to the region's healing."[44] In both countries, there is a feeling that audiences need to confront the factual reality of the recent past. What is specific to the region of the former Yugoslavia is that documentary art and theater is inextricably linked to the experiences of war. As Dijana Milošević and Jadranka Andjelić, co-founders of Dah Theater in 1991 in Belgrade, state, they were driven "perhaps subconsciously, to oppose the destruction with creation; to create, in the midst of a world falling apart, a microcosm of theater."[45]

Since violence often appears as an inexplicable act, almost impossible to understand, the power of representation, with its symbolic force, gives an ability to restore the meaning inherent in the traumatic act through *reenactment*.[46] Therefore, in documentary theater, as one of many justice seeking strategies besides truth commissions, trials, public rituals, to name a few, lies huge potential to bring some sense of justice and restoration of dignity to survivors.

VIVID MEMORIES: HYPERMNESIA[47]

> "Is this a war?"
> "Yes, a war."
> "What we will do now?"
> "We'll put the blankets on our windows."
> "Why?"
> "To black out. The bullet may also embroil in them."[48]

People who have lived through an armed conflict have stories to tell, truths that have been silenced. All of the actors in Spahić's award winning performance *Hypermnesia* were children when the war started, but their memories are still strong and vivid almost two decades after the war ended.[49] Their experiences left scars and numerous other consequences. The idea for this performance came from Spahić, a Sarajevo-born theater director, who wanted to make a performance that would work with issues that are often silenced. She also wanted to bring together young artists from BiH, Serbia, and Kosovo to work together in such a play. To realize her idea, she sent a public invitation to citizens to send her a letter that they would write to an unknown person about something they had never said to anyone. These letters arrived in her email account and most were written to parents about things that the authors of the emails had never communicated for various

FIGURE 1: Heartefact Fund and Belgrade's Bitef Theater, Original Scene from *Hypermnesia*. Reproduced with permission of Nataša Govedarica. Actors: Maja Izetbegović, Ermin Bravo, Alban Ukaj, and Damir Kustura.

reasons, such as fear, shame or love. This methodology helped Spahić and her team to confirm that they wanted to make a play about the relationship between parents and children.

For Spahić, the most interesting part of documentary theater is that it creates a possibility to face personal fears, prejudices, hatred, and evil. The theater has a "social responsibility to confront us first with [the] personal and intimate in order to then be able to talk about [the] collective."[50] Spahić believes that the performance aims at being both straightforward and a testimony without accusatory character and argues that in this setting the emphasis is not on what has been silenced, but on the persons who have spoken up "because it is not easy to speak up; that act can change a whole life."[51]

After she received the letters from the citizens, Spahić asked the actors to write their own brief biography with emphasis on unspoken events and issues that had happened in their family. Actors would also come to the rehearsals with stories from their lives, which were then transmitted in stage improvisations, and adapted to theater mechanisms of expression.[52] In this performance, eight actors tell their intimate stories which are shaped by the extreme sociopolitical conditions of war. The actors were originally from Sarajevo, Belgrade, and Pristina. By putting together their stories on stage, it was

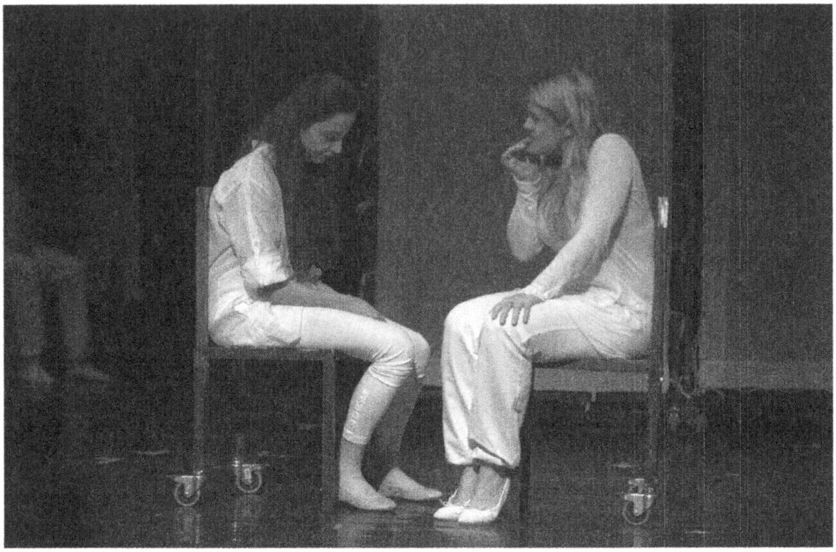

FIGURE 2: Heartefact Fund and Belgrade's Bitef Theater, Original Scene from *Hypermnesia*. Reproduced with permission of Nataša Govedarica. Actors: Milica Stefanović and Tamara Krcunović.

inevitable that a political context would emerge. They had different visions and "truths" about the violent past that had marked their childhood, and they brought these multiple heritages, histories, and embodied knowledge to the theater scene. These stories were challenging for both the actors and the audience, as they exposed the naked lives of actors, their vulnerabilities, and also their resilience and coping mechanisms. The process of making this performance took place in two cities: Belgrade and Sarajevo. Although initially the play was about relationship between parent and child, as Govedarica notes, "we got this performance that talks a lot about war, a sort of political play that was not necessarily our initial aim."[53]

Hypermnesia provides space for actors to go through processes of self-definition and even catharsis, creatively and collectively. It has become a venue where everyone is allowed to tell her or his own truth, crossing the political and physical borders of the places they live. The performance has been described by actress Jelena Ćuruvija-Đurica as a "psycho-drama," and she expressed her motivation to act in this play as wanting other people to hear her "personal story."[54] To tell an intimate narrative was a completely new and different experience for actors in this performance. Ćuruvija-Đurica also tells how the performance has been viewed differently by audiences in BiH and

FIGURE 3: Heartefact Fund and Belgrade's Bitef Theater, Original Scene from *Hypermnesia*. Reproduced with permission of Nataša Govedarica. Actors: Damir Kustura, Milica Stefanović, Jelena Ćuruvija, Ermin Bravo, Tamara Krcunović, Alban Ukaj, Maja Izetbegović, and Sanin Milavić.

Serbia: "There is a scene in which Sanjin [one of the actors] tells his personal story in which he and his family tried to reach [the] Muslim part of Sarajevo during the siege . . . The story is tragic but he made this part funny and that moment in a show is a comedy . . . The people in Bosnia always laugh a lot at it because they recognise this situation from their own experience, they survived it and they know that in these tragic situations there is always a funny moment . . . Here [in Serbia] though people think it is funny, they are afraid to react because they know how hard it must have been, how dangerous it was, so they try to cover their laugh . . . That is the most evident difference between these two audiences."[55]

Govedarica confirms this statement by noting that "in Sarajevo people laugh the most, while in Belgrade the audience does not know whether it would be politically correct [to laugh] during scenes that are politically incorrect."[56] The Belgrade audiences did not experience the siege and some even feel responsible for the terrible hardship it brought to Sarajevo residents. Rather than laughing, they feel embarrassed and uncomfortable. Also, in Banjaluka, a town in BiH with a predominantly Serb population, there were times when the audience "froze" and appeared to feel "uncomfortable to be a Serb."[57] *Hypermnesia* is a performance that crossed important ethnic borders between Serbia and Kosovo. It was the first performance which came "from

Belgrade to Priština after the 1970s, so this fact in itself was a big triumph for all of us to play it there." Most importantly, Alban Ukraj, a Kosovo-born actor, said that the audience in Kosovo, in particular the younger generation, had seen and heard in this play something they had not heard from the mainstream media or their parents before: that other people understand their pain, other ethnic groups suffered as well, and not all of them supported nationalist governments. He said that after the show, in informal gatherings with the audience, "I had feeling that people experienced some enlightenment."[58] They also had to confront polar opposite views and experiences of the same event, the NATO bombing of Serbia. There is a scene in which a Serbian actor Tamara talks about her experience of the first day of bombing and running to the shelter, and then Ukraj talks about celebrations he participated in because the NATO started bombing Serbia. As Ćuruvija-Đurica explains, "this scene makes people uncomfortable and they are often silent, they don't know how to react." This is probably because they hear "the other" for the first time and may have some empathy for her or his experience. Comments after watching the performance were that this show "was something completely different from anything I saw before in theater ... It is great that actors used their personal stories at stage," and "This is very difficult and courageous performance ... to come bare naked before the public, very courageous ... really courageous performance act."[59]

The play was released on May 8, 2011, and since then has played more than thirty times in the countries of the former Yugoslavia, in BiH, Serbia, Kosovo, and Montenegro, but also in Germany and Greece. In Greece, the performance was enacted for the participants of the "Balkan Forum" that was held in February 2013. According to Govedarica, the play had an overwhelmingly positive response from the audience, prompting such comments as: "This performance is the most important contribution to transitional justice that they have ever seen."[60] In November 2013, the actors and directors took the play to Switzerland.

MISSING PERSONS: PRESENCE OF ABSENCE

The Way
Every step,
Every tear,
Every touch
Lead you to light
Where at last
You will find yourself in peace

FIGURE 4: Dah Theater, Original Scene from *Presence of Absence*. Reproduced with permission of Dah Theater. Actors: Nemanja Ajdačić and Sanja Krsmanović Tasić. Photo by Una Škandro.

So be careful where you tread!
You, man, who in vain
Seeks outside
What has been inside you forever!
My dearest, unrepeatable,
With your tears
Cleanse humanity
So that the ones to come
Will keep the memory of you.[61]

In July 2013, I entered a well-known theater in Belgrade. As someone who has an ongoing personal and professional relationship with Milošević, the director of Dah Theater company (Dah) in Belgrade, I had been invited to watch rehearsals of the theater's new play *Presence of Absence* that was scheduled to be released in November. I was seated next to the director. I had an idea what was the performance about, but I needed to feel and see it alive. While watching the personal dramas spoken by actors in front of me, I was drowned in a world of loss and pain. "People cannot just disappear, they can die of illness, or they can be killed in wars or be murdered, but they cannot just disappear."[62] These were the words spoken by the "Few Hundred

Years Old Woman Who Saw It All," a role played by Maja Vujović, an actress from the Dah. Watching, from a close distance, Vujović with her eyes half shut while gazing over what would be the audience, I felt a shiver down my spine.

The performance is based on authentic testimonies of women from around the world by drawing on secondary sources, including literature, poems, and other documents that have considered issues of missing persons. Dah also did qualitative research and interviewed women in January 2013 in Đulići, BiH, and the essence of this show can be explained in one sentence, as related by the actor who in the performance is searching for his missing brother: "I have to know what had happened."[63] Dah took these words from Madres de Plaza de Mayo in Argentina, but they also heard them in Đulići, a small village in BiH where they recorded testimonies of women whose husbands and other family members disappeared. In April 1992, members of the Serb army committed a massacre against the male civilians in this and surrounding villages. They first deported from Đulići and surrounding villages around 700 men, held them as hostages, and later killed them. Some of these bodies were found and some have not yet been discovered.

Dah decided to work with women survivors of massacre, since they know them from when they had come to present the documentary performance *Crossing the Line* a year before.[64] The village is almost completely made up of women and children, since sons, husbands, and fathers were killed. During an informal lunch in one of the women's houses one afternoon, a time of conversation and mutual exchange, the directors and actors asked about fifteen women who were there to tell them what had happened, how and whom they lost, how they preserved memory of their loved ones, and what sort of belongings they kept to remember them. It was not a one-on-one interview, but a collective remembrance and discussion. According to Milošević, "some of these stories have been recorded in [the NGO] Women in Black's Belgrade book *Women's Side of the War* but many of them we heard for the first time . . . It was a very sensitive process since these women were asked many times by journalists, lawyers, judges, and civil society [representatives] to tell their stories, so it was all so emotional to me and all the time I was asking myself what we can do for them."[65]

From these recorded conversations and dialogues, the theater director took sentences and paragraphs and constructed a script for the performance. The play *Presence of Absence* is a part of the larger project "The Power of Remembrance," which deals with post-traumatic memories of members of families, in particular women, of their close family members who disappeared. The project consists of three parts: the research process,

FIGURE 5: Dah Theater, Original Scene from *Presence of Absence*. Reproduced with permission of Dah Theater. Actors: Sanja Krsmanović Tasić and Maja Vujović. Photo by Una Škandro.

creation of a music installation, and the performance *Presence of Absence*. By creating a performance based on research about the essence of such remembrance, the Dah theater wants to help families that have gone through such painful experiences, to speak publicly about them, and through this to help them to move on with their lives. With this performance, Dah hopes to facilitate the process of confronting the past in the Balkans, but also in other places where people suffered from the disappearance of their loved ones.[66]

The performance *Presence of Absence* is meant to be a universal story about the disappeared and the impact of transgenerational trauma. It conveys bigger questions such as: "How does disappearance affect us? How does it affect generations to come? What is the meaning of disappearance? What is the meaning of remembrance?"[67] It is about the universality of a traumatic experience of disappearance and painful loss. As Milošević, director of the play, says: "Listening to the accounts of those incredibly brave women from Bosnia, Serbia or Kosovo who have disappeared loved ones in their families, I realized that their lives are inhabited with a constant presence. The presence of absence; the presence of the absent ones. Reading of the men and women from all over the world who live with that tragic experience, I was intrigued that often they use identical words to explain their feelings and what happened to them. Reading testimonies from the women in Argentina, I thought about women from Kosovo, listening to testimonies of women from Bosnia, I thought about women from Chile, and so on. Their experience erased all boundaries."[68]

The performance finishes with the planting of fields of roses on bricks that before had represented ruins and despair. The bricks are an important element of the play since, according to Milošević, they signify at the same time "a wreck left after demolition of house but also life, new beginning, building a shelter." Little papers giving information about missing persons had been stuck on them. In the praxis of women's truth seeking campaigns roses have a significant meaning. They were carried by mothers from Plaza del Mayo in Argentina, in their eternal circling, searching for the truth about their missing. The Saturday mothers from Turkey too carried roses and put them in front of main state institutions, seeking truth about their missing.

Roses have a very symbolic presence in the region of former Yugoslavia, too. Hundreds of roses were carried by families of the disappeared from Đulići, who left the flowers on sites of concentration camps where their dearest had been taken, and where all traces of these loved ones had disappeared. With

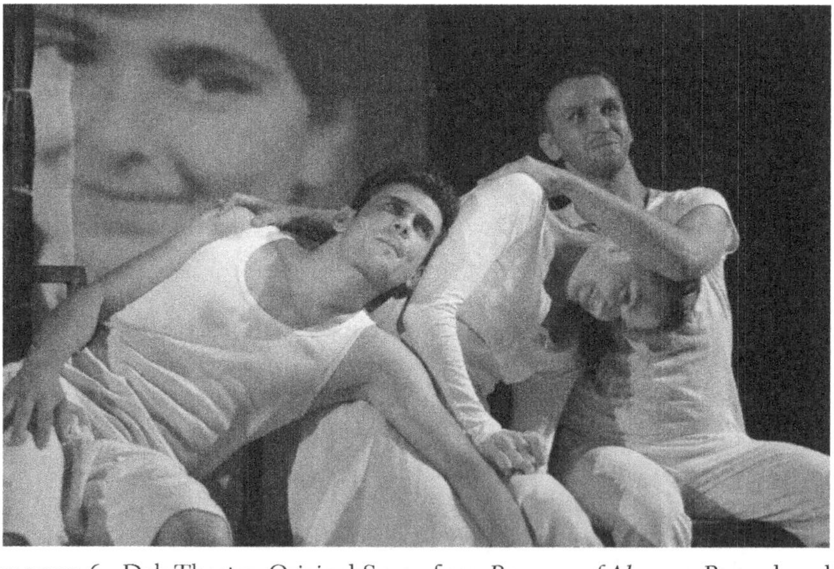

FIGURE 6: Dah Theater, Original Scene from *Presence of Absence*. Reproduced with permission of Dah Theater. Actors: Sanja Krsmanović Tasić, Nemanja Ajdačićand, and Maja Vujović. Photo by Una Škandro.

Presence of Absence, Dah not only raises awareness of a theme that is silenced and ignored by the state, but also warns about the traumatic impact that people's disappearances leave on future generations. Dah has been invited by the International Committee for Missing Persons in Sarajevo to come to that city and present their play on December 10, 2013, the International Day of Human Rights.

WOMEN'S LIVES SHATTERED BY WAR: SEVEN BREATHS

On the initiative of a young actress, Mirela Mijačank-Kordić, the director of the Mostar Youth Theater, Tanja Miletić Oručević, created a play based on the authentic testimonies of seven women who survived recent wars in the former Yugoslavia. *Seven Breaths* (sometimes titled *Seven Sighs*) ultimately served as Mijačank-Kordić's final exam performance for her university theater studies. *Seven Breaths* was a graduation play for Mijačank-Kordić who had spent time in Srebrenica with women survivors and listened to their stories. That experience affected her emotionally and she was interested in working on a play that would bring women's stories to the light. The seven stories were chosen from the Women in Black Belgrade's collection "Women's side of war."[69] *Seven Breaths* is a play about "tragic women's experiences of war which happened to women from all [ethnic] sides in the recent war."[70] All testimonies are from victims who are "the most silenced and hidden in our society whose stories were pushed under the carpet and who were never encouraged to talk about their experience."[71] As with other small theaters, the Mostar Theater of Youth struggles financially, so the play was designed to be simple, straightforward and economical. The play was released on July 11, 2013, and has since been played a few times in Mostar and once in Sarajevo.

Reactions from the audience to the performance were largely positive, but some people were surprised since, as Miletić Oručević reported, they did not expect this "type of play." According to her, a few people said after the play that "we should not talk about the war anymore; that these are difficult issues to discuss." She admits that "it is not easy to listen and watch an actress acting out women's testimonies of rape and loss, but although these narratives are uncomfortable, it is important to go through this 'uncomfortability.'" Still, a majority of audience members did think it was important to talk about the issues and to deal with them. In general, reactions to the play have been very emotional and audience members have often cried during the performances. The director of the play strongly believes that it is important to discuss wartime issues: "I think we still need to discuss war and past events. Regardless [of] how

FIGURE 7: Mostarski Teatar Mladih, Original Scene from *Seven Breaths*. Reproduced with permission of Mostarski Teatar Mladih. Actor: Mirela Mijačank-Kordić.

understandable is [the] human desire to forget some things and move on with their life in peace, to look at the future and development, many questions and issues and traumas related to war are not adequately worked through, but rather pushed under the carpet because of the political and cultural circumstances in which we live. Because they are pushed under the carpet, it affects how we live today, that is why I think that no matter how this play can raise uncomfortable and painful experiences and memories, it is necessary and it has some catharsis potential. We have to deal with [the] past and questions that we are so burdened with in order to move to [the] future; in order to become a democratic society; we still have perpetrators walking free, people who need to be accountable for what they did."

Seven Breaths was the director's second documentary theater performance. In 2012, she directed and released a play *Bio je lijep i sunčan dan* [It Was a Nice and Sunny Day] based on a book with the same title, which collected seventy-eight authentic testimonies from people who survived the siege in Sarajevo. In this book, they use their memories to describe May 2, 1992, the day when the siege started. In that play, she encountered documentary theater methodology for the first time and found this work exciting, valuable, and inspiring in the "process of creating a new documentary

FIGURE 8: Mostarski Teatar Mladih, Original Scene from *Seven Breaths*. Reproduced with permission of Mostarski Teatar Mladih. Actor: Mirela Mijačank-Kordić.

theater."[72] Miletić Oručević told me that the reason why documentary theater is increasingly popular in the region is because "the theater artists feel that in all narratives in public discourse the manipulation and lies exist and lasted for too long, so we lost trust in narratives that are in the public domain. So it seems to use a document, to rely on something that has not been processed in any way but only in theater is much better especially when we talk about war."

After each play the audience often spontaneously gathers with the director and actress at the verandah at the top of the theater house, and they talk in an informal way about the play. Most young people know little about war, says Miletić Oručević, and even the little that they hear in school or from their families is "one ideological content, politicized in order to sustain national myths which are empty and lack any human story and content and that is why it is important that we play this performance." She has heard many times from young people after watching the performance that "we did not know anything about this, so in that sense the play has an educational function, too." Local media have not shown any interest in the performance so far. This is partially due to the difficulty of getting media attention for any play that "was not produced in Sarajevo." The director and actress have been

FIGURE 9: Mostarski Teatar Mladih, Original Scene from *Seven Breaths*. Reproduced with permission of Mostarski Teatar Mladih. Actor: Mirela Mijačank-Kordić.

invited to Slovenia to play and hope to tour this play in the region, in particular Belgrade.

LEARNING FROM DOCUMENTARY THEATER

The new wave of documentary theater in the Balkans is born from the directors' "urge for authenticity" for information that was "undressed"[73] and raw. It is a form of resistance to the denial and collective amnesia that has infected the region. The theater directors and artists strongly believe that there is no future without proper responding, dealing and working through the past human rights violations committed during the 1990s, rather than "running away from something that we cannot run from."[74] Simply put, it is not possible to fully turn to the future without resolving a common, difficult past and acknowledging the pain, loss, and destruction that generations of people in the Balkans have survived. The question of the war inheritance is present but, as my interviewees mentioned, is often swept "under the carpet." Silence about the past is still prevailing and there are too few people, such as artists, who are whistleblowers, who call for accountability for past wrongdoings, or demand justice. With their plays these directors and actors are collectively contributing to symbolic reparation for all people who have not been heard in the public, and whose stories have been left buried in tons of archival documents. The plays also serve as an important educational tool, in particular for younger generations.

What these and similar artistic projects show, at least, is that it is possible and desirable to bring together young artists from the previous warring parties (for example, Belgrade and Pristina), and talk about "the other" without judgments and blame. The lesson that theater sends to the community and government is: "We can work together and talk about painful issues together."[75] It is necessary to document past experiences, to raise one's voice, to be courageous, and to talk about things that have tended to be silenced or remained unspoken. Building peace in the region requires encouraging citizens to remember the past in meaningful ways, and to participate in activities that can transform social relations in their community.[76] Art can make an important contribution to the ongoing transitional justice processes in the former Yugoslavia by exposing naked narratives of survivors, through which audience members not only can recognize themselves and their own experiences, but can also empathize and hopefully better understand the universality of loss.

NOTES

1. Text from the play *Presence of Absence*, Dah Theater Company, Belgrade.
2. Miguel Rubio is a founding member and director of the Lima-based theater group Grupo Cultural Yuyachkani. Cited in Francine A'ness, "Resisting Amnesia: Yuyachkani, Performance, and the Postwar Reconstruction in Peru," *Theater Journal* 56 (2004): 395.
3. Serbia has never admitted its participation in the wars in BiH and Croatia. Also, it has never been proven that it bears responsibility for the war crimes committed on the territory of these two countries, in particular, accountability for the genocide in BiH. International Court of Justice, *Bosnia and Herzegovina v. Serbia and Montenegro*, February 26, 2007, available at: http://www.icj-cij.org/docket/files/91/13685.pdf (accessed October 13, 2013).
4. Stan uses the term "unofficial projects" for those led by non-state actors. Lavinia Stan, *Transitional Justice in Post-Communist Romania: The Politics of Memory* (New York: Cambridge University Press, 2013), 205.
5. Craig Zelizer, "The Role of Artistic Processes in Peacebuilding in Bosnia-Herzegovina," *Peace and Conflict Studies* 10 (2003): 62–75.
6. Max Stafford Clark, *Verbatim: Contemporary Documentary Theater* (London: Oberon Books, 2008), 7.
7. Ivan Medenica, "Novi vidovi političkog pozorišta: Slučaj ex-Yu," *Teatron* 154/155, Prolece/leto 2011, 18.
8. Ibid., 2.

9. Alison Forsyth and Chris Megson, eds., *Get Real: Documentary Theater Past and Present* (London: Palgrave, 2009), 1.
10. For example, Alexander Laban Hinton, ed., *Transitional Justice: Global Mechanisms and Local Realities after Genocide and Mass Violence* (New Brunswick, NJ: Rutgers University Press, 2010); Patricia Lundy and Mark McGovern, "The Role of Community in Participatory Transitional Justice," in *Transitional Justice from Below: Grassroots Activism and the Struggle for Change*, ed. Kieran McEvoy and Lorna McGregor (Oxford: Hart Publishing, 2008), 1–13; Rosalind Shaw and Lars Waldorf, with Pierre Hazan, eds., *Localizing Transitional Justice: Interventions and Priorities after Mass Violence* (Stanford, CA: Stanford University Press, 2010); Lia Kent, "Local Memory Practices in East Timor: Disrupting Transitional Justice Narratives," *International Journal of Transitional Justice* 5 (2011): 434–455; David Baker, "Civil Society and Transitional Justice: Possibilities, Patterns and Prospects," *Journal of Human Rights* 2 (2003): 297–313. Olivera Simić and Zala Volcic, eds., *Transitional Justice and Civil Society in the Balkans* (New York: Springer, 2013); Peter Rush and Olivera Simić, eds., *The Arts of Transitional Justice: Culture, Activism, and Memory after Atrocity* (New York: Springer, 2013).
11. Personal interview with Nataša Govedarica, October 7, 2013, Brisbane–New York City.
12. Ruti Teitel, *Transitional Justice* (New York: Oxford University Press, 2000), 148.
13. Jacqueline O'Connor, *Documentary Trial Plays in Contemporary American Theater* (Carbondale: Southern Illinois University Press, 2013), 2.
14. Ibid.
15. Teitel, *Transitional Justice*, 146.
16. Cath Collins, *Post-Transitional Justice: Human Rights Trials in Chile and El Salvador* (Philadelphia: Pennsylvania State University Press, 2010), 12.
17. Catherine Cole, "Performance, Transitional Justice, and the Law," *Theater Journal* 59 (2007): 170.
18. Martha Minow, *Between Vengeance and Forgiveness: Facing History after Genocide and Mass Violence* (Boston: Beacon Press, 1998), 47.
19. Shoshana Felman and Dori Laub, eds., *Testimony: Crises of Witnessing in Literature, Psychoanalysis, and History* (New York: Routledge, 1991).
20. Lavinia Stan, "Conclusions: Memory, Courts, and Justice in Transition," in *Transitional Criminal Justice in Post-Dictatorial and Post-Conflict Societies*, eds. Agata Fijalkowski and Raluca Grosescu (Cambridge: Intersentia, forthcoming).
21. Attilio Favorini, *Voicing: Ten Plays from the Documentary Theater* (New York: Ecco Press, 1995), 141.
22. Cole, "Performance, Transitional Justice, and the Law," 171.
23. O'Connor, *Documentary Trial Play*, 9.
24. Peter Rush, "After Atrocity: Foreword to Transition," in Rush and Simić, *The Arts of Transitional Justice: Culture, Activism, and Memory after Atrocity*, v–xi.
25. Cole, "Performance, Transitional Justice, and the Law," 180.
26. Nadia Siddiqui, Hadi Marifat, and Sari Kouvo, "Culture, Theater and Justice: Examples from Afghanistan," in Rush and Simić, *The Arts of Transitional Justice*, 113–135.

27. Cited in Gary Fisher Dawson, *Documentary Theater in United States: An Historical Survey and Analysis of Its Contents, Form, and Stagecraft* (Westport, CT: Greenwood Press, 1999), 5.
28. Serbian/Croatian/Bosnian is my mother tongue. Unless otherwise noted, all translations are my own.
29. Ksenija Bilbija, Jo Ellen Fair, Cynthia E. Milton, and Leigh A. Payne, eds., *The Art of Truth-Telling about Authoritarian Rule* (Madison: University of Wisconsin Press, 2005), 10.
30. Olivera Simić and Dijana Milošević, "Enacting Justice: The Role of Dah Theater Company in Transitional Justice Processes in Serbia and Beyond," in Rush and Simić, *The Arts of Transitional Justice: Culture, Activism, and Memory after Atrocity*, 99–113.
31. Salomón Lerner Febres, "Memory of Violence and Drama in Peru: The Experience of Truth Commission and the Yuyachkani Theater Group," keynote speech delivered at the Just Performance: Enacting Justice in the Wake of Violence symposium at Brandeis University, USA, December 1–2, 2011.
32. Amina Hamzić, "Docu Genre Answers Bosnian's Postwar Hunger for Facts," *Balkan Insight*, August 28, 2012, available at: http://www.balkaninsight.com/en/article/docu-genre-answers-bosnia-s-postwar-hunger-for-facts (accessed October 25, 2013).
33. A'ness, "Resisting Amnesia," 402.
34. Ibid.
35. Hamzić, "Docu Genre Answers Bosnian's Postwar Hunger for Facts."
36. Personal interview with Nataša Govedarica, October 7, 2013, Brisbane–New York City.
37. Laura McLeod, Jovana Dimitrijević and Biliana Rakočević, "Artistic Activism, Public Debate and Temporal Complexities: Fighting for Transitional Justice in Serbia," in Rush and Simić (eds.), *The Arts of Transitional Justice: Culture, Activism, and Memory after Atrocity*, 99–113.
38. Ibid.
39. Doris Živković, "Intervju, Oliver Frljić: Govorim o onome što svi znaju, a o čemu šute," *Novi List*, June 11, 2012, available at: http://www.novilist.hr/Kultura/Kazaliste/Oliver-Frljic-Govorim-o-onome-sto-svi-znaju-a-o-cemu-sute (accessed September 7, 2013).
40. Ibid.
41. Kathy Daly, "Conventional and Innovative Justice Responses to Sexual Violence," *Australian Center for the Study of Sexual Assault* 12 (2011): 2.
42. Bilbija, Fair, Milton and Payne, *The Art of Truth-Telling*, 3.
43. Vikki Bell, "Contemporary Art and Transitional Justice in Northern Ireland: The Consolation of Form," *Journal of Visual Culture* 10 (2011): 325.
44. Dijana Milošević, "Theater as a Way of Creating Sense: Performance and Peacebuilding in the Region of the Former Yugoslavia," in *Acting Together: Performance and the Creative Transformation of Conflict*, Volume I: *Resistance and Reconciliation in Regions of Violence*, eds. Cynthia Cohen, Roberto Gutiérrez Varea, and Polly Walker (New York: New Village Press, 2011), 23.
45. Dubravka Knežević, "Do poslednjeg daha," *Scena* 5/6, September–December 1995.

46. Salomon Lerner Febres, "Foreword: The Rebellion of the Masks," in *Acting Together: Performance and the Creative Transformation of Conflict*, Volume II: *Building Just and Inclusive Communities*, eds. Cynthia Cohen, Roberto Gutiérrez Varea, and Polly Walker (New York: New Village Press, 2011), x.
47. Hypermnesia is the condition of having an unusually vivid or precise memory.
48. Hypermensia, text of the performance: Sanin-beginning of the war. On file with author.
49. For an excellent insight into the war-time experience of children in BiH, see Lynne Jones, *Then They Started Shooting: Growing Up in Wartime Bosnia* (Cambridge: Harvard University Press, 2004).
50. Filip Vujošević, "Hipermnezija: Rediteljka o predstavi." Document on file with author.
51. Ibid.
52. Vujošević, "Hipermnezija: Rediteljka o predstavi."
53. Personal interview with Nataša Govedarica, October 7, 2013, Brisbane-New York City.
54. Jelena Ćuruvija-Đurica,"Hipermnezija-Prica o prici," May 24, 2012, available at: http://www.youtube.com/watch?v=Wap1IWSjNJQ (accessed September 7, 2013).
55. Ibid.
56. Personal interview with Nataša Govedarica, October 7, 2013, Brisbane-New York City.
57. Ibid.
58. Alban Ukraj, "Hipermnezija-Prica o prici," and supra endnote 54.
59. Impressions after the performance *Hypermnesia*, available at: http://www.youtube.com/watch?v=yooSJN5f-yY (accessed October 14, 2013).
60. Personal interview with Nataša Govedarica, October 7, 2013, Brisbane-New York City.
61. Maja Vujović, Dah Theater, internal office document on file with author.
62. Text from the play *Presence of Absence*, Dah Theater Company, Belgrade.
63. Ibid.
64. On this performance, see Olivera Simić, "Breathing Sense into Women's Lives Shattered by War: the DAH Theater Company of Belgrade," *Law Text Culture* 14 (2010): 117–133.
65. Personal interview with Dijana Milošević, July 16, 2013, Belgrade.
66. Dah Theater, internal document, on file with author.
67. Personal interview with Dijana Milošević, July 16, 2013, Belgrade.
68. Document on file with author.
69. Women in Black Belgrade, ed., *Women's Side of War* (Belgrade: Art grafik Beograd, 2007).
70. Personal interview with Tanja Miletić Oručević, October 6, 2013, via Skype, Mostar-Brisbane.
71. Ibid.
72. "U SARTR-u premijerno izvedena predstava 'Bio je lijep i sunčan dan,'" Abrasmedia, May 18, 2012, available at: http://www.abrasmedia.info/content/u-sartr-u-premijerno-izvedena-predstava-bio-je-lijep-i-sun%C4%8D-dan (accessed September 11, 2013).
73. Michael Balfour, "Mapping Realities: Representing War through Affective Place Making," *New Theater Quarterly* 28 (2012): 33.

74. Personal interview with Nataša Govedarica, October 7, 2013, Brisbane–New York City.
75. Ibid.
76. Olivera Simić and Kathleen Daly, "'One Pair of Shoes, One Life': Steps towards Accountability for Genocide in Srebrenica," *International Journal of Transitional Justice* 5 (2011): 479.

13

Vigilante Justice and Unofficial Truth Projects

Lavinia Stan

The scholarship available to date identifies state and civil society actors as instrumental in advancing or blocking programs that redress past human rights abuses. This chapter points to yet another actor with a key role in promoting truth-telling initiatives in post-communism: individual justice seekers who speak on behalf of no civil society group and act in isolation from other state and non-state agents. Five such private initiatives have taken place in Central and Eastern Europe during the first twenty-five years of post-communist transitional justice. Their close examination reveals that the array of transitional justice actors active in post-communist settings is more diverse than the literature suggests. It further raises questions relative to the effectiveness of such vigilante initiatives and their relationship with truth, justice, and reconciliation, the main goals of reckoning programs in post-communist countries and beyond.[1]

The chapter starts with a brief overview of the literature, with an emphasis on non-state actors instrumental in truth-telling efforts of publicly naming communist-era secret agents. It then chronologically describes the five initiatives, explaining how they came about, who their initiators were, what information they released publicly under which conditions, and how the government and the larger society in those countries received them. As I argue, these initiatives cannot be ascribed to civil society because their promoters are individuals representing themselves, not organized groups. Neither can they be ascribed to the state, since their promoters were non-state actors working in defiance of state authorities to de-block official programs. The chapter then identifies similarities and differences among these initiatives, and discusses the lessons they teach us about transitional justice in Central and Eastern Europe and other settings.

TRUTH-TELLING BETWEEN THE STATE AND CIVIL SOCIETY

According to their authors, the five disclosure initiatives discussed here aimed to assist official truth-telling programs that named secret agents who had infringed other people's rights. Notwithstanding the serious flaws affecting their validity and accuracy, these disclosures stemmed out of frustration with official programs and the authorities' refusal to unmask former secret agents from among post-communist elites or to open the secret archives needed for identification. Official arguments that the identification was inopportune as long as the post-communist democracy remained unstable were dismissed by these authors as protecting the unsavory past of high-ranking government officials who sought to keep the secret files closed and the identity of former spies protected.

According to scholars, these unofficial disclosures are forms of "wild lustration" that undermine state-led reckoning programs. They provoked public scandal, rocked the political scene, and prompted "a hostile reaction to those named."[2] They had serious social repercussions because those named had not yet admitted to their past secret collaboration and were thus surprised to see themselves identified as secret agents in the absence of official investigations.[3] They mirrored the inquisitorial stance of official programs, and failed to verify information from a variety of sources of information.[4] They instrumentalized secret files,[5] and this amounted to a dangerous "sweeping blacklisting" that re-victimized secret collaborators by not explaining that they had been often recruited through the use of "compromising documents, extortion, beatings," or that "their collaboration was falsified."[6]

Naming former perpetrators has been seen as a needed step in the quest to unveil the true nature of past repressive regimes and show that not only abstract and impersonal political institutions and mechanisms but also specific individuals bear responsibility for past crimes.[7] The importance of publicly naming former perpetrators in post-communist Europe is two-fold. First, the scarcity of court proceedings against those responsible for the gruesome crimes of the Stalinist era (1945–1953) or the widespread surveillance programs of the 1970s and the 1980s and the complete lack of truth commissions conducting public hearings have often made identification programs the only source of information that can tell the public which persons were responsible for which crimes. Through their proceedings, the hearing of depositions, the interviewing of witnesses, and the arguments of the prosecution and defense, court trials and truth commissions can allow the public to find out the details of past human rights infringements and the identity of the perpetrators. Such court trials have been the exception, not the rule, in post-communist Europe. Trials organized to date have provided information on only a few high-ranking officials (including the Polish martial law leader Wojciech Jaruzelski) or low-level soldiers (the Berlin Wall border guards).[8] In addition, post-communist commissions have worked behind closed doors, without conducting public hearings, bringing victims and victimizers together, visiting detention centers, or engaging in outreach activities.[9]

Second, the identification takes on added significance in the case of former secret informers, whose collaboration had been kept secret even from their closest relatives and friends. Their public unveiling is sure to put a stop to their secret activities, which in many cases have continued after 1989. Not naming them risks subjecting the victims to new human rights abuses incompatible with the new democracy. Identifying former part-time secret agents has more urgency than identifying former full-time secret officers because informers far outnumbered officers and they engaged in activities far more damaging to the victims. Officers at least were officially working for the secret police and what they did was part of their job description. Since most of them were wearing uniforms at least some of the time, victims had the necessary cues to refrain from giving out sensitive personal information and even from speaking to secret agents. The situation differed in the case of informers, whose identity remained hidden to the victim at all times and who could be individuals very close to the victim, with intimate knowledge about the victim's political views, personal preferences, and day-to-day behavior. Particularly bothersome is the refusal of the overwhelming majority of informers to acknowledge their past collaboration and to admit that their actions damaged the victims' lives.

Locating the five disclosure campaigns within the literature proves challenging. Until recently the literature on post-communist transitional justice has emphasized the role of the state, not of the civil society.[10] This emphasis may derive from an understanding of the communist past as a period of repression carried out by an all-powerful state against a powerless society. As it bears responsibility for those rights violations, the state should redress the crimes, former victims insist. Civil society may prompt the state to adopt relevant legislation to initiate, speed up or improve specific programs, and keep transitional justice in the public eye. However, authors have drawn attention to the limitations of programs carried out by the civil society without the full cooperation of state authorities.[11]

Unofficial truth projects have also been recognized for promoting transitional justice. Such projects are "geared toward revealing the truth about crimes committed in the past as a component of a broader strategy of accountability and justice," and they "self-consciously or coincidentally resemble official truth commissions," but are "rooted in civil society – hosted and driven by human rights [non-governmental organizations], victim groups, universities, and other societal organizations – and are not primarily state-based efforts."[12] In contexts where official truth commissions "are not feasible because of political constraints, are ineffective or politically compromised, or human rights activists and their allies in government choose not to create them," the unofficial projects "may represent viable alternative strategies" and "more legitimate interlocutors for the task of confronting the past."[13] Civil society bodies resembling official truth commissions, citizens' tribunals, documentation projects, as well as art, theatre, poetry, literature projects, memorials, museums, and traveling exhibits that focus on the past are examples of such unofficial projects, as Simic's chapter suggests.

The five cases presented here do not neatly fit the categories of civil society groups or unofficial truth projects. First, their authors were individuals working in isolation, not organized groups. These individuals were connected with civil society groups representing former communist-era victims and their disclosure campaign was facilitated by other people, who either granted them access to the lists of former secret agents or helped them to hide the lists before, during, and after the public disclosure, but they did not act in the name of any group, and in some cases they did not even want to assume responsibility for their acts. Second, these private initiatives sought to thwart the post-communist political careers of those named and to harm their chances of being elected or nominated to public positions as much as they wished to uncover the truth about the communist past and to make it available to the public, goals shared by both the civil society actors engaged in transitional justice and the unofficial truth projects.

Given their propensity for revenge, these disclosures represent instances of vigilante justice, meted out by self-appointed inquisitors who believed they furthered the common good by publicly releasing the information without delay. By championing the interests of ordinary citizens – to know the identity of those connected to the communist secret police and to be represented by post-communist politicians untainted by association with the repressive regime – the vigilante sought to compel state officials to de-block key procedures like lustration, access to the secret files, and the reform of the intelligence services. For them, the need to disclose names was more urgent and more compelling than the need to verify the accuracy of the lists. The danger of falsely identifying an innocent person as a former perpetrator or of discrediting the list by including incomplete or very common names was apparently of little concern in the cases presented below.

FIVE UNOFFICIAL INITIATIVES

This section presents five disclosure campaigns that provoked intense public scandals in Czechoslovakia, Romania, Slovenia, Poland, and the Czech Republic. As they are introduced chronologically, my narrative starts and ends in Prague. Except for Czechoslovakia/the Czech Republic, all these countries have remained laggards in secret file access and court trials against former communist officials and secret agents.[14] By the time the scandals occurred, none of these other countries had adopted radical lustration, created truth commissions to investigate communist crimes, or allowed citizens to access significant sections of the secret archives.

Czechoslovakia: The Cibulka Lists

In its short existence (1989–1992), post-communist Czechoslovakia adopted radical lustration in 1991, but was less forthcoming with public access to the files of the communist political police (Státní bezpecnost or the StB). Some secret files were destroyed both before and after the regime change. To keep the extant materials safe from further manipulation and cleanse parliament of people tainted by collaboration with the former regime, in January 1991 parliament created the special legislative November 17th Commission to vet all deputies. To fulfill its mandate, the commission asked the federal government to publish all names of secret agents. Instead of complying with the request, the government warned that "the publication [of the names], at a time when democratic institutions and habits are not yet consolidated, would expose these persons and their families to harassment, and would therefore be an ill-considered step."[15] Some disagreed with this position.

Just before the June 1992 parliamentary elections, Petr Cibulka published the names of 160,000 alleged StB secret officers and informers, some 80 percent of whom worked for the Second Department, which was charged with domestic repression. Cibulka was a former member of Charter 77, Czechoslovakia's most important anticommunist group that demanded authorities observe fundamental human rights. In 1979, he conducted a hunger strike, and he was five times jailed from 1979 to 1989. The list was acquired by blind luck on two floppy disks from an unnamed source with access to StB records, as Cibulka stated.[16] It was entirely unauthorized and unofficial, and included Category C candidates for collaboration – that is, individuals targeted for recruitment who might have refused such an offer for various reasons. Still, the list was very accurate in relation to the StB registers, leading experts familiar with the communist political police to conclude that someone simply took the register out of the archive and copied it.[17] Cibulka continued to publish names of secret agents until 1996, and then again in 1999, when he named 15,000 other StB agents.[18] He also published the names in book format and released an electronic version of the list with an easy search function.

In interviews that blended facts and conspiracy theories, Cibulka detailed the reasons why he chose to disclose the information. For him, with the list's publication, "for the first time the people had the chance to read the truth about the level of infiltration and the level of control of this [Czech, post-communist] society by Communist [Party] and StB powers and structures."[19] Public disclosure was important because Cibulka was convinced that "the communists and their secret services, connected to Moscow, never lost any power in the Czech Republic" after 1989. Not surprisingly, the Cibulka Lists rocked Czech and Slovak politics, prompting a hostile reaction to those named that escalated into what some labeled a witch-hunt against informers.[20] Cibulka was bitterly contested by leftist successors to the Communist Party, and even by President Vaclav Havel, a former Charter 77 member who objected to the uncontrolled release of information.

Many of those named in the lists argued that the situation was extremely unfair because, with the secret files still off-limits to the public, there was no way for them to defend themselves by pointing to exonerating or mitigating contextual documents.[21] This situation made it necessary to open the files because "it would not be just to have just the names of people with no background information."[22] For the Czechs, the opening happened only in 1997. After years of speculation over the reliability of the Cibulka's lists, in 2003, the Czech Interior Ministry released an official list of 75,000 names, including 3,000 names of collaborators from abroad. The Ministry argued that its list was shorter than Cibulka's because it included only those who collaborated with the StB knowingly, not potential informants, and only the names of Czech, not Slovak, citizens.[23] These reasons failed to explain why notorious known collaborators were not on the official list.[24]

The Romanian "Armageddon 7"

From 2001 to 2007, a series of anonymous and controversial emails were distributed to the Romanian press for publication under the general title *Armageddon*. The first to receive attention was "Armageddon 2," which accused the Social Democrat Prime Minister Adrian Nastase of corruption. The government's reaction was swift. In January 2002, the General Prosecutor ordered the arrest of journalist Ovidiu Cristian Iane and the search of former government official Mugur Ciuvica's home, claiming that the two suspected authors of the document damaged national security and violated the Criminal Code by disseminating false information (a provision intended to cover acts that posed a threat to the public, such as making a false bomb threat, not to limit freedom of the press). Nastase later acknowledged that he had overreacted.

In March of that year, "Armageddon 7" created a scandal by publicly listing former officers of the communist Securitate who continued to hold key posts in the post-communist intelligence services. The email reached the press when the country was about to join NATO, which, journalists argued, had asked for the vetting of former Securitate "dinosaurs" from the country's intelligence services as a pre-condition of accepting Romania as a member. The author of "Armageddon 7" remained unknown, but rumors had it that the list originated with historian Marius Oprea. The press further suggested that the Interior Ministry or the Romanian Information Service might know something and hoped that, by printing the text, the government would confirm or disconfirm the list's accuracy. The newspaper *Ziua*, which published "Armageddon 7," believed that only part of the information was true, as the list included mistakes, but insisted that "the names in this list are not names of ghosts. The persons in question have acquaintances, neighbors, who can deny or confirm the facts. We are inviting them to the debate."[25]

"Armageddon 7" alleged that since 1990, when the Information Service was established, it had "systematically and shamelessly lied about its composition" to the public. Instead of "becoming a modern intelligence service, in which the number of Securitate officers is continuously decreasing," the Service was controlled by the Securitate, whose officers prevailed in its leadership. Responding to claims that the Service had hired Securitate officers as experts, the "Armageddon" asked for the disclosure of information about the expertise of Securitate officers and Service leaders involved in political scandals, and claimed that the Service had kept the Securitate officers "who shamelessly made every possible move to get ahead, polishing the shoes of figurehead politicians, hanging around talking and pretending they were good at something, or putting up for bid documents that could be used for blackmail." As such, the Service included "people who pull strings behind the scenes, engage in intrigues, or are good for nothing," that is, the active and retired Securitate officers who "troubled our society."[26]

The influence of retired Securitate officers allegedly extended to financial institutions, as they were "managing public and private money" and private security and protection firms "in permanent conflict with the law," and exploited banks "under the pretext of assuring their protection, but the banks they protected have collapsed, one by one." The document further tied former Securitate officers to the "great robber" Sorin Ovidiu Vantu, the controversial owner of the Financial Investment Fund, whose collapse made many ordinary Romanians lose their life savings. The relationship was allegedly proved by the fact that "320 Securitate and Intelligence Service reservists worked, shoulder to shoulder, for this profoundly dubious man, cashing in their shares" when ordinary people went bankrupt, and by the fact that "our vigilant domestic intelligence service pretended not to notice anything when Vantu's clay empire was riding on top of the wave." Even more disconcerting, according to "Armageddon 7", was the Securitate officers' penetration of the legislature after Law 187/1999 asked members of parliament and cabinet to disclose their past collaboration. "Armageddon 7" claimed that it had identified six or seven former Securitate agents close to Nastase and wondered why the "highly educated" prime minister put up with agents who were "poor in spirit" or were "nobody in their profession," unless "there is a dictatorship in store for us" that satisfied both the prime minister and the secret agents.[27]

The anonymous authors claimed that they compiled a list of over 1,600 names of former Securitate officers connected to the post-communist intelligence services from 1990 to 2002. However, they offered to the press for publication a list of only 287 individuals, of which 232 were identified by their full names and 25 others were identified only by their family names. Each name was followed by a short paragraph detailing that person's association with the Securitate, the post-communist intelligence services, political parties, state agencies, or public utilities. However, except for the recognizable names, the identities of the listed persons were difficult to make out, since many names were among the most common in Romania and no further details, like the birth place and place of residence, were provided. In a handful of cases where only the family name was listed, it was even difficult to make out the person's gender.

"Armageddon 7" hoped to assist in the removal of former Securitate officers from post-communist intelligence services. By the time it reached the press, the identification of former secret agents was seriously stalling, although the civil society had repeatedly underscored the need to make a clear break with the communist past and emphasized that former Securitate agents were engaged in notorious corruption scandals. Law 187/1999 launched the public identification of Securitate agents, regardless of whether they occupied public positions after 1989, and created the governmental agency responsible for the identification. During its first years of activity, the National Council for the Study of Securitate Archives was obstructed by the Information Service, which housed 60 percent of Securitate extant files, and the Social Democrat cabinet of Prime Minister Nastase, which kept under lock files touching on the "national interest". By the time "Armageddon 7" was released, the Council had publicly unveiled 29 of the 486,000–700,000 part-time informers who had worked for the Securitate before 1989 and none of its 13,275 full-time officers.[28]

Months after the release, the Council identified the first Securitate officers and accelerated the identification of informers.

The UDBa.net Scandal in Slovenia

In April 2003, the police and secret police file references to one million Slovenes were published online. For each listed name, the website provided the secret file number, parents' names, the citizenship/nationality status, employment history, criminal record, and birth date. Only some 100,000 of those listed were secret agents of the Yugoslav communist Department of State Security (Uprava drzavne bezbednosti or the UDBa). The others were victims of the secret police, persons who came in contact with the UDBa, and even common criminals. Some of those named were prominent Slovenian politicians and public figures. Most of the disclosed UDBa file references were for "persons registered in criminal evidence" or for "criminal activities," and only a few were political police files. Most secret files "refer to people who simply had or were suspected of having a run-in with the law, people considered part of preliminary evidence in an investigation that remained open since the communist era, and individuals who had contact with the police or criminal investigators."[29] We know from other sources that the police files contained subcategories of targets of investigation, agents, and collaborators. The disappearance of most secret files and the destruction of the most sensitive files in the 1990s meant that, by the time the UDBa scandal erupted, the archive contained no incriminating evidence. Thus, there was no way to ascertain the relationship to the secret police of the named persons and to distinguish between informers, collaborators, agents, or victims.[30]

According to the website, the posted file details had come from the secret archives. Neither the secret services nor the government confirmed their authenticity, which was nevertheless supported by independent experts and historians. The National Archives director noted that the website offered an incomplete list of secret files, thus confirming the authenticity of the disclosed files. Leopold Vidmar, who oversaw the transfer of information from the paper-based system to an electronic system, confirmed that the UDBa.net files were authentic.[31] Soon thereafter, the press announced that Slovenia's Honorary Consul for Australia and New Zealand, Dusan Lajovic, had made the list public. Lajovic was known for supporting lustration, which post-communist Slovenia had stubbornly refused to implement. The Slovenian press intensively debated the scandal.[32] Attention focused on the way Lajovic accessed sensitive information, with the Oversight Commission of the Work of Security and Information Services concluding that he could have accessed one of the microfilm copies created before 1986 as duplicates of UDBa paper files. Marjan Antoncic, a data protection expert with the Interior Ministry, confirmed that the UDBa.net data came from the microfilm copies made in the 1980s.[33] Created for cases of emergency, the microfilm copies were stored in army locations unknown to the public.

In 1991, Lajovic received from a secret service official the microfilm that contained the UDBa.net data. He handed the microfilm over to an unnamed friend. From Slovenia, the microfilm arrived in 1992 in Australia, where expert analysis was used to find out what information it contained. Lajovic believed that the Slovenian government would disclose the secret files to the public to signal a clear break with the communist past. Working on this assumption, he decided to withhold the information for fear of jeopardizing Slovenia's entry into the European Union. As the Slovenian politicians refused to make the files public even after the country was invited to join the Union in 2002, Lajovic felt it was time to deal with the unresolved issue of secret collaboration among high state officials. He published a book about the communist secret police[34] and posted the information on the internet in the interest of "uncovering the barbarism of communist times" and of "rethinking those times."[35]

Despite the proven authenticity of the file references, the UDBa.net and Lajovic's book provided incomplete information and, as such, generated no renewed political support for lustration, although the secret files exposed on the UDBa.net referred to high-profile center-left politicians. Leaders of the opposition Democratic Party insisted that the list proved that their call for lustration was morally right. The parties that supported Slovenia's change from communism to democracy had long sought the opening of the secret files of all post-communist politicians in the hope of discrediting their center-left rivals. However, the UDBa.net proved that the extant archive included files on politicians from other formations, including the nationalist Slovenian National Party. The party split into factions after the UDBa.net unveiled leader Zmago Jelincic Premeniti as a secret agent of the UDBa. In 1993, Jelincic had called for the destruction of the communist secret files on agents and informers, not victims. The website proved that his call was motivated by a desire to hide his secret collaboration. Center-right parties felt vindicated by the length of the list, since it went against claims that Slovenia had no past to atone to. Those named were not quick to admit guilt. For example, former Prime Minister Lojze Peterle (1990–1992) denied his past collaboration, but admitted that calls for lustration were grounded, because the web-based list confirmed the fact that the "Slovenian UDBa has a longer list [of collaborators] than the Stasi," the feared East German communist secret political police.[36]

Lajovic also asked for the opening of the secret archives, for citizens to know the past of their elected officials. In reply, politicians argued that making the files public infringed upon the privacy rights of those named in the list and thus endangered the rule of law. That view was adopted by the governmental Inspectorate for Personal Data Protection, which took the extraordinary measure to ask Slovenian internet service providers to block access to the website. Within days, the order was revoked, when it became clear that the site could not be shut down, as it was registered in New York and operated from a server in Thailand. Blocking access to it through the Slovenian internet service providers was unable to prevent the dissemination of the information, while the order to block access was controversial.[37]

The government also enforced the privacy laws, which blocked access to archived secret material for 75 years following its creation or ten years after the death of the individual on whom the file was compiled. Individuals may access their own files, from which the names of the full-time agents and part-time informers who contributed information are removed. Even after the UDBa affair, few Slovenians sought to read their secret files, and there was no renewed public call for lustration. The Oversight Commission of Security and Intelligence Services deemed the internet publication of secret data a violation of the rights of victims, agents, and collaborators of the UDBa. Similarly, the Public Prosecutor indicted Lajovic for illegal publication of personal data, although the data came from an internet account housed outside Slovenia. The UBDa.net failed to launch lustration in Slovenia. As communist leaders still enjoy public support, lustration has been treated as a "historical curiosity and a political strategy more than a contemporary political exercise required to ensure liberal democracy."[38] Access to secret files remains curtailed by a privacy law that protects "even those public figures who may have grossly violated the law."[39]

The Wildstein List in Poland

The slow pace at which files were made available by the Institute for National Remembrance (Instytut Pamieci Narodowej or the IPN) and the Institute's failure to fulfill its mandate of publicly naming secret agents prompted former dissident Bronislaw Wildstein, a journalist with the conservative daily *Rzeczpospolita*, to "steal" from the Institute a working list of some 240,000 names of former communist-era secret agents, military intelligence, secret covert informers, prospective candidates to informer positions, and victims, and to post it on the internet in February 2005. The list did not distinguish between perpetrators and victims of the communist secret police (Służba

Bezpieczeństwa or the SB), thus exposing all those named to the suspicion that they had collaborated and arousing concern that the incomplete data may be used for political purposes or personal vendetta. Prosecutors launched an inquiry into the case, but were unable to identify the IPN employee who helped Wildstein. Refusing to name his accomplice, Wildstein defended his action as legitimate, since "this is not our past, this is our present. Those people are present and play important roles in our reality."[40] IPN leaders accused Wildstein of being irresponsible, and Prime Minister Marek Belka asked the post-communist intelligence services to ensure that agents on active duty were not affected by the revelations.[41] Many of those on the list asked the IPN to allow them to read their secret file.

Wikipedia suggests that Wildstein "rose to nationwide prominence" after smuggling the list from the IPN and distributing it to the public.[42] His purported theft revived the public debate on de-communization in Poland. True, his disclosure of names was strongly criticized by politicians, intellectuals, former communist officials, and some journalists, but no charges were ever brought against him by the Polish authorities. In fact, barely one year after the incident, the government appointed Wildstein as head of the national, state-owned television station, Telewizja Polska, proof that at least some political parties gave support to transitional justice effected through any means possible.

The list's publication increased pressure on Polish authorities to open up the SB archives, and to adopt a more radical lustration program that would bar former communist decision-makers from post-communist politics. Indeed, until the Wildstein scandal many key secret documents were out of reach for the general public. Almost two years after the scandal, in 2006 Poland adopted a new lustration law that both expanded the number of public officials whose past had to be investigated and specified that failure to disclose past collaboration with the communist secret political police resulted in job loss. The first Polish lustration law, adopted in 1997, had affected only the few politicians who chose to hide their past collaboration by denying it. Lustration liars could be excluded from public office, if their attempts to cover up their former secret collaboration were proven by the court.[43]

The Penc Internet Databases in Prague

The Czech Republic was the first Central European country to provide public access to state security service archives through the state-run Institute for the Study of Totalitarian Regimes, which can interpret the secret documents compiled by the communist authorities. In 2009, the Institute got an unlikely competitor. On July 6, the newspaper *Lidové Noviny* published an article titled "New List Posted on the Internet," reporting that several thousand names had been made available by former dissident and human rights campaigner Stanislav Penc. Penc claimed he received the data in electronic format from Ján Langos, the first head of the Slovak National Memory Institute who lost his life in a road accident in 2006. Langos was frustrated at the failure of the state authorities to lift the veil of secrecy covering the communist-era secret records.

The two StB databases released through the internet disclosed whether the StB had kept a file on a particular individual in its Record of Persons of Interests, without specifying whether the file was a victim or an informer file. The databases offered the numbers of all relevant files where the names introduced in the search motor were mentioned. The website showed that the StB included the Jewish names of individuals (in case they or their relatives had changed them), as well as all surnames of married women and other people who changed their names.[44] So many Czechs wanted to access the databases in order to check the information that the high demand caused the computer server to crash when the records first went online.[45] As many as 140,000 hits were registered on the website during its first three days of operation.[46]

Although an initiator of the Institute, Penc criticized the governmental agency for monopolizing "the interpretation of history" and for releasing only data on cases that "will not upset a majority of the population" or "big names cases."[47] He blamed the Institute for improperly handling the archives and refusing to publish an index of all the files that would let citizens know the archive's contents. Penc maintained that making the databases available online helped to reduce the risk of blackmail against post-communist luminaries formerly involved with the StB. Pavel Zácek, the Institute director, retorted that Penc engaged in an "amateur attempt"[48] and was "kicking down doors that were already open."[49] The Institute argued that the secret archives contained many errors that could be misleading to the general public, and thus had to be carefully reviewed by trained historians.[50] The new databases differed from the Cibulka lists in both content and format. *Lidové Noviny* explained that the Penc list allowed people to check if the secret police had targeted them but warned that information available on the internet may not be enough to distinguish the many shades of collaboration and resistance under communism.

Three days after Penc published the two databases, the Institute launched a pilot project permitting researchers and ordinary citizens to search four million digitized documents. Critics pointed out that the digitized documents represented just a tiny fraction of the Institute's archive, which included as many as 280 million pages amounting to twenty kilometers of material. The documents can be read only during visits at the Institute's library, after obtaining a username and password. The Institute claimed that the launch of the pilot project was not connected in any way to Penc's databases, since "we could [not] digitize these documents within four days of his website's going live."[51] While indeed the pilot project had been under way for some time, its launch seemed to have been speeded up by the Penc scandal.

The government took action after the scandal. In late 2009, the Office for Personal Data Protection sued Penc for processing personal data without the consent of those who were the subject of the information.[52] In February 2011, the court ruled that the electronic publication of the StB databases was "not illegal," and thus Penc won the civil dispute in which he faced a potential fine of up to 400,000 Euros.[53]

TRUTH, JUSTICE, AND THE VIGILANTE

These five cases share several similarities and differences. Some similarities relate to the background of their authors, who, without exception, were isolated individuals not speaking on behalf of any group and not claiming to represent anybody but themselves. At the time when they disclosed the secret information, these individuals occupied no positions in the government, public administration or state-led independent agencies charged with implementing access to secret files or lustration. All authors were former communist-era dissidents who expressed dissatisfaction with the slow pace of public identification of former secret agents involved in human rights violations and the fact that former communist decision-makers continued to occupy positions of power and responsibility after 1989. These observations also apply to Oprea in Romania, if indeed he was the author of "Armageddon 7," as the historian distributed anti-regime pamphlets and was questioned for his actions by the Securitate months before the collapse of the communist regime. When "Armageddon 7" reached the press, Oprea occupied no public post. Last, in all cases the people who leaked the information to the public (the "authors" of the five cases of information disclosures) had received it from other persons with direct access to it. Having betrayed the trust of the intelligence services or independent transitional justice agencies they were working for, these other persons were adamant to protect their identity.

Other similarities relate to the way in which information was disseminated and received by the general public and the political elite. In all cases, the disclosed lists claimed to link names of individuals with the communist secret police structures, not the Communist Party structures or other repressive structures of the old regime. Similarly, in all five cases the disclosed information was basic, including only names and sometimes some other basic identification markers, but not enough background to assess the nature and extent of the individual relationship with the communist secret services. In all cases but "Armageddon 7", the lists included both informers and victims of the communist political police without distinguishing between these two groups, thus casting suspicion on former victims and victimizing them again. In all cases but Cibulka's Lists, the internet played a vital role in providing access to information and even search functions for easy retrieval, and in making the lists known to the press (through the emails used to circulate "Armageddon 7"). Therefore, the five cases described here were precursors to Wikileaks, the organization that seeks to provide wide electronic access to sensitive state information to the general public. Whereas for Wikileaks the citizens' right to information takes precedent over the states' right to secrecy in the name of national interest, for the five vigilantes mentioned here the citizens' right to information trumps the perpetrators' right to privacy.

In none of these five cases was the publicly released information confirmed by the government, that is, the Ministries of Interior or the post-communist intelligence services that inherited the personnel and archives of the communist political police. While they knew who the former spies were, these government agencies kept silent to protect the identity of the communist spies they had retained as active agents or informers after 1989. All five unofficial disclosures provoked public scandal and were commented on in the local press, but none led to vigorous debates on the communist past among politicians or civil society groups. The press reported very few statements and declarations of representatives of parties belonging to the government or the opposition, no deputy or senator believed that these unofficial disclosures were important enough to mention them in parliament, and no legislative proposal (de-blocking lustration, public identification of secret informers, or access to secret files) directly resulted from these disclosure drives. The civil society was equally silent, and no major association representing former communist-era victims or political prisoners supported these unofficial disclosures. Most likely, the reason lies in the suspicion that the lists cast over the victims, who were named alongside their former victimizers (the informers).

There are also important differences among the five cases. The first is their timing relative to 1989. Except for Cibulka's Lists, all other initiatives occurred during the 2000s, over a decade after the collapse of the communist regime. The interest and curiosity of the general public remained high in all five cases, suggesting that Eastern Europeans continue to be interested in the communist past, truth, and justice even for the milder forms of repression, as was secret surveillance by unnamed informers. Second, the five cases of unofficial disclosures differ in terms of their timing relative to file access and lustration. According to their authors, the five cases responded to a perceived lack of willingness, on the part of the political elite and the state-led transitional justice agencies, to name former secret collaborators, some of them endangering the new democracy by occupying public positions or remaining active in the intelligence services. At least in some cases, however, file access and lustration legislation were adopted before these unofficial disclosures. Wildstein and Penc made their lists available after

Polish and Czech citizens already gained the right to access secret archives and thus to find out the names of former secret agents directly from the files. Cibulka, Penc, and Wildstein released their lists after their countries enacted lustration, a policy that either identified agents from secret files or asked politicians to self-identify as former agents. Finally, the cases differ in terms of the impact the information disclosures had on their authors. In Slovenia and the Czech Republic, authorities invoked privacy laws and prosecuted Lajovic and Penc.

The debates provoked by these unofficial disclosures suggest that at least some Eastern Europeans have remained profoundly dissatisfied with the slow pace of public identification of communist secret agents. True, these five vigilantes could release information almost instantly because they skipped one crucial step: the verification of the data included on the lists. By contrast, the independent state agencies had to prove secret collaboration with secret documents and to provide those named with the right to appeal the decision of identification before the name is released. These stages require time to be completed. By skipping these key stages, the authors of the five unofficial disclosures named former communist secret agents at the cost of allowing innocent people to be tainted by association with the communist political police.

CONCLUSION

The cases examined above teach us at least three important lessons. First, scholars should recognize that the current scholarship does not identify all actors with a significant input in truth-telling mechanisms. The five individual initiatives presented here could easily be overlooked, if one believes that only state agencies and organized non-state groups can design and implement reckoning programs. As the chapter suggests, these initiatives' ability to revive the debate on the communist past was minimal, but at least some of these information leaks led to the partial de-blocking of official state-sponsored programs to publicly identify former communist agents.

Second, the cases demonstrate the limits of non-state input in reckoning with the past. On the one hand, they show that courageous individuals with initiative and access to secret information can make a difference by releasing that information to the public. In contexts where neither state agents nor organized civil society groups are willing or able to de-block lustration and secret file access, private individuals can unexpectedly further these programs. On the other hand, the indiscriminate release of sensitive information serves truth only to a limited degree, blurring the difference between victims, victimizers, and bystanders, confusing the public as to the meaning of resistance and collaboration under the communist regime, and exposing those named to the trauma of re-victimization. The authors of the five initiatives believed that the public's need to know took precedence over the rights of those named, but evidence suggests that untruth and partial truth (the naming of former victims alongside victimizers, the absence of clear instructions on the roles those named played in connection to the communist secret services, and the inclusion of incomplete identification details) cannot ultimately serve as truth.

Last, these cases warn us against the use of heavy-loaded words to characterize non-state initiatives. Labeling them as "wild," as some authors do, reflects the fear that their growing number could further divide former perpetrators and victims, pro-identification and anti-identification political parties. Note, however, that post-communist state authorities also pursued "wild" truth-telling initiatives before any transitional justice legislation was adopted in their countries. In Albania, through successive purges various governments sought to weaken the opposition during election campaigns more than to unveil the truth about communist crimes.[54] In Poland, the "wild" identification attempt of May 1992 involved the Minister of Interior Antoni Macierewicz, who presented legislators with a list of persons allegedly named in the secret archives as informers.[55] The cases discussed here reveal the power of individual initiative, while cautioning against publicly disclosing incomplete data that blur the lines between victims, victimizers, and by-standers.

NOTES

1. This chapter is based on a text first published as Lavinia Stan, "Vigilante Justice in Post-Communist Europe," *Communist and Post-Communist Studies* 44 (2011): 319–327. I thank Dr. Lucy Kerner for allowing me to publish this updated version.

2. Nadya Nedelsky, "Czechoslovakia and the Czech and Slovak Republics," in Lavinia Stan, ed., *Transitional Justice in Eastern Europe and the Former Soviet Union: Reckoning with the Communist Past* (London: Routledge, 2009), 51.
3. Françoise Mayer, *Les Tcheques et leur communism* (Paris: Les Editions de l'Ecole des Hautes Etudes en Sciences Sociales, 2004), 197.
4. Muriel Blaive, "L'ouverture des archives d'une police politique communiste: le cas tcheque de Zdena Salivarová à Milan Kundera," in Sonia Combe, ed., *Archives et histoire dans les societes postcommunistes* (Paris: La Decouverte, 2004), 203–225.
5. Valentin Behr, "La production du récit historique à l'Institut de la mémoire nationale. Une etude des usages politiques du passe en Pologne," MA thesis, Universite de Strasbourg (2008), available at: http://scd-theses.u-strasbg.fr/2008/01/BEHR_Valentin_2010.pdf (accessed on December 17, 2013), 29.
6. Jan Stojaspal, "Blowing the Whistle on the Past," *Time* (April 24, 2000), available at: http://www.time.com/time/world/article/0,8599,2056342,00.html (accessed on December 17, 2013).
7. Priscilla Hayner, *Unspeakable Truths. Facing the Challenge of Truth Commissions* (London: Routledge, 2002).
8. Tina Rosenberg, *The Haunted Land: Facing Europe's Ghosts after Communism* (London: Random House, 1996); James McAdams, *Judging the Past in Unified Germany* (New York: Cambridge University Press, 2001); Stan, *Transitional Justice in Eastern Europe and the Former Soviet Union.*
9. See Chapter 10 in this volume, and Lavinia Stan, "Truth Commissions in Post-Communism: The Overlooked Solution?" *Open Political Science Journal* 2 (2009): 1–13.
10. An excellent contribution is Nadya Nedelsky, "State, Civil Society, and Media Interactions in Slovak Transitional Justice," paper presented at the Legal Frames of Memory conference, Warsaw, November 28, 2013. For Romania, see Raluca Grosescu, "The Role of Civil Society and Anticommunist Political Actors in the Romanian Transitional Justice Partial Failure," in *Lustration and Consolidation of Democracy and the Rule of Law in Central and Eastern Europe*, eds. Vladimira Dvorakova and Andelko Milardovic (Zagreb: Political Science Research Center, 2007), 183–196; and Lavinia Stan, "Civil Society and Post-Communist Transitional Justice in Romania," in *Transitional Justice and Civil Society in the Balkans*, eds. Olivera Simić and Zala Volcic (New York: Springer, 2013), 17–31.
11. Noel Calhoun, *Dilemmas of Justice in Eastern Europe's Democratic Transitions* (New York: Palgrave Macmillan, 2004).
12. Louis Bickford, "Unofficial Truth Projects," *Human Rights Quarterly* 29 (2007): 994–995.
13. Bickford, "Unofficial Truth Projects," 995.
14. Stan, *Transitional Justice in Eastern Europe and the Former Soviet Union*, 247–270.
15. Nedelsky, "Czechoslovakia and the Czech and Slovak Republics," 51.
16. Jan Malina, "In Eastern Europe Things Are Not What They Seem. An Interview with Petr Cibulka" (March 10, 2003), available at: http://www.jrnyquist.com/petr_cibulka_2003_0310.htm (accessed on December 17, 2013); Karel Vrana, "Getting Even," *Transitions on Line* (April 25, 2003), available at: http://www.tol.org/client/article/9348-getting-even.html (accessed on December 17, 2013).

17. "Cibulka StB Files Accurate," *The Slovak Spectator* (May 9, 2002), available at: http://spectator.sme.sk/articles/view/7554/10 (accessed on December 17, 2013).
18. Jan Stojaspal, "Blowing the Whistle on the Past," *Time* (April 24, 2000), available at: http://www.time.com/time/world/article/0,8599,2056342,00.html (accessed on December 17, 2013).
19. Malina, "In Eastern Europe Things Are Not What They Seem."
20. Miroslav Balastik, "Two Stories: Kundera and the Conclusion of the Velvet Revolution," *Eurozine* (July 11, 2008), available at: http://www.eurozine.com/articles/2008-11-07-balastik-en.html (accessed on December 17, 2013).
21. Zdena Salivarova-Skvorecka, ed., *Osoceni: Pravdive pribehy lidi z "Cibulkova seznamu"* (Toronto: Sixty-Eight Publishers, 2000). Also Kazi Statsna, "The Czechs' Unfinished Business," *Foreign Policy* (July 7, 2010), available at: http://www.foreignpolicy.com/articles/2001/09/01/europes_fake_id (accessed on January 9, 2014).
22. Jiri Pehe cited in Nedelsky, "Czechoslovakia and the Czech and Slovak Republics," 51.
23. Dita Asiedu, "Czechs Wait Thirteen Years for Official Names of Secret Police Collaborators," Radio Praha (March 24, 2003), available at: http://www.radio.cz/en/section/curraffrs/czechs-wait-thirteen-years-for-official-names-of-secret-police-collaborators (accessed on December 17, 2013).
24. "Official Lists of StB Collaborators Full of Mistakes," Europe Intelligence Wire (March 27, 2003), available at: http://www.accessmylibrary.com/coms2/summary_0286-22820063_ITM (accessed on December 18, 2003).
25. "Romanian Daily Publishes List of Securitate Agents Working in Intelligence," Foreign Broadcast Information Service, FBIS-EEU-2002-0405 (March 28, 2002), available at http://cryptome.org/ro-spy-list.htm (accessed February 20, 2011).
26. Ibid.
27. Ibid.
28. Lavinia Stan, "Spies, Files and Lies: Explaining the Failure of Access to Securitate Files," *Communist and Post-Communist Studies* 37 (2004): 348.
29. Tamara Kotar, "Slovenia," in Stan, *Transitional Justice in Eastern Europe and the Former Soviet Union*, 220.
30. Ales Gaube, "Slovenia: A Sorry Spy Hunt," *Transitions Online* (April 28, 2003), available at: http://www.tol.org/client/article/9366-slovenias-sorry-spy-hunt.html?print (accessed on December 18, 2013).
31. Kotar, "Slovenia," 214.
32. "UDBa.net Stir up Controversy," *Voice of Slovenia* (2003), available at: http://www.glasslovenije.com.au/acrobat/voice-april2003.pdf (accessed on December 17, 2013), 2.
33. Zoran Savin, "UDBa in Cenzura," *Mladina* (April 18, 2003), available at: http://www.mladina.si/tednik/200315/ (accessed December 10, 2013).
34. Dusan Lajovic, *Med Svobodo in Rdeco Zvezdo* (Ljubljana: Nova obzorja, 2003).
35. Kotar, "Slovenia," 214.
36. Kotar, "Slovenia," 207.
37. Kotar, "Slovenia," 213.
38. Kotar, "Slovenia," 206.
39. Kotar, "Slovenia," 201.
40. Stan, *Transitional Justice in Eastern Europe and the Former Soviet Union*, 89.

41. "Poland in Uproar over Leak of Spy Files," *The Guardian* (February 5, 2005), available at: http://www.guardian.co.uk/international/story/0,3604,1406281,00.html (accessed December 10, 2013), and D. Dastych, "Better Late than Never: Retarded De-communization in Poland," *The Gazette* (January 9, 2007), available at: http://www.axisglobe.com/article.asp?article.1192 (accessed on January 28, 2011).
42. "Bronisław Wildstein," Wikipedia (December 13, 2012), available at: http://en.wikipedia.org/wiki/Bronisław_Wildstein (accessed on December 18, 2013).
43. Dastych, "Better Late than Never."
44. "Declassified Archive Shows StB Kept Track of Jews," Aktualne.cz (July 24, 2009), available at: http://aktualne.centrum.cz/kultura/film/recenze/clanek.phtml?id.643270 (accessed December 10, 2013).
45. Rob Cameron, "The Czech Secret Police Files," Euranet (October 28, 2009), available at: http://www.euranet.eu/eng/layout/set/print/Dossier/The-fall-of-Communism/Restricted-access-The-Czech-secret-police-files (accessed on December 10, 2013).
46. Sarah Borufka, "Communist Secret Police Database Goes Online," *The Prague Post* (July 15, 2009), available at: http://www.praguepost.com/news/1738-communist-secret-police-database-goes-online.html (accessed April 10, 2011).
47. Nada Strakova, "Row Blows Up as Ex-dissident Publishes Secret Cop Files," Czechnews (July 8, 2009), available at: http://aktualne.centrum.cz/pda/clanek.phtml?id=641966 (accessed on December 17, 2013).
48. Borufka, "Communist Secret Police Database Goes Online."
49. Martin Simecka, "In the Shadow of the Archives," *Presseurop* (July 9, 2009), available at: http://www.presseurop.eu/en/content/article/51111-shadow-archives (accessed December 18, 2013).
50. Strakova, "Row Blows up as Ex-dissident Publishes Secret Cop Files."
51. Borufka, "Communist Secret Police Database Goes Online."
52. "Declassified Archive Shows StB Kept Track of Jews."
53. Jan Schneider, "Publication of StB Database 'Not Illegal', Court Rules," CzechPosition.com (February 21, 2011), available at: http://www.ceskapozice.cz/en/news/politics-policy/publication-stb-database-%92not-illegal%92-court-rules (accessed December 17, 2013).
54. See Robert C. Austin's chapter in this volume. Also Robert C. Austin and Jonathan Ellis, "Albania," in Stan, *Transitional Justice in Eastern Europe and the Former Soviet Union*, 176–199.
55. Stan, "Truth Commissions in Post-Communism," 81.

Conclusion: Some Lessons Learned

Nadya Nedelsky

What can twenty-five long years of experience in Central and Eastern Europe teach us about transitional justice? Through both case studies and broad comparative studies, this volume's authors offer many important lessons. Some are explanatory and some practical; some are hopeful and others deeply cautionary. In this concluding section, I explore some lessons that twine through the analyses, emerging from a variety of contexts and across the volume's three sections. This is by no means a comprehensive list; I identify five. These are: *beware the overly narrow view of* elite motivations, transitional justice actors and methods, goals, timing, and comparative cases. I take each in turn.

To start, the volume indicates that we must beware the overly narrow view of elite motivations with regard to transitional justice. At the volume's outset, Grodsky notes that both scholars and primary actors alike should analyze transitional justice in the context of many other relevant policy issues that governments must consider concurrently in the aftermath of conflict and dictatorship. Looking at Serbia, Croatia, and Poland, he emphasizes that elites must provide constituents some goods to remain in office, and this hard constraint often drives transitional justice decision-making; economic and material considerations play a critical (if not definitive) role. Austin, taking up the Albanian case, argues that there the post-communist elites ignored public opinion and as a result transitional justice became so politicized that it has functioned primarily as intra-elite blackmail. Beattie and Ciobanu, as well, note that elites' self-promoting motives can drive truth commissions and other reckoning processes and practices as much as concern for victims.

At the same time, the volume shows that normative considerations clearly played a determining role in some cases. Looking at Poland, Szczerbiak argues that we should expand our focus beyond narrow political strategy and take seriously elites' ideological orientations and perspectives on historical memory. Elite positions on transitional justice may also respond to just demands for political renewal in deeply corrupt states. Taking a broader comparative approach, Welsh, as well, observes that ideas and methods flowed across borders and influenced policy, most effectively when values and goals were shared (leading her to emphasize dialogue and assistance over coercion in promoting policies).

Furthermore, diverse elite motivations are important for understanding how common projects like the redevelopment of historical memory may lead to very different methods and outcomes. For example, Ciobanu argues that memory of national victimization was used as a tool by Romanian elites to re-legitimize themselves after a deficient revolution, and Subotic shows that Serb and Croat elites used memory to undergird nationalist mobilization. By contrast, the Polish reconsideration of memory that Szczerbiak considers (described above) prompted what seems to be a renewed serious push for more straightforward transitional justice, including a fresh and more radical in scope lustration law. Likewise, Beattie notes that post-communist truth commissions were motivated not only by elite self-interest, but also other concerns, such as solidifying state legitimacy during highly unstable transitional times. The volume thus makes a very strong case for the need to avoid mono-causal or narrow assumptions regarding elite motivations, as these motivations are usually complex, multi-faceted, and evolving, and as such shape both policy and outcomes in many ways.

A second lesson the volume offers is to avoid a too-narrow view of the region's transitional justice actors and the methods they employed. As Light and Young argue in their multi-country study, scholars have focused largely on what may be considered "hard" aspects of transitional justice, such as lustration, restitution, and truth commissions, and much less on "soft" aspects such as memorialization, which nevertheless provide important venues for both state and non-state actors to redefine memory and history. Even regarding the "hard" methods, intergovernmental organizations, such as the International Criminal Court for the Former Yugoslavia (discussed by Grodsky), NATO, and the European Union (Ciobanu) have not received much attention in analyses of the region, though accession and other pressures have played some role in post-communist developments.

Likely even more important, the volume's analyses suggest, are a number of understudied international, civil society and non-state actors. These include associations such as European Network for Solidarity and Remembrance (Welsh) that have contributed importantly to regional norm and policy diffusion. Domestic actors have been crucial but overlooked as well. As Light and Young argue, state elites cannot claim a monopoly on the development of memory, and many civil society and private actors have shaped societies' relationship to the past via memorials in public spaces, often in ways that may be more lastingly influential than "hard" transitional justice methods. Simić similarly points to the role of documentary theatre in the Balkans in breaking official/societal silences regarding conflict and human rights abuses. These theatrical productions invite citizens to interact within and across communities and thereby to develop empathy and a more encompassing understanding of loss. Like Light and Young, Simić hopes that such groups could shift perspectives in the longer term, including by educating the young. Finally, Stan points to the importance of certain individuals who shook their societies by unilaterally exposing communist secret police lists of agents and informers. Non-state actors have thus shaped and at times transformed transitional justice. As such, regional developments cannot be understood, and potential future progress envisioned, without them.

A third lesson warns us – and especially policymakers – to beware the overly narrow focus on particular goals. Looking at the Czech case, David discusses the ramifications of an approach that, while comprehensive, sought justice with little concern for reconciliation. As he argues, the former without the latter is troublingly incomplete. By contrast, Subotic explores the implications in Serbia and Croatia of prioritizing national reconciliation over a thorough reckoning with all key periods of a society's dark past. Ciobanu likewise explores the implications of focusing on the wrongs of one past (narrowly conceived) over other "competing" pasts. In both cases, reckoning left gaping and crucial portions of previous periods out and, because it overlooked numerous human rights violations as a result, proved divisive and ethnically and religiously exclusionary. Beattie, as well, notes that a narrow focus on reconciliation can obscure the other potential goods truth commissions can deliver. Looking at five cases of "wild" file disclosures, Stan also warns against the overzealous pursuit of truth and the potential re-victimization of certain individuals. Focus on a particular concern to the exclusion of other related issues can thus be dangerous in a number of ways.

A further policy question where narrowness is a real concern is lustration. In their large comparative study, involving not only formerly communist Europe but also Latin America, Lynch and Marchesi find, counter to the expectations of many studies published to date, that lustration and trials may actually negatively affect political rights and physical integrity rights. What seems to counter this potentially negative relationship is comprehensiveness of lustration – the breadth of its reach and quality of implementation. Austin's case study of the sham lustration in Albania backs up the importance of these elements.

A fourth lesson concerns an overly narrow view of timing. Based on her large comparative study, Horne finds that the timing of lustration matters much less for trust in government and democratization than many expected (a dominant previous view held that there was likely a small early window for such policies). Indeed, somewhat delayed lustration had better outcomes than early policies. That said, Horne finds, along with Lynch and Marchesi, that a far more important factor is the quality of the reforms and policies. Welsh also cautions that trans-national diffusion may start slowly and take some time to have significant effects.

An important corollary to this timing lesson warns against a too-narrow view of reforms without regard to the possible importance of sequencing. Austin, Ciobanu, and Lynch and Marchesi all note that a non-independent or insufficiently vetted judiciary can become a serious impediment to transitional justice measures, since the judiciary must be in the driver's seat for key "hard" transitional justice methods such as court trials and lustration to ever be pursued. This finding leads Lynch and Marchesi to suggest that lustration programs that target the judiciary may lay key groundwork for its potential to support the development of a rights culture via subsequent free and fair trials and further legitimate lustration. Likewise, Horne argues that delayed lustration might be more efficacious because other foundational institutions already exist to properly execute reform measures.

A final lesson the volume offers warns against a too-narrow view of the post-communist region with regard to broader transitional justice issues and questions. Without denying its distinctive features and experiences, Beattie argues that seeing Central and Eastern Europe as overly special or exceptional can obscure commonalities with other cases outside the region. Lynch and Marchesi, as well, call for broader comparative study to test conclusions regarding post-communist lessons, and Horne observes that the region's lessons could be useful for many other cases, including the Middle East, Central America, and Asia.

Indeed, this project was animated by the hope that identifying the hard-learned lessons of post-communist Europe's first twenty-five years may not only contribute to our understanding of that period of history but also lay groundwork for a better future in the region and beyond. The editors are grateful to all the volume's authors for their contribution to these aims as we celebrate this important anniversary.

Bibliography

AA. 2012. "Draža, Srbi i Hrvati," *Novi magazin*, March 31.
Abrahams, Fred. 1996. *Human Rights in Post-Communist Albania*. New York: Human Rights Watch.
Act No. 451/1991 on Conditions for Holding Certain Positions in State Bodies and Organizations (October 4, 1991), the Screening ("Lustration") Law, translated in *Transitional Justice: How Emerging Democracies Reckon with Former Regimes*, ed. Neil Kritz. Washington, D.C.: United States Institute of Peace Studies, 1995, 3: 312–321.
Akhavan, Payam. 2001. "Beyond Impunity: Can International Criminal Justice Prevent Atrocities?" *American Journal of International Law*, 95: 7–31.
"Albania Blast Trial Sentences Disappoint Victims," *Balkan Insight*, March 13, 2012, available at: http://www.balkaninsight.com/en/article/light-sentences-in-albania-deadly-blast-trial (accessed October 10, 2013).
Albanian Constitution, 2008, available at: http://www.ipls.org/services/kusht/cp2.html (accessed October 9, 2013).
Albanian Telegraph Agency (ATA), February 16, 2009, as provided by BBC Monitoring.
Albu, Mihai. 2008. *Informatorul: studiu asupra colaborării cu Securitatea*. Iaşi: Polirom.
Alderman, Derek H. 2004. "Memory and Place: Geographies of a Critical Relationship," *Social and Cultural Geographies*, 5: 347–355.
Allcock, John B. 2000. *Explaining Yugoslavia*. New York: Columbia University Press.
Amnesty International. 2003. "Argentina: The Full Stop and Due Obedience Laws and International Law" (April 1), available at: http://www.refworld.org/docid/3f13d9d34.html (accessed November 15, 2013).
2010. *Commissioning Justice: Truth Commissions and Criminal Justice*. London: Amnesty International Publications.
2007. *Truth, Justice and Reparation: Establishing an Effective Truth Commission*. London: AI International Secretariat.
Anderson, Benedict. 2006. *Imagined Communities: Reflections on the Origin and Spread of Nationalism*, 2nd ed. London: Verso.
A'ness, Francine. 2004. "Resisting Amnesia: Yuyachkani, Performance, and the Postwar Reconstruction in Peru," *Theatre Journal*, 56: 395–414.

Angelovska, Despina. 2013. "The Failure of Macedonian Post-Communist Transitional Justice: Lustration, between Cleansing and Parody," in *Transitional Justice and Civil Society in the Balkans*, eds. Olivera Simić and Zala Volcic. New York: Springer, 51–67.

Apostol, Lucia and Rudy Marcovici. 2011. "The Romanian Heritage: Rehabilitation, Restoration and Options for Preservation," *Studia Hebraica*, IX-X: 199–211.

Appel, Hilary. 2005. "Anti-Communist Justice and Founding the Post-Communist Order: Lustration and Restitution in Central Europe," *East European Politics and Societies*, 19: 379–405.

Argenbright, Robert. 1999. "Remaking Moscow: New Places, New Selves," *Geographical Review*, 89: 1–22.

Arthur, Paige. 2009. "How 'Transitions' Reshaped Human Rights: A Conceptual History of Transitional Justice," *Human Rights Quarterly*, 31: 321–367.

Asiedu, Dita. 2003. "Czechs Wait Thirteen Years for Official Names of Secret Police Collaborators," Radio Praha (March 24), available at: http://www.radio.cz/en/section/curraffrs/czechs-wait-thirteen-years-for-official-names-of-secret-police-collaborators (accessed on December 17, 2013).

Austin, Robert. 1993. "What Albania Adds to the Balkan Stew," *ORBIS*, 37: 259–279.

Austin, Robert and Jonathan Ellis. 2009. "Albania," in *Transitional Justice in Eastern Europe and the Former Soviet Union*, ed. Lavinia Stan. London: Routledge, 176–199.

2008. "Post-Communist Transitional Justice in Albania," *East European Politics and Societies*, 22: 370–401.

Avello, María. 2008. "European Efforts in Transitional Justice," FRIDE Working Paper no. 58 (June).

Azaryahu, Maoz. 1996. "The Power of Commemorative Street Names," *Environment and Planning D: Society and Space*, 14: 311–330.

Bădica, Simina. 2010. "The Black Hole Paradigm: Exhibiting Communism in Post-Communist Romania," in *History of Communism in Europe*, Volume 1: *Politics of Memory in Post-Communist Europe*. Bucharest: Zeta Books, 83–101.

Baehr, Peter. 2000. "Controversies in the Current International Human Rights Debate," *Human Rights Review*, 2: 7–32.

Baker, David. 2003. "Civil Society and Transitional Justice: Possibilities, Patterns and Prospects," *Journal of Human Rights*, 2: 297–313.

Bălan, Ion. 2000. *Regimul Concentraţionar din România: 1945–1964*. Bucharest: Civic Academy Foundation.

Balastik, Miroslav. 2008. "Two Stories: Kundera and the Conclusion of the Velvet Revolution," *Eurozine* (July 11), available at: http://www.eurozine.com/articles/2008-11-07-balastik-en.html (accessed on December 17, 2013).

Balcerowicz, Leszek. 1995. *Socialism, Capitalism, Transformation*. Budapest: Central European University Press.

Balfour, Michael. 2012. "Mapping Realities: Representing War through Affective Place Making," *New Theatre Quarterly*, 28: 30–40.

Banjeglav, Tamara. 2012. "Sjećanje na rat ili rat sjećanja?" in *Re:vizija prošlosti: Politike sjećanja u Bosni i Hercegovini, Hrvatskoj i Srbiji od 1990. godine*, eds. Tamara Banjeglav, Nataša Govedarica, and Darko Karačić. Sarajevo: ACIPS, 91–162.

Barahona De Brito, Alexandra, Carmen Gonzales-Enriquez, and Paloma Aguilar, eds. 2001. *The Politics of Memory: Transitional Justice in Democratizing Societies*. Oxford: Oxford University Press.

Barsalou, Judy and Victoria Baxter. 2007. *The Urge to Remember: The Role of Memorials in Social Reconstruction and Transitional Justice*. Washington, D.C.: United States Institute of Peace, available at: http://www.usip.org/publications/the-urge-remember-the-role-of-memorials-in-social-reconstruction-and-transitional (accessed on October 3, 2013).

Batson, Charles. 1991. *The Altruism Question: Toward a Social Psychological Answer*. Hillsdale, NJ: Erlbaum.

Baumann, Gabriele and Nina Müller. 2006. "Vergangenheitsbewältigung und Erinnerungskultur in den Ländern Mittelost- und Südosteuropas," Konrad-Adenauer-Stiftung Working Paper no. 164.

Beattie, Andrew H. 2013. "Ein neuer Historikerstreit? Kommunismus und Nationalsozialismus in der deutschen Erinnerungs- und Geschichtspolitik seit 1990," in *Ein Kampf um Deutungshoheit: Politik, Opferinteressen und historische Forschung: Die Auseinandersetzung um die Gedenk- und Begegnungsstätte Leistikowstraße Potsdam*, ed. Wolfgang Benz. Berlin: Metropol Verlag, 16–36.

2009. "An Evolutionary Process: Contributions of the Bundestag's Inquiries into East Germany to an Understanding of the Role of Truth Commissions," *International Journal of Transitional Justice*, 3: 229–249.

2009. *Playing Politics with History: The Bundestag Inquiries into East Germany*. New York: Berghahn Books.

Behr, Valentin. 2008. "La production du récit historique à l'Institut de la mémoire nationale. Une etude des usages politiques du passe en Pologne," MA thesis, Universite de Strasbourg, available at: http://scd-theses.u-strasbg.fr/2008/01/BEHR_Valentin_2010.pdf (accessed on December 17, 2013), 29.

Bell, James. 1999. "Redefining National Identity in Uzbekistan: Symbolic Tensions in Tashkent's Official Public Landscape," *Ecumene*, 6: 184–213.

Bell, Vikki. 2011. "Contemporary Art and Transitional Justice in Northern Ireland: The Consolation of Form," *Journal of Visual Culture*, 10: 324–353.

Benomar, Jamal. 1995. "Justice after Transitions," in *Transitional Justice: How Emerging Democracies Reckon with Former Regimes*, ed. Neil Kritz. Washington, D.C.: United States Institute of Peace Press, 1: 31–41.

Benyamin, Lya. 2011. "Politica antievreiască a regimului Antonescu 1940–1944," *Holocaust Studii şi Cercetări*, 1: 1–9.

"Berisha: All Files Will Be Opened." *Republika*, Tirana, November 27, 2007.

Bertschi, Charles. 1995. "Lustration and the Transition to Democracy: The Cases of Poland and Bulgaria," *East European Quarterly*, 28: 435–452.

Biberaj, Elez. 1998. *Albania in Transition: The Rocky Road to Democracy*. Boulder, CO: Westview Press.

Bickford, Louis. 2007. "Unofficial Truth Projects," *Human Rights Quarterly*, 29: 994–1035.

Bilbija, Ksenija, Jo Ellen Fair, Cynthia E. Milton, and Leigh A. Payne, eds. 2005. *The Art of Truth-Telling about Authoritarian Rule*. Madison: University of Wisconsin Press.

Billig, Michael. 1995. *Banal Nationalism*. London: Sage.

Blaive, Muriel. 2004. "Einige Etappen der Bewältigung der kommunistischen Vergangenheit seit 1989 in der Republik Tschechien," in *Die Überlieferung der Diktaturen*, eds. Agnès Bensussan, Dorota Dakowska and Nicolas Beauprè. Essen: Klartext Verlag, 111–126.

2011. "The Memory of the Holocaust and of Communist Repression in a Comparative Perspective: The Cases of Hungary, Poland and Czechoslovakia/the Czech Republic," in *Clashes in European Memory: The Case of Communist Repression and the Holocaust*, eds. Muriel Blaive, Christian Gerbel, and Thomas Lindenberger. Innsbruck: Studien Verlag, 154–172.

2004. "L'ouverture des archives d'une police politique communiste: le cas tcheque de Zdena Salivarová à Milan Kundera," in *Archives et histoire dans les societes postcommunistes*, ed. Sonia Combe. Paris: La Decouverte, 203–225.

Bodnar, John. 1994. "Public Memory in an American City: Commemoration in Cleveland," in *Commemorations: The Politics of National Identity*, ed. John R. Gillis. Princeton, NJ: Princeton University Press, 74–89.

1992. *Remaking America: Public Memory, Commemoration, and Patriotism in the Twentieth Century*. Princeton, NJ: Princeton University Press.

Boed, Roman. 1999. "An Evaluation of the Legality and Efficacy of Lustration as a Tool of Transitional Justice," *Columbia Journal of Transitional Law*, 37: 357–402.

Borodziej, Włodzimierz. 2006. "Der Kommunismus in der deutschen Erinnerungskultur. Kommentar aus polnischer Sicht," in *Woran erinnern? Der Kommunismus in der deutschen Erinnerungskultur*, eds. Peter März and Hans-Joachim Veen. Cologne: Böhlau Verlag, 205–212.

Borufka, Sarah. 2009. "Communist Secret Police Database Goes Online," *The Prague Post* (July 15), available at: http://www.praguepost.com/news/1738-communist-secret-police-database-goes-online.html (accessed April 10, 2011).

Börzel, Tanja A. and Thomas Risse. 2012. "When Europeanisation Meets Diffusion: Exploring New Territory," *West European Politics*, 35: 193–207.

Brahm, Eric. 2009. "What Is a Truth Commission and Why Does It Matter," *Peace and Conflict Review*, 3: 1–14.

Brems, Eva. 2011. "Transitional Justice in the Case of the European Court of Human Rights," *International Journal of Transitional Justice*, 5: 282–303.

Buckley-Zistel, Susanne. 2013. "Vergangenes Unrecht aufarbeiten. Eine globale Perspektive," *Aus Politik und Zeitgeschichte*, 63: 36–37.

Budryte, Dovile. 2013. "International Commission for the Evaluation of the Crimes of the Nazi and Soviet Occupation Regimes in Lithuania," in *Encyclopedia of Transitional Justice*, eds. Lavinia Stan and Nadya Nedelsky. New York: Cambridge University Press, 3: 218–222.

Bugaj, Ryszard. 2010. "Osierocona idea IV RP," *Rzeczpospolita*, July 6.

Bunce, Valerie and Sharon Wolchik. 2011. "International Diffusion and Democratic Change," *The Dynamics of Democratization. Dictatorship, Development, and Diffusion*, ed. Nathan J. Brown. Baltimore: Johns Hopkins University Press, 286–287.

2010. "Transnational Networks, Diffusion Dynamics, and Electoral Change in the Postcommunist World," in *The Diffusion of Social Movements. Actors, Mechanisms, and Political Effects*, eds. Rebecca Kolins Givan, Kenneth

M. Roberts, and Sarah A. Soule. Cambridge: Cambridge University Press, 140–162.
Cabledrum for this cable from Ambassador Withers, "Lustration Law Passes, but What Next?" Tirana, December 23, 2008, available at: https://www.cabledrum.net/cables/08TIRANA899 (accessed October 14, 2013).
Cabledrum for this cable from the U.S. Embassy in Tirana, "President Topi Leaning Against Veto of Lustration Law," Tirana, January 13, 2009, available at: https://www.cabledrum.net/cables/09TIRANA18 (accessed October 10, 2013).
Calhoun, Noel. 2004. *Dilemmas of Justice in Eastern Europe's Democratic Transitions*. Basingstoke: Palgrave Macmillan.
2002. "The Ideological Dilemma of Lustration in Poland," *East European Politics and Societies*, 16: 494–520.
"Cambodia: Bringing the Khmers Rouges to Justice," *The Economist*, October 7, 2004.
Cameron, Rob. 2009. "The Czech Secret Police Files," Euranet (October 28), available at: http://www.euranet.eu/eng/layout/set/print/Dossier/The-fall-of-Communism/Restricted-access-The-Czech-secret-police-files (accessed on December 10, 2013).
Castillo, Mariano. 2013. "Guatemala Confronts a Dark Chapter," *CNN*, April 11.
Cenckiewicz, Sławomir and Piotr Gontarczyk. 2008. *SB a Lech Wałęsa. Przyczynek do biografii*. Warsaw: IPN.
Centrum pro Výzkum veřejného mínení. 2012. "Názor veřejnosti na roli církví ve společnosti a na navrácení církevního majetku" (October 23), available at: http://cvvm.soc.cas.cz/media/com_form2content/documents/c1/a6901/f3/pi121023b.pdf (accessed October 13, 2013).
Cesereanu, Ruxandra. 2008. "The Final Report on the Holocaust and the Final Report on the Communist Dictatorship in Romania," *East European Politics and Societies*, 22: 240–281.
2004. *Decembrie'89. Deconstrucţia unei revoluţii*. Iaşi: Polirom.
Český Statistický Úřad, n. d. "Výsledky voleb a referend," available at: http://volby.cz (accessed January 20, 2014).
Chapman, Audrey and Patrick Ball. 2001. "The Truth of Truth Commissions: Comparative Lessons from Haiti, South Africa, and Guatemala," *Human Rights Quarterly*, 23: 1–43.
Choi, Susanne Y. P. and Roman David. 2012. "Lustration Systems and Trust: Evidence from Survey Experiments in the Czech Republic, Hungary, and Poland," *American Journal of Sociology*, 117: 1172–1201.
Church, Gordon. 1979. "Bucharest: Revolution in the Townscape Art," in *The Socialist City: Spatial Structure and Urban Policy*, eds. R. A. French and F. E. I. Hamilton. Chichester: Wiley, 493–506.
"Cibulka StB Files Accurate," *The Slovak Spectator* (May 9, 2002), available at: http://spectator.sme.sk/articles/view/7554/10 (accessed on December 17, 2013).
Cienski, Jan. 2007. "Polish Witch-Hunt 'Risks Business Chaos,'" *Financial Times*, March 14.
Ciobanu, Monica. 2013. "Recent Restorative Justice Measures in Romania (2006–2010)," *Problems of Post-Communism*, 60: 45–57.

"Čistka v ÚSTR: Nová šéfka se zbavuje lidí napojených na exředitele, nechtějí s ní mluvit," *iHned.cz*, April 18, 2013, available at: http://zpravy.ihned.cz/c1-59717020-sefka-ustr-foglova-zahajila-cistku (accessed October 13, 2013).

Clark, Janine N. 2013. "Reconciliation through Remembrance? War Memorials and the Victims of Vukovar," *International Journal of Transitional Justice*, 7: 136–156.

Closa, Carlos. 2013. "Spain," in *Encyclopedia of Transitional Justice*, eds. Lavinia Stan and Nadya Nedelsky. New York: Cambridge University Press, 2: 459–464.

Cole, Catherine. 2007. "Performance, Transitional Justice, and the Law," *Theatre Journal*, 59: 167–187.

Collins, Cath. 2010. *Post-Transitional Justice: Human Rights Trials in Chile and El Salvador*. Philadelphia: Pennsylvania State University Press.

"Communist Repression at the End of the Second World War," *Hereticus*, 9, nos. 1–2, 2011, available at: http://www.hereticus.org/wp-content/uploads/2011/Hereticus%201-2%202011.pdf (accessed January 13, 2014).

Corey, Allison and Sandra F. Joireman. 2004. "Retributive Justice: The Gacaca Courts in Rwanda," *African Affairs*, 103: 73–89.

Council of Europe. 1996. Measures to Dismantle the Heritage of Former Communist Totalitarian Systems. Resolution 1096, available at: http://assembly.coe.int/Documents/AdoptedText/ta96/ERES1096.HTM (accessed December 7, 2013).

Council of Europe Parliamentary Assembly. 1996. *Resolution 1096 (1996) on Measures to Dismantle the Heritage of Former Communist Totalitarian Systems*, available at: http://assembly.coe.int/main.asp?Link=/documents/adoptedtext/ta96/eres1096.htm (accessed October 9, 2013).

"Croatia: Premier Says Decision to Cooperate with Hague Tribunal Was Inevitable," *BBC Monitoring Europe – Political*, July 8, 2001.

"Croatian PM Tells BBC He Would Personally Arrest Indicted Gen Gotovina," *BBC Monitoring International Reports*, April 26, 2005.

"Croatian PM Urges Support in War Crimes Confidence Vote," *Agence France Presse*, July 15, 2001.

"Croatian Prime Minister Asks Vatican for Help in Pushing for EU Membership Talks," *Associated Press Worldstream*, February 22, 2005.

Crowley, David and Susan E. Reid. 2002. "Socialist Spaces: Sites of Everyday Life in the Eastern Bloc," in *Socialist Spaces: Sites of Everyday Life in the Eastern Bloc*, eds. David Crowley and Susan E. Reid. Oxford: Berg, 1–22.

ČTK [Czech Press Agency], "Babis Says He Need Not Be in Czech Government, Will Not Seek Lustration," November 6, 2013, available at: http://www.ceskenoviny.cz/zpravy/babis-says-he-need-not-be-in-czech-govt-will-not-seek-lustration/1004873 (accessed November 14, 2013).

"Dcera Rudého kata rozdala dědictví těm, kterým ublížil," *Aktualne.cz*, August 30, 2013, available at: http://aktualne.centrum.cz/domaci/spolecnost/clanek.phtml?id=789080&utm_source=email&utm%5Fmedium=email&utm_campaign=posli (accessed October 13, 2013).

Culic, Irina. 2005. "Re-writing the History of Romania after the Fall of Communism," *History Compass*, 1: 1–21.

Ćuruvija-Đurica, Jelena. 2012. "Hipermnezija-Prica o prici," May 24, available at: http://www.youtube.com/watch?v=Wap1IWSjNJQ (accessed September 7, 2013).

Cvetković, Srdjan. 2011. *Izmedju srpa i čekića: Politička represija u Srbiji*. Belgrade: Institut za savremenu istoriju.

Czarnota, Adam. 2009. "Lustration, Decommunisation and the Rule of Law," *Hague Journal on the Rule of Law*, 1: 307–336.

Czepczyński, Marius. 2008. *Cultural Landscapes of Post-Socialist Cities: Representations of Powers and Needs*. Aldershot: Ashgate.

Dakowska, Dorota. 2005. "German Political Foundations: Transnational Party Go-betweens in the Process of EU Enlargement," in *Transnational European Union*, eds. Wolfram Kaiser and Peter Starie. London: Routledge, 150–169.

Daly, Kathy. 2011. "Conventional and Innovative Justice Responses to Sexual Violence," *Australian Center for the Study of Sexual Assault*, 12, available at: http://www.aifs.gov.au/acssa/pubs/issue/i12/ (accessed February 16, 2014).

Dancy, Geoff. 2013. "The Impact of Human Rights Law in Time," Ph.D. Dissertation. University of Minnesota.

Dancy, Geoff, Bridget Marchesi, Tricia Olsen, Leigh Payne, Andrew Reiter, and Kathryn Sikkink. 2013. "Stopping State Agents of Violence or Promoting Political Compromise? The Powerful Role of Transitional Justice Mechanisms," paper presented at the American Political Science Association annual meeting, Chicago, August 30.

Danilović, Rajko. 2010. *Upotreba neprijatelja: Politička suđenja 1945–1991 u Jugoslaviji*. Belgrade: Zavod za udžbenike.

Dastych, D. 2007. "Better Late than Never: Retarded De-communization in Poland," *The Gazette* (January 9), available at: http://www.axisglobe.com/article.asp?article.1192 (accessed on January 28, 2011).

David, Roman. 2006. "In Exchange for Truth: The Polish Lustration and the South African Amnesty Process," *Politikon: South African Journal of Political Studies*, 32: 81–99.

2011. *Lustration and Transitional Justice: Personnel Systems in the Czech Republic, Hungary and Poland*. Philadelphia: University of Pennsylvania Press.

2003. "Lustration Laws in Action: The Motives and Evaluation of Lustration Policy in the Czech Republic and Poland (1989–2001)," *Law and Social Inquiry*, 28: 387–489.

2012. "Twenty Years of Transitional Justice in the Czech Lands," *Europe-Asia Studies*, 64: 761–784.

The Utility of Transitional Justice in the Czech Republic, Grant SG-54378, 2009, funded by the British Academy.

David, Roman and Houda Mzioudet. 2014. "Personnel Change or Personal Change? Rethinking Libya's Political Isolation Law," *Brookings Doha Center – Stanford University Project on Arab Transitions Paper Series*, 4 (March).

David, Roman and Susanne Y. P. Choi. 2009. "Getting Even, or Getting Equal? Retributive Desires and Transitional Justice," *Political Psychology*, 30: 161–192.

2006. "Forgiveness and Transitional Justice in the Czech Republic," *Journal of Conflict Resolution*, 50: 339–367.

2005. "Victims on Transitional Justice: Lessons from the Reparation of Human Rights Abuses in the Czech Republic," *Human Rights Quarterly*, 27: 392–435.

Davis, Laura. 2010. "The European Union and Transitional Justice," International Center for Transitional Justice – Initiative for Peace Building (June), available at: http://www.initativeforpeacebuilding.eu (accessed January 10, 2014).

"Declassified Archive Shows StB Kept Track of Jews," Aktualne.cz (July 24, 2009), available at: http://aktualne.centrum.cz/kultura/film/recenze/clanek.phtml?id. 643270 (accessed December 10, 2013).
Deletant, Dennis. 1995. *Ceauşescu and the Securitate: Coercion and Dissent in Romania, 1965–1989*. Armonk, NY: M.E. Sharpe.
"Decretul 40 din 9 ianuarie 1990 privind comemorarea eroilor revoluţiei," *Monitorul Oficial*, January 6, 1990.
Djikić, Ivica. 2004. *Domovinski obrat: Politička biografija Stipe Mesića*. Zagreb: VBZ.
Dobrincu, Dorin, and Constantin Iordachi. eds. 2005. *Ţărănimea şi puterea. Procesul de Colectivizare a agriculturii în România (1949–1962)*. Bucharest: Polirom.
Dobrincu, Dorin, Mihai Stamatescu, Raluca Grosescu, Liviu Pleşa, Sorin Andresscu, and Andrei Muraru. 2008. *O istorie a comunismului din România. Manual pentru liceu*. Bucharest: Polirom.
Donovan, Mark, Carolyn Tolbert, and Daniel Smith. 2009. "Political Engagement, Mobilization, and Direct Democracy," *Public Opinion Quarterly*, 73: 98–118.
Dvořáková, Vladimíra and Anđelko Milardović. eds. 2007. *Lustration and Consolidation Of Democracy and Rule of Law in Central and Eastern Europe*. Zagreb: Political Science Research Centre Zagreb.
Edensor, Tim. 2002. *National Identity, Popular Culture and Everyday Life*. Oxford: Berg.
1997. "National Identity and the Politics of Memory: Remembering Bruce and Wallace in Symbolic Space," *Environment and Planning D*, 15: 175–194.
Ellis, Mark. 1997. "Purging the Past: The Current State of Lustration Laws in the Former Communist Bloc," *Law and Contemporary Problems*, 59: 181–196.
Elster, Jon. 2004. *Closing the Books: Transitional Justice in Historical Perspective*. Cambridge: Cambridge University Press.
Eriksen, Svein. 2007. "Institution Building in Central and Eastern Europe: Foreign Influences and Domestic Responses," *Review of Central and East European Law*, 32: 333–369.
European Court of Human Rights. 2007. *Case of Matyvek v. Poland*, Judgment 38184/03, April 24. Strasbourg: Council of Europe.
2006. *Case of Ždanoka v. Latvia*, Judgment 58278/00, March 16, Strasbourg: Council of Europe.
2004. *Case of Sidabras and Dziautas v. Lithuania*, Final 55480/00 and 59330/00, July 27, Strasbourg: Council of Europe.
Explanatory Note Contained in a Note Verbale Handed to the Secretary General at the Time of Deposit of the Instrument of Ratification of Treaty No. 009: Protocol to the Convention for the Protection of Human Rights and Fundamental Freedoms, October 2, 1996, available at: http://conventions.coe.int/Treaty/Commun/Liste Declarations (accessed October 9, 2013).
Favorini, Attilio. 1995. *Voicing: Ten Plays from the Documentary Theatre*. New York: Ecco Press.
Featherstone, Kevin and Claudio M. Radaelli. eds. 2003. *The Politics of Europeanization*. Oxford: Oxford University Press.
Felman, Shoshana and Dori Laub. eds. 1991. *Testimony: Crises of Witnessing in Literature, Psychoanalysis, and History*. New York: Routledge.

Fendrych, Martin. "Gottwaldovec kádruje Čunase, *Aktualne.cz*, August 19, 2013, available at: http://aktualne.centrum.cz/blogy-a-nazory/komentare/clanek.phtml?id=788006 (accessed October 13, 2013).

"Začíná rudý úklid, antikomunista Herman končí," *Aktualne.cz*, April 11, 2013, available at: http://aktualne.centrum.cz/blogy-a-nazory/komentare/clanek.phtml?id=776608 (accessed October 13, 2013).

Finnemore, Martha and Kathryn Sikkink. 1998. "International Norm Dynamics and Political Change," *International Organization*, 52: 887–917.

Fisher Dawson, Gary. 1999. *Documentary Theatre in United States: An Historical Survey and Analysis of Its Contents, Form, and Stagecraft*. Westport, CT: Greenwood Press.

Florian, Alexandru. 2011. "The Treatment of the Jews in Romanian Legislation," *Holocaust: Studii şi Cercetări*, 1: 36–57.

Foote Kenneth, E., and Maoz Azaryahu. 2007. "Towards a Geography of Memory: Geographical Dimensions of Public Memory and Commemoration," *Journal of Political and Military Sociology*, 35: 125–144.

Foote, Kenneth E., Atilla Tóth, and Annet Árvay. 2000. "Hungary after 1989: Inscribing a New Past on Place," *Geographical Review*, 90: 301–334.

Forest, Benjamin and Juliet Johnson. 2002. "Unravelling the Threads of History: Soviet-Era Monuments and Post-Soviet National Identity in Moscow," *Annals of the Association of American Geographers*, 92: 524–547.

Forest, Benjamin, Juliet Johnson, and Karen Till. 2004. "Post-totalitarian National Identity: Public Memory in Germany and Russia," *Social and Cultural Geography*, 5: 357–380.

Forsyth, Alison and Chris Megson. eds. 2009. *Get Real: Documentary Theatre Past and Present*. London: Palgrave.

Freeman, Mark. 2006. *Truth Commissions and Procedural Fairness*. New York: Cambridge University Press.

Friling, Tuvia, Radu Ioanid, and Mihail E. Ionescu. eds. 2005. *Raport Final: Comisia Internaţională pentru Studierea Holocaustului în România*. Bucharest: Polirom.

Garton Ash, Timothy. 2000. *History of the Present: Essays, Sketches and Dispatches from Europe in the 1990s*. London: Penguin.

Gaube, Ales. 2003. "Slovenia: A Sorry Spy Hunt," *Transitions Online* (April 28), available at: http://www.tol.org/client/article/9366-slovenias-sorry-spy-hunt.html?print (accessed on December 18, 2013).

Gauck, Joachim in collaboration with Helga Hirsch. 2009. *Winter im Sommer – Frühling im Herbst. Erinnerungen*. Munich: Siedler.

Geiger, Vladimir. 1997. *Nestanak folksdojčera*. Zagreb: Nova stvarnost.

Geiger, Vladimir, Mate Rupić, Mario Kevo, Egon Kraljević, and Zvonimir Despot. eds. 2005. *Partizanska i komunistička represija i zločini u Hrvatskoj 1944–1946*. Slavonski brod: Hrvatski institut za povijest.

Georgescu, Vlad. 1991. *The Romanians: A History*. Columbus: Ohio State University Press.

German Parliament, ed. 1995. *Materialien der Enquete-Kommission "Aufarbeitung von Geschichte und Folgen der SED-Diktatur in Deutschland" (12. Wahlperiode des Deutschen Bundestages)*, vol. 1. Frankfurt am Main: Suhrkamp.

Gibson, James L. 2004. "Does Truth Lead to Reconciliation? Testing the Causal Assumptions of the South African Truth and Reconciliation Process," *American Journal of Political Science*, 48: 201–217.

Gillis, John R. 1994. "Memory and Identity: The History of a Relationship," in *Commemorations: The Politics of National Identity*, ed. John R. Gillis. Princeton: Princeton University Press, 3–24.

Gledhill, John. 2011. "Integrating the Past: Regional Integration and Historical Reckoning in Central and Eastern Europe," *Nationalities Paper*, 39: 481–506.

Gmyz, Cezary. 2010. "IPN wedlug Platformy," *Rzeczposolita*, March 19.

Goldstein, Ivo and Slavko Goldstein. 2001. *Holokaust u Zagrebu*. Zagreb: Novi liber.

Govedarica, Nataša. 2012. "Zemlja nesigurne prošlosti," in *Re:vizija prošlosti: Politike sjećanja u Bosni i Hercegovini, Hrvatskoj i Srbiji od 1990. godine*, eds. Tamara Banjeglav, Nataša Govedarica, and Darko Karačić. Sarajevo: ACIPS, 162–240.

Grancea, Mihaela. 2007. "Retorica morţii eroice în epitaful revoluţionarilor din decembrie'89," in *Revoluţia Română din Decembrie 1989: Istorie şi Memorie*, ed. Bogdan Murgescu. Iaşi: Polirom, 47–50.

Grigorescu, Alexandru. 2006. "The Corruption Eruption in East-Central Europe: The Increased Salience of Corruption and the Role of Intergovernmental Organizations," *East European Politics and Societies*, 20: 516–549.

Grodsky, Brian. 2011. "Exploring the Schelling Conjecture in Reverse: 'International Constraints' and Cooperation with the International Criminal Tribunal for the Former Yugoslavia," *European Journal of International Relations*, 17: 121–143.

2010. *The Costs of Justice: How New Leaders Respond to Previous Rights Abuses*. Notre Dame, IN: University of Notre Dame Press.

2009. "Beyond Lustration: Truth-Seeking Efforts in the Post-Communist Space," *Taiwan Journal of Democracy*, 5: 21–43.

2007. "Producing Truth: The Politics of Investigating Past Human Rights Violations in Post-Communist States," *World Affairs*, 169: 125–133.

Grosescu, Raluca. 2007. "The Role of Civil Society and Anticommunist Political Actors in the Romanian Transitional Justice Partial Failure," in *Lustration and Consolidation of Democracy and the Rule of Law in Central and Eastern Europe*, eds. Vladimira Dvorakova and Andelko Milardovic. Zagreb: Political Science Research Center, 183–196.

Grosescu, Raluca and Raluca Ursachi. 2009. *Justiţia penală de tranziţie. De la Nuremberg la Postcomunimul românesc*. Bucharest: Institutul de Investigare a Crimelor Comunismului din România.

Großbölting, Thomas. 2013. "Commission of Inquiry for the Assessment of History and Consequences of the SED Dictatorship in Germany," in *Encyclopedia of Transitional Justice*, eds. Lavinia Stan and Nadya Nedelsky. New York: Cambridge University Press, 3: 57–61.

Gulińska-Jurgiel, Paulina. 2010. "Transnational References in Times of Radical Changes. 'Europe' as a Function of Coming to Terms with the Past," paper presented at the 18th Conference of the Council of European Studies, Barcelona, Spain, June 20–22.

"Half of the Croats Support Extradition of War Crimes Suspects," *Deutsche Presse-Agentur*, July 9, 2001.
Hall, Derek. 2001. "Brand Development, Tourism and National Identity: The Re-imaging of Former Yugoslavia," *Brand Management*, 9: 323–334.
1999. "Destination Branding, Niche Marketing and National Image Projection in Central and Eastern Europe," *Journal of Vacation Marketing*, 5: 227–237.
Hall, Michael C. 2005. *Tourism: Rethinking the Social Science of Mobility*. London: Routledge.
1994. *Tourism and Politics: Policy, Power and Place*. Chichester: Wiley.
Hall, Richard Andrew. 1999. "The Uses of Absurdity: The Staged War Theory and the Romanian Revolution of December 1989," *East European Politics and Societies*, 13: 501–542.
Halmai, Gábor. 2007. "Lustration and Access to the Files in Central Europe," in *Lustration and Consolidation of Democracy and the Rule of Law in Central and Eastern Europe*, eds. Vladimíra Dvořáková and Anđelko Milardović. Zagreb: Political Science Research Centre, 19–45.
Hamber, Brendon, Liz Ševčenko, and Ereshnee Naidu. 2010. "Utopian Dreams or Practical Possibilities? The Challenges of Evaluating the Impact of Memorialization in Societies in Transition," *International Journal of Transitional Justice*, 4: 397–420.
Hamilton, Michael and Antoine Buyse. 2011. "Introduction," in *Transitional Jurisprudence and the ECHR. Justice, Politics and Rights*, eds. Antoine Buyse and Michael Hamilton. Cambridge: Cambridge University Press, 1–23.
Hamzić, Amina. 2012. "Docu Genre Answers Bosnian's Postwar Hunger for Facts," *Balkan Insight*, August 28, available at: http://www.balkaninsight.com/en/article/docu-genre-answers-bosnia-s-postwar-hunger-for-facts (accessed October 25, 2013).
Harmsen, Robert and Thomas M. Wilson. 2000. "Introduction: Approaches to Europeanization," *Yearbook of European Studies*, 14: 13–26.
Hayner, Priscilla. 2010. *Unspeakable Truths: Transitional Justice and the Challenge of Truth Commissions*. New York: Routledge.
Helsinki Committee for Human Rights in Serbia. 2011. *Human Rights Reflect Institutional Impotence*. Belgrade: HCHRS.
Hiio, Toomas, Meelis Maripuu and Indrek Paavle. eds. 2009. *Estonia since 1944: Reports of the Estonian International Commission for the Investigation of Crimes against Humanity*. Tallinn: Estonian Foundation for the Investigation of Crimes against Humanity.
eds. 2006. *Estonia 1940–1945: Reports of the Estonian International Commission for the Investigation of Crimes against Humanity*. Tallinn: Estonian Foundation for the Investigation of Crimes against Humanity.
Horne, Cynthia. 2012. "Assessing the Impact of Lustration on Trust in Public Institutions and National Government in Central and Eastern Europe," *Comparative Political Studies*, 45: 412–446.
2009. "Late Lustration Programmes in Romania and Poland: Supporting or Undermining Democratic Transitions," *Democratization*, 16: 344–376.
2009. "International Legal Rulings on Lustration Policies in Central and Eastern Europe: Rule of Law in Historical Context," *Law and Social Inquiry*, 34: 713–744.

Horne, Donald. 1984. *The Great Museum: The Re-presentation of History*. London: Pluto.

Horovitz, Sigall. 2006. "Transitional Criminal Justice in Sierra Leone," in *Transitional Justice in the Twenty-First Century: Beyond Truth Versus Justice*, eds. Naomi Roht-Arriaza and Javier Mariezcurrena. New York: Cambridge University Press, 43–69.

Hristov, Hristo and Alexander Kashumov. 2012. "Justice and Accountability Mechanisms in Bulgaria in the Transition Period (1989–2008)," in *After Oppression: Transitional Justice in Latin America and Eastern Europe*, eds. Vesselin Popovski and Mónica Serrano. Tokyo: United Nations University Press, 273–297.

Human Rights Watch. 2004. *Justice at Risk: War Crimes Trials in Croatia, Bosnia and Herzegovina, and Serbia and Montenegro*. New York: Human Rights Watch, October 13.

Huntington, Samuel. 1991. *The Third Wave: Democratization in the Late Twentieth Century*. Norman: University of Oklahoma Press.

Huyse, Luc. 1995. "Justice after Transition: On the Choices Successor Elites Make in Dealing with the Past," *Law & Social Inquiry*, 20: 51–78.

Iancu, Bogdan. 2010. "Post-Accession Constitutionalism with a Human Face: Judicial Reform and Lustration in Romania," *European Constitutional Law Review*, 6: 28–58.

"IICCMER Is Investigating 35 People under Suspicion of Having Committed War Crimes during the Communist Regime," *Jurnalul National*, April 11, 2013, available at: http://jurnalul.ro/stiri/observator/iiccmer-investigheaza-35-de-persoane-suspectate-ca-au-comis-crime-in-timpul-regimului-comunist-641060.html (accessed February 19, 2013).

Iliescu, Ion. 2004. *După 20 de ani: 1989 an de cotitură în istoria naţională şi în viaţa internaţională*. Bucharest: Semne, 218–223.

Imholz, Kathleen. 1997. "States of Emergency as Pretexts for Gagging the Press: Word Play at Albania's Constitutional Court," *East European Constitutional Review*, 6: 57–63.

1997. "Albania," *East European Constitutional Review*, 6: 2–5.

1995 "Decommunization in Albania," *East European Constitutional Review*, 4: 54–60.

International Commission for the Evaluation of the Crimes of the Nazi and Soviet Occupation Regimes in Lithuania. 1999. "Outline of Work Plan," August 29, available at: http://www.komisija.lt/en/body.php?&m=1173548714 (accessed December 4, 2013).

n.d. "Conclusions of the Commission (List)," available at: http://www.komisija.lt/en/naujiena.php?id=1187780828 (accessed December 4, 2013).

n.d. "Partners," available at: http://www.komisija.lt/en/body.php?&m=1182947575 (accessed December 4, 2013).

n.d. "Publishing," available at: http://www.komisija.lt/en/body.php?&m=1150461059 (accessed on December 4, 2013).

n.d. "Sessions: 8th Meeting of the Commission, 18–20 April 2005," available at: http://www.komisija.lt/en/naujiena.php?id=1175272773 (accessed December 4, 2013).

n.d. "Sessions: 4th Meeting of the Commission, 1–2 June 2000," available at: http://www.komisija.lt/en/naujiena.php?id=61 (accessed December 4, 2013).

International Court of Justice. 2007. *Bosnia and Herzegovina v. Serbia and Montenegro*, February 26, available at: http://www.icj-cij.org/docket/files/91/13685.pdf (accessed October 13, 2013).
Ioanid, Radu. 2000. *The Holocaust in Romania: The Destruction of Jews and Gypsies under the Antonescu Regime, 1940–1944*. Chicago: Ivan R. Dee.
IPN. 2007. *Ustawa z dnia 18 października 2006r o ujawnianiu informacji o dokumentach organów bezpieczeństwa z lat 1944–1990 oraz treści tych dokumentów*, available at: http://ipn.gov.pl/__data/assets/pdf_file/0009/49284/1-7967.pdf (accessed May 3, 2012).
Jacoby, Wade. 2006. "Inspiration, Coalition, and Substitution: External Influences on Post-Communist Transformations," *World Politics*, 58: 623–651.
James, Beverly. 1999. "Fencing in the Past: Budapest's Statue Park Museum," *Media, Culture and Society*, 21: 291–311.
Janjetović, Zoran. 2000. *Between Hitler and Tito: The Disappearance of the Vojvodina Germans*. Belgrade: s.n.
Jaskovska, Eva and John P. Moran. 2006. "Justice or Politics? Criminal, Civil and Political Adjudication in the Newly Independent Baltics," *Journal of Communist Studies and Transition Politics*, 22: 485–506.
Jelin, Elizabeth. 2007. "Public Memorialization in Perspective: Truth, Justice and the Memory of Past Repression in the Southern Cone of South America," *International Journal of Transitional Justice*, 1: 138–156.
Johnson, Nuala. 2004. "Public Memory," in *A Companion to Cultural Geography*, eds. James S. Duncan, Nuala C. Johnson, and Richard H. Schein. Oxford: Blackwell, 316–327.
Jones, Lynne. 2004. *Then they Started Shooting: Growing Up in Wartime Bosnia*. Cambridge, MA: Harvard University Press.
Jordana, Jacint, David Levi-Faur, and Xavier Fernández Marin. 2011. "The Global Diffusion of Regulatory Agencies: Channels of Transfer and Stages of Diffusion," *Comparative Political Studies*, 44: 1343–1369.
Jović, Josip. 2010. "Državni terorizam: UDBA ubila 69 emigranata," *Slobodna Dalmacija*, June 18.
Kaczyński, Andrzej, Ewa K. Czaczkowska, and Paweł Siennecki. 2005. "Donosił z Wiecznego Miasta," *Rzeczpospolita*, April 28.
Kaminski, M. and Monika Nalepa. 2006. "Judging Transitional Justice: A New Criterion for Evaluating Truth Revelation Procedures," *Journal of Conflict Resolution*, 50: 383–408.
Keck, Margaret E. and Kathryn Sikkink. 1998. *Activists Beyond Borders. Advocacy Networks in International Politics*. Ithaca, NY: Cornell University Press.
Kent, Lia. 2011. "Local Memory Practices in East Timor: Disrupting Transitional Justice Narratives," *International Journal of Transitional Justice*, 5: 434–455.
Killingsworth, Matt. 2010. "Lustration and Legitimacy," *Global Society*, 24: 71–90.
Kim, Hunjoon and Kathryn Sikkink. 2010. "Explaining the Deterrence Effect of Human Rights Prosecutions for Transitional Countries," *International Studies Quarterly*, 54: 939–963.
Kiss, Csilla. 2010. "Transitional Justice and the Reconstruction of Identity in Post-Communist Countries," in *Diktaturüberwindung in Europa. Neue nationale und*

transnationale Perspektiven, eds. Birgit Hofmann, Katja Wezel, Katrin Hammerstein, Regina Fritz, and Julie Trappe. Heidelberg: Universitätsverlag, 69–83.

2006. "The Misuses of Manipulation: The Failure of Transitional Justice in Post-Communist Hungary," *Europe-Asia Studies*, 58: 925–940.

Kligman, Gail and Katherine Verdery. 2011. *Peasants Under Siege: The Collectivization of Romanian Agriculture, 1949–1962*. Princeton, NJ: Princeton University Press.

Knežević, Dubravka. 1995. "Do poslednjeg daha," *Scena* 5/6, September–December.

Knill, Christoph. 2005. "Introduction: Cross-National Policy Convergence: Concepts, Approaches and Explanatory Factors," *Journal of European Public Policy*, 12: 764–774.

Kolsto, Pal. 2010. "Bleiburg: The Creation of a National Martyrology," *Europe-Asia Studies*, 62: 1153–1174.

Kopecký, Josef. 2013. "Zeman chce změnu restitucí, aby církve dostaly méně peněz," *iDnes* (September 1), available at: http://zpravy.idnes.cz/zeman-je-pro-zmenu-zakona-o-cirkevnich-restitucich-f8g-/domaci.aspx?c=A130901_112141_domaci_kop (accessed October 13, 2013).

Kornai, János and Susan Rose-Ackerman. eds. 2004. *Building a Trustworthy State in Post-Socialist Transition*. New York: Palgrave/Macmillan Press.

Kotar, Tamara. 2009. "Slovenia," in *Transitional Justice in Eastern Europe and the Former Soviet Union*, ed. Lavinia Stan. London: Routledge, 200–221.

Kovras, Iosif. 2013. "Explaining Prolonged Silences in Transitional Justice: The Disappeared in Cyprus and Spain," *Comparative Political Studies*, 46: 730–756.

Kritz, Neil. 1995. *Transitional Justice: How Emerging Democracies Reckon with Former Regimes*. Washington, D.C.: United States Institute of Peace Press, 3 vols.

Krobová, Tereza. 2013. "Rada ÚSTR rozhodla: Hermana nahradí Pavla Foglová," *Aktualne.cz* (April 10), available at: http://aktualne.centrum.cz/domaci/zivot-v-cesku/clanek.phtml?id=776543 (accessed October 13, 2013).

Ku, Julian and Jide Nzelibe. 2006. "Do International Criminal Tribunals Deter or Exacerbate Humanitarian Atrocities?" *Washington University Law Review*, 84: 777–833.

Kublik, Agnieszka and Wojciech Czuchnowski. 2005. "Wildstein wyniósł listę 240,000 nazwisk z IPN," Gazeta.pl, January 31, available at: http://serwisy.gazeta.pl/kraj/2029020,34317,2520547.html (accessed January 31, 2005).

Kurski, Jacek and Piotr Semka. 1993. *Lewy Czerwcowy*. Warsaw: Editions Spotkania.

Hinton, Alexander Laban. ed. 2010. *Transitional Justice: Global Mechanisms and Local Realities after Genocide and Mass Violence*. New Brunswick, NJ: Rutgers University Press.

Lajovic, Dusan. 2003. *Med Svobodo in Rdeco Zvezdo*. Ljubljana: Nova obzorja.

Lamont, Christopher K. 2009. *International Criminal Justice and the Politics of Compliance*. Burlington, VT: Ashgate.

Lampe, John R. 1996. *Yugoslavia as History: Twice There Was a Country*. Cambridge: Cambridge University Press.

Latvian Constitutional Court. 2005. Case No. 2004–13–0106, Judgment, March, 22, available at: www.satv.tiesa.gov.lv/upload/2004-13-0106E.rtf (accessed December 21, 2013).

Law Nr. 8001 of September 22, 1995, "On Genocide and Crimes Against Humanity Committed in Albania during the Communist Regime for Political, Ideological and Religious Reasons" (the Genocide Law), translated by Kathleen Imholz, available at: http://www.lustration.net/albania_documentation.pdf (accessed February 2, 2011).

Law Nr. 8043 of November 30, 1995, "On the Control of the Moral Figure of Officials and Other Persons Connected with the Protection of the Democratic State" (the Verification Law), translated by Kathleen Imholz, available at: http://www.lustration.net/albania_documentation.pdf (accessed February 2, 2011).

Law 8151 of September 9, 1996, On Amendments to Law No. 7573 *On Elections of the Organs of Local Authorities in Explanatory Note Contained in a Note Verbale Handed to the Secretary General at the Time of Deposit of the Instrument of Ratification of Treaty No. 009: Protocol to the Convention for the Protection of Human Rights and Fundamental Freedoms*, October 2, 1996, available at: http://conventions.coe.int/Treaty/Commun/ListeDeclarations (accessed October 9, 2013).

Law on Background Checks to be Conducted on Individuals Holding Certain Important Positions, Law No. 23/1994 (March 9, 1994), translated in *Transitional Justice: How Emerging Democracies Reckon with Former Regimes*, ed. Neil Kritz. Washington, D.C.: United States Institute of Peace Studies, 1995, 3: 418–425.

Leebaw, Bronwyn A. 2008. "The Irreconcilable Goals of Transitional Justice," *Human Rights Quarterly*, 30: 95–118.

Lehti, Marko, Matti Jutila and Markku Jokisipilä. 2008. "Never-Ending Second World War: Public Performances of National Dignity and the Drama of the Bronze Soldier," *Journal of Baltic Studies*, 39: 393–418.

Lerner Febres, Salomón. 2011. "Memory of Violence and Drama in Peru: The Experience of Truth Commission and the Yuyachkani Theater Group," keynote speech delivered at the Just Performance: Enacting Justice in the Wake of Violence symposium at Brandeis University, USA, December 1–2.

2011. "Foreword: The Rebellion of the Masks," in *Acting Together: Performance and the Creative Transformation of Conflict (Volume II: Building Just and Inclusive Communities)*, eds. Cynthia Cohen, Roberto Gutiérrez Varea, and Polly Walker. New York: New Village Press, ix–xiii.

Letki, Natalia. 2002. "Lustration and Democratization in East-Central Europe," *Europe-Asia Studies*, 54: 529–552.

"Libya's Government and the Militias: Is the Tide Turning?" *The Economist*, June 15, 2013.

"Lista Macierericza," Y-Elita Pl, n. d., available at: http://yelita.pl/artykuly/art/lista-macierewicza (accessed December 16, 2013).

Light, Duncan. 2006. "Romania: National Identity, Tourism Promotion and European Integration," in *Tourism in the New Europe: The Challenges and Opportunities of EU Enlargement*, eds. Derek Hall, Melanie Smith, and Barbara Marciszewska. Wallingford: CABI, 256–269.

2004. "Street Names in Bucharest, 1990–1997: Exploring the Modern Historical Geographies of Post-Socialist Change," *Journal of Historical Geography*, 30: 154–172.

1995. "Heritage as Informal Education," in *Heritage, Tourism and Society*, ed. David T. Herbert. London: Mansell, 117–145.

Lithuania: Decree Banning KGB Employees and Informers from Government Positions. Decree No. 418 (October 12, 1991), translated in *Transitional Justice:*

How Emerging Democracies Reckon with Former Regimes, ed. Neil Kritz. Washington, D.C.: United States Institute of Peace Studies, 1995, 3: 427.

Lopušina, Marko. 2013. "Srđan Cvetković: Osvetljavamo mračne godine Srbije," *Večernje novosti*, October 13.

Łoś, Maria. 1995. "Lustration and Truth Claims: Unfinished Revolutions in Central Europe," *Law and Social Inquiry*, 20: 117–161.

Los, Maria and Andrzej Zybertowicz. 2000. *Privatizing the Police-State: The Case of Poland*. Basingstoke: Palgrave Macmillan.

Lundy, Patricia and Mark McGovern. 2008. "The Role of Community in Participatory Transitional Justice," in *Transitional Justice from Below: Grassroots Activism and the Struggle for Change*, eds. Kieran McEvoy and Lorna McGregor. Oxford: Hart Publishing, 1–13.

Lutz, Ellen and Kathryn Sikkink. 2001. "The Justice Cascade: The Evolution and Impact of Foreign Human Rights Trials in Latin America," *Chicago Journal of International Law*, 2: 1–33.

Machcewicz, Paweł. 2012. "The Institute of National Remembrance and the Legacy of Communism in Poland," in *Politics, History and Collective Memory in East Central Europe*, eds. Zdzisław Krasnodębski, Stefan Garsztecki, and Rüdiger Ritter. Hamburg: Reinhold Krämer Verlag, 79–97.

Magaš, Branka. 1993. *The Destruction of Yugoslavia: Tracking the Break-up 1980–92*. London: Verso.

Maier, Charles S. 2000. "Doing History, Doing Justice: The Narrative of the Historian and of the Truth Commission," in *Truth v. Justice: The Morality of Truth Commissions*, eds. Robert I. Rotberg and Dennis Thompson. Princeton, NJ: Princeton University Press, 261–278.

Malina, Jan. 2003. "In Eastern Europe Things Are Not What They Seem. An Interview with Petr Cibulka" (March 10), available at: http://www.jrnyquist.com/petr_cibulka_2003_0310.htm (accessed on December 17, 2013).

Mälksoo, Lauri. 2001. "Soviet Genocide? Communist Mass Deportations in the Baltic States and International Law," *Leiden Journal of International Law*, 14: 757–787.

Malksoo, Maria. 2014. "Criminalizing Communism: Transnational Mnemopolitics in Europe," *International Political Sociology*, 8: 82–99.

2009. "The Memory Politics of Becoming European: The East European Subalterns and the Collective Memory of Europe," *European Journal of International Relations*, 15: 653–680.

Marieş, Teodor. 2012. "Despre dosarele revoluţiei," in *Şcoala Memoriei 2011*, ed. Călin Uba. Bucharest: Civic Academy Foundation, 390–412.

Mark, James. 2010. *The Unfinished Revolution. Making Sense of the Communist Past in Central-Eastern Europe*. New Haven, CT: Yale University Press.

Marsh, David, and J. C. Sharman. 2009. "Policy Diffusion and Policy Transfer," *Policy Studies*, 30: 274–275.

Marshall, Monty G. and Keith Jaggers. 2012. "Polity IV Project: Political Regime Characteristics and Transitions 1800–2012," available at: http://www.systemicpeace.org/polity/polity4.htm (accessed February 6, 2014).

Mayer, Françoise. 2004. *Les Tcheques et leur communism*. Paris: Les Editions de l'Ecole des Hautes Etudes en Sciences Sociales.

Mayer-Rieckh, Alexander and Pablo De Greiff. eds. 2007. *Justice as Prevention: Vetting Public Employees in Transitional Societies*. New York: ICTJ and Social Science Research Council.
McAdams, James. 2001. *Judging the Past in Unified Germany*. New York: Cambridge University Press.
McLean, Fiona. 1998. "Museums and the Construction of National Identity: A Review," *International Journal of Heritage Studies*, 3: 244–252.
McLeod, Laura, Jovana Dimitrijević and Biliana Rakočević. 2013. "Artistic Activism, Public Debate and Temporal Complexities: Fighting for Transitional Justice in Serbia," in *The Arts of Transitional Justice: Culture, Activism, and Memory after Atrocity*, eds. Peter Rush and Olivera Simić. New York: Springer, 99–113.
Medenica, Ivan. 2011. "Novi vidovi političkog pozorišta: Slučaj ex-Yu," *Teatron* 154/155, Prolece/leto, 18.
Mendeloff, David. 2004. "Truth-Seeking, Truth-Telling, and Postconflict Peacebuilding: Curb the Enthusiasm?" *International Studies Review*, 6: 355–80.
Michnik, Adam and Vaclav Havel. 1993. "Justice as Revenge?" *Journal of Democracy*, 4: 20–27.
Mihajlović Trbovc, Jovana and Tamara Pavasović Trošt. 2013. "Who Were the Anti-Fascists? Multiple Interpretations of WWII in Post-Yugoslav Textbooks," in *The Use and Abuse of Memory: Interpreting World War Two in Contemporary European Politics*, eds. Christian Karner and Bram Mertens. New Brunswick, NJ: Transaction Publishers, 173–192.
Milosavljević, Olivera. 2010. *Savremenici fašizma*. Belgrade: Helsinški komitet za ljudska prava.
Milošević, Dijana. 2011. "Theatre as a Way of Creating Sense: Performance and Peacebuilding in the Region of the Former Yugoslavia," in *Acting Together: Performance and the Creative Transformation of Conflict*, Volume I: *Resistance and Reconciliation in Regions of Violence*, eds. Cynthia Cohen, Roberto Gutiérrez Varea, and Polly Walker. New York: New Village Press, 23–43.
Milošević, Srdjan. 2012. "Rehabilitacija kneza Pavla: Zbir netačnih podataka i pogrešnih tumačenja," *Novi magazin*, October 4.
Mink, George. 2013. "Institutions of National Memory in Post-Communist Europe: From Transitional Justice to Political Uses of Biographies (1989–2010)," in *History, Memory and Politics in Central and Eastern Europe*, eds. George Mink and Laure Neumayer. Houndmills: Palgrave Macmillan, 155–170.
Minow, Martha. 1998. *Between Vengeance and Forgiveness: Facing History after Genocide and Mass Violence*. Boston: Beacon Press.
Mncwabe, Nokukhanya. 2013. "Truth Commissions," in *Encyclopedia of Transitional Justice*, eds. Lavinia Stan and Nadya Nedelsky. New York: Cambridge University Press, 3: 98–106.
Mociolca, Simona. 2010. "Pelerinaj la Bucureşti, Popeşi-Leordeni şi Slatina-Olt pentru comemorarea victimelor Revoluţiei," *Memorial 1989*, 1: 191–194.
Moran, John. 1994. "The Communist Torturers of Eastern Europe – Prosecute and Punish or Forgive and Forget," *Communist and Post-Communist Studies*, 27: 95–109.
Morgan, Nigel and Annette Pritchard. 1998. *Tourism, Promotion and Power: Creating Images, Creating Identities*. Chichester: Wiley.

Müller-Enbergs, Helmut. 2012. "Aufarbeitung der Vergangenheit in Mittel- und Osteuropa – Dimension der Staatssicherheiten," in *Der allmächtige Geheimdienst. Ein Relikt der Vergangenheit. Zur Transformation der Geheimdienste Mittel- und Osteuropas nach 1990*, eds. Wolbert K. Smidt, Irina Mohr, and Helmut Müller-Enbergs. Berlin: LIT Verlag, 37–45.

Muraru, Andrei. 2008. *Dicţionarul Penitenciarelor in România Comunista (1945–1967)*. Iaşi: Polirom.

Nalepa, Monika. 2013. "Institute of National Remembrance – Commission for the Prosecution of Crimes against the Polish Nation/Instytut Pamięci Narodowej – Komisja Scigania Zbrodni przeciwko Narodowi Polskiemu," in *Encyclopedia of Transitional Justice*, eds. Lavinia Stan and Nadya Nedelsky. New York: Cambridge University Press, 3: 200–205.

2013. "Lustration," in *Encyclopedia of Transitional Justice*, eds. Lavinia Stan and Nadya Nedelsky. New York: Cambridge University Press, 1: 46–51.

2010. "Captured Commitments: An Analytic Narrative of Transitions with Transitional Justice," *World Politics*, 62: 341–380.

2010. *Skeletons in the Closet: Transitional Justice in Post-Communist Europe*. New York: Cambridge University Press.

2008. "To Punish the Guilty and Protect the Innocent: Comparing Truth Revelation Procedures," *Journal of Theoretical Politics*, 20: 221–245.

"Nečasově vládě už věří jen necelá pětina lidí. Ztrácí i podporu stoupenců ODS," *iHned*, October 5, 2012, available at: http://zpravy.ihned.cz/c1-57779990-necasove-vlade-uz-veri-jen-necela-petina-lidi-ztraci-i-podporu-stoupencu-ods (accessed October 13, 2013).

Nedelsky, Nadya. 2013. "State, Civil Society, and Media Interactions in Slovak Transitional Justice," paper presented at the Legal Frames of Memory conference, Warsaw, November 28.

2009. "Czechoslovakia and the Czech and Slovak Republics," in *Transitional Justice in Eastern Europe and the Former Soviet Union: Reckoning with the Communist Past*, ed. Lavinia Stan. London: Routledge, 37–75.

2004. "Divergent Responses to a Common Past: Transitional Justice in the Czech Republic and Slovakia," *Theory and Society*, 33: 65–115.

"New Premier on Croatia's Economy, Media, Relations with Hague Tribunal, Bosnia," *BBC Monitoring Europe – Political*, January 29, 2000.

Neier, Aryeh. 1990. "What Should Be Done about the Guilty?" *New York Review of Books* (February 1).

Ní Aoláin, Fionnuala and Colm Campbell, 2005. "The Paradox of Transition in Conflicted Democracies," *Human Rights Quarterly*, 27: 172–213.

Nováková, Michaela. 2013. "Ekonomové změřili, jak se po každých volbách opakuje hra o 'trafiky,'" *iDnes* (September 11), available at: http://zpravy.idnes.cz/ies-vydal-studii-o-propojeni-politiky-s-verejnym-sektorem-pan-/domaci.aspx?c=A130911_170759_domaci_ael (accessed October 13, 2013).

Oberländer, Erwin. 2011. "Soviet Genocide in Latvia? Conflicting Cultures of Remembrance of Stalin's Policy, 1940–1953," in *Forgotten Pages in Baltic History: Diversity and Inclusion*, eds. Martyn Housden and David J. Smith. Amsterdam: Rodopi, 239–261.

O'Connor, Jacqueline. 2013. *Documentary Trial Plays in Contemporary American Theater*. Carbondale: Southern Illinois University Press.

O'Donnell, Guillermo and Philippe C. Schmitter. 1986. "Tentative Conclusions about Uncertain Democracies," in *Transitions from Authoritarian Rule: Prospects for Democracy*, eds. Guillermo O'Donnell, Philippe C. Schmitter, and Laurence Whitehead. Baltimore: Johns Hopkins University Press, 3–78.

Offe, Claus. 1996. *Varieties of Transition: The East European and East German Experience*. London: Cambridge University Press.

Office for Democratic Institutions and Human Rights. 2005. *Republic of Albania Parliamentary Elections 3 July 2005*, November 7, available at: http://www.osce.org/odihr/elections/albania/16856 (accessed September 25, 2013).

2001. *Republic of Albania Parliamentary Elections 24 June-19 August 2001*, October 11, available at: http://www.osce.org/odihr/elections/albania/13560 (accessed September 25, 2013).

1996. *Observation of the Parliamentary Elections Held in the Republic of Albania, May 26 and June 2, 1996*, July 2, available at: http://www.osce.org/odihr/elections/albania/13567 (accessed October 9, 2013).

Office of the United Nations High Commissioner for Human Rights. 2006. *Rule of Law Tools for Post-Conflict States: Truth Commissions*. New York: United Nations.

"Official Lists of StB Collaborators Full of Mistakes," Europe Intelligence Wire (March 27, 2003), available at: http://www.accessmylibrary.com/coms2/summary_0286-228 20063_ITM (accessed on December 18, 2003).

Olsen, Tricia D., Leigh A. Payne and Andrew G. Reiter. 2010. *Transitional Justice in Balance: Comparing Processes, Weighing Efficacy*. Washington, D.C.: United States Institute of Peace Press.

2010. "Transitional Justice in the World, 1970–2007: Insights from a New Dataset," *Journal of Peace Research*, 47: 803–809.

Onken, Eva-Clarita. 2007. "The Baltic States and Moscow's 9 May Commemoration: Analysing Memory Politics in Europe," *Europe-Asia Studies*, 59: 23–46.

2007. "The Politics of Finding Historical Truth: Reviewing Baltic History Commissions and Their Work," *Journal of Baltic Studies*, 38: 109–116.

2003. *Demokratisierung der Geschichte in Lettland: Staatsbürgerliches Bewußtsein und Geschichtspolitik im ersten Jahrzehnt der Unabhängigkeit*. Hamburg: Krämer.

Oprea, Marius. 2002. *Banalitatea răului. O istore a Securităţii în documente*. Iaşi: Polirom.

Orenstein, Mitchell, Stephen Bloom, and Nicole Lindstrom. 2008. "A Fourth Dimension of Transition," in *Transnational Actors in Central and East European Transitions*, eds. Mitchell A. Orenstein, Stephen Bloom, and Nicole Lindstrom. Pittsburgh: University of Pittsburgh Press, 1–18.

Orentlicher, Diane F. 1991. "Settling Accounts: The Duty to Prosecute Human Rights Violations of a Prior Regime," *Yale Law Journal*, 100: 2539–2568.

"Otevřel se Ústav pro studium totalitních režimů," *iHned*, February 1, 2008, available at: http://zpravy.ihned.cz/c1-22871540-otevrel-se-ustav-pro-studium-totalitnich-rez imu (accessed October 13, 2013).

Paczynska, Agnieszka. 2005. "Inequality, Political Participation, and Democratic Deepening in Poland," *East European Politics and Societies*, 19: 573–613.

Palade, Rodica. 2011. "Profitorii Revoluţiei," 22 (August 1).

Palmer, Catherine. 2005. "An Ethnography of Englishness: Experiencing Identity through Tourism," *Annals of Tourism Research*, 32: 7–27.

Pavelić, Boris. 2013. "Croatia Confirms Ex-Minister's WWII Killing Charges," *Balkan Insight* (October 29), available at: http://www.balkaninsight.com/en/article/croatian-ex-minister-wwii-crimes-indictment-confirmed (accessed January 13, 2014).

2013. "Croatia Changes Controversial Extradition Law," *Balkan Insight* (October 7), available at: http://www.balkaninsight.com/en/article/croatia-changes-lex-perkovi c (accessed January 13, 2014).

2013. "Exploring the Power of Memory in Croatia," *Balkan Insight* (October 4), available at: http://www.balkaninsight.com/en/article/croatia-personal-war-mem ories-collection-presented (accessed January 13, 2014).

2013. "Croatia Monument to Serb War Victims Vandalised," *Balkan Insight* (September 16), available at: http://www.balkaninsight.com/en/article/croatia-monument-to-serb-victims-vandalised/1460/5 (accessed January 13, 2014).

Pearce, Susan, C. 2011. "Delete, Restart or Rewind? Post-1989 Public Memory Work in East-Central Europe," *Sociology Compass*, 5: 256–272.

Perović, Latinka. 1991. *Zatvaranje kruga: Ishod političkog rascepa u SKJ 1971/1972*. Sarajevo: Svjetlost.

Pertoch, Philippe. 2011. "History as a Tool for Foreign Policy in the Baltic States after Independence," in *Geschichtspolitik im erweiterten Ostseeraum und ihre aktuellen Symptome – Historical Memory Culture in the Enlarged Baltic Sea Region and Its Symptoms Today*, eds. Oliver Rathkolb and Imbi Sooman. Göttingen: V&R unipress, 242–256.

Peskin, Victor. 2008. *International Justice in Rwanda and the Balkans: Virtual Trials and the Struggle for State Cooperation*. Cambridge: Cambridge University Press.

Pettai, Eva-Clarita. 2013. "Commission of Latvia's Historians," in *Encyclopedia of Transitional Justice*, eds. Lavinia Stan and Nadya Nedelsky. New York: Cambridge University Press, 3: 74–78.

2013. "Estonian International Commission for the Investigation of Crimes against Humanity," in *Encyclopedia of Transitional Justice*, eds. Lavinia Stan and Nadya Nedelsky. New York: Cambridge University Press, 3: 117–121.

2011. "The Convergence of Two Worlds: Historians and Emerging Histories in the Baltic States," in *Forgotten Pages in Baltic History: Diversity and Inclusion*, eds. Martyn Housden and David J. Smith. Amsterdam: Rodopi, 263–280.

2011. "Establishing 'Holocaust Memory': A Comparison of Estonia and Latvia," in *Geschichtspolitik im erweiterten Ostseeraum und ihre aktuellen Symptome – Historical Memory Culture in the Enlarged Baltic Sea Region and Its Symptoms Today*, eds. Oliver Rathkolb and Imbi Sooman. Göttingen: V&R unipress, 159–173.

Pettai, Vello. 2013. "Estonia," in *Encyclopedia of Transitional Justice*, eds. Lavinia Stan and Nadya Nedelsky. New York: Cambridge University Press, 2: 161–167.

Petrescu, Cristina and Dragoş Petrescu. 2009. "Retribution, Remembering, Representation: On Romania's Incomplete Break with the Communist Past," in *Geschichtsbilder in den postdiktatorischen Ländern Europas. Auf der Suche nach historisch-politischen Identitäten*, eds. Gerhard Besier and Katarzyna Stokłosa. Berlin: LIT Verlag, 155–182.

Petrović, Vladimir. 2007. "Modeli zaštite javnog sećanja u borbi protiv poricanja zločina," *Forum za tranzicionu pravdu*, April: 131–139.

Phillips, Ann L. 2000. *Power and Influence after the Cold War. Germany in East-Central Europe*. Lanham, MD: Rowman and Littlefield.

Piana, Daniela. 2009. *Judicial Accountabilities in New Europe: From Rule of Law to Quality of Justice*. Farnham: Ashgate.
Plakans, Andrejs. 2011. *A Concise History of the Baltic Sates*. Cambridge: Cambridge University Press.
Poe, Steven C. and C. Neal Tate. 1994. "Repression of Human Rights to Personal Integrity in the 1980s: A Global Analysis," *American Political Science Review*, 88: 853–872.
Poe, Steven C., C. Neal Tate and Linda Camp Keith. 1999. "Repression of the Human Right to Personal Integrity Revisited: A Global Cross-National Study Covering the Years 1976–1993," *International Studies Quarterly*, 43: 291–313.
"Poland in Uproar over Leak of Spy Files," *The Guardian* (February 5, 2005), available at: http://www.guardian.co.uk/international/story/0,3604,1406281,00.html (accessed December 10, 2013).
Polish Constitutional Tribunal, Judgment of 11th May 2007, file Ref. No. K 2/07 LUSTRATION (2007), available at: http://www.trybunal.gov.pl/eng/summaries/documents/K_2_07_GB.pdf (accessed December 23, 2013).
"Poslanci schválili, že diskriminovat bude trestné," *Aktualne.cz*, March 19, 2008, available at: http://aktualne.centrum.cz/domaci/politika/clanek.phtml?id=600192 (accessed October 13, 2013).
Posner, Eric and Adrian Vermeule. 2004. "Transitional Justice as Ordinary Justice," *Harvard Law Review*, 117: 761–825.
"Premier-Elect Says Political System Needs Changing," *BBC Summary of World Broadcasts*, January 13, 2000.
President of Latvia. n.d. "Commission of Historians," available at: http://www.president.lv/pk/content/?cat_id=7 (accessed December 4, 2013).
2011. "Former Presidents of Latvia, Valdis Zatlers, Commission of Historians, Events 2010," available at: http://www.president.lv/pk/content/?cat_id=9055&lng=en (accessed December 4, 2013).
President of Lithuania. 2012. "Decree on the International Commission for the Evaluation of the Crimes of the Nazi and Soviet Occupation Regimes in Lithuania," No. 1K-1245 Vilnius, October 16, available at: http://www.komisija.lt/Files/www.komisija.lt/File/Decree%2020121016%20-Unofficial%20translation.pdf (accessed December 4, 2013).
Přibán, Jiri. 2009. "From 'Which Rule of Law?' to 'The Rule of Which Law?' Post-Communist Experiences of European Legal Integration," *Hague Journal on the Rule of Law*, 1: 337–358.
2007. "Oppressors and Their Victims: The Czech Lustration Law and the Rule of Law," in *Justice as Prevention: Vetting Public Employees in Transitional Societies*, eds. Alexander Mayer-Rieckh and Pablo De Grieff. New York: Social Science Research Council.
Purves, Gillian, ed. 2013. *A Reader for Older Secondary School Students Anywhere in Europe*. Prague: Institute for the Study of Totalitarian Regimes.
Raabe, Stephan with Denny Schlüter. 2011. "Auf den Spuren des 'Europäischen Netzwerks Erinnerung und Solidarität,'" *Länderbericht*, Konrad-Adenauer-Stiftung: Auslandsbüro Polen (January 6), available at: http://www.kas.de/polen/de/publications/21555/ (accessed June 20, 2013).
Radanović, Milan. 2011. "Istorijska politika u Srbiji nakom 2000. godine: Primeri manifestovanja sprege između akademskog istorijskog revizionizma i državne

revizije prošlosti," in *Izgubljeno u tranziciji: Kritička analiza procesa društvene transformacije*, eds. Ana Veselinović, Petar Atanacković, and Željko Klarić. Belgrade: Rosa Luxemburg Stiftung, 258–305.

Radonić, Ljiljana. 2012. "Standards of Evasion: Croatia and the Europeanization of Memory," *Eurozine* (April 6), available at: http://www.eurozine.com/articles/2012-04-06-radonic-en.html (accessed January 13, 2014).

2011. "Croatia – Exhibiting Memory and History at the 'Shores of Europe,'" *Culture Unbound*, 3: 355–367.

Ramet, Sabrina P. 2007. "The Denial Syndrome and Its Consequences: Serbian Political Culture since 2000," *Communist and Post-Communist Studies*, 40: 41–58.

2006. *The Three Yugoslavias: State-building and Legitimation, 1918–2005*. Washington, D.C.: Woodrow Wilson Center Press.

Ramet, Sabrina P. and Ola Listhaug. eds. 2011. *Serbia and the Serbs in World War Two*. New York: Palgrave Macmillan.

"Rehabilitation Law, 25 April 2006," *Službeni glasnik Republike Srbije* 33/2006.

Risse, Thomas, Steven C. Ropp, and Kathryn Sikkink. 1999. *The Power of Human Rights: International Norms and Domestic Change*. Cambridge: Cambridge University Press.

Roehrig, Terence. 2002. *The Prosecution of Former Military Leaders in Newly Democratic Nations*. Jefferson, NC: McFarland.

Ristić, Marija. 2013. "Exposing the Secret Crimes of Communism in Serbia," *Balkan Insight* (September 9), available at: http://www.balkaninsight.com/en/article/ser bia-still-unaware-of-communist-era-crimes (accessed January 13, 2014).

Roknić, Aleksandar. 2008. "Iz podruma Udbe u podrum Arhiva," *Danas*, October 9.

"Romanian Daily Publishes List of Securitate Agents Working in Intelligence," Foreign Broadcast Information Service, FBIS-EEU-2002-0405 (March 28, 2002), available at http://cryptome.org/ro-spy-list.htm (accessed February 20, 2011).

Rose-Redwood, Reuban, Derek Alderman, and Maoz Azaryahu. 2010. "Geographies of Toponymic Inscription: New Directions in Critical Place-Name Studies," *Progress in Human Geography*, 34: 453–470.

Rosenberg, Tina. 1996. *The Haunted Land: Facing Europe's Ghosts after Communism*. London: Random House.

1995. "Overcoming the Legacies of Dictatorship," *Foreign Affairs*, 74: 134–152.

Rothstein, Bo and Eric Uslaner. 2005. "All for All: Equality, Corruption, and Social Trust," *World Politics*, 58: 41–72.

Rusan, Romulus. 2007. *Chronology and Geography of Communist Repression in Romania*. Bucharest: Civic Academy Foundation.

Rush, Peter. 2013. "After Atrocity: Foreword to Transition," in *The Arts of Transitional Justice: Culture, Activism, and Memory after Atrocity*, eds. Peter Rush and Olivera Simić. New York: Springer, v-xi.

Rush, Peter and Olivera Simić. eds. 2013. *The Arts of Transitional Justice: Culture, Activism, and Memory after Atrocity*. New York: Springer.

Sa'adah, Anne. 1998. *Germany's Second Chance: Trust, Justice and Democratization*. Cambridge, MA: Harvard University Press.

Sadurski, Wojciech. 2005. *Rights Before Courts: A Study of Constitutional Courts in Postcommunist States of CEE*. Dordrecht: Springer.

Safjan, Marek. 2007. "Transitional Justice: The Polish Example, the Case of Lustration," *European Journal of Legal Studies*, 1, 2, available at: http://www.ejls.eu/2/29UK.htm (accessed October 15, 2013).

Sajó, András. 2004. "Militant Democracy and Transition towards Democracy," in *Militant Democracy*, ed. András Sajó. The Hague: Eleven International Publishing, 209–230.

Salivarova-Skvorecka, Zdena. ed. 2000. *Osoceni: Pravdive pribehy lidi z "Cibulkova seznamu."* Toronto: Sixty-Eight Publishers.

Sather-Wagstaff, Joy. 2011. *Heritage That Hurts: Tourists in the Memoryscapes of September 11*. Walnut Creek: Left Coast Press.

Savin, Zoran. 2003. "UDBa in Cenzura," *Mladina* (April 18), available at: http://www.mladina.si/tednik/200315/ (accessed December 10, 2013).

Schabas, William. 2003. "The Relationship between Truth Commissions and International Courts: The Case of Sierra Leone," *Human Rights Quarterly*, 25: 1035–1066.

Schindler, John. 2010. Interview, *Studia Croatica*, February 11, available at http://studiacroatica.blogspot.com/2010/02/dr-john-r-schindler-agents-provocateurs.html (accessed January 13, 2014).

Schneider, Jan. 2011. "Publication of StB Database 'Not Illegal', Court Rules," CzechPosition.com (February 21), available at: http://www.ceskapozice.cz/en/news/politics-policy/publication-stb-database-%91not-illegal%92-court-rules (accessed December 17, 2013).

Schultz, Deborah and Alina Serban. 2010. "Public Memory and National Identity under Construction: The Trajectory of Monuments in Romania in the Communist and Post-Communist Periods," *Centropa*, 10: 56–66.

Sejm, "Sprawozdanie Stenograficzne," Sejm (Kadencja X, 49 posiedzenia, 1991).

Senate, *Dziennik Ustaw* (I Kadencja, 45 posiedzenia, March 15 1991).

Senate, *Dziennik Ustaw* (I Kadencja, 45 posiedzenia, April 19, 1991).

Senate of the Parliament of the Czech Republic. 2008. *Prague Declaration on European Conscience and Communism*, June 3, available at: http://www.praguedeclaration.eu/ (accessed February 23, 2012).

"Serb General Pavkovic to Surrender to Hague," *Reuters*, April 22, 2005.

"Serbia Ready to Arrest Two Indicted Generals – Official," SeeNews, March 14, 2005.

"Serbian Premier Confident Feasibility Study to Be Positive," *BBC Monitoring International Reports*, March 4, 2005.

"Serbian Premier Says Cooperation with Icty 'Necessary,' *BBC Monitoring Europe – Political*, November 22, 2004.

Shaw, Rosalind and Lars Waldorf, with Pierre Hazan. eds. 2010. *Localizing Transitional Justice: Interventions and Priorities after Mass Violence*. Stanford, CA: Stanford University Press.

Siani-Davis, Peter. 2006. *The Romanian Revolution of December 1989*. Ithaca, NY: Cornell University Press.

Siddiqui, Nadia, Hadi Marifat and Sari Kouvo. 2013. "Culture, Theatre and Justice: Examples from Afghanistan," in *The Arts of Transitional Justice: Culture, Activism, and Memory after Atrocity*, eds. Peter Rush and Olivera Simić. New York: Springer, 113–135.

Sikkink, Kathryn. 2011. *The Justice Cascade: How Human Rights Prosecutions Are Changing World Politics*. New York: Norton.

Simecka, Martin. 2009. "In the Shadow of the Archives," *Presseurop* (July 9), available at: http://www.presseurop.eu/en/content/article/51111-shadow-archives (accessed December 18, 2013).

Simić, Olivera. 2010. "Breathing Sense into Women's Lives Shattered by War: the DAH Theater Company of Belgrade," *Law Text Culture*, 14: 117–133.

Simić, Olivera and Kathleen Daly. 2011. "'One Pair of Shoes, One Life': Steps towards Accountability for Genocide in Srebrenica," *International Journal of Transitional Justice*, 5: 477–491.

Simić, Olivera and Dijana Milošević. 2014. "Enacting Justice: The Role of Dah Theatre Company in Transitional Justice Processes in Serbia and Beyond," in *The Arts of Transitional Justice: Culture, Activism, and Memory after Atrocity*, eds. Peter Rush and Olivera Simić. New York: Springer, 99–113.

Simić, Olivera and Zala Volcic. eds. 2013. *Transitional Justice and Civil Society in the Balkans*. New York: Springer.

Skapska, Grazyna. 2003. "Moral Definitions in Constitutionalism in East Central Europe: Facing Past Human Rights Violations," *International Sociology*, 18: 199–218.

Slaivorova-Skvorecka, Zdena. 2000. *Osočení: pravdivé příběhy lidí z "Cibulkova seznamu,"* Brno: Host.

Smith, Laurajane. 2012. "The Cultural 'Work' of Tourism," in *The Cultural Moment in Tourism*, eds. Laurajane Smith, Emma Waterton, and Steve Watson. London: Routledge, 210–234.

Sólyom, László. 2003. "The Role of Constitutional Courts in the Transition to Democracy: With Special Reference to Hungary," *International Sociology*, 18: 133–161.

Śpiewak, Paweł. 2010. "Pięć lat po czwartej," *Polityka*, June 26.

Stafford Clark, Max. 2008. *Verbatim: Contemporary Documentary Theater*. London: Oberon Books.

Stan, Lavinia. Forthcoming. "Conclusions: Memory, Courts, and Justice in Transition," in *Transitional Criminal Justice in Post-Dictatorial and Post-Conflict Societies*, eds. Agata Fijalkowski and Raluca Grosescu. Cambridge: Intersentia, pages.

2013. "Civil Society and Post-Communist Transitional Justice in Romania," in *Transitional Justice and Civil Society in the Balkans*, eds. Olivera Simić and Zala Volcic. New York: Springer, 17–31.

2013. *Transitional Justice in Post-Communist Romania: The Politics of Memory*. New York: Cambridge University Press.

2013. "Reckoning with the Communist Past in Romania: A Scorecard," *Europe-Asia Studies*, 65: 127–146.

2012. "Witch-Hunt or Moral Rebirth? Romanian Parliamentary Debates on Lustration," *East European Politics and Societies*, 26: 274–295.

2011. "Vigilante Justice in Post-Communist Europe," *Communist and Post-Communist Studies*, 44: 319–327.

2009. "Truth Commissions in Post-Communism: The Overlooked Solution?" *Open Political Science Journal*, 2: 1–13.

ed. 2009. *Transitional Justice in Eastern Europe and the former Soviet Union: Reckoning with the Communist Past*. London: Routledge.
2009. "Introduction: Post-Communist Transition, Justice, and Transitional Justice," in *Transitional Justice in Eastern Europe and the Former Soviet Union*, ed. Lavinia Stan. London: Routledge, 1–14.
2009. "Conclusion: Explaining Country Differences," in *Transitional Justice in Eastern Europe and the Former Soviet Union*, ed. Lavinia Stan. London: Routledge, 261–262.
2004. "Spies, Files and Lies: Explaining the Failure of Access to Securitate Files," *Communist and Post-Communist Studies*, 37: 341–359.
2002. "Access to Securitate Files: The Trials and Tribulations of a Romanian Law," *East European Politics and Societies*, 16: 145–181.
Stan, Lavinia and Nadya Nedelsky. eds. 2013. *Encyclopedia of Transitional Justice*. New York: Cambridge University Press.
Stănescu, Mircea. 2010. *Reeducarea in România Comunistă (1945–1952). Aiud, Suceava, Piteşti, Braşov*. Iaşi: Polirom.
Statsna, Kazi. 2010. "The Czechs' Unfinished Business," *Foreign Policy* (July 7), available at: http://www.foreignpolicy.com/articles/2001/09/01/europes_fake_id (accessed on January 9, 2014).
Ştoicuţa Maria, and Flavia Biianu. 2009. *Monumente memoriale ale Revoluţiei din Timişoara. Ghidul oraşului*. Timişoara: Artpress.
Stojanović, Dubravka. 2013. "Vinovnici i žrtve u srpskim udžbenicima istorije," *Peščanik* (September 19), available at: http://pescanik.net/2013/09/vinovnici-i-zrtve-u-srpskim-udzbenicima-istorije (accessed January 13, 2014).
2010. "U ogledalu 'drugih,'" in *Novosti iz prošlosti: Znanje, neznanje, upotreba i zloupotreba istorije*, eds. Dubravka Stojanović, Radina Vučetić, Sanja Petrović Todosijević, Olga Manojlović Pintar, and Radmila Radić. Belgrade: Beogradski centar za ljudska prava, 13–32.
Stojaspal, Jan. 2000. "Blowing the Whistle on the Past," *Time* (April 24), available at: http://www.time.com/time/world/article/0,8599,2056342,00.html (accessed on December 17, 2013).
Stover, Eric and Harvey Weinstein. eds. 2004. *My Neighbor, My Enemy: Justice and Community in the Aftermath of Mass Atrocity*. Cambridge: Cambridge University Press.
Stransky, Zbynek Z. 1992. "Museums in Post-Communist Countries," in *Museums and Europe* 1992, ed. Susan Pearce. London: Athlone Press, 194–186.
Subotić, Jelena. 2013. "Stories States Tell: Identity, Narrative, and Human Rights in the Balkans," *Slavic Review*, 72: 306–326.
2012. "Transformation of International Justice Agency," *International Journal of Transitional Justice*, 6: 106–125.
2009. *Hijacked Justice: Dealing with the Past in the Balkans*. Ithaca, NY: Cornell University Press.
Sutter, Daniel. 1995. "Settling Old Scores: Potholes Along the Transition from Authoritarian Rule," *Journal of Conflict Resolution*, 39: 110–128.
Szczerbiak, Aleks. 2002. "Dealing with the Communist Past or the Politics of the Present? Lustration in Post-Communist Poland," *Europe-Asia Studies*, 54: 553–572.

"Talks Stall on Extraditing Milošević to Hague: Serb Minister," *Agence France Presse*, June 4, 2001.

Tamm, Marek. 2013. "History as Cultural Memory: Mnemohistory and the Construction of the Estonian Nation," in *Contested and Shared Places of Memory: History and Politics in North Eastern Europe*, eds. Jörg Hackmann and Marko Lehti. New York: Routledge, 116–133.

Tănase, Stelian. 2002. *Acasă se vorbeşte in şoaptă. Dosar si jurnal din anii tirzii ai dictarurii*. Bucharest: Compania.

Tauber, Joachim. 2011. "Vergangenheitsbewältigung in Litauen: Politik, Gesellschaft und der Holocaust nach 1945," in *Geschichtspolitik im erweiterten Ostseeraum*, eds. Oliver Rathkolb and Imbi Sooman. Göttingen: V&R unipress, 175–193.

Teitel, Ruti. 2000. *Transitional Justice*, New York: Oxford University Press.

2003. "Transitional Justice Genealogy," *Harvard Human Rights Journal*, 16: 69–94.

Terlikowski, Tomasz P. 2007. "Arcybiskup Stanisław Wielgus byl agentem wywiadu PRL," *Rzeczpospolita*, January 4.

"The Arab Uprisings: Democracy's Hard Spring," *The Economist*, March 10, 2011.

The "European Network of Official Authorities in Charge of the Secret-Police Files". A Reader on Their Legal Foundations, Structures and Activities (Berlin: Der Bundesbeauftragte für die Unterlagen des Staatssicherheitsdienstes der ehemaligen Deutschen Demokratischen Republik, December 2009), available at: http://www.bstu.bund.de/DE/Wissen/Publikationen/Publikationen/E_netzwerkreader_englisch.html (accessed January 14, 2014).

Thoms, Oskar, James Ron and Roland Paris. 2008. *The Effects of Transitional Justice Mechanisms: A Summary of Empirical Research Findings and Implications for Analysts and Practitioners*. Ottawa: Centre for International Policy Studies.

Till, Karen. 2005. *The New Berlin: Memory, Politics, Place*. Minneapolis: University of Minnesota Press.

1999. "Staging the Past: Landscape Designs, Cultural Identity and Erinnerungspolitik at Berlin's Neue Wache," *Ecumene*, 6: 251–283.

Tismaneanu, Vladimir, Dorin Dobrincu and Cristian Vasile. eds. 2007. *Raport Final: Comisia Prezidenţială pentru Analiza Dictaturii Comuniste din România*. Bucharest: Humanitas.

Todorova, Maria. 2006. "The mausoleum of Georgi Dimitrov as *lieu de mémoire*," *Journal of Modern History*, 78: 377–411.

"To nie jest lista agentów," *Rzeczpospolita*, January 31, 2005.

Traynor, Ian. 1999. "Franjo Tudjman," *Guardian*, December 12.

Troebst, Stefan. 2008. "Wiederbelebung einer 'Totgeburt'? Das Europäische Netzwerk Erinnerung und Solidarität," *Polen-Analysen*, 33: 2–7.

2006. *Vertreibungsdiskurs und europäische Erinnerungskultur. Deutsch-polnische Initiativen zur Institutionalisierung. Eine Dokumentation*. Veröffentlichungen der Deutsch-Polnischen Gesellschaft Bundesverband e.V. Volume 11. Osnabrück: Fibre, 22–23.

Tudjman, Franjo. 1998. *Address of the President of the Republic of Croatia on the State of the Nation*. Zagreb: Croatian Parliament.

Tudor, Cristina and Cornel Seracin. 2010. "Proclamaţia de la Timişoara: document al Revoluţiei Române din decembrie 1989," *Memorial* 1989, 1: 24–37.

Tupy, Marian. 2006. "The Rise of Populist Parties in Central Europe: Big Government, Corruption, and the Threat to Liberalism," *Development Policy Analysis*, No. 1. Washington, D.C.: Cato Institute: Center for Global Liberty & Prosperity.

Tzortzi, Ellie. 2005. "Serb Ex-General to Surrender to UN," *Reuters*, March 3.

"U SARTR-u premijerno izvedena predstava 'Bio je lijep i sunčan dan,'" Abrasmedia, May 18, 2012, available at: http://www.abrasmedia.info/content/u-sartr-u-premijerno-izvedena-predstava-bio-je-lijep-i-sun%C4%8D-dan (accessed September 11, 2013).

"UDBa.net Stir up Controversy," *Voice of Slovenia* (2003), available at: http://www.glasslovenije.com.au/acrobat/voice-april2003.pdf (accessed on December 17, 2013).

Ugrešić, Dubravka. 1996. "The Confiscation of Memory," *New Left Review*, I: 26–39.

Unger, Thomas. 2010. "The European Union and Transitional Justice," Center for the Law of EU External Relations (CLEER) Working Paper no. 1.

United Nations. 2006. *Rule of Law Tools for Post-Conflict States: Vetting: An Operational Framework*. Office of the UN High Commission on Human Rights, New York, United Nations HR/PUB/06/5.

Ursachi, Raluca. 2007. "In Search of a Theoretical Model of Transitional Justice," in *Lustration and Consolidation of Democracy and the Rule of Law in CEE*, eds. Vladimira Dvořáková and Anđelko Milardović. Zagreb: Political Science Research Centre, 65–83.

Vaduchova, Milada. 2005. *Europe Undivided. Leverage and Integration after Communism*. Oxford: Oxford University Press.

Varga, László. 2005. "Vom Erbe des kommunistischen Staatssicherheitsdienstes in Ungarn," in *Lustration, Aktenöffnung, demokratischer Umbruch in Polen, Tschechien, der Slowakei und Ungarn. Referate der Tagung des BStU und der Akademie für politische Bildung Tutzing vom 26.-28. 10. 1998*, eds. Dagmar Unverhau with Roland Lucht. Münster: LIT Verlag, 161–176.

Vasić, Miloš. 2005. *Atentat na Zorana Đinđića*. Beograd: Politika.

Velikonja, Mitja. 2009. "Lost in Transition Nostalgia for Socialism in Post-socialist Countries," *East European Politics and Societies*, 23: 535–551.

Venice Commission. 2009. *Amicus Curiae Opinion on the Law on the Cleanliness of the Figure of High Functionaries of the Public Administration and Elected Persons of Albania*, Strasbourg, October 13, Opinion no. 524/2009, available at: http://www.venice.coe.int/webforms/documents/?pdf=CDL-AD(2009)044-e (accessed October 14, 2013).

Verdery, Katherine. 1999. *The Political Lives of Dead Bodies: Reburial and Postsocialist Change*. New York: Columbia University Press.

1996. *What Was Socialism and What Comes Next?* Princeton, NJ: Princeton University Press.

"Vojislav Koštunica, Moderate Nationalist and Old Milošević Foe," *Agence France Presse*, September 24, 2000.

Vrana, Karel. 2003. "Getting Even," *Transitions on Line* (April 25), available at: http://www.tol.org/client/article/9348-getting-even.html (accessed on December 17, 2013).

Waldman, Felicia. 2010. "Holocaustul în manualele şcolare postcomuniste din România," in *Holocaustul la periferie*, eds. by Wolfgang Benz and Brigitte Mihok. Bucharest: Cartier, 320–335.

Walicki, Andrzej. 1997. "Transitional Justice and the Political Struggles in Post-Communist Poland," in *Transitional Justice and the Rule of Law in New Democracies*, ed. A. James McAdams. Notre Dame, IN: University of Notre Dame Press, 185–237.

Weber, Matthias. 2010. "Gemeinsam Erinnern. Das Europäische Netzwerk 'Erinnerung und Solidarität,'" available at: http://www.bundesregierung.de/Content/DE/_Anlagen/BKM/2010-02-18-weber-zum-eruopaeischen-netzwerk-erinnerung-solidaritaet.pdf?__blob=publicationFile (accessed August 12, 2013).

Weiffen, Brigitte. 2012. "From Domestic to International Instruments for Dealing with a Violent Past: Causes, Concomitants and Consequences for Democratic Transitions," in *Memory and Political Change*, eds. Aleida Assmann and Linda Shortt. Houndmills, Basingstoke: Palgrave Macmillan, 89–111.

Welsh, Helga. 1996. "Dealing with the Communist Past: Central and East European Experiences after 1990," *Europe-Asia Studies*, 48: 413–438.

Wilke, Cristiane. 2013. "Remembering Complexity? Memorials for Nazi Victims in Berlin," *International Journal of Transitional Justice*, 7: 136–156.

Williams, Kieran, Brigid Fowler, and Aleks Szczerbiak. 2005. "Explaining Lustration in Central Europe: A 'Post-Communist Politics' Approach," *Democratization*, 12: 22–43.

Witcombe, Andrea. 2013. "Using Immersive and Interactive Approaches to Interpreting Traumatic Experiences for Tourists," in *Heritage and Tourism: Place, Encounter, Engagement*, eds. Russell Staiff, Robyn Bushell, and Steve Watson. London: Routledge, 152–170.

Women in Black Belgrade. ed. 2007. *Women's Side of War*. Belgrade: Art grafik Beograd.

Wood, Nicholas. 2005. "Serbia Moves a Step Closer to the European Union," *New York Times*, April 13.

Wulff, Meike. 2010. "Politics of History in Estonia: Changing Memory Regimes 1987–2009," *History of Communism in Europe*, 1: 245–267.

Wulf, Meike and Pertti Grnholm. 2010. "Generating Meaning across Generations: The Role of Historians in the Codification of History in Soviet and Post-Soviet Estonia," *Journal of Baltic Studies*, 41: 351–382.

Zalaquett, Jose. 1995. "Confronting Human Rights Violations Committed by Former Governments: Principles Applicable and Political Constraints," in *Transitional Justice: How Emerging Democracies Reckon with Former Regimes*, ed. Neil J. Kritz. Washington, D.C.: United States Institute of Peace Press, 1: 3–31.

1992. "Balancing Ethical Imperatives and Political Constraints: The Dilemma of New Democracies Confronting Past Human Rights Violations," *Hastings Law Journal*, 43: 1425–1438.

Zelizer, Craig. 2003. "The Role of Artistic Processes in Peacebuilding in Bosnia-Herzegovina," *Peace and Conflict Studies*, 10: 62–75.

Živković, Doris. 2012. "Intervju, Oliver Frljić: Govorim o onome što svi znaju, a o čemu šute," *Novi List*, June 11, available at: http://www.novilist.hr/Kultura/Kazaliste/Oliver-Frljic-Govorim-o-onome-sto-svi-znaju-a-o-cemu-sute (accessed September 7, 2013).

Zolkos, Magdalena. 2006. "The Conceptual Nexus of Human Rights and Democracy in the Polish Lustration Debates 1989–97," *Journal of Communist Studies and Transition Politics*, 22: 228–248.

PERSONAL INTERVIEWS

Grodsky

Advisor to Prime Minister Zoran Djindjić, February 11, 2005, Belgrade.
Bronislaw Geremek, January 20, 2004, Warsaw.
Cedomir Jovanovic, February 3, 2005, Belgrade.
Dragor Hiber, December 16, 2004, Belgrade.
Dusan Petrovic, December 9, 2004, Belgrade.
European Union Official 1, December 6, 2004, Belgrade.
European Union Official 2, December 2004, Belgrade.
European Union Official 3, November 16, 2004, Belgrade.
Gordana Matkovic, December 9, 2004, Belgrade.
Grazyna Staniszewska, December 17, 2003, Warsaw.
Ivan Simonovic, March 18, 2005, Zagreb.
Ivica Račan, March 4, 2005, Zagreb.
Ivo Josipovic, March 18, 2005, Zagreb.
Milan St. Protic, December 20, 2004, Belgrade.
Miroslav Filipovic, February 2, 2005, Belgrade.
Rebeka Bozovic, January 28, 2005, Belgrade.
United States Government Official, April 2005, Zagreb.
Vuk Obradovic, December 20, 2004, Belgrade.
Zarko Korac, February 4, 2005, Belgrade.

Austin

Arben Imami, Tirana, June 24, 2005.
Genc Ruli, Tirana, May 5, 2006.
Gent Ibrahimi, Tirana, June 2005.
Rustem Gjata, Tirana, June 24, 2005.
Sali Berisha, Tirana, June 23, 2005.
Spartak Ngjela, Tirana, June 21, 2005.

Horne

Dimitar Markov, Sofia, Bulgaria, July 2, 2012.
Gabriel Andreescu, Bucharest, Romania, October 10, 2012.
Georgö Bendegúz Cseh, Budapest, Hungary, April 4, 2013.
János Kornai, Budapest, Hungary, April 8, 2013.

Ciobanu

Adrian Cioflâncă, Bucharest, March 23, 2013.

Welsh (email correspondence with:)

Antoni Dudek, Division of International Relations, Office of the President of the Institute of National Remembrance, translated and transmitted by Katarzyna Holopiak, April 24, 2012.
Claudiu Secaşiu, CNSAS board member, February 22, 2012.
Ekaterina Boncheva, facilitated and translated by Antoinette Primatarova, March 7, 2012.
Hristo Hristov, Bulgarian journalist, January 19, 2013.
Roman David, February 15, 2012.

Simić

Dijana Milošević, July 16, 2013, Belgrade.
Nataša Govedarica, October 7, 2013, Brisbane-New York City.
Tanja Miletić Oručević, October 6, 2013, via Skype, Mostar-Brisbane.

WEBSITES

"Bronisław Wildstein," Wikipedia (December 13, 2012), available at: http://en.wikipedia.org/wiki/Bronisław_Wildstein (accessed on December 18, 2013).
Bundesstiftung Aufarbeitung, available at: http://www.bundesstiftung-aufarbeitung.de (accessed December 4, 2013).
Croatian Memories, http://www.croatianmemories.org/en.
Impressions after the Performance Hypermnesia, available at: http://www.youtube.com/watch?v=yooSJN5f-yY (accessed October 14, 2013).
"Memorialul Victimelor comunismului şi al Rezistenţei," available at: http://www.memorialsighet.ro/ (accessed 18 October 2013).
Museum website, http://mij.rs/poseta/izlozbe/66/jugoslavija-od-pocetka-do-kraja.html.
"Museum of the Occupation of Latvia 1940–91," available at: http://okupacijasmuzejs.lv/en/about-museum/mission-and-history (accessed on October 18, 2013).
"Terror," available at: http://www.terrorhaza.hu/ (accessed October 19, 2013).
"The Berlin-Hohenschönhausen Memorial," available at: http://en.stiftung-hsh.de/document.php?cat_id=CAT_231&special=0 (accessed October 19, 2013).
"The memorial," available at: http://gloriavictis.hu/en/memorial.html (accessed on January 6, 2014).
The Sighet Memorial website, available at: http://www.sighet.memorial.ro (accessed October 20, 2013).

Theatrical Works

Kad su cvetale tikve by Dragoslav Mihailović, 1968.
Presence of Absence, Dah Theatre Company, Belgrade.

Documents with Simić
Hypermensia, text of the performance: Sanin-beginning of the war. On file with author.
Filip Vujošević, "Hipermnezija: Rediteljka o predstavi." Document on file with author.
Maja Vujović, Dah Theatre, internal office document on file with author.
Dah Theatre, internal document, on file with author.

Index

Lightning Source UK Ltd.
Milton Keynes UK
UKOW06n2119250815

257524UK00003B/58/P

9 781107 065567